The Economics of Recreation, Leisure and Tourism

D1341337

The Economics of Recreation, Leisure and Tourism

John Tribe

ELSEVIER

AMSTERDAM   BOSTON   HEIDELBERG   LONDON   NEW YORK   OXFORD   PARIS   SAN DIEGO
SAN FRANCISCO   SINGAPORE   SYDNEY   TOKYO

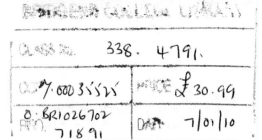

CLASS No. 338.4791.

007.0003552

PRICE £30.99

0: BR1026702

71891

DATE 7/01/10

Butterworth-Heinemann is an imprint of Elsevier
The Boulevard, Langford Lane, Kidlington, Oxford, OX5 1GB
30 Corporate Drive, Suite 400, Burlington, MA 01803, USA

First edition 1995
Reprinted 1996, 1997, 1998
Second edition 1999
Reprinted 2000, 2001
Third edition 2005
Reprinted 2005, 2006, 2007, 2008 (twice)

Copyright © 2005, John Tribe. Published by Elsevier Ltd. All rights reserved

The right of John Tribe to be identified as the author of this work has been
asserted in accordance with the Copyright, Designs and Patents Act 1988

No part of this publication may be reproduced, stored in a retrieval system
or transmitted in any form or by any means electronic, mechanical, photocopying,
recording or otherwise without the prior written permission of the publisher

Permissions may be sought directly from Elsevier's Science & Technology Rights
Department in Oxford, UK: phone (+44) (0) 1865 843830; fax (+44) (0) 1865 853333;
email: permissions@elsevier.com. Alternatively you can submit your request online by
visiting the Elsevier web site at http://elsevier.com/locate/permissions, and selecting
Obtaining permission to use Elsevier material

Notice
No responsibility is assumed by the publisher for any injury and/or damage to persons
or property as a matter of products liability, negligence or otherwise, or from any use
or operation of any methods, products, instructions or ideas contained in the material
herein. Because of rapid advances in the medical sciences, in particular, independent
verification of diagnoses and drug dosages should be made

British Library Cataloguing in Publication Data
A catalogue record for this book is available from the British Library

Library of Congress Cataloging-in-Publication Data
A catalog record for this book is available from the Library of Congress

ISBN: 978-0-7506-6180-5

For information on all Butterworth-Heinemann publications
visit our website at www.elsevierdirect.com

Printed and bound in *Great Britain*

08 09 10 10 9 8 7 6

Working together to grow
libraries in developing countries

www.elsevier.com | www.bookaid.org | www.sabre.org

ELSEVIER   BOOK AID International   Sabre Foundation

Contents

v

Preface to the third edition

Recreation, leisure and tourism continue to provide a fascinating field of study for economists. The first edition of this text was written just after a period of intense recession in the UK economy. The second edition was prepared during a period of growth in the economies of the UK, the USA and Europe. But elsewhere, the economies of Japan – the second largest in the world – Brazil, Russia, and what were once referred to as the Asian tiger economies had suffered decline. This third edition has been written in a period where the economic significance of China has continued to grow whilst the rest of the world economy has suffered a mixture of low growth and economic stagnation. Additionally, whilst the broad economic activity of recreation and leisure continues to grow, tourism suffered a severe shock in the wake of 9/11 and the war in Iraq. It is, of course, impossible to predict the economic conditions that will prevail in the year when, or the region where, this text will be read. But it is important to understand what has happened over the course of economic business cycles to prepare for what may happen in the future.

The changes in fortunes of various economies are mapped out through the updated statistics which are a central feature of this third edition. The effects of these changes on the leisure sector are also evident in these statistics and more so in the many new and updated exhibits that illustrate the text. In some cases original exhibits have been retained so as to provide the reader with contrasting evidence and a sense of the dynamics of the economy. In terms of geographical coverage, this text attempts to use examples from around the world to illustrate its points.

The aim of this text remains that of offering those involved in the business of recreation, leisure and tourism an understanding of the practicalities of economics. To support this aim real-world examples continue to be emphasized in this text rather than economic theory for theory's sake. Thus in contrast to general economics introductory texts, the marginal productivity theory of labour theory is excluded, but pricing of externalities is included on the grounds that the latter is more useful to students of leisure and tourism than the former.

The key themes of the book focus on a series of questions:

- How is the provision of leisure and tourism determined?
- Could it be provided in a different way?
- How are organizations affected by the competitive and macro-economic environments?
- What are the economic impacts of leisure and tourism?
- What are the environmental impacts of leisure and tourism?
- How can economics be used to manage leisure and tourism?

The other key features of this text are:

- Visual mapping of the content of each chapter.
- Liberal use of press cuttings to illustrate points.
- Chapter objectives.
- Learning outcomes.
- Key points summarized.
- Data response questions.
- Short answer questions.
- Integrated case studies.
- Useful web sites.

The third edition also includes illustrations in each chapter, multiple choice questions at the end of each chapter and a set of PowerPoint slides available on the companion web site.

It is hoped that this text will create a lasting interest in the economics of leisure and tourism and generate a spirit of critical enquiry into leisure and tourism issues affecting consumers, producers and hosts.

John Tribe, 2004

Acknowledgements

The author would also like to thank students and colleagues at Buckinghamshire Chilterns University, (BCUC) and friends in the wider community of leisure and tourism academics who have assisted directly and indirectly in the preparation of this book. In particular, at BCUC, the Director, Professor Bryan Mogford and Assistant Director Gill Fisher and at Butterworth-Heinemann, Kathryn Grant and Sally North have each provided much encouragement and support.

Introduction

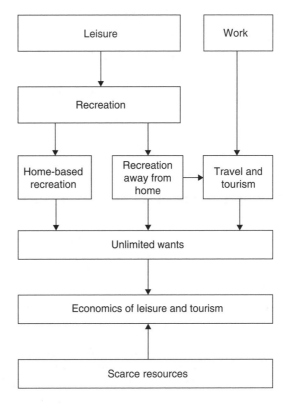

Objectives and learning outcomes

- How important are recreation, leisure and tourism to national economies?
- Why do these industries provide so many new jobs?
- What is the globalization of recreation and leisure?
- Are recreation, leisure and tourism shares good investments?
- Is the growth of recreation, leisure and tourism sustainable?

This book will help you investigate these issues. The objectives of this chapter are to define and integrate the areas of study of this book. First the scope of recreation, leisure and tourism will be discussed, and second the scope and techniques of economics will be outlined. The final part of the chapter explains how the study area of recreation, leisure and tourism can be analysed using economic techniques.

By studying this chapter students will be able to:

- understand the scope of recreation, leisure and tourism and their interrelationship;
- explain the basic economic concerns of scarcity, choice and opportunity costs;
- outline the allocation of resources in different economic systems;
- explain the methodology of economics;
- understand the use of models in economics;
- understand the use of economics to analyse issues in recreation, leisure and tourism;
- access sources of information.

Definition and scope of recreation, leisure and tourism

Like all definitions, those pertaining to recreation, leisure and tourism encounter some problems. For example, a common element in many definitions of leisure is that of free time. Thus working, sleeping and household chores are excluded. However, should we then include people who are sick or recovering from illness? Similarly, recreation is commonly applied to the pursuits that people undertake in their leisure time. But what about things people do to support their employment in their spare time? For example, is a computer programmer's use of computers in non-working time a leisure activity? Similar questions arise in defining tourism. The common element in definitions of tourism is that of 'temporary visiting'. Questions of scope immediately arise. Are people who are engaged in study overseas tourists? Are people travelling on business tourists? Aware of the problems involved, some working definitions of travel and tourism are now attempted.

Working definitions

- Leisure: *discretionary time* is the time remaining after working, commuting, sleeping and doing necessary household and personal chores which can be used in a chosen way.
- Recreation: *pursuits undertaken in leisure time*. Recreational pursuits include home-based activities such as reading and watching television, and those outside the home including sports, theatre, cinema and tourism.
- Tourism: *visiting for at least one night for leisure and holiday, business and professional or other tourism purposes*. Visiting means a temporary movement to destinations outside the normal home and workplace.
- Recreation, leisure and tourism sector organizations: *organizations producing goods and services for use in leisure time*, organizations seeking to influence the use of leisure time and organizations supplying recreation, leisure and tourism organizations. Many organizations produce goods and services for recreational and non-recreational use, for example computer manufacturers. Figure 1.1 shows the relationship between recreation, and tourism and the constituent parts are discussed below.

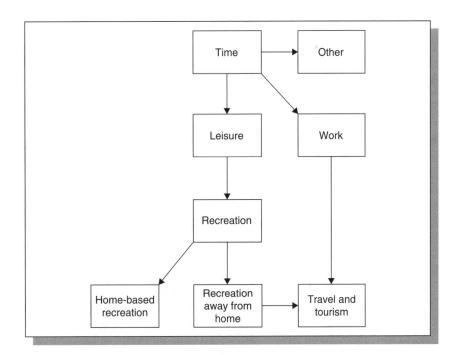

Figure 1.1
Leisure and tourism

Home-based recreation

This includes:

- listening to music,
- watching television and videos,
- listening to the radio,
- reading,
- do it yourself (DIY),
- gardening,
- playing games,
- exercise,
- hobbies,
- leisure use of computers.

Recreation away from home

This includes:

- sports participation,
- watching entertainment,
- hobbies,
- visiting attractions,
- eating and drinking,
- betting and gaming.

Travel and tourism

This includes:

- travelling to destination,
- accommodation at destination,
- recreation at destination.

Definition, scope and methodology of economics

The nature of economics

Resources and wants • • •

Economics arises from a basic imbalance that is evident throughout the world. On the one side there are resources which can be used to make goods and services. These are classified by economists into land (raw materials), labour and capital (machines). Additionally we sometimes include the entrepreneur (the person that brings factors of production together) as a resource. On the other side we have people's wants. The worldwide economic fact of life is that people's wants appear unlimited and exceed the resources available to satisfy these wants. This is true not just for people with low incomes, but for people with high incomes too. Clearly the basic needs of rich people are generally satisfied in terms of food, clothing and shelter, but it is evident that their material wants in terms of cars, property, holidays and recreation are rarely fully satisfied.

Scarcity and choice ● ● ●

The existence of limited resources and unlimited wants gives rise to the basic economic problem of scarcity. The existence of scarcity means that choices have to be made about resource use and allocation. Economics is concerned with the choice questions that arise from scarcity:

- What to produce?
- How to produce it?
- To whom will goods and services be allocated?

Opportunity cost ● ● ●

Since resources can be used in different ways to make different goods and services, and since they are limited in relation to wants, the concept of opportunity cost arises. This can be viewed at different levels.

At the individual level, consumers have limited income. So if they spend their income on a mountain bike, they can consider what else they could have bought with the money, such as 50 compact disks (CDs). Individuals also have limited time. If an individual decides to work extra overtime, leisure time must be given up.

At a local or national government level the same types of choices can be analysed. Local councils have limited budgets. If they decide to build a leisure centre, that money could have been used to provide more home help to the elderly. Even if they raised local taxes to build the new leisure centre there would be an opportunity cost, since the taxpayers would have to give up something in order to pay the extra taxes. Similar examples exist at a national government level. For example, subsidizing the arts means that there is less money available for student grants.

Opportunity cost is defined as the alternatives or other opportunities that have to be foregone to achieve a particular thing. Figure 1.2 illustrates this concept by use of a production possibility frontier (PPF). It is assumed first

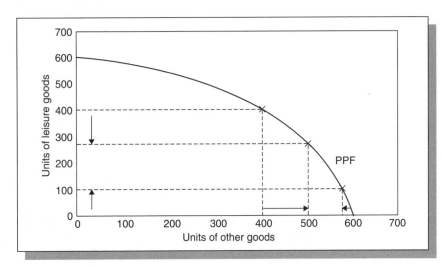

Figure 1.2
Opportunity cost and the PPF

that the economy only produces two types of goods (leisure goods and other goods) and second, that it uses all its resources fully.

Curve PPF plots all the possible combinations of leisure goods and other goods that can be produced in this economy. It is drawn concave to the origin (bowed outwards) since, as more and more resources are concentrated on the production of one commodity, the resources available become less suitable for producing that commodity.

Curve PPF shows that if all resources were geared towards the production of leisure goods, 600 units could be produced with no production of other goods. At the other extreme, 600 units of other goods could be produced with no units of leisure goods. The PPF describes the opportunity cost of increasing production of either of these goods. For example, increasing production of leisure goods from 0 to 100 can only be done by diverting resources from the production of other goods, and production of these falls from 600 to 580 units. Thus the opportunity cost at this point of 100 units of leisure goods is the 20 units of other goods that must be foregone. Similarly, if all resources are being used to produce a combination of 400 units of leisure goods and 400 units of other goods, the opportunity cost of producing an extra 100 units of other goods would be 100 units of leisure goods.

Allocative mechanisms • • •

The existence of scarcity of resources and unlimited wants means that any economy must have a system for determining what, how and for whom goods are produced. The main systems for achieving this are:

- free market economies,
- centrally planned economies,
- mixed economies.

Free market economies work by allowing private ownership of firms. The owners of such firms produce goods and services by purchasing resources. The motive for production is profit and thus firms will tend to produce those goods and services which are in demand. Figure 1.3 shows the market mechanism in action.

Centrally planned economies do not allow the private ownership of firms which instead are state owned. Production decisions are taken by state planning committees and resources are mobilized accordingly. Consumers generally have some choice of what to buy, but only from the range determined by state planners.

Mixed economies incorporate elements from each system. Private ownership of firms tends to predominate, but production and consumption of goods and services may be influenced by public ownership of some enterprises and by the use of taxes and government spending.

The allocative mechanism has important implications for leisure and tourism. The collapse of communism in the eastern bloc has meant that many economies are now in transition from centrally planned to market

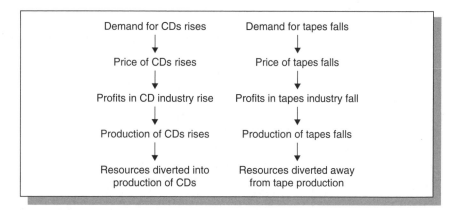

Figure 1.3
The price mechanism in action

Plate 1
The McDonald's Golden Arches in Beijing, China

systems. Tourism facilities, such as hotels and restaurants, in these countries are having to revolutionize their organizational culture and become more customer oriented. The economies of Cuba and China are still nominally centrally planned, but free enterprise is currently flourishing under the economic reforms in China, and a visit to the Great Wall is repaid by privately owned souvenir shops jostling for custom. Plate 1 and Exhibit 1.1 illustrate the boom in private enterprise in China.

In the UK, the 'Thatcher revolution', which involved 'rolling back the frontiers of the state', had an important impact on recreation, leisure and tourism production. It involved privatization of British Airways (BA) and the British Airports Authority (BAA), and also limited the spending powers of local government, thus reducing public provision in arts and leisure. Exhibit 1.2 illustrates the popularity of privatization across Europe particularly in

---

Exhibit 1.1   Private sector leisure revolution in communist China

In Forbes magazine's recently published list of the richest people in China's rich, Huang Qiuling, a former farmer is rated at No. 44. Mr Huang runs a leisure empire and the jewel in his crown is his Song Dynasty theme park in Hangzhou. Attractions in the Song Dynasty Park include a full-size replica of the White House and scaled down versions of the Washington Monument and Mount Rushmore. Visitors to the park can sit in a buffalo cart, dress up in imperial costume, and watch Chinese opera. The success of Huang Qiuling's leisure empire means that he has now accumulated assets worth US $150 million.

Mr Huang and the Song Dynasty Park illustrate the massive changes that have occurred in the political economy of China over the last 25 years. Under the regime of Chairman Mao Zedong communism was kept as pure as possible. Enterprises were owned by the state and individualism and consumerism were frowned upon. Few foreign tourists managed to enter China. It was Mao's successor Deng Xiaoping who introduced a complete turn around in policy. For him economic development was seen as the top priority for China and under him limited private enterprise and foreign investment was encouraged allowing the free market to grow.

By 1999, private Chinese companies had grown to account for nearly one-quarter of industrial output. If the contribution of foreign companies is added the total accounts for nearly 40 per cent. This means that there are now nearly as many private companies as state-owned enterprises. The latter decreased by 10 per cent in the 1990s, shedding hundreds of thousands of workers in the process. Between 2000 and 2005 the private sector in Shanghai is expected to grow by a further 40 per cent. Leisure, tourism and recreation are the key sectors in the new Chinese economy. The relative cheapness of production in China means that it is a growing centre of the manufacture of recreation goods – from tennis racquets to sports clothes and electronic leisure equipment. The diverse cultural attractions make China a growing tourist destination and the rapidly growing economy has caused a growth in the domestic leisure and recreation markets.

Source: Adapted from *The Guardian*, 5 November 2002.

---

relation to state-owned airlines. Indeed these moves are actively encouraged by the European Commission.

The debate surrounding the mix of private versus public provision tends to centre on several key issues. Advocates of the free market argue that the system allows maximum consumer choice or sovereignty. They point to the efficiency of the system as firms compete to cut costs and improve products, the fact that the system does not need wastefully to employ officials to plan and monitor production, and lower taxes under free market systems. Their evidence is the one-way flow of human traffic observed across the Florida Straits from Cuba and past the former Iron Curtain from Eastern Europe in search of the free market.

> **Exhibit 1.2   Privatization in the skies of Europe**
>
> - *Greece*: The Greek government plans to privatize Olympic Airways and use the proceeds to cover the old airline's debt. It wants to sell at least 51 per cent of the new carrier, to be named Olympic Airlines. Three Greek banks – National, Alpha and Commercial Bank – have started talks with potential buyers to privatize a new airline from the remnants of debt-burdened Olympic Airways.
> - *France*: The state wants to cut its holding in Air France to below 20 per cent from 54.4 per cent early next year or 'when market conditions permit'. This privatization move would raise more than €1 billion, but trade unions are deeply hostile to any sale.
>
> *Sources*: Adapted from *The Guardian*, 13 September 2002 and 30 August 2003.

Critics of the free market argue that choice is an illusion. Thus, although by day the shops in major shopping districts in London, New York and Paris are full of every conceivable product, by night their doorways are full of homeless people. What this illustrates is that only those with purchasing power can exercise choice and purchasing power is unequally distributed in free market economies. Additionally public provision is able to provide services which may be socially desirable but not profitable.

Macroeconomics and microeconomics ● ● ●

Economics is often subdivided into the separate areas of microeconomics and macroeconomics. Microeconomics studies individual consumer and household behaviour as well as the behaviour of firms. It analyses how these interact in particular markets to produce an equilibrium price and quantity sold. Thus microeconomics looks at the price of air travel, the output of running shoes and the choice between leisure and work.

Macroeconomics looks at the economy as a whole. The national economy is composed of all the individual market activities added together. Thus macroeconomics looks at aggregates such as national product and inflation.

Marginal analysis ● ● ●

The concept of 'the margin' is central to much economic analysis. Consumer, producer and social welfare theories are based on the idea that an equilibrium position can be achieved which represents the best possible solution. This position can theoretically be found by comparing the marginal benefit (MB) of doing something with the marginal cost (MC). For example, MC to a firm is the cost of producing one extra unit. MB is the revenue gained from selling one extra unit. Clearly a firm can increase its profit by producing more if MB > MC. It should not expand such that MC > MB, and thus profits are maximized, and the firm is in equilibrium, because it cannot better its position, where MC = MB.

The methodology of economics

Economics is a social science. As such it draws some of its methodology or way of working from other sciences such as physics or chemistry, but also has important differences.

The 'science' of social science • • •

The science part of economics is that it is a discipline that attempts to develop a body of principles. Economic principles attempt to explain the behaviour of households and firms in the economy. It therefore shares some common methods with other sciences.

The first of these is the need to distinguish between positive and normative statements. Positive statements are those which can be tested by an appeal to the facts. They are statements of what is or what will be. 'Swimming cuts cholesterol' is a positive statement. It can be tested, and accepted or refuted. Normative statements are those which are statements of opinion, and therefore cannot be tested by an appeal to the facts. 'There should be a swimming pool in every town' is a normative statement.

Second, economics uses scientific method. The scientific method acts as a filter which determines which theories become part of the established body of principles of economics, and whether existing theories should maintain their place. Figure 1.4 illustrates the scientific testing of theories.

New and existing theories are subject to testing and are accepted, rejected, amended or superseded according to the results of testing. Thus the body of economic principles is, like that of other sciences, organic in the sense that knowledge is being extended and some theories are shown to be no longer valid.

This can be illustrated by considering the shape of the earth. Hundreds of years ago, people were in agreement that the earth was flat. This theory was confirmed by scholars who reasoned that if it was not flat people would fall off it. It was further reasoned that the stars were attached to a canopy above the earth and this fitted observations nicely. This then was the accepted set of principles until the theory no longer tested true. It was developments in geometry and astronomy that first led to serious questioning of the accepted principles and circumnavigation of the earth endorsed such findings. Modern space programmes continue to confirm our current belief in a round earth by providing supporting photographic evidence.

Academic journals in economics, leisure and tourism provide the arena for testing old and new hypotheses in this field.

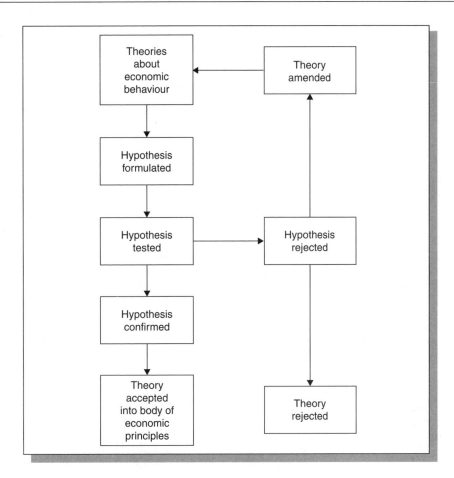

Figure 1.4
Scientific testing of theories

The 'social' of social science ● ● ●

The difference between social sciences such as economics, sociology and psychology and natural sciences such as physics and chemistry is that the former study people rather than inanimate objects. This means first that their investigative methods are often different. It is difficult to perform laboratory experiments in economics and often data must be collected from historical records or from surveys. Second it means that economic 'laws' are different from physics laws. If interest rates increase it can be predicted that the demand for credit will fall but we cannot predict that will be true for every individual. The law of gravity, on the other hand, applies universally.

Economic models ● ● ●

Economic models are built to describe relationships between economic variables and predict the effects of changing these variables. They can be compared to models used elsewhere. For example, civil engineers build models of bridges and subject them to stress in a wind tunnel. The purpose of the model is to predict what will happen in the real world, and in the case of a bridge ensure that the design is safe in extreme conditions.

Models are generally simplified abstractions of the real world. They have two key components. First assumptions are made which build the foundations for the model. For example, the model of firms' behaviour under perfect competition assumes that firms maximize profits, that there are many buyers and sellers, and that the products bought and sold are identical. Second implications or outcomes are predicted by the working of the model. For example, theory predicts that firms operating under conditions of perfect competition will not be able to earn abnormally high profits in the long run. As the channel crossing becomes a more competitive environment, since the opening of the tunnel, the predictions of competition theory can be tested empirically, or in other words by making observations.

The term *ceteris paribus* is often used in economic analysis, meaning all other things remaining unchanged. This is important because in the real world several factors often occur at the same time, some exaggerating a particular effect, and some countering it. So for example it can be said that for most goods an increase in price will lead to a fall in demand *ceteris paribus*. Thus a rise in cinema ticket prices should cause a fall in demand. Clearly if other things are allowed to change this might not happen. For example, if incomes rose significantly this might more than offset the increase in price and we might observe demand for cinema tickets rising whilst prices rise.

The economics of recreation, leisure and tourism

Economic questions in general as well as those specific to recreation, leisure and tourism result form scarcity. Scarcity arises from the imbalance between the resources available to make goods and services and people's demand for those goods and services. Economics is a social science which studies how limited resources are used to try to satisfy unlimited wants. Economic theories and models are constructed to describe the relationship between economic variables (e.g. the level of income and the demand for fitness club membership) and to make predictions. Economics is generally divided into microeconomics focussing on individuals, firms and markets and macroeconomics, focussing on the whole economy generally at the national level. There is also a growing movement concerned with environmental economics.

At the microeconomic level, in market economies, it is consumer preferences expressed through patterns of demand that largely determine which recreation, leisure and tourism goods and services will be supplied. On the demand side rising incomes have stimulated strong growth in this sector. On the supply side technological advances have led to the introduction of new leisure products (e.g. digital cameras and MP3 players) and the reduction in prices of many existing ones (e.g. televisions and stereos). Changing patterns of demand and supply create relative shortages, gluts and price changes in different recreation, leisure and tourism markets. These signals are picked up by profit-seeking producers who adjust production and economizing consumers who adjust purchases accordingly until there is an equilibrium reached in each market at a price where demand equals supply. This is the 'invisible hand' of the market which was first explained by the early economist Adam Smith. It demonstrates in general how leisure resources are allocated amongst competing uses and specifically how, for example, CDs have replaced vinyl and tapes in music stores. It also demonstrates why in a sports stadium a cleaner might earn US $5 per hour (high supply and limited demand) whereas a top international sportsperson can earn US $300 an hour (limited supply and high demand).

Most economies incorporate a degree of government intervention and so recreation, leisure and tourism production and consumption is not left totally to market forces. For example some leisure pursuits (e.g. the consumption of recreational drugs) are banned and not available through regular markets. Similarly, some leisure pursuits (e.g. gambling and smoking) are discouraged by governments through taxation. Other leisure pursuits (e.g. opera, arts and children's playgrounds) are deemed to be beneficial to society at large. These so-called merit goods are therefore encouraged by governments and offered at reduced prices or at no charge through government subsidy. In some instances (e.g. television stations, parks and swimming pools) leisure services are not provided by private firms (the private sector) but rather by state or local government (the public sector). However, over the last 20 years there has been a move towards privatization of public sector organizations – most notably airlines in the leisure sector. Privatization and deregulation of markets are both designed to promote competition which in turn encourages cost cutting, low prices and product innovation. Similarly governments intervene in markets for the purposes of consumer protection which includes actions to prevent the formation of monopolies that may be against the public interest. In the UK the government has acted to prevent the formation of monopolies in the brewing industry and in cross-Channel ferries.

As well as making choices in the market between different leisure goods and services, and other goods and services, individuals are also faced with the choice of allocating time between work and leisure. An interesting economic question is the way in which individuals react to an increase in wages. On the one hand an increase in wages stimulates our desire for leisure time because we have more income to enjoy it. On the other hand as earnings per hour increase workers are faced with a notional increase in the cost of not working (i.e. the opportunity cost of leisure increases). Hence rational individuals may be tempted to reallocate time towards paid work or at least increase the intensity of their leisure consumption. Empirical evidence points to a modest reduction in time devoted to work and research in the UK suggests that between the 1950s and the end of the 1990s, British people had decreased their working hours by 2 hours 40 minutes per week. The labour market is also subject to government intervention and in the European Union for example, the European Work Directive has capped the working week at 35 hours for most employees.

At the macroeconomic level, recreation and tourism are major contributors to national income and prosperity. Their main economic impacts include expenditure, incomes, employment and foreign currency earnings but is difficult to determine the exact contribution of recreation and tourism to the macroeconomy because the boundaries between leisure and other activities can be blurred. For example motoring can include business and leisure uses as can computing and Internet use. Nevertheless leisure expenditure was estimated to account for a quarter of total expenditure in the UK in 1997, and contribute to over 6 per cent of employment. In some countries economic impacts are particularly strong and tourism for example represents approximately 50 per cent of the economic activity of islands of Bermuda and the Bahamas (Conlin and Baum, 1995). In terms of foreign currency earnings, by the mid-1990s tourism contributed over US $11 million to the balance of payments account of France. Different aspects of the leisure industry are of importance in different countries. For example the film industry is particularly significant in the USA, the music industry in the UK and the tourism industry in Spain.

The economic importance of recreation and tourism also depends on the stage of a county's economic development. As countries become richer, leisure assumes an increased economic importance. In low-income economies, resources are typically used mainly to satisfy basic demands of food, clothing and shelter with little available for leisure. In high-income economies resources and incomes are more plentiful and the production and consumption of leisure goods and services become significant economic activities. This is reflected in economic data so that for low-income countries the primary sector of the economy (agriculture, mining, etc.) accounts for the majority of economic activity, whereas for developed economies it is the manufacturing and the services sector. However in mature developed countries deindustrialization is a common phenomenon where traditional manufacturing industries decline and the services sector (especially financial services, leisure and information technology) has become the major source of economic growth.

The leisure industry is increasingly seen as an appropriate vehicle to aid economic growth. For developing countries, tourism especially can be an important part of an economic development strategy, although resources need to be found for investment in infrastructure. Leisure projects are also important for developed countries. For example there was considerable competition between European countries to host the new Disney theme park which was eventually established near Paris, France. Such projects bring income and employment both in the construction and running phases and can have significant multiplier effects on the local and national economy. Because of this governments may favour leisure developments as part of a regeneration strategy for regions which have been affected by a decline in traditional industries. In situations such as these where wider benefits beyond immediate profitability are important, governments may use cost benefit analysis to determine whether a scheme should go ahead.

The growth of multinational corporations through integration, franchising and international tourism has led to an increasing globalization of leisure. In economic terms this means that production and marketing of leisure goods and services are increasingly unconstrained by national boundaries. Examples of global brands in leisure include Nike, Manchester United Football Club, Holiday Inn Hotels and Time Warner. Multinationals such as Nike are able to locate production where labour and other costs are lowest whilst marketing products to high-income consumers. Additionally production for global markets enables multinationals to benefit from economies of scale. These factors can bring benefits to shareholders in higher profits and consumers in lower prices. However, some multinationals have been criticized for exploitation of labour in developing countries. Similarly whilst multinationals can provide investment for tourism development, they may result in lower-multiplier benefits since they tend to import more and repatriate profits to their corporate headquarters.

The production and consumption of leisure goods and services also gives rise to a series of externalities. For example on the positive side, increased use of fitness facilities results in lower use of public health provision. On the negative side increased air travel causes environmental impacts of air and noise pollution. Environmental economics seeks to extend conventional economic analysis to include consideration of environmental externalities, the use of renewable and non-renewable resources, and the carrying capacity of the environment. Taking the example of air travel, environmental economists would advocate the following. First, airlines should pay for the pollution they cause (for example they should finance double-glazing for those directly affected by aircraft noise). Second, airlines should monitor and control their effects on resources such as the ozone layer. Third, since the atmosphere has a limited carrying capacity for absorbing pollution before global warming occurs, airline contribution to this should be monitored and controlled. Environmental taxes are advocated so that polluting firms pay the full costs of any negative environmental impacts and non-government organizations (NGOs) such as Tourism Concern, World Wide Fund for Nature (WWF) and Greenpeace lobby governments to provide better environmental protection.

Finally, the limitations of economics in analysing the leisure world should be noted. Economics tends to concentrate on how markets work and how to increase economic efficiency and economic growth. The market is the mechanism that decides which leisure goods and services will be produced and who will enjoy them. It does not raise or answer questions about what leisure goods and services should be produced or who should enjoy them or indeed about what kind of a leisure society would be desirable. Such questions are generally tackled under ethics and philosophy.

Review of key terms

- Leisure: discretionary time.
- Recreation: pursuits undertaken in leisure time.
- Tourism: visiting for at least one night for leisure and holiday, business and professional or other tourism purposes.
- Economic problem: scarcity and choice.
- Leisure and tourism sector organizations: organizations producing goods and services for use in leisure time, and organizations seeking to influence the use of leisure time.
- Opportunity cost: the alternatives or other opportunities that have to be foregone to achieve a particular thing.
- Free market economy: resources allocated through price system.
- Centrally planned economy: resources allocated by planning officials.

- Mixed economy: resources allocated through free market and planning authorities.
- Microeconomics: study of household and firm's behaviour.
- Macroeconomics: study of whole economy.
- Marginal analysis: study of effects of one extra unit.
- Positive statement: based on fact.
- Normative statement: based on opinion.
- *Ceteris paribus*: other things remaining unchanged.

Data Questions

Task 1.1   The uses and misuses of economics

Economics is a discipline which can help to understand leisure and tourism and provides tools to help decision-making. But it is only one of a number of ways of looking at leisure and tourism. For example, the disciplines of sociology, psychology, anthropology and philosophy each investigate different aspects of leisure and tourism and use different methods and theories in their investigations. So philosophy may look at meaning (what is the concept of leisure?), aesthetics (is a football stadium attractively designed?) and ethics (are violent video games good or bad?). Focussing on video games can help to see how different disciplines tackle different issues. Psychology might investigate human motivation for playing video games. Economics may forecast the demand for them. Sociology can help to understand the effects of video games on society.

A complex field of study such as leisure and tourism often requires a multidisciplinary approach. That is we may seek understanding not just from one discipline but from a number of disciplines. In addition, there are approaches which are interdisciplinary. Here a new set of methods, theories and language emerge from those working collaboratively across disciplines. Environmentalism, which uses economics, sociology, biology, physics and chemistry, is an example of an interdisciplinary approach.

Then there are functional approaches to leisure and tourism. These have a more distant relationship to disciplines and their specific focus is on management. Examples here include accounting, law, marketing and human resource management. Whilst disciplines are nurtured in universities and concentrate on the development of theories, functional approaches are developed in the practising field. The main differences between disciplinary knowledge and functional knowledge are summarized in Table 1.1. The importance of this discussion is that we

Table 1.1 Differences between disciplinary and functional approaches to leisure and tourism

	Disciplinary	Functional
Knowledge	Knowing that	Knowing how
Site of knowledge creation	Universities	Industry
Interest	Is it true?	Does it work?
Emphasis	Theory	Practice

live in a society of specialists with a highly developed division of labour. It is easy for people to become highly knowledgeable in one area while being ignorant of other significant aspects of a situation. It is therefore important to understand the limits of any single approach and the fact that most leisure and tourism issues are multifaceted. It is always worth asking what kind of a question is being investigated (is it an economic, philosophical, psychological question, or one of law or marketing?). Of course, the wider the approach, the more difficult decision-making can become.

Recap Questions

1 What contribution can economics make to environmentalism?
2 What kinds of questions are each of the following?
   (a) The level of a minimum wage for the hotel industry.
   (b) Whether violent video games should be banned.
   (c) The effects of a rise in interest rates.
   (d) Maximizing profits from the sales of video games.
   (e) Imposing a tax on aviation fuel.
   (f) Ending duty-free sales.
   (g) The location of the next Olympic Games.
3 Is there a correct answer to any of these questions?
4 Frame two leisure and tourism questions which are exclusively economic.

Task 1.2   The importance of leisure to the US economy

In their publication 'White Paper No. 3' The American Academy of Leisure Sciences claims that leisure is becoming the new centre of America's economy. The authors initially note that 'identifying leisure's economic importance is difficult' and that it is 'hard even to find the word "leisure" in government economic statistics'. The main part of the report then goes on to provide an insight into the contribution of leisure to the US economy. In terms of leisure spending the report initially considers recreation. 'The Department of Commerce defines recreation spending to include spending on home electronics, radio and television, music, entertainment, sporting goods, amusements, home gardening, toys, books and magazines, and recreation equipment like boats, motor homes and bicycles. In 1990 consumers spent US $280 billion on these recreational goods and services, constituting 7 per cent of all consumer spending. This is 3 times what consumers spent for new cars in 1990.'

However the report notes that 'US $280 billion is only a small part of all leisure spending' and that 'the majority of leisure spending is classified elsewhere'. It notes that much of spending under general categories such as transportation, housing, clothing and food can be attributed to leisure uses. 'Add all of this up' say the authors 'and leisure easily accounts for over US $1 trillion or about a third of all consumer spending ... this makes leisure America's number one economic activity.'

Turning to tourism, the report quotes Robert Crandall, Chairman of American Airlines, who reckons that 'the US's top three industries ... are tourism with US $621 billion in spending, health care with US $604 billion and education with US $331 billion.' In terms of jobs the report notes that 'Crandall claims that travel and tourism employs 9 million people in the US'. It adds that leisure is responsible for '25 million jobs about a quarter of all jobs in 1990'. What makes particularly interesting reading is the comparisons that the report makes with other sectors of the US economy. For example it notes that 'depending on which measure of economic importance you choose to accept, leisure is between 5 and 20 times the size of the automobile industry in the US'. Despite its importance though the authors claim that the significance of leisure to the economy is often overlooked. One reason they attribute for this is that government statistics are slow to catch up with and mirror changes in the economy. Because of this, there are detailed statistics available for example on agricultural and automobile production but it is still difficult to find detailed or aggregate statistics on the contribution of recreation, leisure and tourism.

Source: Adapted from *White Paper No. 3: Leisure: The New Center of the Economy?* published by The Academy of Leisure Sciences (www.academyofleisuresciences.org).

Recap Questions

1 What kind of jobs are provided in recreation, leisure and tourism?
2 How might these activities affect US imports and exports?
3 Explain
  (a) How the US market economy works to produce changing patterns of output of automobiles, agriculture and leisure?
  (b) What are the main determinants of the level of outputs?
  (c) How the 'allocative mechanism' of the USA differs from that in Cuba?
4 Are there any negative economic impacts of recreation, leisure and tourism industries?
5 How significant are recreation, leisure and tourism industries to the economy of the country where you are studying?
6 How would you expect the economic significance of leisure industries to differ between the USA, the UK, Australia, India, Saudi Arabia and Nepal?

Task 1.3   Economic impact of hosting Olympics

While the 2008 Olympic Games are scheduled to last only 16 days, their effects on host cities will be felt long after the final gold medals are awarded, according to Jones Lang LaSalle and LaSalle Investment Management. The report, *Reaching beyond the Gold: The Impact of the Olympic Games on Real Estate Markets* examines the legacies of four recent Olympic hosts – Seoul (1988), Barcelona (1992), Atlanta (1996) and Sydney (2000) – and forecasts the potential impacts on Athens, the Olympics' 2004 host.

'History clearly demonstrates that the 2008 Olympics host city will enjoy significant long-term benefits,' said Melinda McKay, Senior Vice President of Marketing and Research, Jones Lang LaSalle, and co-author of the study. 'While the Games generate short-term economic gains, such as more jobs and increased revenue, other indirect effects – such as changes in the host city's urban form and governance – are farther reaching and longer lasting.'

It is estimated that the Sydney Olympics will add approximately US $4.3 billion to the Australian gross domestic product (GDP) and create as many as 100 000 full-time jobs over the 12-year period from 1994 to 2006. Equally impressive figures have been cited for the Seoul, Barcelona and Atlanta Games. While the data in Table 1.2 is not directly comparable, given differences in methodology and scope of the studies between cities, it does illustrate the large positive economic impacts generated by each of the past four Olympics. The total of US $16.6 billion of investment generated by the Barcelona Games was sufficient to delay (but not prevent) the

Table 1.2 Summary of economic impact

	Estimated net economic impact (US $billion)*	Size of economy (GDP US $billion)**	Per cent impact
Seoul	2.6	182.0	1.4
Barcelona	16.6	577.3	2.9
Atlanta	5.1	7388.0	0.07
Sydney	4.3	429.1	1.0

* All figures in US $, based on average exchange rates during Olympic Year.
** GDP in Olympic Year.

Barcelona economy from suffering the impact of the economic downturn that swept Europe in the early 1990s. The Seoul Olympics acted as an important catalyst, promoting Korea as one of the leading Asian Tiger economies.

'Each of the recent host cities has capitalized on the Olympics to revitalize run-down urban areas,' said McKay. 'For example, the Sydney Games were hosted on a site that had previously been home to an unusable swamp, brick works, a meat-packing house and a munitions dump. As a result of the Games, this area is now one of the most accessible locations in Sydney, boasting world-class sporting facilities and one of the largest and best-serviced new residential communities in the city.' Atlanta, which had experienced many of the classic problems associated with urban sprawl, made a determined effort to revitalize inner city areas, with the area around Centennial Olympic Park currently undergoing a revival.

'The design, location and form of Olympic Villages also can have a dramatic impact on urban development of the host city,' said McKay. Seoul and Barcelona constructed full-scale new urban centres – including housing, retail and other community facilities – that now are fully integrated into their respective metropolitan areas. Sydney's Olympic village of Newington eventually will house 5000 residents and form the world's largest solar-powered settlement. Athens will follow the same model, transforming the 80 hectares (198 acres) Olympic site into a residential, commercial and public use site after the games.

Infrastructure development has been another major benefit for Olympic host cities. As an example, the Seoul Games were used as the catalyst for undertaking a number of upgrades including the expansion of Kimpo International Airport, new roads and underground stations.

'For a host city's tourism and convention industries, the long-term payback of the Olympics is potentially profound,' said McKay. 'Consider the case of Sydney, which transformed Australia into a living postcard.' The 2000 Olympics has been widely recognized as the biggest marketing event in the nation's history, with an estimated US $2 billion of global publicity for Sydney and Australia over the last 4 years. An early indication of success is that total visitor arrivals for 2000 were up by 11 per cent, with the highest monthly total arrivals achieved in December 2000, 3 months after the Games themselves.

Source: Adapted from Press release from Jones Lang Lasalle, Lasalle Investment Management.

Recap Questions

1 How can projects such as hosting the Olympic Games help in regeneration? What other examples are there of this?
2 What negative economic impacts might there be from the hosting of the Olympic Games?
3 What is the opportunity cost of public sector investment in hosting of the Olympic Games?
4 Which industries are most likely to benefit from hosting the Olympic Games?

Multiple choice

1 **Which of the following is not considered a resource?**

(a) Demand
(b) Land
(c) Labour
(d) Capital

2 *Ceteris paribus* **means**

(a) Everything changes in the long run
(b) All other things remain unchanged
(c) Equal wages
(d) Inflation is rising

3 **What does the term macroeconomic mean?**

(a) An embedded programme in economics
(b) The absence of scarcity
(c) To do with the whole economy
(d) The economy is growing

4 **Opportunity cost measures**

(a) An alternative that has to be given up in order to produce something
(b) Average cost plus MC
(c) Average cost divided by MC
(d) Environmental cost

5 **Which of the following is a positive statement?**

(a) The minimum wage should be increased
(b) Pigs can fly
(c) The price of bacon is too high
(d) Unemployment should be reduced

Review questions

1 What is the opportunity cost of watching television?
2 Explain in terms of marginal analysis at what point you will turn off the television.

3 Formulate a hypothesis that links the level of unemployment to the demand for video rentals. How would you test this hypothesis and what problems might you encounter?
4 Explain how the market mechanism responds to a change in consumer tastes or demand using an example from the leisure or tourism sector.
5 Distinguish between the kinds of problems which physics, biology, psychology and economics might address in the area of sports. What similarities and differences in investigative methods are there between these disciplines?

Web sites of interest

Leisure opportunities: daily news www.leisureopportunities.co.uk
Institute of Leisure and Amenity Management: www.ilam.co.uk
World Tourism Organization: www.world-tourism.org/
World Travel and Tourism Council: www.wttc.org/
Learning help in economics and business studies www.bized.ac.uk
Tourism Education Web site: www.touriseducation.org
The ALTIS guide to Internet resources in hospitality, leisure, sport and tourism: www.altis.ac.uk

Part One

Organizations and Markets

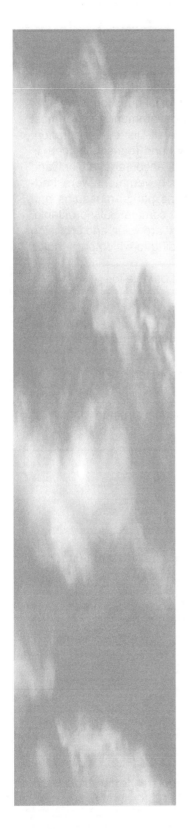

CHAPTER 2

Recreation, leisure and tourism organizations

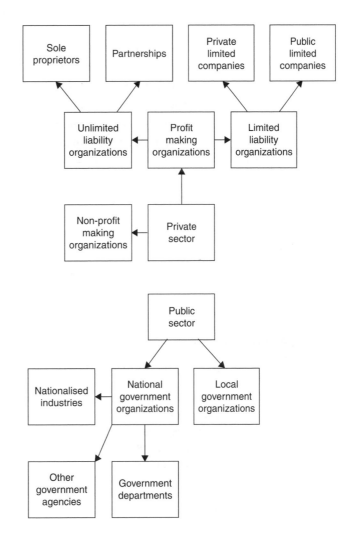

Objectives and learning outcomes

In order to analyse and understand the behaviour of organizations in the recreation, leisure and tourism sector, we need to be able to clarify their aims and objectives. An important initial question is whether the organization is in the private sector or government run. For most private sector organizations such as The Walt Disney Corporation, profits are the main objective. On the other hand Tourism Concern is a not-for-profit organization and exists to encourage ethical and sustainable tourism. Organizations run by government were traditionally set up to provide services such as parks, museums and swimming pools that were desirable but not commercially profitable. But the attitudes to the extent of government provision and provision of subsidies varies across countries according to which party holds political power.

By studying this chapter students should be able to:

- distinguish between private sector and public sector organizations,
- understand the differences in finance, control, structure and objectives of organizations,
- understand ways in which capital can be raised,
- analyse movements in share prices,
- analyse the effects of different organizational structures on organizational behaviour.

Public sector organizations

Public sector organizations are those owned by the government. This can be national government or local government.

Local government organizations

Leisure and tourism provision in the local government sector may include:

- leisure centres and swimming pools,
- libraries,
- arts centres,
- parks and recreation facilities,
- tourism support services.

It should be noted that sometimes services are free, sometimes they are subsidized and sometimes they are provided at full commercial rates. For example, charges for swimming pools are often subsidized but sometimes cover the full cost of provision. On the other hand facilities such as parks, libraries and children's playgrounds are generally provided without charge.

Sources of finance • • •

The finance of these organizations comes from:

- charges for services where applicable,
- central government grants,
- grants from other sources (e.g. the Arts Council of Great Britain),
- local government taxation,
- local government borrowing.

Ownership and control • • •

In essence local government organizations are owned by the local population. Policy decisions or decisions of strategic management are taken on their behalf by the local council. Each local government area elects councillors or members to represent them. The political party which holds the majority of seats on the council will generally be able to dictate policy and such policy will be determined through a series of committees such as:

- libraries and arts,
- recreation and leisure,
- planning and resources.

The planning and resources committee is a particularly powerful one as it determines the medium- to long-term strategy of the council and thus provides the financial framework within which the other committees must operate. The day-to-day or operational management of local government-run services depends on the nature of the service being provided. Council employees are responsible for overall management and services which are spread out across a local government area, such as parks, will be run from the council offices. Larger services such as leisure centres will have their own management which in turn will be responsible to a service director at the council offices.

Aims and missions • • •

The aims of local government and its organizations are largely determined by the political party or coalition of parties who hold the majority. This often means that leisure provision for example will vary between neighbouring local authorities which have different political parties in power. Administrations to the right of the political spectrum favour lower local taxes and market-driven provision. Those to the left favour public provision financed out of tax revenues and offered free or at subsidized prices. To determine the differing aims of political parties we need to consult their manifestos as well as review their actual provision. However, political parties do not operate in a vacuum. They will be influenced by:

- pressure groups,
- trade unions,
- local press,
- national government.

Edgecombe (2003) examines a major dilemma facing local government leisure facility managers in Australia – that of providing recreation services, whilst at the same time minimizing financial deficits and avoiding significant negative impacts on private enterprises providing similar services.

National government organizations

National government-owned organizations can be further sub-divided into public corporations, government departments and other government agencies.

Public corporations are sometimes known as nationalized or state-run industries. They generally supply goods or services to the public. Examples of these include:

- the British Broadcasting Corporation (UK),
- SNCF (National Rail Network) (France),
- Air India.

But the extent of nationalization of recreation, leisure and tourism industries depends on the politics of individual countries (Exhibit 2.1). So in the US most television stations and airlines are in the private sector and in the UK railways are run by private sector organizations.

Government departments perform an executive role on behalf of governments in implementing policy. There are a number of government departments which impinge on the recreation leisure and tourism sector of the economy. Examples include:

- the Department of Culture, Media and Sport (DCMS) (UK) which has responsibility for tourism, arts and libraries, sport and broadcasting;
- the Department of the Interior (US) which has responsibility for the National Parks Service;
- the Department of Industry, Tourism and Resources (Australia).

Exhibit 2.1   Nationalization of Air India

Air India, originally known as Tata Airlines started life with two planes, one palm-thatched shed, one full-time pilot, one part-time engineer and two apprentice-mechanics. In its first full year of operations (1933), it flew 160 000 miles, carrying155 passengers and 10.71 tonnes of mail. Tata Airlines was converted into a Public Company and renamed Air India in August 1946.

However by the early 1950s the financial condition of airlines operating in India had deteriorated so that the Government made the decision to nationalize the air transport industry. On 1 August 1953 Indian Airlines was formed with the merger of eight domestic airlines to operate domestic services and Air India International was established to operate the overseas services.

Source: Author, adapted for Air India Corporate Information (www.airindia.com).

Other government agencies tend to work at a smaller level than government departments and provide more specific services. Examples include:

- the Australian Tourist Commission,
- the British Tourist Authority.

Aims and missions ● ● ●

The aims of nationalized industries vary from country to country. In some cases public corporations aim for public service provision without the limitations imposed by the profit motive and are able to provide services that are loss making. In these instances the rigours of efficiency and private sector management styles may not be apparent. In other parts of the world (notably the UK and the US) public corporations have been subjected to efficiency targets, performance indicators, and target rates of return on investment, all of which have made them more closely mimic private sector organizations. Nationalized industry's aims are generally contained within their charters or constitutions.

The aim of government departments is to carry out the policy of the government of the day and includes the planning, monitoring and reviewing of provision and legislation. Exhibit 2.2 illustrates the aims of The Department of Culture, Media and Sport in the UK. The aims of other government agencies are specific to each organization and are generally targeted to a quite narrow field.

Exhibit 2.2   The Department of Culture Media and Sport (DCMS) (UK)

The DCMS's aim is to improve the quality of life for all through cultural and sporting activities, to support the pursuit of excellence and to champion the tourism, creative and leisure industries. Our vision is to extend excellence and improve access in all our many sectors.

To achieve this, we have developed four strategic priorities around which we organize our work:

- *Children and Young People*: enhancing access to a fuller cultural and sporting life for children and young people and giving them the opportunity to develop their talents to the full.
- *Community*: opening up our institutions to the wider community to promote lifelong learning and social cohesion.
- *Economy*: maximizing the contribution which the tourism, creative and leisure industries can make to the UK's economy.
- *Delivery*: modernizing the way we deliver our services by ensuring our sponsored bodies are set and meet targets which put consumers first.

What does the DCMS do?

The DCMS is responsible for Government policy on the arts, sport, the National Lottery, tourism, libraries, museums and galleries, broadcasting, film, the music industry, press freedom and regulation, licensing, gambling and the historic environment.

It is also responsible for the listing of historic buildings and scheduling of ancient monuments, the export licensing of cultural goods, the management of the Government Art Collection and for the Royal Parks Agency.

Our Public Service Agreement targets which we have agreed with the Treasury for 2003–2006 are:

- to enhance the take-up of sporting opportunities by 5–16 year olds by increasing the percentage of school children who spend a minimum of 2 hours on PE and sport within and beyond the curriculum from 25 to 75 per cent;
- to increase significantly the take-up of cultural and sporting opportunities by new users aged 20 and above from priority groups;
- to improve the productivity of the tourism, creative and leisure industries;
- to improve significantly the value for money of the Department's sponsored bodies.

Source: Department for Culture, Media and Sport web site (www.dcms.gov.uk).

Sources of finance • • •

National organizations in the public sector are financed in the main from:

- taxes,
- trading income.

The dependence on tax funding can mean that public sector organizations are very sensitive to the changing priorities of the government of the day. Equally if the state of the economy as a whole is unhealthy, spending cuts will generally be imposed through the public sector.

Ownership and control • • •

National government organizations are owned by the government on behalf of the population at large. However, each type of organization is controlled in a different way. At the point of nationalization a law is passed outlining the aims, organization and control mechanism for each industry. Nationalized industries are typically given some autonomy and generally have a legal identity separate from the government. A typical structure is one where a board of directors is established responsible for the day-to-day running of the industry. The chair of the board and its other members are appointed by an appropriate government minister and strategic decisions will be taken by the minister in consultation with the government.

Government departments are headed by a minister and staffed by government employees. Their actions are directly accountable through a minister to the national assembly such as parliament. The offices of government departments are generally located close to the national assembly. The degree of political control exerted over government departments is thus more direct than for nationalized industries.

Private sector organizations

Private sector organizations are those which are non-government-owned. They can be further sub-divided into profit-making organizations and non-profit-making organizations.

Profit-making organizations

Profit-making private sector organizations consist of those with unlimited liability, those with limited liability and companies which are quoted on the stock exchange.

Unlimited liability • • •

Unlimited liability means that the owners of such companies face no limit to their contribution should the organization become indebted. Most of their personal assets can be used to settle debts should the business cease trading. This includes not only the value of anything saleable from the business, but also housing, cars, furniture and stereos. Because of the discipline that unlimited liability brings, there are often very few formalities required to start trading as this form of business. Sole proprietorships and partnerships are examples of this type of business organization and advantages include:

- independence,
- motivation,
- personal supervision,
- flexibility.

Equally there are some disadvantages which include:

- unlimited liability,
- long hours of work,
- lack of capital for expansion,
- difficulties in case of illness (Plate 2).

Limited liability ● ● ●

In contrast the formation of a limited liability company enables its owners to create a separate legal identity and this enables them to limit their exposure and liability in the case of company failure. Incorporation confers separate legal identity on the company. This may be contrasted with the position of

Plate 2
Small scale enterprise:
Bike Hire in Zimbabwe
Source: The author

unlimited liability organizations where the owners and the organization are legally the same. Limited liability places a limit to the contribution by an investor in an organization to the amount of capital that has been contributed. Should one of these organizations cease trading with debts, an investor may well lose the original investment, but liability would cease there and personal assets would not be at risk.

The benefits of the limited liability company mean that they are bound by closer rules and regulations than are unlimited liability organizations. Typically such companies need to provide details of:

- the name and address of the company,
- details of the directors,
- the objectives of the company,
- details of share capital issued,
- details of the internal affairs of the company including procedures for annual general meetings,
- audited accounts.

Limited liability companies are further sub-divided into private companies and public companies. It is the latter's shares which are freely tradable on the stock exchange. Examples of companies that have been floated on the stock market (i.e. changed from private to public limited companies) include:

- Thistle Hotels (hotels) (UK) 1996.
- Thomson (tour operator) (UK) 1998 (see Exhibit 2.3).
- Virgin Blue (Airline) (Australia) 2003.

Exhibit 2.3   Post-flotation: Thomson shares sink then get lifeline

In May 1998, Thomson was floated by its Canadian parent company Thomson Corporation on the London stock exchange who want to concentrate on their core business of publishing in North America. It became the Thomson Travel Group (TTG) plc with an estimated value of £1.7 billion. The group's main brands include Thomson Holidays (the market leader in the UK), Lunn Poly Travel Agents, Britannia Airways and the Holiday Cottages Group, 1 billion shares were offered at a flotation price of 170*p*. In the period immediately following flotation share prices rose to a peak of 195*p*, but by September 1998 prices had fallen to below 130*p*, This followed a fall in first-half profits in 1998 from £12.2 million to £5.5 million. Shares subsequently reached a low of 80*p*.

In May 2000 the company announced that it had recommended shareholders to accept a bid from rival German group Preussag. The 180*p* per share offer valued the company at £1.8 billion and means that Preussag will remain Europe's largest travel company.

Source: The author (1999, 2002).

> **Exhibit 2.4   Trade weighs taking the plunge**
>
> Airtours profits rocketed from £2 million in 1987 to £45 million in 1993 – that could never have happened without Airtours floating on the stock market. Perhaps that explains why travel companies continue to make cash calls on the city either by going public or seek venture capital investment. One person who believes more holiday companies should float did it himself – Inspirations managing director Vic Fatah. 'If you float on the stock exchange you give up less than if venture capitalists come in,' said Mr Fatah. Companies could also consider raising private funds. 'The advantage of venture capitalists is that you can get people in at an earlier stage of your development.' Another advantage in taking the private route is that a company does not have to pay fees to advisors such as merchant bankers, brokers, lawyers and public relations firms. Expense is one reason why former Eurocamp group sales and marketing director Julian Rawel advises caution before opting to float. Mr Rawel helped steer Eurocamp through its flotation in 1991. The demands on a quoted company are always great, says Chris Parker, who has taken Unijet to the brink of floatation on two separate occasions: 'A quoted company always has to perform in the short-term, which can be very difficult in a volatile industry.'
>
> *Source*: *Travel Trade Gazette*, 9 March 1994 (adapted).

Exhibit 2.4 illustrates some of the debate in the travel sector in the 1990s over the benefits and drawbacks of moving from a private limited company to a public limited company. Airtours saw access to more capital as being a key advantage of becoming a public limited company. On the other hand Eurocamp stressed the fact that there are considerable extra costs associated with flotation and Unijet voiced concerns about the constant need to perform and produce high profits in the short term as a public limited company, and the possible loss of control. The extent of share ownership and lack of control on transfer of shares mean that it is more difficult to retain control of public than private limited companies as groups of shareholders can build up controlling interests.

Sources of finance • • •

Sources of finance available to sole proprietors and partnerships are limited to:

- capital contributed by the owners,
- ploughed-back profits,
- bank loans.

This is a key reason why small firms remain small. Companies are able to raise capital through the additional routes of:

- shares (equity),
- debentures.

Table 2.1   Financing Eurotunnel

1986	Concession to build the channel Tunnel awarded to Eurotunnel £46 million seed corn equity raised £206 million share placing with institutions
1987	£5 billion loan facility agreed with 200-bank syndicate 770 million equity funding from public offer in UK and France
1990	£1.8 billion additional debt from syndicate £300 million loan from European investment bank £650 million rights issue
1994	£700 million raised from banks £850 millon rights issue, priced at 26 per cent discount and entirely underwritten.

Source: Adapted from *The Guardian*, 27 May 1994.

A share, or equity or stock (US) represents a small portion of ownership of a company. The price of shares goes up and down according to relative demand and supply. Shares can be seen from the shareholder and company perspective. From the company point of view, share capital is generally low-risk since if the company doesn't make any profits then no dividends are issued. Shareholders are attracted to shares by the prospect of dividend payments (related to the level of company profits) as well as growth in the value of shares.

Debentures can be seen as a form of loan as they carry a fixed rate of interest. Thus to the company they pose a problem when profits are low because they still have to pay out the fixed interest, but their fixed interest rate is attractive when profits are high. Debenture holders get a guaranteed rate of return and are paid before shareholders so they are generally less risky than shares.

Eurotunnel is the name given to the rail tunnel that was built between England and France in the 1990s. Several points emerge from Table 2.1 which illustrates the financing of Eurotunnel. First, Eurotunnel's capital represents a mixture of loans from banks which carry interest payments until they are repaid, and share issues which will not pay dividends until profits are earned. If profits from the tunnel are insufficient to repay loans and interest, the company may be forced into liquidation by the banks. The assets of the company would then be sold to repay the banks. Under this scenario, shareholders would get nothing. However because their liability is limited, neither would they stand to lose any personal assets. Under a more optimistic, high-profit scenario, payments to the banks are limited to previously negotiated rates, leaving substantial profits to be distributed in the form of high dividends to shareholders. Second, three different forms of share issue are illustrated:

- A placing in 1986. This is where Eurotunnel's shares were placed directly with institutions such as pension funds and insurance companies.

- An offer for sale in 1987. This is where shares are advertised and offered to the public.
- A rights issue in 1990 and 1994. This is where existing shareholders are able to buy new shares at a discount.

Finally, the underwriting of share issues means that insurance has been taken out against the eventuality of shares remaining unsold.

Share prices and the stock market ● ● ●

Shares which are sold on the stock market are second-hand shares and thus their purchase doesn't provide new capital to companies. Prices of shares are determined by supply and demand. The stock market approximates to a perfect market (see Chapter 3) and thus prices are constantly changing to bring supply and demand into equilibrium. The demand for and the supply of shares depend upon the following:

- Price of shares.
- Expectations of future price changes. This can be very important when the market suffers a long period of price falls (bear market) or a period of sustained price rises (bull market).
- Profitability of the firm. This increases the prospect of higher dividends.
- Price of other assets. The price of gold and property prices can influence the attractiveness of holding shares.
- Interest rates. A rise in interest rates can cause a fall in demand for shares by making savings more attractive.
- Government policy.
- Tax considerations.

Aims, missions, ownership and control ● ● ●

Aims in the private sector are generally to maximize profits. For example Exhibit 2.5 illustrates the mission statement of the Sony Corporation. The private sector consists of both small- and medium-sized enterprises (SMEs)

Exhibit 2.5 Sony Corporation's mission statement

Our mission is to offer the opportunity to create and fulfil dreams to all kinds of people, including shareholders, customers, employees, and business partners. We pledge to continue to take on the challenge of preserving Sony's position as a unique and creative company.

Source: Sony Corporation.

---

and large corporations. Understanding small business organization is straightforward. The owner is the manager and this can act as a strong incentive to maximize profits. However it may also mean that profit maximization is subject to personal considerations such as environmental concerns or hours worked. Indeed the term 'lifestyle entrepreneur' has been used to describe small business owners who construct a business around a hobby that enables them to earn an income whilst pursuing their interest.

For companies, size of operations and number of shareholders make the picture more complex. Companies are run along standard lines: the managing director is responsible for directing managers in the day-to-day running of the organization. The board of directors is responsible for determining company policy and for reporting annually to the shareholders. This can lead to a division between ownership (shareholders) and control (managers) and a potential conflict of interests. Shareholders generally wish to see their dividends and capital gains, and thus company profits, maximized. Managers will generally have this as an important objective since they are ultimately answerable to shareholders. However, they may seek other objectives – in particular, maximizing personal benefit – which may include kudos from concluding deals, good pension prospects and a variety of perks such as foreign travel, well-appointed offices and high specification company cars.

Non-profit-making organizations

Non-profit organizations in the private sector vary considerably in size and in purpose. They span national organizations with large turnovers, smaller special interest groups, professional associations and local clubs and societies, and include:

- *The National Trust (UK)*: This is a charity and independent from the government. It derives its funds from membership subscriptions, legacies and gifts, and trading income from entrance fees, shops and restaurants. It is governed by an act of parliament – the National Trust Act 1907. Its main aim is to safeguard places of historic interest and natural beauty.
- *The New York Road Runners/NYC Marathon (USA)*: This non-profit organization is dedicated to promoting the sport of running for health, recreation and competition. It organizes over 75 races each year.
- *Surf Life Saving Australia*: (SLSA) This is Australia's major water safety and rescue authority and one of the largest volunteer organizations in the world. Their mission is 'to provide a safe beach and aquatic environment throughout Australia'. SLSA provides lifesaving patrol services on most of Australia's populated beaches in the swimming season.
- *Indigenous Tourism Rights International (USA)*: This is an Indigenous Peoples' organization collaborating with Indigenous communities and networks to protect their territories, rights and cultures. Their mission is to exchange experiences in order to understand, challenge and take control of the ways in which tourism affects our lives.

- *Tourism Concern (UK)*: Their mission statement is 'to effect change in the tourism industry by campaigning for fair and ethically traded tourism' Tourism Concern works with communities in destination countries to reduce social and environmental problems connected to tourism and with the out-going tourism industry in the UK to find ways of improving tourism so that local benefits are increased.

The aims and missions of voluntary groups include protection of special interests, promotion of ideas and ideals, regulation of sports and provision of goods and services which are not catered for by the free market.

Review of key terms

- Public sector: government owned.
- Private sector: non-government owned.
- Council member: elected councillor.
- Council officer: paid official.
- Private limited company: company with restrictions governing transfer of shares.
- Public limited company: company whose shares are freely transferable and quoted on stock market.
- Public corporation: public sector commercial-style organization.
- Dividend: the distribution of profits to shareholders.
- Limited liability: liability limited to amount of investment.
- Flotation: floating a private limited company on the stock market, thus becoming a public limited company.

Data Questions

Task 2.1   Mission types

- The National Trust of Australia (NSW) is a non-government, community organization which promotes the conservation of both the built and natural heritage (e.g. buildings, bushland, cemeteries, scenic landscapes, rare and endangered flora and fauna, and steam engines may all have heritage value). The trust has approximately 30 000 members in New South Wales. Its mission is 'to lead the community in the identification, conservation, interpretation, promotion and celebration of cultural and natural heritage through involvement, education and by engendering a sense of pride'.
- The Australian Tourist Commission (ATC) is an Australian Government Statutory Authority established in 1967 to promote Australia as an international tourism destination. Its mission is to 'market Australia internationally to create a sustainable advantage for our tourism industry – for the benefit of all Australians.' The principle objectives of the ATC under the Australian Tourist Commission Act 1987 are to:
  (a) increase the number of visitors to Australia from overseas;
  (b) maximize the benefits to Australia from overseas visitors;

(c) work with other relevant agencies to promote the principles of ecologically sustainable development and to seek to raise the awareness of the social and cultural impacts of international tourism in Australia.

- the BAA (British Airports Authority) owns London Heathrow and other major UK airports. Its mission is as follows:' Our mission is to make BAA the most successful airport group in the world. This means:
  (a) Always focusing on our customers' needs and safety.
  (b) Achieving continuous improvements in the profitability, costs and quality of all our processes and services.
  (c) Enabling us all to give of our best.
  (d) Growing with the support and trust of our neighbours.'

Figure 2.1 sets out a number of features that may be found in an organization's mission statement.

↓ Mission Agenda Example →	NTA	ATC	BAA
Maximising profits			
Corporate success			
Customer satisfaction			
Employee welfare			
Environmental sensitivity			
Product safety			
Employment policy			
Community activity			
Ethical considerations			
Benefits to society			
Political considerations			

Figure 2.1
What's in a mission?

Recap Questions

1 Identify the different aspects of the mission agenda that are evident for each of the above organizations using figure 2.1.
2 Which aspects of the mission agenda are most likely to be found for
  (a) A private sector corporation,
  (b) A not-for-profit organization,
  (c) A local government organization.
3 Why is it important for economists to identify organizational type if they are to understand the pricing policy of recreation, leisure and tourism organizations?

Task 2.2   In and out of the Stock Exchange

London 1980s • • •

Richard Branson started his business career with a student magazine at the age of 17, followed by a discount mail-order record company. This was the beginning of the Virgin empire which demonstrated its maturity when he floated the company on the London Stock Exchange. However in his autobiography, 'Losing My Virginity', Branson explains why he changed his mind about the benefits of being a public company so that the company's management executed a management buyout to take Virgin private again. He particularly pointed to the 'onerous obligations' which included the duty of appointing and working with outside directors. He also felt that he had lost the ability to make quick decisions: 'Our business was not one that could be boxed into a rigid timetable of meetings. We had to make decisions quickly, off-the-cuff: if we had to wait 4 weeks for the next board meeting before authorizing Simon to sign UB40, then we would probably lose them altogether.'

Branson found the British tradition of paying a large dividend difficult to fit with his business philosophy which was to reinvest profits to increase the company's value and stated that the one year when Virgin was quoted on the stock exchange was the company's least creative year because the executives where taken away from management and strategy by the need to explain their business to fund managers and financial advisers.

Sydney 2003 • • •

Virgin launched its low-cost carrier Virgin Blue in Australia in 2001. In the year to the end of March 2003 the airline had made a pre-tax profit of A $158 million on revenues of A $924 million and it is expected to report profits of about A $150 million for 2003–04.

Its owner Richard Branson has announced plans to the float the company on the stock market by Christmas 2003. Virgin Blue was originally expected to come to the market in summer 2003 but a listing was postponed because of the adverse effects on the aviation sector from the impact of the Sars outbreak and the war in Iraq.

The float is expected to value the group at up to A $2 billion (£832million). The airline is expected to raise about A $400 million from the flotation on the Australian Stock Exchange. One of the principle reasons for the strategy is to give the company enough cash to expand internationally without having to obtain the money from existing shareholders. The airline is expected to use the cash raised to help fund its plans to launch a low cost airline in the US next spring and Virgin Blue is also planning new routes to New Zealand, Papua New Guinea and the Polynesian islands. The group is also looking at speeding up the expansion of its Virgin Mobile operations in the US.

Commenting on the float, Grant Williams of brokerage firm Reynolds & Co said, 'There seems to be a strong interest in Virgin Blue's float but this is not a lot of money and there won't be much around for the retail market.'

A Virgin spokesman said the money from Virgin Blue would be used to increase the Virgin group's 'war chest'. Plans for a low-cost carrier in the US are described as 'quite advanced'.

Recap Questions

1 What is meant by floating a company?
2 How does a flotation raise money for a company? Where does the money come from?
3 What does Grant Williams mean when he says 'there won't be much around for the retail market'?
4 What are the advantages and disadvantages of floating a company?

Task 2.3   Right to roam

While Finland has 'Everyman's Right' (the right to walk unheeded across any land), the UK equivalent 'The Right to Roam' has yet to become law (1999).The Ramblers Association has conducted an opinion poll which shows that 85 per cent of those questioned support such a right becoming law. The Ramblers Association commissioned the poll to exert pressure on the Department of Transport, the Environment and the Regions which is seen to be wavering on pre-election promises to legislate on the right to roam. The government has also come under a major campaign by the Country Landowners Association (CLA) to accept a voluntary code instead of legislation.

Source: The author (1999).

Recap Questions

1 Distinguish between the missions, finance and organization of a government department, the Ramblers Association and the CLA.
2 What other organizations might have an interest in this issue?
3 Evaluate 'The Right to Roam' from an economic perspective.

Multiple choice

1 **Which of the following is most likely to contribute to a fall in the share price of British Airways?**

(a) A fall in interest rates.
(b) A rise in profits.
(c) A bear market.
(d) None of the above.

2 **Unlimited liability means:**

(a) A firm can be sued for damages.
(b) A firm's owner is liable for all of its debts.
(c) A firm has been incorporated.
(d) A firm may be sued for libel.

3 **Tourism Concern is:**

(a) A non-profit making organization.
(b) A local government organization.
(c) A nationalized industry.
(d) Quoted on the stock exchange.

4 **Which of the following is a valid reason for holding shares:**

(a) A chance to benefit from a company's profit.
(b) Guaranteed to get your investment back.
(c) The avoidance of risk.
(d) Guaranteed minimum dividends.

5 **Which of the following statements is not true?**

   (a) Public sector organizations are government owned.
   (b) Debentures are less risky than shares.
   (c) Shareholders are not liable for more than their initial investment.
   (d) Nationalized industries always seek to maximize profits.

Review questions

1 Distinguish between the public sector, public limited companies and nationalized industries, giving examples of each in the recreation, leisure and tourism sector.
2 What is the major benefit of incorporation?
3 Who determines strategic policy for:
   (a) Local government organizations?
   (b) Public limited companies?
   (c) Nationalized industries?
4 What are the benefits and drawbacks for a company thinking of floating on the stock exchange?
5 Identify four quoted corporations in the leisure and tourism sector.
   (a) Research and record movements in their share prices over the past 24 months.
   (b) Suggest reasons for the movements in these share prices.

Web sites of interest

Adam Smith Institute www.adamsmith.org.uk/
British Airways www.ba.com
Department for Culture, Media and Sport www.culture.gov.uk
Learning help in economics and business studies www.bized.ac.uk
Surf Life Saving Australia www.slsa.asn.au
The Australian Tourist Commission www.atc.net.au
The National Trust www.nationaltrust.org/
Time Warner Corporation www.timewarner.com
Tourism Concern www.tourismconcern.org.uk
Tourism Education www.tourismeducation.org
UK share prices www.moneyworld.co.uk/stocks/
Virgin Atlantic www.bized.ac.uk/compfact/vaa/vaaindex.htm

The market for recreation, leisure and tourism products

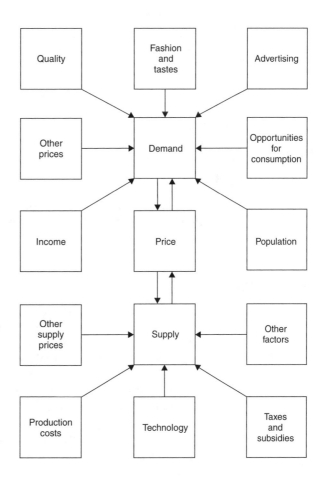

Objectives and learning outcomes

Prices in a market economy are constantly on the move. For example, the price of package holidays has fallen considerably in real terms over the last decade, whilst the price of foreign currency changes many times in a single day. Price has a key function in the market economy. On the one hand it signals changes in demand patterns to producers, stimulating production of those products with increasing demand and depressing production of those products where demand is falling. At the same time price provides an incentive for producers to economize on their inputs. This chapter will investigate how price is formed in the market. It will investigate the factors which determine the demand for and the supply of a good or service and see how the forces of demand and supply interact to determine price.

After studying this chapter students will be able to:

- identify a market and define the attributes of a perfect market;
- analyse the factors that affect the demand for a good or service;
- analyse the factors that affect the supply of a good or service;
- understand the concept of equilibrium price;
- analyse the factors that cause changes in equilibrium price;
- relate price theory to real-world examples.

Definitions

Effective demand

Effective demand is more than just the wanting of something, but is defined as 'demand backed by cash'.

Ceteris paribus

Ceteris paribus means 'all other things remaining unchanged'. In the real world there are a number of factors which affect the price of a good or service. These are constantly changing and in some instances they work in opposite directions. This makes it very difficult to study cause and effect. Economists use the term *ceteris paribus* to clarify thinking. For example, it might be said that a fall in the price of a commodity will cause a rise in demand, *ceteris paribus*. If this caveat were not stated then we might find that, despite the fact that the price of a commodity had fallen, we might observe a fall in demand, because some other factor might be changing at the same time, for example a significant rise in income tax.

Perfect market assumption

A market is a place where buyers and sellers come into contact with one another. In the model of price determination discussed in this chapter we make a simplifying assumption that we are operating in a perfect market.

The characteristics of a perfect market include:

- many buyers and sellers;
- perfect knowledge of prices throughout the market;
- rational consumers and producers basing decisions on prices;
- no government intervention (e.g. price control).

The stock exchange is an example of a perfect market – equilibrium price is constantly changing to reflect changes in demand and supply. There is some evidence to suggest that the Internet is leading to markets becoming less imperfect as consumers are able to get more information about prices and products, and source their purchases from a wider range of suppliers.

The demand for recreation, leisure and tourism products

Demand and own price

Generally, as the price of a good or a service increases, the demand for it falls, *ceteris paribus*, as illustrated in Table 3.1. This gives rise to the demand curve shown in Figure 3.1.

The demand curve slopes downwards to the right and plots the relationship between a change in price and demand. The reason for this is that as prices rise consumers tend to economize on items and replace them with other ones if possible. Notice that as price changes we move along the demand curve to determine the effect on demand so that in Figure 3.1 as price rises from $100 to $120, demand falls from 4400 to 4000 units a day.

The main exceptions to this are twofold. Some goods and services are bought because their high price lends exclusivity to them and thus they become more sought after at higher prices. A good example of this is a top class five-star hotel such as the Ritz-Carlton. Also, if consumers expect prices to rise in the future, they might buy goods even though their prices are rising. However this is difficult to do with services.

Table 3.1 The demand for four-star hotel rooms

Price ($ US)	220	200	180	160	140	120	100
Demand (per day)	2000	2400	2800	3200	3600	4000	4400

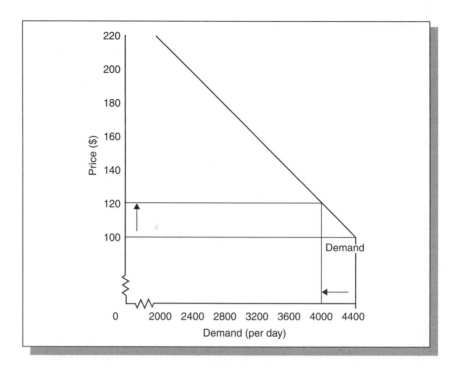

Figure 3.1
The demand curve for
four-star hotel rooms

Demand and other factors

The following factors also affect the demand for a good or service:

- income,
- other prices,
- comparative quality/value added,
- fashion and tastes,
- advertising,
- opportunities for consumption (e.g. leisure time),
- population,
- other factors.

Since the demand curve describes the relationship between demand and price, these other factors will affect the position of the demand curve and changes in these factors will cause the demand curve to shift its position to the left or the right.

Disposable income • • •

Disposable income is defined as income less direct taxes but including government subsidies. The effect of a change in disposable income on the demand for a good or service depends on the type of good under consideration. First, for normal or superior goods, as disposable income rises, so does demand. This applies to most hotels, holidays abroad, compact discs (CDs)

Exhibit 3.1   UK seaside resorts: from superiority to inferiority

In Victorian England the place to be for the British monied, leisured classes was a British seaside resort. Queen Victoria herself had a residence at Osborne House near Cowes on the Isle of Wight and the Victorian boom brought railways, piers, promenades and seafront hotels to resorts such as Brighton, Ventnor and Eastbourne. Today, piers have collapsed, accommodation has shrunk and resorts are in decline. Since 1970 long holidays taken abroad by UK residents have increased from 5 million to over 30 million and the number spent in the UK has shown a steep decline. The resort of Morecombe has suffered a severe reduction in visitor spending in real terms. In 1974 it was over €63 million, but had fallen to €9 million by 1990. Increased incomes made Spain the major destination for UK holidaymakers in the 1980s and 1990s, but as incomes continue to rise Spanish resorts are becoming inferior substitutes for more exotic, distant destinations.

Source: The author.

---

and membership of leisure clubs. However some goods or services are bought as cheap substitutes for other ones. These are defined as inferior goods and examples might include cheap hotel rooms, bed and breakfast accommodation, domestic holidays, cheap-range hi-fi systems, or trainers without a leading brand name. As income rises the demand for these goods and services declines as people start to demand the normal goods that they can now afford. Exhibit 3.1 shows that Morecombe can be classified as an 'inferior' destination in economic terms. It is likely to suffer continued decline as a seaside resort as people's standard of living continues to increase.

An income consumption curve shows the relationship between changes in income and changes in the demand for goods and services and Figure 3.2 shows the different income consumption curves for superior and inferior goods. As income rises from A to B, the demand for superior goods rises from C to E, whilst the demand for inferior goods falls from C to D.

Price of other goods ● ● ●

Changes in the prices of other goods will also affect the demand for the good or service in question. In the case of goods or services which are substitutes, a rise in the price of one good will lead to a rise in the demand for the other. In the skiing market, for example, Verbier in Switzerland, Ellmau in Austria, and Courcheval in France are to some extent substitutes for each other and changes in relative prices will cause demand patterns to change.

Some goods and services are complements or in joint demand. In other words, they tend to be demanded in pairs or sets. In this case an increase in the price of one good will lead to a fall in the demand for the other. So in

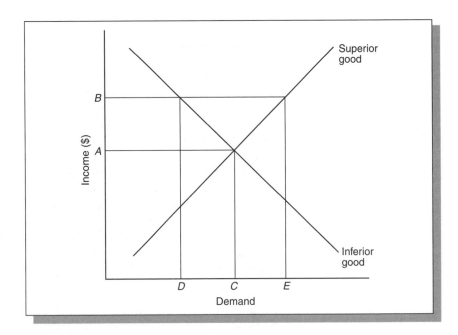

Figure 3.2
Income consumption
curves for superior and
inferior goods

Exhibit 3.2 the demand for ski holidays in Borovets, Bulgaria may well be lifted by the relative cheapness of those items that are in joint demand with a ski holiday – lift passes and meals. Other examples include such goods include CDs and CD players, holiday destinations and transport costs and Exhibit 3.3 reports on the link between the restaurant sales and a cigarette ban in the US.

Comparative quality/value added • • •

Consumers do not just consider price when comparing goods and services – they also compare quality. Improvements in the quality of a good or service can be important factors in increasing demand and Exhibit 3.4 describes how airlines have been rated by passengers over a number of key quality issues. This is an important consideration for airlines' strategies for increasing market share.

Fashion and tastes • • •

Fashion and tastes affect demand for leisure goods and services as in other areas. For example, the demand for tennis facilities and accessories rises sharply during tennis tournaments such as Wimbledon. Similarly, World Cup rugby and football events have a big impact on sales of sports clothing and merchandise as do the successes of teams in national leagues. Holiday destinations move in and out of fashion. Bali was particularly affected by the publicity surrounding the deaths of tourists during a terrorist attack in 2002 and subsequent attacks in Indonesia have continued to affect tourism in that region. Exhibit 3.5 shows how the fortunes of destinations can quickly change.

Exhibit 3.2   Skiing: unpacking the price

The demand for skiing at different resorts is affected by a range of price factors. The price of accommodation in the resort (own price) will be a key factor. But other prices will also affect demand. Demand will be sensitive to substitute prices which includes prices in other resorts and prices of other alternative activities (e.g. diving holidays). Demand will also be affected by the price of other essential parts of a ski package (complementary goods and services). Lift pass prices, equipment hire and tuition are key factors here. The table shows some of these for ski resorts in Europe. Of the three roughly comparable resorts of Ellmau (Austria), Courcheval (France) and Verbier (Switzerland), Ellmau offers the best value in terms of a complete package.

Price comparisons for ski package elements, 1999 (€)

Resort	Local lift pass (week)	Boot and ski hire	Ski school (adult)	Three-course meal	Bottle of house wine
Borovets, Bulgaria	82	60	90	8	6
Ellmau, Austria	110	52	86	10	14
Courcheval, France	140	92	106	30	12
Verbier, Switzerland	166	110	84	34	8

Source: Adapted from data collected by Thomas Cook.

Exhibit 3.3   New York's smoke-free regulations: effects on employment and sales in the hospitality industry

This study found that neither sales nor employment is hurt when smoke-free regulations are put in place. The findings are contrary to claims that smoke-free regulations cause decreases in hospitality–industry sales, The findings are based on an examination of changes in restaurants' and hotels' business levels in five populous New York State areas that have implemented smoke-free regulations (namely Erie, Monroe, Suffolk and Westchester counties, and the five boroughs of New York city). Using state sales data and employment data for eating and drinking establishments and for hotels, the study compared those statistics for the year before the regulation was implemented with the same statistics for the first year following implementation. The study examined trends in per capita levels of sales and employment, as well as the fraction of restaurant sales to total retail sales. Instead of damaging hospitality sales and employment, the onset of smoke-free regulations was associated with increases in per capita taxable sales for eating and drinking establishments and hotels (controlling for other economic factors). Employment rose in hotels, while no measurable change was observed for employment in restaurants operating under smoke-free regulations. The study concludes that smoke-free regulations have not been bad for business in New York State restaurants or hotels.

Source: Hyland et al. (2003).

Exhibit 3.4   Airline reputation study finds Singapore Airlines and Southwest Airlines soaring

Harris Interactive reported in April 2000 on its new study of airline reputations. It found that Southwest Airlines, Delta Air Lines, Singapore Airlines and Deutsche Lufthansa are soaring above the competition. The study measured the attitudes of over 20 000 consumers on issues ranging from safety and trust to customer service and food. The reputation quotient (RQ) study was designed and conducted by the Reputation Institute, a private research organization dedicated to advancing knowledge about corporate reputations, and Harris Interactive, a global Internet research firm.

The data also showed that consumers rate airlines primarily on their perceptions of each airline's service quality, reliability, management strength, workplace and growth prospects.

Other notable findings from the Harris Study include:

- *Customer service*: Singapore Airlines and Southwest Airlines scored high marks for their customer service, followed by Delta Air Lines and Lufthansa.
- *Business vs. leisure travellers*: Business travellers awarded Southwest Airlines and United Airlines the highest marks, while leisure travellers gave the highest ratings to Southwest and Delta Air Lines among US airlines.
- *Food quality*: Singapore Airlines came first for airline food quality, and only two US carriers appeared in the top 10 (Delta Air Lines, No. 7, and American Airlines, No. 10).
- *Safety*: Qantas Airways, Singapore Airlines, and Southwest Airlines were perceived as the safest airlines.

Source: Adapted by author from report at www.harrisinteractive.com

---

Exhibit 3.5   From dreams to nightmares on a Greek island

'The half-forgotten island of Cephallonia rises improvidently and inadvisedly from the Ionian Sea,' writes Dr Iannis, a character in Louis de Bernière's bestselling novel *Captain Corelli's Mandolin*. The book has sold over half a million copies in the 5-year period following its publication in 1994. The publication of the book coupled with a BBC holiday programme on the island and the strong pound prompted an increase of 62 per cent in the British holidaymakers in 1997, and 10 000 thousand tourists arrived at the island airport in May 1998 alone.

But this marketer's dream turned suddenly to a nightmare when the brutal murder of two pensioners who had retired to the island hit the newspaper headlines. Roy Eccles, a former Royal Air Force (RAF) electrical engineer, and his wife Judith were murdered in their beds by burglars. Dicky Dawes, a retired computer programmer living on the island explains how things have changed. 'Even the Greeks are now putting up their shutters and locking doors when they go out, which they would never have done before.' Dawes had his life savings stolen by the murderers.

Source: The author, from press cuttings, 1999.

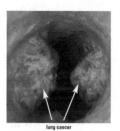

WARNING
CIGARETTES CAUSE LUNG CANCER

85% of lung cancers are caused by smoking. 80% of lung cancer victims die within 3 years.

Health Canada

WARNING
TOBACCO USE CAN MAKE YOU IMPOTENT

Cigarettes may cause sexual impotence due to decreased blood flow to the penis. This can prevent you from having an erection.

Health Canada

Plate 3
Health Canada anti-smoking campaign
Source: Reproduced by kind permission of Health Canada.

Advertising • • •

The aim of most advertising is to increase the demand for goods and services. The exception to this is advertising that is designed to inhibit the demand for some goods and services. For example, many governments fund advertising campaigns to inhibit the demand for cigarettes and drugs. Plate 3 reproduces two graphic labels used in cigarette packaging to dissuade people from smoking by Health Canada.

Opportunities for consumption • • •

Unlike many sectors of the economy, many leisure and tourism pursuits require time to participate in them. Thus the amount of leisure time available

Table 3.2 Time (hours/minutes) spent on various activities: by sex, 2000–01 (UK adults 16+ years)

	Males	Females
Other	2.35	2.52
Entertainment and culture	0.10	0.10
Childcare	0.17	0.48
Sports and outdoor activities	0.30	0.18
Shopping and services	0.38	0.62
Social life	0.85	1.02
Eating	1.38	1.45
Travel	1.48	1.37
Household and family care	1.65	2.88
TV and video	2.65	2.25
Employment/study	4.28	2.57
Sleeping	8.40	8.57

Source: Adapted from *UK Time 2000 Use Survey*, Office for National Statistics.

will be an important enabling factor in demand. The two main components here are the average working week and the amount of paid holidays. The level of unemployment is also an important consideration, but the unemployed lack effective demand. Table 3.2 illustrates time use in the UK. This shows that women still do the majority of the household chores, spending nearly 3 hours a day on average on housework (excluding shopping and childcare) compared with 1 hour and 40 minutes spent by men. Women also spent more time than men on childcare. However, men worked or studied on average for nearly 2 hours a day more than women (4 hours and 20 minutes a day for men compared with 2 hours and 30 minutes for women). Fredman and Heberlein (2003) suggest that the changes in mountain tourism that are apparent in Sweden during the last 20 years may be related to the occurrence of shorter vacations and increased demand on people's time. These factors have caused increased visits to the Dalarna mountain region close to the Swedish population centres.

Population • • •

Population trends are an important factor in the demand for recreation leisure and tourism. Demand will be influenced by the size of population as well as the composition of the population in terms of age, sex and geographical distribution; for example, the leisure requirements of a country are likely to change considerably as the average age of the population increases. Football pitches may need to give way to bowling greens. The location of leisure facilities similarly needs to be tailored to the migration trends of the population. Tourism marketing also needs to be informed by relevant population data. The dramatic growth in extended winter sun breaks in Europe reflects the demands of an ageing population. Table 3.3 shows different

Table 3.3 Selected world population data

Demographic variable	Australia	USA	China	India	Spain
Population mid-2003	19 900 000	291 500 000	1 288 700 000	1 068 600 000	41 300 000
Birth rate (annual number of births per 1000 total population)	13	14	13	25	10
Death rate (annual number of deaths per 1000 total population)	7	9	6	8	9
Rate of natural increase (birth rate minus death rate, expressed as a %)	0.6	0.6	0.6	1.7	0.1
Population change 2003–50 (projected %)	48	45	8	52	0
Population 2025 (projected)	25 000 000	351 100 000	1 454 700 000	1 363 000 000	43 500 000
Population 2050 (projected)	29 500 000	421 800 000	1 393 600 000	1 628 000 000	41 300 000
Population under age 15 (%)	20	21	22	36	15
Population over age 65 (%)	13	13	7	4	17

Source: Adapted from Population Reference Bureau web site www.prb.org

population trends from around the world. The population of India is set to increase by over 50 per cent between 2003 and 2050 and this growth in the population will mean the average age of the population remains low. In contrast the population of Spain is forecast to decline in total size between 2025 and 2050. This is because of a low birth rate and therefore the average age of the Spanish population is likely to increase. Bouchet (2002) examines the demand for high-end tourism by senior age groups and finds this demand is being satisfied by the introduction of specific products that are more or less adapted to the needs of this client group. Similarly, Grant (2002) outlines the demand for active leisure in the Australian seniors market and concludes that those in the leisure industry need to understand not only the changing demographics but also the special demand characteristics of this group. The future of leisure services for the elderly in Canada is explored in the light of ageing of the baby-boom generation by Johnson (2003).

Other factors • • •

Terrorism has had a significant impact particularly on some types of tourism in recent years. For example, Tate (2002) examines the impact of the

11 September 2001 events on the world tourism and travel industry and reviews some of the recovery strategies adopted by the industry. These are lower prices, shorter duration of visits, changes in booking habits, changes in motivation for travel, and new approaches to product and service promotion. Ingra (2001) anticipates the following impacts of 11 September on the tourism industry: a growing demand for security; a shift in focus towards tourism in domestic markets (i.e. less foreign travel); for foreign travel, an increasing tendency to travel to relatively close and familiar destinations (i.e. those in the same geographic region); greater importance being placed on visiting friends and relatives as a reason for travelling; a growth in the number of short trips and city breaks (although not to large city destinations); a decreasing interest in adventure tourism; and a growing interest in travel that emphasizes experiencing local cultures or proximity to nature.

The supply of recreation, leisure and tourism products

Supply and own price

Generally as the price of a good or a service increases, the supply of it rises, *ceteris paribus*. This gives rise to the supply curve which is illustrated in Table 3.4 and Figure 3.3. The supply curve slopes upwards to the right and plots the relationship between a change in price and supply. The reason for this is that, as prices rise, the profit motive stimulates existing producers to increase supply and induces new suppliers to enter the market. Notice that as price changes we move along the supply curve to determine the effect on supply so that in Figure 3.3, as price rises from $100 to $120, supply rises from 2000 units a week to 2400 units a day.

Supply and other factors

The following factors also affect the supply of a good or service:

- prices of other goods supplied,
- changes in production costs,
- technical improvements,
- taxes and subsidies,
- other factors (e.g. industrial relations).

Since the supply curve describes the relationship between supply and price, these other factors will affect the position of the supply curve and changes in these factors will cause the supply curve to shift its position to the left or the right. Exhibit 3.6 describes the increase in the supply of cruise ships over recent years.

Table 3.4 The supply of four-star hotel rooms

Price ($)	220	200	180	160	140	120	100
Supply (per day)	4400	4000	3600	3200	2800	2400	2000

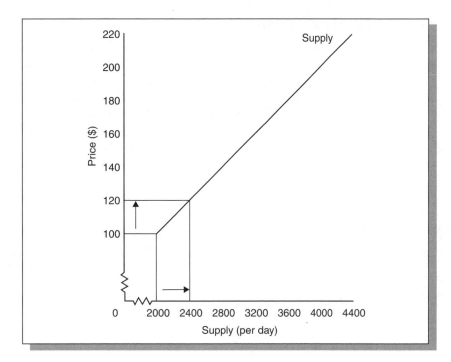

Figure 3.3
The supply curve for
four-star hotel rooms

Exhibit 3.6 Carry on cruising

The cruise industry is undergoing a period of remarkable change and rapid growth. In North America particularly the cruise industry is undergoing phenomenal growth with a record 5.5 million cruise passengers in 1998, representing an 8.6 per cent increase in passengers over the previous year. To meet this demand over 30 new ships costing in excess of US $10 billion were ordered for delivery early in the new millennium. The industry body, Cruise Lines International Association (CLIA), explains the reasons for this growth under several factors. These include the increased capacity as new ships are introduced combined with a stronger focus by travel consultants on selling cruises. The cruise ships currently being built are designed for a new generation of passengers with broader, more varied interests and these ships embrace a number of innovations such as large multi-level hotel-style atrium-lobbies, fitness complexes and business centres. The cruise industry has considerable economic impacts, with the US sector alone generating more than 450 000 jobs accounting for US $15 billion in wages and billions of dollars in the purchase of goods and services.

Source: Based on Dowling (2000).

Prices of other goods supplied • • •

Where a producer can use factors of production to supply a range of goods or services, an increase in the price of a particular product will cause the producer to redeploy resources towards that particular product and away from other ones. For example, the owners of a flexible sports hall will be able to increase the supply of badminton courts at the expense of short tennis, if demand changes. In the long run a rise in the price of hotel rooms will cause owners of buildings and land to consider changing their use.

Changes in production costs • • •

The main costs involved in production are labour costs, raw material costs and interest payments. A fall in these production costs will tend to stimulate supply shifting the supply curve to the right, whereas a rise in production costs will shift the supply curve to the left.

Technical improvements • • •

Changes in technology will affect the supply of goods and services in the leisure and tourism sector. An example of this is aircraft design: the development of jumbo jets has had a considerable impact on the supply curve for air travel. The supply curve has shifted to the right, signifying that more seats can now be supplied at the same price. Technology has had a large impact on the production of leisure goods such as television (TVs), video cassette recorders (VCRs), personal computers (PCs) and video cameras. The supply curve for these goods has shifted persistently to the right over recent years, leading to a reduction in prices even after allowing for inflation.

Taxes and subsidies • • •

The supply of goods and services is affected by indirect taxes such as sales taxes and also by subsidies. In the event of the imposition of taxes or subsidies, the price paid by the consumer is not the same as the price received by the supplier. For example, assume that the government imposes a $20 sales tax on hotel rooms. Where the price to the consumer is $200 the producer would now only receive $180. The whole supply curve will shift to the left since the supplier will now interpret every original price as being less $20. Table 3.5 shows the effects of the imposition of a tax on the original supply data. The effects of an imposition of a tax are illustrated in Figure 3.4. Notice that the supply curve has shifted to the left. In fact the vertical distance between the old (S0) and the new (S1) supply curves represents the amount of the tax. Similarly, the effects of a subsidy will be to shift the supply curve to the right.

Table 3.5 The effects of the imposition of a tax on supply

Price ($)	220	200	180	160	140	120	100
Original supply (per day S0)	4400	4000	3600	3200	2800	2400	2000
New supply (per day S1)	4000	3600	3200	2800	2400	2000	

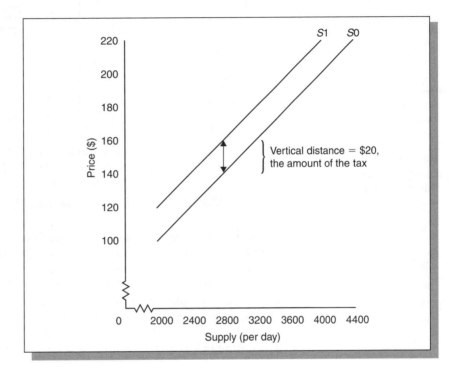

Figure 3.4
The effects of the imposition of a tax on supply

Other factors • • •

There are various other factors which can influence the supply of leisure and tourism goods and services, including strikes, wars and the weather.

Equilibrium price

Equilibrium is a key concept in economics. It means a state of balance or the position towards which something will naturally move. Equilibrium price comes about from the interaction between the forces of demand and supply. There is only one price at which the quantity that consumers want to demand is equal to the quantity that producers want to supply. This is the equilibrium price. Figure 3.5 brings together the demand schedule from Table 3.1 and the supply schedule from Table 3.4. The equilibrium price in this case is $160, since this is where demand equals supply, both of which are 3200 units per day.

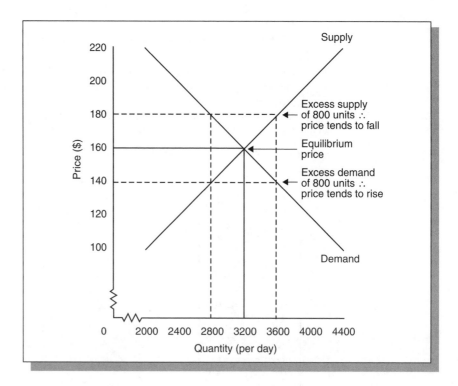

Figure 3.5
Equilibrium price in the market for four-star hotel rooms

It can be demonstrated that this is the equilibrium by considering other possible prices. At higher prices supply exceeds demand. In the example, at a price of $180 there is excess supply of 800 units a day. Excess supply will tend to cause the price to fall. On the other hand, at lower prices demand exceeds supply. At a price of $140 there is excess demand of 800 units a day. Excess demand causes the price to rise. Thus the equilibrium price is at $160, since no other price is sustainable and market forces will prevail, causing price to change until the equilibrium is established.

Changes in equilibrium price

Equilibrium does not mean that prices do not change. In fact, prices are constantly changing in markets to reflect changing conditions of demand and supply.

The effect of a change in demand

We have previously identified the factors that can cause the demand curve to shift its position. Table 3.6 reviews these factors, distinguishing what will cause the demand curve to shift to the right from that which will cause it to shift to the left.

In the example of four-star hotel rooms, a fall in the price of substitutes, for example five-star hotels, will cause the demand curve to shift to the left from $D0$ to $D1$. The supply curve will remain unchanged at $S0$. This is illustrated

Table 3.6 Shifts in the demand curve

Demand curve shifts to the left	Demand curve shifts to the right
Fall in income (normal goods)	Rise in income (normal goods)
Rise in income (inferior goods)	Fall in income (inferior goods)
Rise in price of complementary goods	Fall in price of complementary goods
Fall in price of substitutes	Rise in price of substitutes
Unfashionable	Fashionable
Less advertising	More advertising
Less leisure time	Increased leisure time
Fall in population	Rise in population

Table 3.7 A shift in demand for four-star hotel rooms

Price ($)	220	200	180	160	140	120	100
Original demand (per day $D0$)	2000	2400	2800	3200	3600	4000	4400
New demand (per day $D1$)		2000	2400	2800	3200	3600	4000
Supply (per day $S0$)	4400	4000	3600	3200	2800	2400	2000

in Table 3.7. Figure 3.6 shows the effect of this on equilibrium price. The original price of $160 will no longer be an equilibrium position, since demand has now fallen to 2800 units a day at this price. There is now excess supply of 400 units per day, which will cause equilibrium price to fall until a new equilibrium is achieved at $150 where demand is equal to supply at 3000 units a day. Similarly, if the demand curve were to shift to the right as a result, for example, of an effective advertising campaign, the excess demand created at the original price would cause equilibrium price to rise.

The effect of a change in supply

The factors which cause a leftward or rightward shift in supply are reviewed in Table 3.8. In the example of four-star hotel rooms the effect of the imposition of a tax is shown in Table 3.9. A tax will cause the supply curve to shift to the left from $S0$ to $S1$ but the demand curve will remain unchanged at $D0$, as illustrated in Figure 3.7. The original price of $160 will no longer be in equilibrium, since supply has now fallen to 2800 units a day at this price. There is now excess demand of 400 units per day, which will cause equilibrium price to rise until a new equilibrium is achieved at $170 where demand is equal to supply at 3000 units a day.

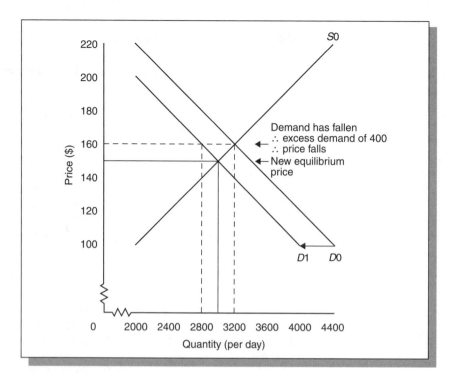

Figure 3.6
The effects on price of a shift in the demand curve

Table 3.8 Shifts in the supply curve

Supply curve shifts to the left	Supply curve shifts to the right
Rise in price of other goods that could be supplied by producer	Fall in price of other goods that could be supplied by producer
Rise in production costs	Fall in production costs
Effects of taxes	Effects of subsidies
Effects of strikes	Technical improvements

Table 3.9 Shifts in the supply of four-star hotel rooms

Price ($)	220	200	180	160	140	120	100
Original demand (per day $D0$)	2000	2400	2800	3200	3600	4000	4400
New demand (per day $S0$)	4400	4000	3600	3200	2800	2400	2000
Supply (per day $S1$)	4000	3600	3200	2800	2400	2000	

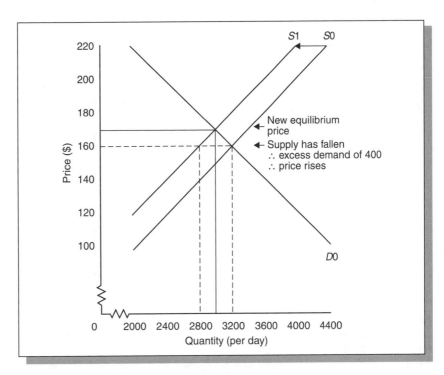

Figure 3.7
The effects on price of a shift in the supply curve

Similarly, if the supply curve were to shift to the right as a result of an improvement in technology, for example, the excess supply created at the original price would cause equilibrium price to fall.

The price mechanism in action

Maximum prices and black markets

It is common in the leisure sector to interfere with free market pricing. The effects of this are particularly evident at prestige sports and music events where the capacity of the stadium is fixed, as illustrated in Figure 3.8. The capacity of the Rugby Football Union (RFU) ground at Twickenham in the UK, for example is about 70 000, and thus the supply curve (S) is fixed and vertical at this point. The demand curve for tickets is downward sloping (D). The RFU fixes a price (P0) which is considerably below the equilibrium price (P1). At the RFU official price there is considerable excess demand (a to b). Equilibrium is restored through the activities of ticket touts in the black market. Prices charged by touts rise and the effects of this can be shown by moving along the demand curve (b to c) until demand falls sufficiently to match supply. Exhibit 3.7 reports on how ticket touts are well aware of elementary economics.

Review of key terms

- Effective demand: demand backed by cash.
- *Ceteris paribus*: all other things remaining unchanged.

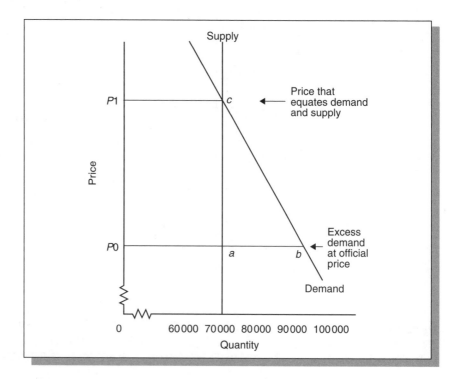

Figure 3.8
The effects of setting a
maximum price below
equilibrium price

Exhibit 3.7   Touts to be tackled

The Australian Rugby Union and the online auction Web site Ebay are to
join forces to combat overpricing of tickets for Ireland's Rugby World Cup
game with the Wallabies in Melbourne on 1 November 2003. This the
most difficult of the pool matches to get into because demand has by far
outstripped supply and touts were getting upwards of AU $1000 (almost
€600) per ticket some weeks ago. This compares with a cover price of €80.
The World Cup marketing manager for the ARU, Shane Harmon, said last
week that Ebay had agreed to start removing advertisements for over-
priced tickets.

Source: The author, from press reports (2003).

- Perfect market: many buyers and sellers, rational players, perfect know-
  ledge, no interference.
- Normal good: demand rises as income rises (also called superior good).
- Inferior good: demand falls as income rises.
- Substitute: good that can replace good in question.
- Complement/joint demand: good that is used with the good in
  question.
- Equilibrium price: where demand equals supply.

Data Questions

Task 3.1

Questions on Figure 3.9

1 If a local authority decided to build OB tennis courts what would happen if they decided to make these free?
2 If the authority wished to create a market equilibrium, what price should they charge?
3 What problems arise from charging an equilibrium price?
4 How would the courts be allocated if they were provided free of charge?

Task 3.2   What am I bid for a week in the sun?

The reporter for a TV holiday programme was looking pleased with himself as he sipped a cocktail on a Caribbean beach. He had managed to book a week in Cuba's winter sun for couple of hundred pounds, and he was keen to make a point. It was not long before his camera crew had found a couple to gloat over. Gill and Tom had paid over £500 each for an identical holiday and they had booked several months before. Enter camera left a man who stole the show £110 – for 2 weeks. So how can the price of the same holiday go up and down like share prices and currencies?

The answer lies back in the UK where the late bookings section of Airtours, the UK's second biggest tour operator, resembles a share dealing room with banks of flickering screens. Here analysts change holiday prices several times a day. They are not alone – Thomson, the industry number one and First Choice, the industry number three, change their holiday prices every day too. Each uses the latest information on their competitors' prices to adjust their own prices to maximize profits. First Choice gets much of its information on competitors' prices through its

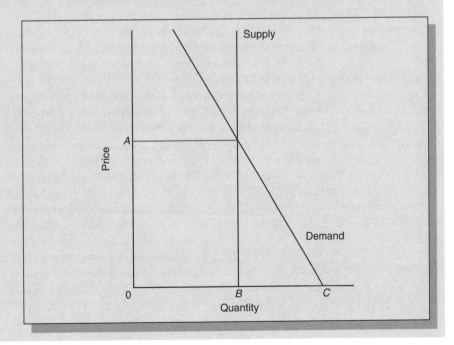

Figure 3.9
The demand and supply curves for tennis courts

ownership of Going Places. When demand for their products is strong and supply is tight, the companies push up prices. However, faced with a half-empty plane departing in 2 days' time, prices plummet as the team tries to get bums on seats that would otherwise earn nothing at all. The First Choice team have developed some ground rules for pricing. There's nothing like grey skies and rain at home to move prices up on the day. Somehow in the face of all this Gill and Tom managed to keep their smiles fixed.

Source: The author, adapted from news cuttings, January 1995.

Recap Questions

1 Illustrate, using demand and supply diagrams, how the Airtours late bookings section sets prices.
2 Why is it difficult to keep to the prices printed in brochures?
3 How does a plane with empty seats represent market disequilibrium and how does Airtours attempt to restore equilibrium?
4 What is the significance of information and knowledge to market prices?
5 What impact has the Internet had on holiday prices?

Task 3.3   Changing demand conditions for UK hotels

In a report which provides forecasts for the UK hotel sector for 2004, PricewaterhouseCoopers note that the current forecast for the UK hotel sector reflects the slightly less favourable economic position, with gross domestic product growth of 1.8 per cent in 2003 (compared to 2.1 per cent in their last forecast) and 3 per cent predicted for 2004 (unchanged). In addition they note that the hotel sector continues to feel the impacts of the economic slowdown both in the UK and globally (particularly in the US) as well as the corporate travel downturn. However, they note that there are now more grounds for optimism and that travel demand continues to improve. They point to several surveys that suggest that business travel is recovering and leisure travel remains buoyant. In addition they note that the UK is becoming more affordable, as a result of the pound's recent fall against the euro and that falling consumer goods prices in the UK adds to its attractiveness as a destination.

One result of this is that increased overseas visitor volumes (particularly from Europe) may well benefit the UK. In recent trading periods there have been severe worries relating to the impacts of Severe Acute Respiratory Syndrome and terrorism on tourism. But these have abated a little. However an uncertain economic outlook and increased security measures and inconvenience at airports continue to impact on business and leisure travel, particularly from the US to Europe.

At the time of their last forecast, indications were that lodging demand would improve sufficiently in the second half of 2003 to 'lift up' the whole year into positive growth. However PricewaterhouseCoopers note that the economic slowdown and widespread discounting now makes it unlikely that room rates will return to growth until 2004 when average room rate (ARR) growth of 2.6, 2.5 and 3.4 per cent is forecast for UK, London and the provinces, respectively. Although in 2003 they forecast that the UK overall may still achieve a slight recovery in revenue per available room (RevPAR) no recovery is likely in RevPAR in London and the Provinces until 2004, when a strong rebound is forecast as economic and corporate travel growth resumes. For 2004, RevPAR growth of 4, 3.7 and 4.7 per cent is expected for UK, London and the provinces.

Source: Adapted from PricewaterhouseCoopers (2003).

Recap Questions

1 List in two columns the factors described above which would tend to
  (a) Shift the demand curve for UK hotels to the left
  (b) Shift the demand curve for UK hotels to the right
2 What are the conditions of demand currently prevailing in the market for hotel rooms in the country in which you are studying?
3 Using supply and demand curves demonstrate the likely effect of a sustained and significant increase in videoconferencing on the price of hotel rooms
4 How would the free market mechanism respond to a long-term fall in hotel prices?

Multiple choice

1 **Which of the following will shift the demand curve for four-star hotel accommodation in New York to the right?**

  (a) A rise in the value of the US dollar against other currencies.
  (b) A fall in incomes of consumers.
  (c) A successful advertising campaign.
  (d) A terrorist threat to New York.

2 **Which of the following statements is not true?**

  (a) As income increases the demand for inferior goods rises.
  (b) As income increases the demand for inferior goods falls.
  (c) As income increases the demand for normal or superior goods rises.
  (d) As income falls the demand for normal or superior goods falls.

3 **Which of the following statements is not true?**

  (a) The income consumption curve for inferior goods is upward sloping to the right.
  (b) The income consumption curve for inferior goods is downward sloping to the right.
  (c) A typically demand is inversely proportionate to price.
  (d) At the point of equilibrium, demand equals supply.

4 **Which of the following is not true?**

  (a) A rise in price the price of air travel causes demand to fall.
  (b) A rise in the price of air travel causes a rise in the demand for train travel over similar routes.
  (c) Where the price of air tickets is above equilibrium, supply will exceed demand.
  (d) Air travel is an inferior good.

5 **Societe National des Chemins de Fer (SNCF) is the monopoly supplier of rail travel in France. This means that:**

  (a) The rail market in France is a perfect market.
  (b) There are no perfect substitutes for a rail journey in France.

(c) Demand for rail travel in France rises as price rises.
(d) *Ceteris paribus* is not useful in analysing the market for French rail travel.

Review questions

1 Distinguish between the factors which cause a movement along a demand curve, and those which cause a shift of the curve.
2 'An increase in the price of a good may arise from an increase in the price of its substitute, *ceteris paribus.*' Explain this statement.
3 Distinguish between a normal and an inferior good using examples from the leisure and tourism sector.
4 What is the likely effect of setting the maximum price of a good below its equilibrium price?

Part Two

Further Issues of Demand and Supply

CHAPTER 4

Demand: time preference, elasticity and forecasting

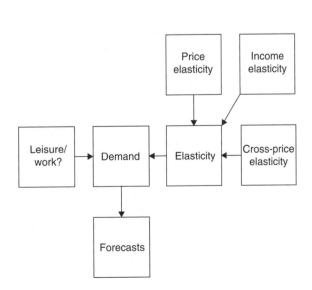

Objectives and learning outcomes

This chapter looks in more detail at demand. First it considers the choice between leisure and work and asks whether we are becoming a leisure society. Various concepts of demand elasticity are explained and the importance of these concepts to the recreation, leisure and tourism sector examined. Finally the chapter considers some techniques of demand forecasting, their uses and shortcomings. By studying this chapter students will be able to:

- evaluate the work/leisure trade-off,
- evaluate the notion of a 'leisure society',
- understand and apply the concept of price elasticity of demand,
- understand and apply the concept of income elasticity of demand,
- understand and apply the concept of cross-price elasticity of demand,
- describe simple methods of demand forecasting,
- evaluate techniques of demand forecasting.

The demand for leisure

We approach the demand for leisure by assuming that consumers act rationally to maximize their satisfaction given a range of economic choices. Leisure time represents an element in the choice set available to consumers, and maximization of consumer satisfaction will therefore also involve choice about how much leisure time to take. Just as when choosing between other goods and services, consumers will consider the extra satisfaction they derive from leisure time against the price or cost of leisure time.

Consumers face the problem of limited time. There are only 24 hours in a day, and thus the most fundamental choice that consumers face is whether to devote their limited time to leisure or work. We can consider the cost or price of leisure time as its opportunity cost or what has to be given up in order to enjoy leisure time. The opportunity cost of leisure time can be thought of as earnings that are lost through not working. An interesting question is what will happen to the trade-off between work and leisure when income changes? Let us consider the case of an increase income. There are two potential effects of an increase in income on the demand for leisure time.

First, an increase in income means an increase in the opportunity cost of leisure time, in terms of greater loss of earnings per hour. In this case we may expect consumers to demand less leisure time. This is called the substitution effect. Consumers will tend to substitute work for leisure to reflect the increased opportunity cost of leisure. However, an increase in income will also result in consumers having more income and spending power. Leisure time can be classed as a 'normal service' and in common with other 'normal' goods and services, as income increases more will be demanded. This is called the income effect. So after an increase in income we are faced with two competing forces that relate to our new demand for leisure time. There are complex set of forces which will determine whether the income or substitution effect is greater. One possibility is that as income increases, consumers have the ability to get more satisfaction out of their leisure time, thus resulting in a strong income effect. The satisfaction derived from labour is also influenced by psychological and social factors. Some individuals may favour long leisure hours which they can happily fill with cheap or free activities such as reading, watching television, sleeping or walking. Other individuals may have a low boredom threshold and thus get less satisfaction from leisure time. Equally there are cultural influences at work. There appears to be a greater work ethic in countries such as Germany and Japan than in other countries, particularly those with warmer climates.

Choice or rigidity?

The extent to which choice can actually be exercised in the work/leisure trade-off depends on flexibility in the labour market. When choosing between most goods and services, consumers can readily vary the amounts consumed in response to changing relative prices. Consumers generally have less choice in their participation in labour markets. Many jobs have standardized hours where individuals cannot choose to add or subtract hours in response to changes in wages. However, workers can express their general preferences through trade unions and staff associations and these may be taken into account in determining the overall work package of pay, hours and holiday benefits.

Some jobs offer flexibility in offering overtime provision, and some individuals may have extra employment in addition to their main job. In these cases individuals will be in a position to exercise more precisely their choice between work and leisure. Finally the unemployed are generally not acting out of choice but by lack of opportunity in their allocation of leisure time. However, there has been considerable debate regarding social security benefits and incentives to work. Right-wing economists argue that benefit levels are distorting the labour market so that some unemployed maximize their satisfaction by remaining unemployed rather than entering the labour market.

Trends in work and leisure: a leisure society?

It was the French sociologist Joffre Dumazedier (1967) who wrote tantalizingly about the imminent arrival of the Leisure Society in the 1960s. Politicians warmed to this theme and in the UK, Prime Minister MacMillan reminded the British electorate that they would never had it so good. Landmarks of the emerging leisure society may be glimpsed in subsequent years. The 1970s witnessed the release of Ian Drury's *Sex and Drugs and*

Rock and Roll, Disneyland conquered Europe and Japan in the 1990s and opened and in 1994 Sony launched the Playstation. Ibiza (Spain), Cancun (Mexico) and the beaches of Southern Thailand seem to have hosted non-stop parties for most of the last decade and Dennis Tito became the first Space Tourist in 2001. So are we having it even better? Have we become a Leisure Society?

Certainly in the developed world the opportunities for leisure have never been better, fuelled by rising incomes, technological advances and a dazzling array of new products. Only a fraction of our income is needed to fulfil basic needs of food, clothing and shelter and much of our rising income is devoted to leisure spending. Almost every household now possesses a television and stereo – all considered luxury items in the 1960s. Labour-saving devices such as washing machines, Hoovers and dishwashers increase our leisure time. So what do we do in our non-working time? Our homes are populated with even more sophisticated leisure devices – TVs, CDs, PCs and increasingly more than one of each. Outside the home we walk, play sports, go to cinemas, clubs, gyms, attractions, restaurants and bars and we shop. We travel further abroad and more frequently. International tourist arrivals reached 600 million in 2000 and are predicted to rise to 1500 million by 2020. Indeed the growth of tourism is such that it now claims to be the world's biggest industry. Other discernible trends include the influence of particular interest groups (witness the importance of the Homo-Euro in Sitges, Spain), the strength of the over 40s leisure markets and the displacement of traditional industries by leisure. On Sundays churches are increasingly deserted in favour of shopping malls. IKEA, the MacDonald Golden Arches and the Spires of the Magic Kingdom of Disneyland all trumpet leisure as our new religion.

But there are several paradoxes surrounding the development of a Leisure Society. The first concerns leisure as a social activity. We have equipped our homes for more comfortable and more sophisticated entertainment with videos, DVDs, wide screen TVs, cable, digital and surround-sound. Yet despite this, cinema attendance grew steadily in the 1990s and admissions in European Union (EU) states increased by 40 per cent. It seems we still like the spectacle of the cinema and the atmosphere created by a larger audience. The cinema at least provides an opportunity for social interaction in leisure. But there are also signs of a retreat from leisure as a social activity to that of a solitary one. This is symbolized in a book called *Bowling Alone* where Robert Putnam (2000) describes the individual who now goes bowling alone, rather than with friends. This phenomenon was confirmed by a paper presented to the 2001 conference of The American Psychological Association which found that the two activities in which a group of young Wall Street brokers spent more time than any other were the non-social ones of jogging and masturbation. (Perhaps the latter explains another economic fact of leisure where Danni's Hard Drive (a porn web site) had a gross turnover of $3.5 million in 1998 and 5 million hits per day.)

A Leisure Society also suggests leisure for all. Certainly there are more opportunities than ever for mass consumption of leisure, but herein lie other problems. First, there is that of involuntary leisure. Unemployment has remained obstinately high in many parts of Europe. This means that a

Plate 4
Porters in Nepal
Source: The author

significant group of people have large swathes of leisure time, but insufficient income to participate in what has become an increasingly marketized activity and this creates a frustrated leisure class. Second, for large populations in many parts of the world, working conditions are harsh, pay is low and paid holidays are uncommon. Plate 4 illustrates porters in action in Nepal. Each porter carries the rucksacks of two to three tourists in the Himalayan mountain range. Not only is the work hard for modest pay but some porters are not equipped with high-altitude clothing (note the flip flops in the picture). In some cases they have lost toes through frostbite.

The phrase 'money rich, time poor' has become a popular mantra for those in employment and suggests that achieving a perfect state of leisure may be illusive. The evidence portrays a mixed picture here. Research in the UK suggests that by the end of the 1990s, British people had decreased their working hours by 2 hours 40 minutes per week since the 1950s, representing a modest gain of 7 extra weekly hours of leisure over the century. The average holiday entitlement of EU manual workers is 4–5 weeks a year. The European Work Directive has capped the working week at 35 hours for most employees. Perhaps the division here is between the Mediterranean and Anglo Saxon traditions since for the latter Juliet Schor (1992) pointed up an unexpected decline of leisure in the book *The Overworked American*. In the USA, annual holidays rarely exceed 2 weeks. In the UK, a survey by the Chartered Institute of Personnel and Development found that over one-fifth of employees are working more than 48 hours a week and 56 per cent of these said the balance between their work and personal life was weighted too much towards their job. This gives rise to contrasting effects. In the UK, the term TINS (Two Incomes No Sex) pithily describes those couples who are too exhausted by work for sex. On the other hand in France and Spain a new architecture of leisure emerges. Bridges are formed by adding leave days to public holidays to form extended weekends and some French workers have constructed ambitious viaducts to take most of May off. Unsurprisingly a study by the French Employment Ministry found that 59 per cent of workers felt their daily lives had improved as a result of the shorter hours.

In terms of working patterns the other significant feature is the steady increase of working women. The up-side of this is the concomitant increase in disposable income available for leisure purchases by women (and a notable result of this, in the UK at least, is a marked increase in female alcohol consumption). However, the amounts of time women have available for leisure depends largely on their ability to reduce their historical burden of unpaid housework activities.

Another intriguing paradox exists between the terms leisure and leisurely. Bertrand Russell wrote *In Praise of Idleness and other Essays* (1932) an essay in favour of the 4 hour working day. In contrast, Staffan Linder's (1970) *The Harried Leisure Class* provided an insight into what might frustrate the opportunities for greater leisure. He noted that as earnings per hour increase workers are faced with a notional increase in the cost of not working. Hence rational individuals will be tempted to reallocate time towards paid work or at least increase the intensity of their leisure consumption. A stark choice arises between less leisure or unleisurely leisure and our growing obsession with fast food is surely the paradigm example of the latter.

A further paradox in leisure is that of individualism versus massification. There are strong forces at work leading to the latter and the homogenization of leisure. Global brands such as Nike, Holiday Inn and Sony are strengthening their grip on their markets and lessening our exposure to global cultural differences. Equally, a particular view of culture is transmitted through the cinema where films from the USA accounted for 75 per cent of total box-office receipts in the EU in 1998. Package holidays still sell in their million by offering low prices based on economies of scale. In his book *The McDonaldization of Society*, Ritzer (1993) describes the spread of the principles of fast food production. In leisure, MacDonalds itself, as well as Disneylands and shopping malls illustrate this process at work with an emphasis on predictable experiences and calculable and efficient production techniques. Against this the French theorist, Bourdieu (1984) stresses the importance of individualism or 'distinction' where leisure enables the individual to construct a distinctive lifestyle and to assert individuality in a modern society. So we face the paradox of searching for difference and distinctiveness in a world of increasing similarity.

We are surrounded by the symbols and signals of a Leisure Society. Our economic circumstances surely permit us to live in a Leisure Society. That we do not always fully claim our leisure or feel the full pleasure of it is due partly to personal and partly to political choices. It is the latter which must cause some worry. Perhaps as leisure has displaced religion it has also become the new opium of the people. Where we used to work and pray we now work and play. This leaves insufficient time for participation in the politics of leisure and decisions about what kind of Leisure Society we want to create. For despite the obvious richness, diversity and accessibility of leisure experiences available we do not appear to be a Society at Leisure. Time seems ever more at a premium. We are not a calm or contemplative

---

Exhibit 4.1   Price elasticity of demand: a worked example

When the price of four-star hotel rooms rose from $160 to $180, demand fell from 3200 to 2800 rooms per week. Calculate elasticity of demand.

1 To calculate percentage change in quantity demanded, divide the change in demand ($\Delta Q = 400$) by the original demand ($D0 = 3200$) and multiply by 100
2 $400/(3200 \times 100) = 12.5$
3 To calculate percentage change in price, divide the change in price ($\Delta P = 20$) by the original price ($P0 = 160$) and multiply by 100
4 $20/(160 \times 100) = 12.5$
5 Elasticity of demand $= 12.5/12.5 = 1$

---

society. Rather we are a frenetic society that not only still works remarkably hard but now plays hard too.

Price elasticity of demand

Price elasticity of demand measures the responsiveness of demand to a change in price. This relationship can be expressed as a formula, and Exhibit 4.1 shows a worked example for calculating price elasticity of demand.

$$\frac{\text{Percentage change in quantity demanded}}{\text{Percentage change in price}}$$

Where demand is inelastic it means that demand is unresponsive to a change in price, whereas elastic demand is more sensitive to price changes.

The range of possible outcomes is summarized in Figure 4.1.

It should be noted that, since a rise in the price of a good causes a fall in demand, the figure calculated for price elasticity of demand will always be negative. Economists generally ignore the minus sign. Note that the demand curve, which has elasticity of demand of 1 throughout its length, is a rectangular hyperbola.

Factors affecting price elasticity of demand

The following are the main factors which influence price elasticity of demand:

- necessity of good or service,
- number of substitutes,
- addictiveness,

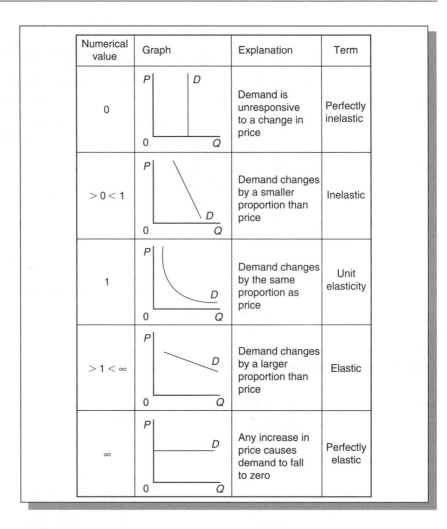

Numerical value	Graph	Explanation	Term
0		Demand is unresponsive to a change in price	Perfectly inelastic
$>0<1$		Demand changes by a smaller proportion than price	Inelastic
1		Demand changes by the same proportion as price	Unit elasticity
$>1<\infty$		Demand changes by a larger proportion than price	Elastic
∞		Any increase in price causes demand to fall to zero	Perfectly elastic

Figure 4.1
Elasticity of demand

- price and usefulness,
- time period,
- consumer awareness.

Necessity of good or service • • •

Goods and services which are necessities generally have a lower price elasticity of demand than goods which are luxuries.

Number of substitutes • • •

Goods and services which are provided in conditions of near monopoly tend to have inelastic demand, since the consumer cannot shop elsewhere should the prices increase. Competition in a market makes demand more elastic.

Addictiveness • • •

Goods such as cigarettes which are addictive tend to have inelastic demand.

Price and usefulness • • •

Cheap and very useful goods and services tend to have inelastic demand since an increase in a low price will have little impact on consumers' purchasing power.

Time period • • •

Demand elasticity generally increases and more time is allowed to elapse between the change in price and the measurement of the change in demand. This is because consumers may not be able to change their plans in the short run. For example, many holiday-makers book holidays 6 months in advance. Thus a fall in the value of the US dollar might have limited effect on the demand for US holidays in the short run since consumers have committed holiday plans. It may not be until the next year that the full effects of such a devaluation on demand can be measured.

Consumer awareness • • •

Package holidays represent a bundle of complementary goods and services which are bought by consumers, and consumers may be attracted to the bottom-line price of a holiday. Consumers may be unaware of destination prices. For this reason, elasticity of demand for services such as ski passes may be inelastic for UK holiday-makers due to lack of information. It should also be noted that the rise of the Internet provides consumers with better knowledge about prices and is therefore likely to lead to demand becoming more price sensitive (elastic). •

Elasticity of demand and total revenue

The concept of price elasticity of demand is useful for firms to forecast the effects of price changes on total revenue received from selling goods and services, as well as for governments wishing to maximize their tax receipts.
Total revenue is defined as:

$$\text{Total revenue} = \text{Price} \times \text{Quantity sold}$$

Consider a rise in the price of a good by 10 per cent. If demand is elastic, quantity sold will fall by more than 10 per cent and thus total revenue will fall. However, if demand is inelastic it will fall by less than 10 per cent and thus total revenue will rise. Similarly, a fall in the price of a good will lead to

---

Exhibit 4.2   Polishing the crown jewels – David Bowen

In 1994, the Queen opened the new Jewel House. The new Jewel House, which cost £10 million, is run by Historic Royal Palaces (HRP), HRP was set up as a 'next steps' agency to look after the Tower, Hampton Court Palace, Kensington Palace state apartments, the Banqueting House, Whitehall and Kew Palace. The agency's staff are civil servants but are not supposed to behave like them.

In 1989, the palaces were generating £11 million in revenue, which was topped up with £10 million from the tax-payer. In 1994, despite the recession, turnover was £26 million and only £6 million came from taxes. The trick has been to apply modern management methods to what is, after all, a substantial business. The first stage was market research. This revealed that tourists were not going to boycott the palaces for the sake of a couple of quid, so HRP increased entrance fees by 50 per cent.

Source: Adapted from *Independent on Sunday*, 20 March 1994.

---

a rise in total revenue in the case of elastic demand and a fall in total revenue where demand is inelastic. Exhibit 4.2 illustrates the application of these principles to the pricing of admission charges to royal palaces in the UK. The exhibit implies that market research was used to estimate elasticity of demand for royal palaces, and since it was found to be inelastic, prices were increased.

Several other studies have been made into price elasticity of demand in the leisure and tourism sector of the economy. For example, Boviard et al. (1984) researched elasticity values for National Trust sites in the UK. Time-series analysis was used and changes in visitor numbers were compared with changes in admission prices, with account being taken of other factors such as changes in the weather, travel costs, unemployment and inflation. Using data from 1970 to 1980, estimates for price elasticity varied from 0.25 at Wallington to 1.05 at Hidcote, but with most results lying in the inelastic range.

Income elasticity of demand

Income elasticity of demand measures the responsiveness of demand to a change in income. This relationship can be expressed as a formula:

$$\frac{\text{Percentage change in quantity demanded}}{\text{Percentage change in income}}$$

Calculation of income elasticity of demand enables an organization to determine whether its goods and services are normal or inferior.

Normal or superior goods are defined as goods whose demand increases as income increases. Therefore their income elasticity of demand is positive

$(+/+ = +)$. The higher the number, the more an increase in income will stimulate demand. Inferior goods are defined as goods whose demand falls as income rises. Therefore their income elasticity of demand is negative $(-/+ = -)$.

Knowledge of income elasticity of demand is useful in predicting future demand in the leisure and tourism sector. For example, Song et al. (2000) undertook an empirical study of outbound tourism demand in the UK. Their results show that the long-run income elasticities for the destinations studied range from 1.70 to 3.90 with an average of 2.367. These estimates of income elasticities imply that overseas holidays are highly income elastic. In other words, demand for outbound tourism should continue to grow with economic growth. The study also considered own-price elasticities and found that the demand for UK outbound tourism is relatively own-price inelastic.

Knowledge of income elasticity of demand also helps to explain some merger and take-over activity as organizations in industries with low or negative income elasticity of demand attempt to benefit from economic growth by expanding into industries with high-positive income elasticity of demand. Such industries show market growth as the economy expands.

Cross-price elasticity of demand

Cross-price elasticity of demand measures the responsiveness of demand for one good to a change in the price of another good. This relationship can be expressed as a formula:

$$\frac{\text{Percentage change in quantity demanded of good A}}{\text{Percentage change in price of good B}}$$

Cross-price elasticity of demand measures the relationship between different goods and services. It therefore reveals whether goods are substitutes, complements or unrelated. An increase in price of good B will lead to an increase in demand for good A if the two goods are substitutes. Thus substitute goods have a positive cross-price elasticity of demand $(+/+ = +)$. For goods which are complements or in joint demand, an increase in the price of good B will lead to a fall in demand for a complementary good, good A. Therefore complementary goods have negative cross-price elasticity of demand $(-/+ = -)$. An increase in the price of good B will have no effect on the demand for an unrelated good, good A. Unrelated goods have cross-price elasticity of demand of zero $(0/+ = 0)$.

Canina et al. (2003) undertook a study to quantify the effects of gasoline price increases on hotel room demand in the US. Their analysis was based on data from 1988 to 2000. They found that each 1 per cent increase in gasoline prices is associated with a 1.74 per cent decrease in lodging demand. In other words, there is a negative cross-price elasticity of demand between gasoline prices and lodging demand which can therefore be seen as complementary items. However, they noted that changes in gasoline price changes do not affect all industry segments equally. The segments that feel the greatest effects of gasoline price increases are full-service mid-market properties and highway and suburban hotels. High-end hotels seem to be immune to the negative effects of fuel price increases.

Demand forecasting

The supply of leisure goods and services cannot generally be changed without some planning and in particular the supply of capital goods such as aircraft requires long planning cycles. Similarly, tour operations require considerable planning to book airport slots and hotel accommodation. Equally, leisure and tourism services are highly perishable. It is not possible to keep stocks of unsold hotel rooms, aircraft and theatre seats, or squash courts. Whilst the supply of some leisure goods, such as golf balls and tennis rackets, can be more readily changed, and stocks of unsold goods held over, there is clearly a need for forecasting of demand for leisure and tourism goods and services.

Exhibit 4.3 reports on forecasts from Airbus Industrie for aircraft demand.

Exhibit 4.3   Aircraft set to for take-off

In a review and forecast of the airline business, the European plane manu-facturer – Airbus Industrie has forecast a doubling in the number of pas-senger aircraft. This is set to rise from 9700 to 17 900 between 2000 and 2020.

Airbus is a consortium of plane manufacturers from Britain, France, Germany and Spain and Mr Adam Brown, its Vice-Chairman for Strategic Planning, has explained how the company plans to meet this demand for aircraft which is linked to a predicted 5 per cent growth of annual passen-gers. First, Airbus is focusing production on large 650-seater aircraft. The Airbus A3XX will be launched in 2004. This is a €8.4 billion project in a plane which will allow passengers to sleep in their own private cabins on long-haul flights.

This optimistic forecast is made despite the poor performance of the Asian economies in 1998–2000. John Leahy, Airbus's Commercial Vice-President, said: 'Our latest forecast confirms that, despite the Asian crisis, this business will enjoy sustained growth.' In fact the projected world's biggest growth area is the Far East and China. Here, 25 new airports are planned in the period 2000–2010. The region is forecast to account for 33 per cent of the world's fleet by 2020, compared with 25 per cent in 2000. The increased demand for air travel will have knock-on effects on airports, demand for fuel and airspace. According to Mr Brown, airlines would be making 88 per cent more flights between 2000 and 2020. 'This will pre-sent a major challenge to airports and air-traffic control capacity. Those involved realize the urgency of the situation. Huge investment will be needed.'

Source: The author, from Airbus Industrie reports and forecasts.

Methods for forecasting demand (Frechtling, 2001) include:

- naive forecasting,
- qualitative forecasts,
- time-series extrapolation,
- surveys,
- Delphi technique,
- models.

Naive forecasts

Naive forecasting makes simple assumptions about the future. At its simplest, naive forecasting assumes that the future level of demand will be the same as the current level. Naive forecasting may also introduce a fixed percentage by which demand is assumed to increase, for example, 3 per cent per annum.

Qualitative forecasts

Qualitative forecasts consider the range of factors which influence the demand for a good or service, as discussed in Chapter 3. These factors are then ranked in order of importance and each of them is in turn analysed to reveal future trends. Although statistical data may be consulted at this stage, no attempt is made to construct a mathematical formula to describe precise relationships between demand and its determinants. Such forecasts rely on a large measure of common sense and are likely to be couched in general terms such as 'small increase in demand' or 'no change in demand envisaged'.

Time-series analysis

A time series is a set of data collected regularly over a period of time. An example of such data is given in Table 4.1.

First, this data can be seen to exhibit seasonal features. Sales of this product rise within each year to a peak in the fourth quarter and drop back sharply in the first quarter of the next year. Second, there seems to be a trend. The figures for each quarter and the yearly totals nearly all display an upward movement. Third, the figure for the first quarter in year 3 does not fit in with the rest of the data and appears as an unusual figure. This may well have been caused by a random variation such as a strike or war or natural disaster.

Forecasting using time-series data first averages seasonal and random variations from the data, to reveal the underlying pattern or trend. The trend can then be used to predict future data, for general yearly totals and adjusted to indicate future seasonal totals. This is illustrated in Figure 4.2 and is a process known as extrapolation.

Table 4.1   Time series of sales of a product

Year	Q1	Q2	Q3	Q4	Total
1	112	205	319	421	1057
2	124	220	350	460	1154
3	90	245	383	503	1221
4	138	267	412	548	1365
5	160	285	450	595	1490

Note: Q1, Q2, etc. = year quarters.

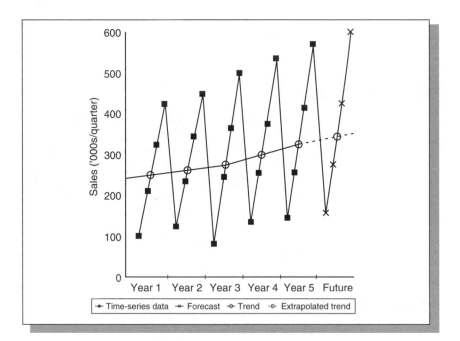

Figure 4.2
Time-series data, trend
and forecast

Time-series forecasting is useful in predicting future seasonal demand and adjusting supply to anticipate seasonal fluctuations. This is particularly important in the leisure and tourism sector where demand tends to be very seasonal (tennis equipment in early summer, leisure centre use after work and at weekends, and holiday demand).

However, care must be taken in using time-series data. Planning ski holiday capacity using time-series data may be useful in predicting market growth, but seasonal fluctuations due to school holidays are not best predicted from past events (which would give the average date) but by looking to see when Easter falls to find the precise date. Equally it is random events that can cause significant changes in the demand for ski holidays. Clearly snowfall and exchange rates are two key factors that cannot be forecast using time-series analysis. It is important therefore that time-series analysis should be used as part of a package of forecasting techniques.

Surveys

Surveys may be carried out by the organization itself or contracted out to a specialist market research organization. Alternatively use may be made of published forecasts constructed using surveys. Surveys can be useful ways of forecasting demand for new or revised products where no time-series data exist. However, survey results are only as valid as their underlying methodology, so care must be taken to ensure that the sample used for the survey is a true reflection of an organization's potential customers, and is of a large enough size to be valid. Additionally, a pilot survey needs to be conducted and analyzed to iron out any problems of interpretation of words or leading questions. In fact, surveys turn out to be more useful for testing ideas such as advertising campaigns or design, where respondents are asked to choose between real and concrete alternatives. Hypothetical questions are generally used in demand forecasting, and respondents' answers may not necessarily reflect what they would actually do if they had to spend money.

Delphi technique

The Delphi technique is a method of forecasting which attempts to harness expert opinion on the subject. Questionnaires are used to discover opinions of experts in a particular field. The results of the forecasts are then fed back to the participants with the aim of reaching a consensus view of the group.

Modelling

More complex forecasting methods attempt to describe accurately the relationship between demand for a product and the factors determining that demand. They consider a number of variables, and use statistical techniques of correlation and regression analysis to test relationships and construct formulae. Some include econometric techniques which forecast key economic variables such as growth rates, interest rates and inflation rates to construct a comprehensive model which relates general economic conditions to the factors affecting demand for a particular product to the demand forecasts for that product.

Problems with forecasts

There are several problems which arise from using forecasts. First, the forecasts are only as good as the assumptions of the model being used. For example, the assumption that the past is a good guide to the future limits the validity of extrapolation using time-series analysis. However, there are equally questionable assumptions included in some very complex models. It is important to know what these assumptions are so that should any of these assumptions prove to be incorrect, forecasts can be re-evaluated. The major problem, however, is the unpredictability of economic trends and outside events such as wars or strikes or disasters. For example, the events of 11 September 2001 undermined the accuracy of many forecasts and caused severe financial problems to those who had relied on overly optimistic predictions of future levels of demand. This does not mean that forecasts are useless, but that those who use them should be constantly monitoring their operating environment to detect any factors which will upset the forecasts they are using.

Sources of forecasts

- *Leisure Futures* (the Henley Centre for Forecasting)
- *Retail Business* (Corporate Intelligence in Retailing)
- *Tourist Intelligence Quarterly*
- *Leisure Forecasts* (Leisure Industries Research Centre/Leisure Consultants)
- *Mintel Leisure Reports* (Mintel)
- *Keynote Market Review* (Key Note)
- *New Leisure Markets* (Marketscope)
- *Travel and Tourism Analyst* (Travel and Tourism Intelligence)
- *International Tourism Reports* (Travel and Tourism Intelligence)

Review of key terms

- Income effect: change in demand caused by change in income.
- Substitution effect: change in demand caused by change in relative prices.
- Price elasticity of demand: the responsiveness of demand to a change in price.
- Inelastic demand: demand is unresponsive to a change in price.
- Elastic demand: demand is responsive to a change in price.
- Income elasticity of demand: the responsiveness of demand to a change in income.
- Cross-price elasticity of demand: the responsiveness of demand for one good to a change in the price of another good.
- Time series: a set of data collected regularly over a period of time.
- Seasonal variation: regular pattern of demand changes apparent at different times of year.
- Extrapolation: extending time-series data into the future based on trend.
- Delphi technique: finding consensus view of experts.

Data Questions

Task 4.1 Teleworking

An office worker who works for 48 weeks a year and has a 90 minute journey to and from work clocks up some alarming statistics. An average of 720 hours each year are spent on commuting. That is 30 whole days. Over the last decade, commuting has reached new heights, largely because of high inner-city house prices and motorways. Cheaper house prices in out-of-city locations, together with the development of a comprehensive network of motorways, have encouraged people to increase their time spent on commuting and to cast a wider net in search of well-paid employment. It may be, though, that we are nearing the peak of commuting. The technological revolution in the office means that the possibility for people to work from home is becoming a reality. Why spend a fortune in time and money sending people to the office, when the office can be sent to the people? The fax, digitalization of information, the telephone network, PCs, modems and videoconferencing are all enabling the spread of teleworking. Meanwhile, environmental concerns have encouraged the government to increase taxes to curb the use of car journeys.

Almost half of major UK companies are experimenting with teleworking schemes. This has resulted in the creation of a new class of over half a million full-time teleworkers. British Telecoms (BT) is a major potential benefactor of increased teleworking, since teleworking means more use of data links. However, BT also uses the scheme itself. Directory enquiries operators can now work at home where they have databases with telephone numbers installed on PCs and calls rerouted. To the customer there is no apparent change in service. The Henley Centre for Forecasting has estimated that more than 15 per cent of hours worked in the UK was worked from home in the mid-1990s, which translates into a figure of over 3 million people.

The choice for workers looks fairly straightforward. It has been estimated that the overall benefit to a $25 000-a-year employee who is able to work at home for 4 days a week and cut commuting to 1 day a week is of the order of $7080 a year. This is calculated mainly in terms of increased leisure time priced at $6335. To these benefits employees can add more flexibility in terms of house location and hours worked, and less commuting stress. On the other hand, some psychologists have pointed out the important functions that a place of work may fulfil, particularly pointing to the friendship factor, and the benefits of a physical separation of work and home. A key question posed by the release of commuting time is how it will be spent. Will people choose to use it as leisure time or might they instead seek to increase their earnings by working more hours?

Source: The author, from news cuttings.

Recap Questions

1 Economic theory assumes that people act rationally and maximize their total satisfaction. Explain this proposition and discuss whether people who spend 30 days a year commuting fulfil these assumptions.
2 'For individuals, the advantages of teleworking are usually believed to have more to do with quality of life than with economics'. Can economic theory consider the quality of life?
3 The value of the extra leisure time made available to the employee cited above is $6335.
   (a) How might this calculation be made?
   (b) What factors will determine what the person will do with the extra leisure time?
4 If the benefit to individuals of teleworking is so clear, why do not more people telework?
5 How might teleworking affect the leisure sector?

Task 4.2 Elasticity

Jensen (1998) estimated income and price elasticities for tourist visitors to Denmark. He found considerable variation in results for different nationalities. His key finding was 'For German tourists, who account for the largest share in Danish tourism, the estimates for price elasticity with respect to the prices in Denmark is close to −1.5 and the long-run income elasticity is found to be near 2' (1998: 101).

Recap Questions

1 Classify German tourism demand in Denmark as elastic/inelastic/inferior/normal.
2 Comment on these findings.
3 What implications do these figures have for policy-makers and tourist organizations in Denmark?
4 Devise a method of estimating price and income elasticity of demand for cinema attendance, explaining any problems foreseen.

Task 4.3 Air-traffic forecasts for the UK

Table 4.2 shows the mid-range forecasts for international air traffic from the UK.

Table 4.2 Mid-range forecasts of international terminal passengers, 2005–20 (million)

Year	Short haul	Long haul	Total
2005	103.4	55.1	158.5
2010	123.7	69.3	193.0
2015	148.4	86.3	234.7
2020	178.2	105.8	284.0

Source: Department for transport.

Recap Questions

1 What additional information would you like before trusting these estimates?
2 What factors would be taken into account in preparing demand forecasts for the air transport industry?
3 Which organizations will use these forecasts, and why?
4 What effects might each of the following have on the forecasts:
   (a) The introduction of an air-pollution tax.
   (b) A change in exchange rates.
   (c) A sustained period of economic recession.
   And why?

Multiple choice

1 **Which of the following statements is always true?**

   (a) An increase in wages increases the opportunity cost of leisure.
   (b) An increase in wages will cause workers to work less.
   (c) US workers have longer holidays than European workers.
   (d) All of the above.

2 **When the price of a leisure good rose by 10 per cent demand remained the same. Which of the following best describes the price elasticity of demand for this good?**

   (a) Perfectly elastic.
   (b) Perfectly inelastic.
   (c) Unit elasticity.
   (d) Neither elastic nor inelastic.

3 **Which of the following will cause the demand for air travel to destination x to be more inelastic?**

   (a) Punctuality of service.
   (b) Consumer awareness of the prices of competitors.
   (c) The absence of close competition.
   (d) x representing a long-haul destination.

4 **Which of the following statements is true?**

   (a) Normal goods have positive income elasticity of demand.
   (b) An increase in price will cause total revenue to rise when demand is elastic.
   (c) Income elasticity of demand for foreign travel tends to be negative.
   (d) An elastic demand curve generally has a steep gradient.

5 **The Delphi technique for forecasting involves:**

   (a) Time-series analysis.
   (b) Regression analysis.
   (c) Extrapolation.
   (d) Asking expert opinion.

Review questions

1 What degree of income elasticity of demand would you expect for summer holiday breaks to an exotic destination?
2 What cross-price elasticity of demand would you expect to find between:
   (a) Price of dollars/holidays in the USA?
   (b) Holidays in Spain/holidays in Greece?
   (c) Sony games consoles/Sony games cartridges?
3 What is meant by extrapolation?

Web sites of interest

Mintel International: a wide range of market intelligence on the leisure sector
www.mintel.co.uk

Supply and costs

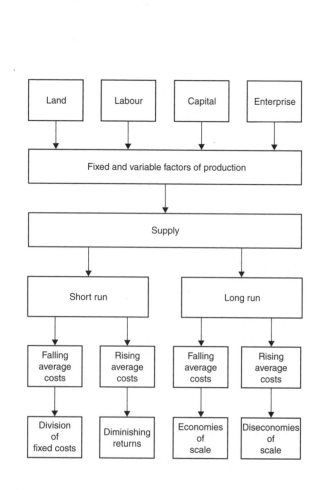

Objectives and learning outcomes

Shuttle services such as British Airways' (BA) London to Belfast service operate on a turn-up-and-fly principle, so BA's operations division has to be able to provide a flexible service in order to meet sudden changes in demand. Air traffic control routes across Europe on the other hand are fairly inflexible – they are sometimes unable to cope with sudden surges in demand and this can lead to long delays in peak times of the year. This chapter looks behind the supply curve at issues such as these. It investigates how easily the supply of leisure and tourism products is able to respond to changes in demand, using the concept of elasticity. It also considers how an organization's costs respond to changes in output and distinguishes between private costs and social or external costs.

By studying this chapter students will be able to:

- understand and utilize the concept of elasticity of supply;
- identify the factors of production;
- distinguish between fixed and variable factors of production;
- analyse the relationship between costs and output in the short run and long run;
- establish the relationship between costs and the supply curve;
- understand the reasons for economies of scale;
- identify methods and rationale for growth;
- distinguish between social and private costs.

Price elasticity of supply

Elasticity of supply measures the responsiveness of supply to a change in price. This relationship may be expressed as a formula:

$$\frac{\text{Percentage change in quantity supplied}}{\text{Percentage change in price}}$$

Exhibit 5.1 shows a worked example of how to calculate elasticity of supply.

Where supply is inelastic it means that supply cannot easily be changed, whereas elastic supply is more flexible. The range of possible outcomes is summarized in Figure 5.1.

Note that any straight line supply curve passing through the origin has supply elasticity of 1.

Exhibit 5.1 A worked example

When the price four-star hotel rooms rose from $160 to $180, supply rose from 3200 to 3600 rooms per week. Calculate elasticity of supply:

1 To calculate percentage change in quantity supplied, divide the change in supply ($\Delta Q = 400$) by the original supply ($S0 = 3200$) and multiply by 100
2 $400/(3200 \times 100) = 12.5$
3 To calculate percentage change in price, divide the change in price ($\Delta P = 20$) by the original price ($P0 = 160$) and multiply by 100
4 $20/(160 \times 100) = 12.5$
5 Elasticity of supply $= 12.5/12.5 = 1$

Numerical value	Graph	Explanation	Term
0		Supply is unresponsive to a change in price	Perfectly inelastic
$>0<1$		Supply changes by a smaller proportion than price	Inelastic
1		Supply changes by the same proportion as price	Unit elasticity
$>1<\infty$		Supply changes by a larger proportion than price	Elastic
∞		Suppliers can supply any amount at the current price but none if price falls	Perfectly elastic

Figure 5.1
Elasticity of supply

Factors affecting price elasticity of supply

The following are the main factors which influence price elasticity of supply:

- time period,
- availability of stocks,
- spare capacity,
- flexibility of capacity/resource mobility.

Time period • • •

Generally the longer the time period allowed, the easier it is for supply to be changed. This is illustrated in Figure 5.2.

In the immediate time scale, it is difficult to change supply and thus supply is relatively inelastic, and a change in price of $P0$ to $P1$ results in supply being unchanged at $Q0$ on curve $S0$. In the short run it may be possible to divert production or capacity from another use and thus supply becomes more elastic. This is shown by supply curve $S1$, where a rise in price from $P0$ to $P1$ results in a small rise in supply from $Q0$ to $Q1$. In the long run it is possible to vary fixed factors of production (e.g. build more factories or invest in more capacity). Supply is thus more elastic during this time period, as shown by curve $S2$, where a rise in price from $P0$ to $P1$ results in a rise in supply from $Q0$ to $Q2$. For example, if there is a sudden increase in demand for air travel from Paris to Lyon due to a rail strike, airlines will not be able to provide more supply. If the increase in demand is sustained airlines could lease extra planes or transfer them from other less well-used routes to increase supply in the short run. In the long run new planes could be purchased to provide increased supply.

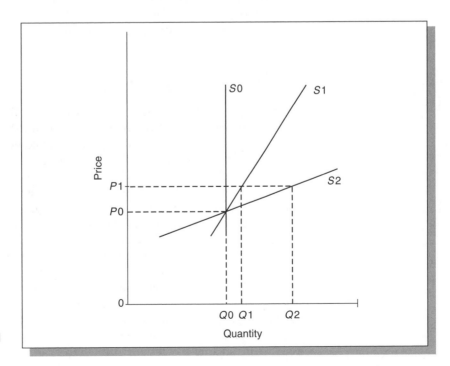

Figure 5.2
The effects of time period on elasticity of supply

Availability of stocks ● ● ●

For manufactured goods the availability of stocks of goods in warehouses will enable supply to be more flexible and more elastic. Modern 'just-in-time' methods of production are geared towards enabling manufacturing to be more sensitive to market needs without recourse to large stocks. However for some leisure services (e.g. theatres and hotels), it is impossible to keep standby stocks and so supply is inelastic in the short run.

Spare capacity ● ● ●

The existence of spare capacity either in terms of service capacity or manufacturing capacity will make supply more elastic. Examples here include airlines that have spare aircraft available for deployment.

Flexibility of capacity/resource mobility ● ● ●

Flexibility of capacity means that resources can easily be shifted from provision of one good or service to another. Flexible sports halls, for example, enable capacity to be shifted from one leisure service to another to respond to changes in demand and thus make supply more elastic. Flexibility of the labour force is also a key factor here and many organizations train staff to be multiskilled to enable them to shift from one task to another when temporary bottlenecks arise. In contrast, changing the supply of specialist goods or services may require the use of specialist skills or machines. These may be difficult or expensive to hire in the short period and hence will tend to make supply inelastic. For example the training period for pilots is lengthy and this can make supply of air travel inelastic in the short period.

Significance of price elasticity of supply to leisure sector

The supply of some tourist attractions is totally inelastic. For example, there is only one tomb of Chairman Mao in Beijing, there is only one Sistine Chapel and there is only one home of Sir Winston Churchill at Chartwell. It is clearly not possible to replicate these sites as it is for other popular attractions such as Disneyworld.

Considerable thought therefore has to be given to managing such sites. The market could establish an equilibrium if prices were allowed to fluctuate, but the heritage aspect of such sites generally precludes such a solution since they are generally meant to be universally accessible. Inevitably, then, there is excess demand for these sites at the given price and this problem is managed differently at each site. At Mao's tomb, capacity is raised substantially by having the queue divided into two to pass each side of Mao's body. White-gloved attendants furiously wave people by and thus queuing is kept to a minimum despite free admission. At the Sistine Chapel large queues do form, but they are accommodated in an imaginative way by making the detour, through the Vatican museum, to the Sistine

Chapel progressively more and more circuitous. The problem of inelastic supply and excess demand at Chartwell is addressed by issuing timed tickets to visitors.

In general terms, price elasticity of supply determines the extent to which a rise in demand will cause either a change in price or shortage. Tour operators generally have relatively fixed capacity in ski resorts, and thus the supply curve is inelastic. When demand rises, for example, during school holiday periods, supply is unable to expand to meet the increased demand and so price rise considerably.

Supply and costs

Leisure and tourism outputs

We need to distinguish between different forms of output in the leisure and tourism sector. Where manufacturing of a product takes place, for example in the production of sports clothing, then output is measured in terms of physical product. Where the provision of a service takes place, output is measured in terms of capacity.

Leisure and tourism inputs

Inputs (or factors of production) are classified in economics under the following general headings.

- *Land*: This includes natural resources such as minerals and land itself, and can be divided into renewable and non-renewable resources (see Chapter 16).
- *Labour*: This includes skilled and unskilled human effort.
- *Capital*: This includes buildings, machines and tools.
- *Enterprise*: This is the factor which brings together the other factors of production to produce goods and services.

For example, a soccer club such as Arsenal FC needs a plot of land. Arsenal's new Ashburton Grove site occupies 27 acres of prime inner city land (although this is quite modest compared with the 100-acre Manchester United site and the 130-acre Wembley complex). Additionally it requires capital to develop the land (mainly the provision of a stadium and facilities). Its labour force would include skilled employees such as players (see Plate 5) and accountants and less skilled stewards and catering staff. But without enterprise, none of these factors of production would be brought together in this way. Enterprise is offered through the club's directors.

In tourism land is a significant resource for some destinations (e.g. beaches for Tobago and Thailand, and Coral for diving in the Red Sea). For other destinations cultural capital is a key attraction (e.g. museums and historical buildings). Williamson and Hirsch (1996) discuss the process of tourism development in Koh Samui, Thailand and the form that this took, in particular, the building of bungalows. It examines the changing control

Plate 5
Arsenal striker Thiery
Henry takes corner kick
in FA cup semi final at
Old Trafford, 2003

over factors of production and the importance of land, labour and capital
in bungalow development.

Factors of production are further classified as:

• fixed factors,
• variable factors.

Fixed factors of production are defined as those factors which cannot be
easily varied in the short run. Examples of fixed factors of production in the
provision of leisure and tourism services include the actual buildings of
theatres and hotels, whilst factories and complex machinery are examples
in leisure manufacturing. Variable factors of production on the other hand
can be changed in the short run and include unskilled labour, energy (e.g.
electricity, gas and oil) and readily available raw materials. The existence
of fixed and variable factors of production means that changes in output
will be achieved by different means in the short run and the long run.

Production

Entrepreneurs bring together factors of production in order to supply
goods and services in the market and maximize their profits. There are generally several possible ways to produce a given level of output or to provide
a service. Profit maximization implies cost minimization and thus entrepreneurs will seek to combine inputs to produce the least-cost method of production. Input prices themselves are constantly changing to reflect changing
conditions in their markets. As input prices change, entrepreneurs will
adapt production methods to maintain lowest costs, substituting where
possible factors of production which are rising in price with cheaper ones.

For example in travel retailing (as in most areas) there is a long-term move to substitute capital for labour. In this case, the Internet is increasingly used for bookings instead of the telephone or high street travel agent.

Short-run costs

Fixed costs • • •

The existence of fixed factors of production means that the costs associated with that factor will also be fixed in the short run. Such costs are sometimes called indirect costs or overheads since they have to be paid irrespective of the level of production. So, for example, whether a plane flies to New York empty or full, its fixed costs or overheads are the same. Exhibit 5.2 illustrates fixed costs for art galleries.

Variable costs • • •

Variable costs are those costs which vary directly with output. They are sometimes called direct costs. For the production of leisure goods they would include raw materials, energy and unskilled labour costs, but for the provision of services such as air transport they are proportionately small and would include such items as meals and passenger handling charges.

Total costs • • •

Total costs are defined as total fixed costs plus total variable costs. This distinction is an important one when deciding whether to continue to operate facilities out of season. A firm which is not covering its costs is making a

---

Exhibit 5.2   High fixed costs for art galleries

The demand for art fluctuates according to the state of the economy. When economic growth is strong, galleries can be full of buyers, but these soon disappear when economic times are hard. During the recession in the early 1990s one commentator reported that 'buyers had gone into hibernation' and many art galleries were forced out of business.

A major factor in this is the high fixed costs that galleries face which can be easily accommodated when sales are strong. But the point about fixed costs is that they cannot be changed in the short term. If demand falls suddenly they can force a gallery into bankruptcy since they must still be paid even when there are few or no customers. Galleries are located in prime locations and so their major fixed costs are rent and property taxes. In addition, galleries typically produce three or four catalogues a year with an average cost of Euros 18 000 per edition.

Source: The author, based on article from *The Independent*.

loss and in the long term will go out of business. However, in the short run a firm which is covering its variable costs and making some contribution to its fixed costs may stay in business. This is because it has to pay for its fixed costs anyway in the short run and thus some contribution to their costs is better than none at all.

Average costs • • •

Average costs (AC) (or unit costs, or cost per item) are defined as total costs divided by output.

Marginal costs • • •

Marginal costs (MC) are defined as the cost of supplying one extra unit of output.

Relationship between output and costs in the short run (production) • • •

Figure 5.3 shows a typical short-run AC curve for the production of goods in the short run. If a manufacturer has planned for a level of output $0Q0$, then $0C0$ represents the AC of production. These will represent the least-cost method of production and combination of factors of production, since profit maximization is assumed. However, if the level of output should subsequently be changed in the short run, then by definition only variable factors of production can be changed and fixed factors remain constant. AC will therefore rise as the mix of inputs resulting in the least-cost method of production cannot be maintained.

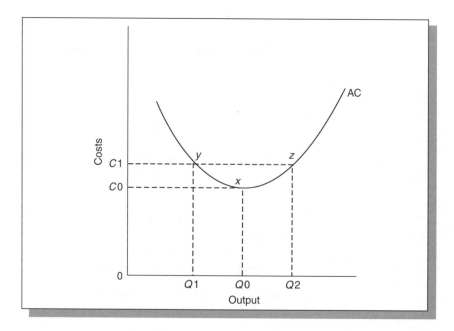

Figure 5.3
Short-run AC for typical manufacturing firm

Consider first a fall in output to 0Q1. AC will rise to 0C1. This is because the fixed costs will now be borne by a smaller level of output. For example, if a UK football premier team is relegated to a lower division it is likely to see its match attendance fall – but it will still have to pay its stadium costs so its AC per spectator will rise. Similarly, if output rises to 0Q2, AC rise to 0C1. The fixed factors of production become overcrowded and production less efficient. This is related to the law of eventual diminishing returns.

Relationship between output and costs in the short run (services) • • •

The provision of services often involves different cost relationships from the provision of goods. For a hotel, a theme park or a theatre, for example, fixed costs represent a large proportion of costs in the short run. MC for extra visitors to a theme park or a theatre are negligible up to the capacity level. Figure 5.4 illustrates typical cost curves for the provision of a service with high fixed costs. Notice that the AC curve falls all the way to short-run capacity and that for much of its range the MC is low and constant. The existence of low or sometimes zero MC explains some marketing activity for the service sector. Theatres sell standby seats to students at low prices but students still have to pay full prices for ice creams.

Long-run costs

In the long run all factors of production are variable and so organizations are not faced with the problems of fixed factors or diminishing returns. Output can be satisfied by the most suitable combination of factors of production. Figure 5.5 illustrates three possible ways in which AC of production

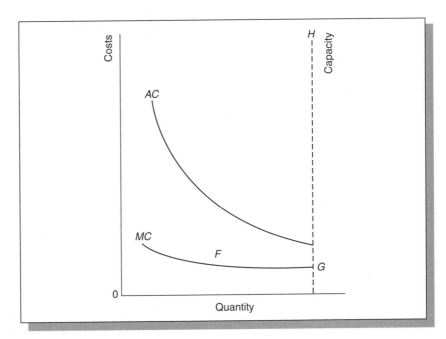

Figure 5.4
Costs for a firm providing a service with high fixed costs

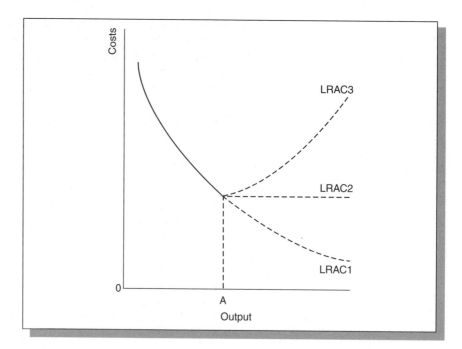

Figure 5.5
LRAC

may vary with output in the long run. In long-run average cost (LRAC) curve 1, average costs fall for the entire range as output rises, illustrating economies of scale. In the case of LRAC2, the curve flattens out after point A when constant returns to scale are achieved. For the curve LRAC3, average costs begin to rise again after point A where diseconomies of scale begin to set in. For Arsenal Football Club a move from its stadium at Highbury with a capacity of only 38 000 to its new stadium at Ashburton Road with a capacity of 60 000 will result in significant economies of scale – particularly economies of increased dimensions.

Internal economies of scale

Economies of scale arise from increases in the size of an organization and can be summarized as follows:

- financial,
- buying and selling,
- managerial/specialization,
- technical,
- economies of increased dimensions,
- risk bearing.

Financial • • •

Large organizations tend to have bigger assets. When they borrow money, they often raise large amounts and these two factors lead to financial economies. Borrowing from banks is likely to be at preferential rates of interest reflecting the security offered by large organizations and the amount borrowed. Additionally, larger organizations have the option of raising funds directly from capital markets by, for example, a rights issue of shares which can be an economical method of financing large projects.

Buying and selling

Buying and selling economies arise from buying and selling in bulk. On the buying side this leads to bulk purchase discounts, and on the selling side costs such as advertising are spread out over a large number of sales.

Managerial/specialization

As firms grow the potential for managerial and specialization economies becomes greater. The proprietor of an independent travel agency, for example, will have to act across a range of managerial functions and may lack specialist knowledge. Large travel agency chains such as Going Places, however, will have the scope for employing experts in functional areas such as accounting marketing and personnel.

Technical

Technical economies are also possible as firms grow. These relate in particular to the utilization of complex and expensive technology and machinery. A large hotel may employ a computerized reservations and accounting system since the cost per guest per year will be relatively insignificant. A small boarding house however may have insufficient business to justify the capital outlay.

Economies of increased dimensions

Economies of increased dimensions are well illustrated by the example of jumbo jets. Although these have the capacity of perhaps three conventional jets, they do not cost 3 times as much to buy or to staff or to run. Thus the cost per seat of a jumbo jet is less than that in a conventional jet. Economies of increased dimension mean that costs rise proportionately less than does capacity.

Risk bearing

Risk-bearing economies derive from the ability of large organizations to weather setbacks. This arises from two factors. First many large organizations have diversified interests and thus a fall in demand in one area can be compensated for by business elsewhere. Second, large organizations with substantial assets are able to sustain short-term losses from their reserves.

External economies of scale

External economies of scale result not from the size of an organization but from the concentration of similar organizations in a particular location. For example, hotels in a particular resort benefit from resort as well as their own advertising, and may attract visitors on the strength of complementary attractions supplied by neighbouring organizations. Another example is that of Dive companies in the Red Sea resorts. The existence of so many companies in a defined area brings benefits to each individual company. These include the existence of a pool of skilled labour (e.g. instructors), the provision of specialist supplies (e.g. dive ships and oxygen suppliers) and the availability of specialist support (e.g. decompression chambers). Additionally the area becomes known for its diving facilities and this offers marketing benefits.

Diseconomies of scale

Internal diseconomies • • •

The main reason for the occurrence of diseconomies of scale is managerial capacity. For some organizations, it becomes difficult to manage efficiently beyond a certain size and problems of control, delegation and communications arise. These may become significant enough to outweigh economies of scale generated in other ways. Diseconomies of scale may also arise from growth due to mergers when the two firms find that there is insufficient fit between themselves in terms of systems of management or organizational culture. Exhibit 5.3 illustrates economies and diseconomies of scale at work in the restaurant and hotels sector.

External diseconomies • • •

The negative side of concentration of organizations in a particular area can be overcrowding and the associated congestion and pollution costs.

How firms grow

The main methods by which firms grow are by:

- internal growth,
- mergers and take-overs.

Internal growth is often a slow process and firms can accelerate their growth by mergers and take-overs. The difference between these is that

> **Exhibit 5.3   Perfect pizzas, synergies Chez Gerard and a marriage made in hell?**
>
> 1998 was a good year for the pizza and pasta sector in the UK which is estimated to be worth approximately € 1170 million a year. Pizza Express moved ahead in the sector when it acquired the Café Pasta chain. The *Guardian* business correspondent described this move as underlining 'the trend towards creating branded chains of restaurants which benefit from economies of scale in financing and property costs'. Pizza Express currently has 175 outlets with expansion plans for an extra 125 outlets. It paid € 8.5 million in cash for the Café Pasta chain.
>
> Advertising and branding are becoming increasingly important in the midrange restaurant sector with names such as Café Rouge and All-Bar-One and a recent Mintel report concludes that branded chains now account for more than a half of all outlets in the pasta and pizza markets. This move by Pizza Express helps bring down the average costs of marketing. David Page of Pizza Express also notes that costs tend to be higher in general for smaller independent companies.
>
> In a similar move, Groupe Chez Gerard has also announced plans to buy the Richoux group of restaurants. Chez Gerard explained that expected marketing, purchasing and head office synergies are a key motive for the acquisition. Commentators have also noted that the move strengthens the position of Chez Gerard in the case of a possible downturn in expenditure since the Richoux group effectively covers the lower end of the market.
>
> Of course there are potential downsides to mergers. One is a possible conflict of personalities between directors. In early 1999, The Ladbroke Group (owners of the non-US Hilton hotels) took over the Stakis hotel chain. This has led the Guardian financial correspondent to describe the new partnership between Mr Peter George (Ladbroke) and Mr David Michels (Stakis) as 'potentially a marriage made in hell'.
>
> *Source*: Adapted from the *Guardian* and *Financial Times* by the author.

mergers are a joint agreement for two organizations to join together whereas a take-over does not necessarily have the agreement of the target firm. It is also useful to identify different types of integration:

- vertical integration,
- horizontal integration,
- conglomerate merger.

Vertical integration

This occurs when a firm takes over or merges with another firm in the same industry but at a different stage of production. It is termed backward integration when the merger is in the direction of suppliers, and forward integration when it is towards the consumer. Thomson Holidays (part of the German Tui group) demonstrates a vertically integrated organization with its ownership of a charter airline, Britannia, and travel agency chain, Lunn Poly.

The key motive in forward vertical integration is in ensuring a market for an operator's product. This may be offensive – selling your product at the expense of your rivals – or defensive – making sure your rivals do not monopolize retail outlets and thus block the selling of your product. Backward integration gives your organization control over suppliers, and means that you have better control over quality. In each case integration can add to profits.

Horizontal integration • • •

This occurs when a firm merges with another firm in the same industry and at the same stage. For example:

- *1998*: Thomas Cook merged with Carlson travel and the Thomson Travel Group bought ski operator Crystal.
- *1999*: the Ladbroke Group owners of The Hilton chain outside of the USA bought up Thistle Hotels.
- *2002*: easyJet was successful in its take-over of a competing low-cost airline, Go.
- *2003*: Air France announces a merger with KLM.

Economies of scale are a prime motive for horizontal integration. For example, advertising costs per holiday fall and bulk purchase discounts can be maximized. Market share and market domination are also key motives. Horizontal acquisition can also occur to purchase firms operating in complementary areas. The interest of the Thomson Travel Group in companies such as Headwater, Crystal and Blakes Cottages is to extend its portfolio beyond the sun markets. There is also scope for cost savings through rationalization of activity (e.g. Air France merger with KLM) and the closing down of sites which duplicate work. Horizontal integration also buys into an existing market (easyJet acquisition of Go) and its customers and can be an effective way of reducing competition. One of the arguments made by Stenna Sealink and P&O (UK ferry operators) for merging was the potential for service improvement. In a study of the lodging industry, Canina (2001) found that the equity markets view lodging mergers and acquisitions in a favourable light. For a sample of 41 acquisitions from 1982 to 1999, the stock-price reaction was significantly positive for both the acquiring firms and their targets. This finding stands in contrast to the results for the overall market, where fewer than half of all mergers add value in terms of equity prices suggesting that the scale economies predicted for mergers may be less than often supposed.

Diversification • • •

A conglomerate merger or diversification occurs when a firm takes over another firm in a completely different industry. The motives for such activity may include first a desire to spread risks. Second growth prospects in a particular industry may be poor, reflecting a low or negative income elasticity of demand. In such circumstances diversification into an industry with high income elasticity of demand may generate faster growth. Third it may be possible to get benefits of synergy, where the benefits of two firms joining exceed the benefits of remaining separate. For example, the Rank Group plc is a UK conglomerate organization with interests across the leisure sector. It has three main business divisions: Gaming, Hard Rock and Deluxe. Gaming includes Mecca Bingo, Grosvenor Casinos and Blue Square. Hard Rock includes 64 owned cafes, 48 franchised cafes and the global rights to the Hard Rock brand. Deluxe owns film processing as well as DVD and VHS replication, distribution and other related services. Similarly, Time Warner is the world's leading media and entertainment company, whose businesses include filmed entertainment, interactive services, television networks, cable systems, publishing and music. Its interests span media and communications:

- America Online,
- Time Warner Book Group,
- Time Warner Interactive Video,
- Time Inc.,
- Time Warner Cable;

and entertainment and networks:

- Home Box Office,
- New Line Cinema,
- Turner Broadcasting System,
- Warner Bros. Entertainment,
- Warner Music Group.

Declutter • • •

A problem that may occur from diversification is that an organization may lose sight of its aims and objectives and find strategic management difficult. Under such circumstances 'decluttering' may take place, whereby an organization disposes of its fringe activities and concentrates on its core business.

Social and private costs

Private costs of production are those costs which an organization has to pay for its inputs. They are also known as accounting costs since they appear in an organization's accounts. However the production of many goods and services may result in side effects. Violent videos may, for example, result in more violent and antisocial behaviour. A nightclub may result in noise pollution. These are classed as external or social costs. They do not appear in an organization's accounts and do not affect its profitability, although they may well affect the well-being of society at large. These issues are discussed more fully in later chapters.

Review of key terms

- Price elasticity of supply: responsiveness of supply to a change in price.
- Factors of production: land, labour, capital and enterprise.
- Fixed factor: one that cannot be varied in the short run.
- Variable factor: one that can be varied in the short run.
- Average cost: total cost divided by output.
- Marginal cost: the cost of producing one extra unit of output.
- Vertical integration: merger at different stage within same industry.
- Horizontal integration: merger at same stage in same industry.
- Conglomerate merger: merger into different industry.
- Private costs: costs which a firm has to pay.
- Social costs: costs which result from output but which accrue to society.

Data Questions

Task 5.1   easyJet

easyJet is a leading low-cost airline. Its principal activity is the provision of a "low-cost–good-value" airline service. It was founded in 1995 when new European Union rules allowed free competition in air transport and grew rapidly becoming a plc in 2000. By 2001 the easyJet network consisted of 35 routes serving 17 airports in 16 cities.

easyJet follows a strategy of low cost and good value. Its fares are determined by a sophisticated yield management system. They are more flexible and generally significantly lower than those of traditional airlines. It keeps costs low in the following ways:

- Use of website to reduce distribution costs: About 90 per cent seats are sold via easyJet.com. No tickets are sold through travel agents saving in commission fees.
- Maximizing the utilization of aircraft: Maximizing the use of each aircraft (by time spent flying and by load factors) reduces the average cost.
- Ticketless operation: This reduces the cost of issuing millions of tickets each year.
- No free on-board catering.
- Simple service model extends to no pre-assigned seats or interline connections.
- Airport use: Smaller airports such as Luton have lower handling charges and suffer less congestion and flight delays. This enables faster turnaround and extra flights.
- Standard aircraft: The use of only Boeing 737 reduces training and servicing costs.
- Paperless office: Management and administration of the company is undertaken entirely on IT systems.
- No expensive corporate Headquarters.
- Flat management structure.

In 2000/01, easyJet's pre-tax profit grew to £40.1 million, on revenues of £356.9 million. This resulted from a 26.4 per cent increase in sold seats and a total of 7.1 million passengers. It achieved aircraft utilization of approximately 12 hours per day and load factors of 83 per cent.

Revenue and profit

Year to end September	Revenue (£ million)	Profit (£ million)
1998	77.0	5.9
1999	139.8	1.3
2000	263.7	22.1
2001	356.9	40.1

Passenger statistics

Year	Total ('000)	Year	Total ('000)
1995	30	1999	3670
1996	420	2000	5996
1997	1140	2001	7664
1998	1880		

An executive team with extensive commercial, operational and financial experience is responsible for overall management of the group and the company adopts a flat management structure. This eliminates unnecessary layers of management and reduces costs. The company holds regular communication meetings and management briefings and publishes an employee newsletter. These channels enable the company to communicate its strategy and direction and receive feedback from employees.

In 2002 easyJet was successful in its take-over of a competing low-cost airline, Go. This was financed through a rights issue of share capital. In the year to 31 March 2002, Go flew 4.3 million passengers generating revenue of £233.7 million and profits before tax of £14.0 million. The benefits of the merger include:

- Market development with the addition of routes not currently operated by easyJet.
- Market penetration with the acquisition of a larger customer base.
- Economies of scale particularly in relation to the purchase of aircraft and fuel, maintenance arrangements, insurance and marketing and advertising.
- The opportunity to achieve significant growth in a single step.
- A stronger and larger group to compete with other low-cost carriers and national flag carriers.
- Ability of enlarged Group to offer passengers a greater choice of destinations at competitive prices.
- Similarity of Go's business model to that of easyJet.
- Go operates Boeing 737 aircraft.
- easyJet and Go have generally complementary networks.
- Cultural fit with both companies emphasizing safety, high utilization, punctuality and value for money.
- Synergy benefits by exploitation of easyJet's brand, yield management system, booking system and pricing system and Go's customer service expertise.

Extracted and adapted from www.easyJet.com (2001).

Recap Questions

1 Explain how easyJet is likely to achieve the following economies of scale:
   (a) Purchase of aircraft and fuel.
   (b) Maintenance arrangements.
   (c) Insurance.
   (d) Marketing and advertising.
2 Are there any areas where the merger with Go may lead to diseconomies of scale?
3 Explain the consequences of the following on easyJet's average costs using a diagram:
   (a) A sharp fall in passengers in the short run.
   (b) A rise in passengers in the long run.
4 Distinguish between social and private costs associated with the activities of easyJet.
5 Why are mergers so common in the airline business and what are the limits to them?

Task 5.2   Merger activity in the hotel sector in the 1990s

American corporations dominate the hotel sector with nine of the top 15 positions in the global league table of companies. In Europe, UK hotel companies dominate the sector where firms that used to make their profits in beer have recently expanded into the hotel marketplace.

For example, Bass is second in the world-wide league table of hotels – ranked by number of rooms rather than number of hotels – compiled annually by the trade magazine *Hotels*. Bass owns the Holiday Inn and Crown Plaza brands. It has recently added InterContinental hotels to its portfolio. Whitbread has also embarked on a strategy of expansion and rebranding with its Travel Inn brand. Ladbroke, owner of the Hilton brand outside the US, made a successful bid for Stakis hotels in 1999. There have been several rumours of an eventual merger with Hilton in America (Table 5.1–5.3).

Melvin Gold, consultant with Pannell Kerr Forster, stresses the importance of branding. 'It is particularly important in some locations. If you are going to Moscow on business, you are more likely to choose a hotel whose name you recognize. You are more likely to choose something

Table 5.1   Major corporate hotel acquisitions 1995–99

Year	Hotel	Purchaser	Cost (million)
1995	Westin Hotels	Starwood	$561
1995	Meridien Hotels (Air France)	Forte	$338
1996	Forte Hotels	Granada	£3870
1996	Metropole Group	Stakis Hotels	
1997	Renaissance Hotels	Marriott International	$1000
1997	Wyndham American	Patriot	$1100
1997	Promus	Doubletree	$4700
1997	Westin Hotels and Resorts	Starwood	$1570
1997	ITT (ITT Sheraton)	Starwood	
1998	InterContinental Hotels (Saison Group)	Bass	£1780
1998	Arctia	Scandia	$100
1999	Stakis	Ladbroke	

Source: Pannell Kerr Foster.

Table 5.2 The 10 largest hotel companies in the UK (1998)

Company	Hotels	Rooms
Forte Hotels (Granada)	161	22 203
Thistle Hotels	97	13 329
Whitbread	206	12 458
Hilton (UK) (Ladbroke)	40	8536
Stakis Hotels	55	8302
Queens Moat Houses UK Ltd	51	7103
Granada Travelodge	155	6621
Holiday Hospitality (Bass)	46	6399
Regal Hotel Group plc	102	5568
Jarvis Hotels	64	5447

Source: Deloitte and Touche.

Table 5.3 Concentration in UK hotel sector

	1991	1996
Number of hotels		
Top 15	15 834	21 039
16–200	6694	8422
Number of rooms		
Top 15	2 155 154	2 698 398
16–200	1 238 090	1 336 237

Source: *Hotels* magazine.

that you can be fairly sure will give you a break from the hustle and bustle of Moscow life.' Other factors such as centralized reservations are also significant in the growth of hotel chains. These allow travellers to make bookings through any same-brand hotel in any location, and therefore represent an important marketing opportunity.

Elsewhere in Europe, France leads in the budget branded sector where Accor, the fourth largest hotel corporation in the world, owns Formule 1 and Ibis. Other European countries, particularly Germany, Spain and Italy, are still relatively underdeveloped in terms of branded chains. The benefits of economies of scale in the hotel sector mean that medium-sized hotel chains such as Jarvis, Thistle and Swallow are likely candidates for future acquisitions particularly by US corporations such as Starwood and Patriot and UK conglomerates such as Bass and Whitbread.

Recap Questions

1 Distinguish between horizontal and vertical integration:
  – What type of integration is occurring in the hotel sector?
  – What form would other types of integration take and what would be its advantages?

2 What economic factors explain the increase in merger activity and concentration of hotel ownership in this sector?

3 What problems might prevent growth of US- or UK-branded hotels into Spain, Germany or Italy?

4 What economic factors determine the limits to the size of hotel chains?

5 Discuss the factors that determine the elasticity of supply of hotel accommodation.

6 Discuss the relationship between fixed costs, average costs and marginal costs for hotels. What are the implications of your analysis for pricing?

7 What have been the major developments in the structure of the hotel industry since the date of this case?

Task 5.3   Record companies: sharks and minnows swim side by side

1998:   Six record companies dominate the UK record industry with the top four accounting for over 55 per cent of sales. But at the same time there still exist a significant number of independent labels. So, on the one hand, the record industry demonstrates a trend towards globalization, larger companies and less competition. In addition, there is a tendency towards global entertainment companies encompassing music, film and the press. But, on the other hand, the creative nature of the industry and the need to be responsive to changes in the market means that there is still an important place for small labels.

Eventually independent labels which are successful are often bought up by larger companies or are linked to them by distribution agreements. Creation Records, an independent famous for signing Oasis, is now 49 per cent owned by Sony having started life in 1984 with a £1000 bank loan. The big six are:

- UK market leader PolyGram incorporating labels such as A&M Island, Mercury and Polydor. PolyGram is part of the Dutch conglomerate Philips Corporation, and has recently been diversifying into films.
- Electrical and Music Industries (EMI) is second in size in the UK to PolyGram and also owns Virgin Music, which it purchased for £510 million in 1992.
- Sony Music is part of the Sony Corporation of Japan. Sony, originally known for its music hardware, entered the recording sector by its purchase of the CBS company. It also owns Colombia and Epic.
- Bertelsmann Music Group (BMG) Entertainment International, UK and Ireland is part of Bertelsmann AG, the third largest media company in the world.
- Warner is part of Time Warner Corporation. This US Corporation has interests in film making, television as well as recorded music.

Distribution is key to the success of recorded music and in the UK record stores are also dominated by a few large chains accounting for 65 per cent of sales.
These include:

- Virgin Our Price, a group which includes 55 Virgin Megastores and the Our Price chain.
- Woolworths which is part of the Kingfisher Group.
- His Master's Voice (HMV) which is part of the EMI group and operates over 1200 HMV outlets.
- WH Smith Retail which operates a chain of 549 shops selling books, magazines, stationery and greeting cards as well as records.

2003

- EMI was facing the prospect of being left on the sidelines once again after US media giant Time Warner spurned its advances in favour of another bidder: Time Warner announced it was selling its recorded music division for $2.6 billion (£1.53 billion) to a consortium led by Edgar Bronfman Jr, the Seagram heir.
- BMG and Sony must overcome tough regulatory hurdles after signing an official agreement to merge their recorded music businesses. The new company, to be called Sony BMG, will be the world's second largest record company, with a 25 per cent share of the global music market, behind Universal Music, which has 26 per cent. Ownership of the new company will be split 50:50 between BMG's parent, the German media group Bertelsmann, and Sony. The new company will aim to cut overheads and merge manufacturing and distribution, an area of vast overcapacity and potential savings.
- Universal Music, the world's largest record company, is to axe 1350 jobs – or 11 per cent of its workforce – in response to a continual fall in global music sales. Universal's competitors already have similar cuts of their own recently. Sony Music Entertainment laid off 1000 people, or 10 per cent of its global work force, in March. EMI has eliminated about 1900 jobs, or about 19 per cent of its total, since late 2001. In all, nearly 8000 jobs – one in five – have gone from the five major record companies.

Sources: Adapted from the *Mintel Report* on records CDs and tapes (1998) and press reports (2003).

Recap Questions

1 Illustrate examples of horizontal, vertical and conglomerate integration in the article.
2 Analyse the motives for and benefits to a record company of:
   (a) Horizontal integration.
   (b) Vertical integration.
   (c) Conglomerate integration.
3 What evidence is there of potential diseconomies of scale existing in the record industry?
4 What is the significance of the terms *elasticity of supply* and *marginal costs* to the record industry?
5 Explain the reactions by record companies to the decline in sales using the terms average costs, variable costs and fixed costs.

Multiple choice

1 **Which of the following is not a factor of production?**

   (a) Land.
   (b) Labour.
   (c) Wages.
   (d) Capital.

2 **When price increases by 10 per cent supply increases by 20 per cent. Which of the following is true?**

   (a) Supply is elastic.
   (b) Supply is inelastic.
   (c) Elasticity of supply is 0.5.
   (d) Marginal cost doubles.

3 **Which of the following is false?**

(a) Average cost is total cost divided by output.
(b) Fixed costs cannot be altered in the short run.
(c) "Economies of scale" means that total costs fall as output rises.
(d) The take-over of the airline Go by its rival easyJet is an example of horizontal integration.

4 **A U-shaped LRAC curve demonstrates:**

(a) Economies of scale followed by diseconomies of scale.
(b) Diseconomies of scale followed by economies of scale.
(c) Falling sales followed by rising sales.
(d) External economies of scale followed by internal economies of scale.

5 **Which of the following is an example of a financial economy of scale?**

(a) American Airlines is able to borrow money more cheaply than smaller airlines.
(b) American Airlines is able to buy aviation fuel cheaper than smaller airlines.
(c) American Airlines has bigger profits than smaller airlines.
(d) American Airlines operates jumbo jets.

Review questions

1 Why may an organization's average cost of production rise as output rises in the short run, but fall in the long run?
2 What is the marginal cost of selling an empty seat on a scheduled flight?
3 Distinguish between private costs and social costs in the provision of air travel.
4 How elastic is the supply of:
   (a) CDs?
   (b) Theatre seats?
   (c) Package holidays?
5 Distinguish between vertical and horizontal integration.
6 Distinguish between fixed costs, variable costs, the short run and the long run.

Web sites of interest

Granada Group plc: www.granada.co.uk
Marriott International: www.marriott.com
McDonald's Corp.: www.mcdonalds.com
Nintendo of America Inc.: www.nintendo.com
Sony Corporation: www.sony.com
Time Warner Corporation: www.timewarner.com
Wilson Sporting Goods Co.: www.wilsonsports.com/
Virgin Atlantic: http://www.bized.ac.uk/compfact/vaa/vaaindex.htm
Learning help in economics and business studies: www.bized.ac.uk

Part Three

Markets in Practice

CHAPTER 6

Market structure and pricing

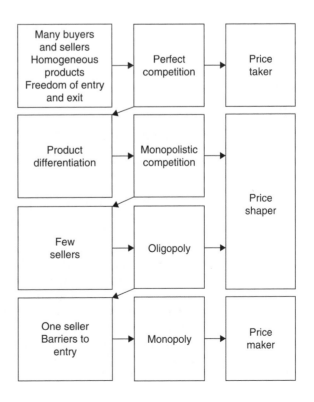

Objectives and learning outcomes

In the real world it is often difficult to relate prices to the simple demand and supply analysis presented in Chapter 3. For example, we find leisure centres and fitness centres offering similar services at vastly different prices. It has been said that an airline running a jumbo jet carrying 350 passengers will charge 100 different prices. A simple T-shirt can cost as little as $5. Print the word 'Evisu' or 'Versace' on it and its price can rise to more than $50. Some shops have as many sale and offer days as normal trading days. This chapter investigates how prices are determined in the real world.

By studying this chapter students will be able to:

- understand how and why firms come to be price takers, price makers or price shapers;
- analyse the pricing strategies that result from different market situations.

Pricing in the private sector

Private sector organizations which seek to maximize profits will attempt to minimize their costs and maximize their revenue. Revenue is composed of price multiplied by quantity sold, and the price that an organization can charge for its product depends largely on the type of market within which it is operating.

Price takers

Perfect competition

At one extreme, economic theory describes the model of perfect competition. In this model there are many buyers, many sellers, identical products, freedom of entry and exit in the market, and perfect knowledge about prices and products in the market. Firms which operate in this type of market have to accept the market price. This is because any attempt to increase their own price over and above market price will lead to consumers purchasing identical goods or services from competitor firms. This is illustrated in Figure 6.1.

Figure 6.1(a) shows the market demand curve DM, the market supply curve SM and the equilibrium price $P0$. Figure 6.1(b) shows the demand curve faced by an individual firm, DF. Note that it is perfectly elastic. This is derived from the conditions of perfect competition. Consumers with perfect knowledge about other prices will buy an identical product from one of the other many sellers if an individual firm attempts to raise prices above the prevailing market rate. What level of profits do firms earn in such markets? They earn normal profits. Normal profit is defined as that

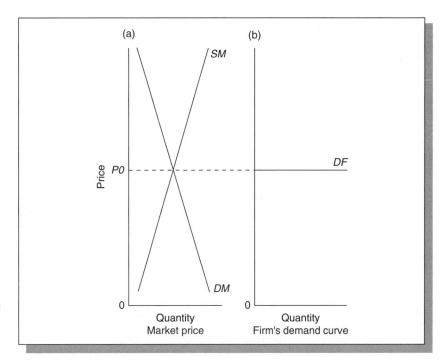

Figure 6.1
(a) The market and (b) the firm under perfect competition (see text for details)

level of return which is just sufficient incentive for a firm to remain in its present business. Any excess profits will lead new firms into the industry and this extra supply will drive prices down to the level where normal profits are restored.

It is interesting to note that consumer ignorance (i.e. lack of perfect knowledge) about other prices means that perfect competition is less prevalent than it might be. For example, in the UK a major supermarket (Tesco) sells top 50 CDs for £9.99. Regular retailers (e.g. HMV) charge £13.99 for an identical product. Even though most towns have both stores near each other, HMV still manages healthy sales of its more expensive CDs. However, it is likely that increasing use of the Internet will lead consumers to better knowledge of prices of competing goods thus promoting more competition and lower prices.

Whilst free market prices and normal profits are good for consumers, profit-maximizing producers will aim to increase and protect profits. Thus there are few examples in the real world of price takers, and if firms are not in the fortunate position of being price makers they will generally take steps to become price shapers. They may achieve this by introducing imperfections into the market.

Price makers

At the other extreme from perfect competition, some firms exist in conditions of monopoly or near monopoly and thus have considerable control over prices.

Monopoly pricing

A monopoly is literally defined as one seller, and monopoly power is maintained by ensuring that barriers to entry into the industry are maintained. In the case of one seller the firm's demand curve is the same as the industry demand curve. Because of this, the monopolist is in a position to be a price maker.

There are examples of near-monopolies in the leisure and tourism sector. For example, there are only two car ferry services to the Isle of Wight (an island off the South coast of the UK) and these operate on different routes, thus giving each operator some control over price. Unique tourist attractions also have some degree of monopoly power. There is no similar attraction to the London Eye in the UK, although to some extent the main visitor attractions in London all compete with each other. Manchester United Football Club, like many other sporting clubs, is unique. Table 6.1 shows typical demand data for a unique attraction. It demonstrates the trade-off that a monopoly producer faces – it can raise prices but as it does so demand falls (but does not disappear as would be the case under perfect competition). So the question that arises for a monopolist is what is the best price to charge? The answer is that price that will maximize total revenue.

The price that maximizes total revenue for this organization is one of £5 when total revenue of £250 per hour is generated. This is illustrated in Figure 6.2. In Figure 6.2(a), D represents the firm's demand curve using the data from Table 6.1. In Figure 6.2(b), TR represents the firm's total revenue curve. This is found by multiplying quantity sold at each price. Price £5 generates total revenue of £250 per hour, whilst a higher price of £8 or a lower price of £2 causes total revenue to fall to £160.

Table 6.1 Monopoly attraction demand data

Price (£)	Quantity demanded (visitors/hour)	Total revenue*	Marginal revenue**
10	0	0	
9	10	90	9
8	20	160	7
7	30	210	5
6	40	240	3
5	50	250	1
4	60	240	−1
3	70	210	−3
2	80	160	−5
1	90	90	−7
0	100	0	−9

* Total revenue: price × quantity sold.
** Marginal revenue: the extra revenue gained from attracting one extra customer ($\Delta TR \div \Delta Q$), where TR = total revenue and Q = quantity.

This confirms the relationship between changes in price, changes in total revenue and elasticity of demand discussed in Chapter 4. Where demand is inelastic a rise in price will cause an increase in total revenue. Where demand is elastic, a rise in price will cause a fall in total revenue. Profit maximization therefore occurs where demand elasticity is $(-)1$. In Figure 6.2 the demand curve is elastic in the range X to Y, inelastic in the range Y to Z and has unit elasticity at point Y.

To summarize, monopolists can choose a price resulting in high profits, without fear of loss of market share to competitors. The actual price chosen

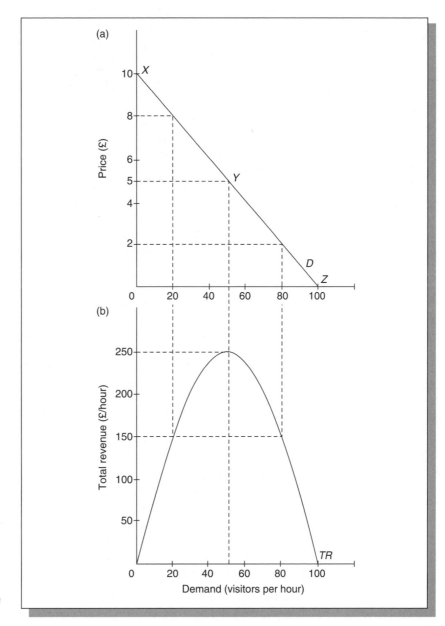

Figure 6.2
(a) Demand and (b) revenue-maximizing price for monopolist

will reflect both demand conditions and the firm's cost conditions. Exhibit 6.1 shows how top UK football clubs are exploiting their market position.

Price-discriminating monopolist/yield management • • •

Some firms sell the same goods or services at different prices to different groups of people. For example, British Airways (BA) return fares from London to New York (summer 1999) are: £5446 (first class), £3213 (club class), £828 (standard economy 1), £417 (APEX), £82.80 (staff 10 per cent standby) and £0 (staff yearly free standby/holders of airmiles or frequent-flyer miles).

In fact BA is not a monopolist since there is much competition on this route, but most fares are subject to International Air Transport Association (IATA) regulation and thus many firms are able to act as monopolists. It should also be recognized that the fare differential for club and first-class passengers is not strictly price discrimination since these represent different services with different costs. But since all economy-class passengers receive an identical service, why should BA charge different prices and why do passengers accept different prices? The answer is that by price discrimination companies can increase their profits by charging different prices according to how much different market segments are prepared to pay.

The conditions for price discrimination to take place are as follows:

- The product cannot be resold. If this were not the case, customers buying at the low price would sell to customers at the high price and the

---

Exhibit 6.1 Chelsea fans: sold out

Price increases for season tickets at Chelsea football Club for the 1998–99 season are in some cases as high as 47 per cent as against inflation of around 2.5 per cent in the UK economy. This means that the cheapest season ticket for supporters is now £525, while the most expensive is £1250.

Top premier clubs find themselves in monopoly positions. Stadiums are full to capacity and price increases do not lead fans to chose alternative products elsewhere. Nearby Fulham or Arsenal do not offer alternative football for Chelsea fans in the way that different brands of beer can be seen as substitutes.

At a meeting with the UK sports minister a Chelsea fan complained: 'I'm an old age pensioner and have been following Chelsea since 1923 ... a season ticket now costs £1250. Me and my five pals have decided to join, but last season we had reduced tickets in the same seats for £600.' The minister replied: 'A number of clubs know that if they put up prices, they will sell them anyway. Football is a drug. But I am increasingly drawn to the conclusion that, sooner or later, a degree of regulation might be necessary.'

Source: Adapted from *The Guardian* by the author.

---

system would break down. Services therefore provide good conditions for price discrimination.

- There must be market imperfections (otherwise firms would all compete to the lowest price).
- The seller must be able to identify different market segments with different demand elasticities (for example, age groups, different times of use).

Figure 6.3 illustrates a typical demand curve for economy-class travel. If a single price of £500 is charged as in Figure 6.3(a), then 250 seats are sold

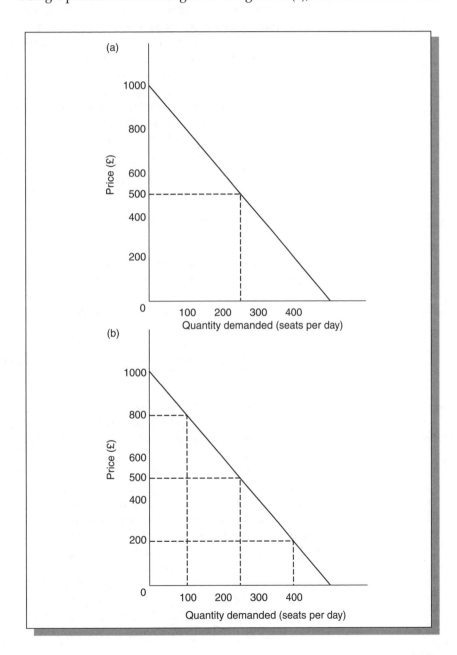

Figure 6.3
(a) Single price and (b) price discrimination

Exhibit 6.2   Orchestras conduct research into pricing

Managers from an airline and a Premier League football club have been approached to help Britain's symphony and chamber orchestras increase their profits from selling concert tickets. A marketing manager for the airline easyJet – Ruth Start – and the marketing manager for Everton FC – Andy Hosie – offered advice at the annual conference of the Association of British Orchestras, which represents 60 orchestras across the country.

The idea is to exploit 'yield management' techniques (Plate 6). This is a favourite device of no-frills airlines whose tickets become more expensive as departure dates approach. Transferring the idea to concerts could mean that concert-goers who book their tickets in advance might pay £10 for the best seat while those buy nearer the day of the concert could pay up to £30.

Sarah Gee, director of communications at the City of Birmingham Symphony Orchestra said: 'At present we do not have the ability to track demand and make prices elastic as it peaks and falls. I know the Chicago Symphony has a marketing director who comes from the airline industry and they have been experimenting with this. I think it is a really interesting concept.'

Source: Adapted from *The Guardian Newspaper* (2003) by the author.

---

and total revenue is £125 000. Figure 6.3(b) shows a situation in which three prices are charged. One hundred seats are sold at £800, the next 150 seats are sold at £500 and the next 150 seats are sold at £200, producing a total revenue of £185 000, an increase of £60 000 over the single price situation.

Airlines must consider the behaviour of costs when price discriminating. Once the decision has been taken to run a scheduled service, marginal costs are low up until the aircraft capacity, when there is a sudden large jump. Airlines are able to discriminate by applying travel restrictions to differently priced tickets. So, for example, full fare economy tickets are fully refundable and flights may be changed at no cost. Cheaper tickets are non-refundable and have advance purchase and travel duration restrictions.

Yield management is a sophisticated form of price discrimination. Hamzaee and Vasigh (1997) discuss a model for establishing the optimal allocation of available seats to different classes of airfare. Computer technology is able to identify patterns of demand for a particular product and compare it with its supply. A request for a hotel reservation or an airline ticket will result in the system suggesting a price that will maximize the yield for a particular flight or day's reservations. So for budget airlines, for example, seats on a Friday or Sunday night or in school holidays tend to be expensive whilst a seat to the same destination on a Tuesday morning would be much cheaper. Exhibit 6.2 shows how orchestras are hoping to exploit this system to maximize revenue at concerts.

Plate 6
Virgin Blue: Ticket prices
determined by yield
management system
Source: The author

Price shapers

Whilst firms operating under conditions of perfect competition are price takers and those operating under conditions of monopoly are price makers, firms operating in markets between these two extremes can exert some influence on price. Such firms are called price shapers. The two main market types which will be examined are:

- oligopoly pricing,
- monopolistic competition.

Oligopoly pricing

An oligopoly is a market dominated by a few large firms. An example of this is the cross-channel (UK to France) travel market. Aguiló et al. (2003) examined the prices of package holidays to the Balearic Islands, Spain, one of the Mediterranean's leading tourist destinations, offered by a sample of 24 German and 20 UK tour operators studied in 2000. They concluded that tour operators' strategies and price structures are characteristic of an oligopolistic market. Oligopoly makes pricing policy more difficult to analyse since firms are interdependent, but not to the extent as in the perfectly competitive model. The actions of firm A may cause reaction by firms B and C, leading firm A to reassess its pricing policy and thus perpetuating a chain of action and reaction. For these reasons firms operating in oligopolistic markets often face a kinked demand curve. This is illustrated in Figure 6.4.

Consider the demand curve D, which might illustrate the demand curve for a cross-channel car ferry firm. The prevailing price is $P0$. Notice that the

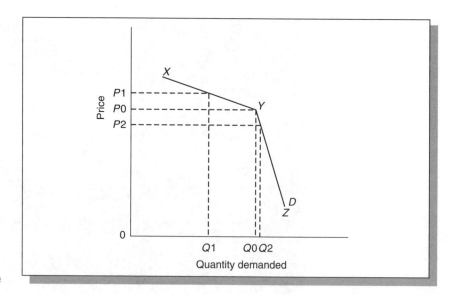

Figure 6.4
The kinked demand curve

demand curve is elastic in the range X to Y. This is because, if a firm decides to increase its price, for example from $P0$ to $P1$, it will lose customers to its competitors and demand will fall sharply from $Q0$ to $Q1$ and the firm will suffer a fall in total revenue. On the other hand, if it should decide to reduce its price from $P0$ to $P2$, it is likely that its competitors will match the reduction in price to protect their market share, and there will be only a small increase in demand from $Q0$ to $Q2$, resulting in a fall in the firm's revenue. Thus the demand curve is inelastic in the range Y to Z, and the demand curve is kinked at point Y. In this situation it is clearly not in the interests of individual firms to cut prices, and thus such markets tend to be characterized by price rigidities. Marketing and competition under oligopoly conditions are often based around:

- advertising,
- free gifts and offers,
- quality of service or value added,
- follow-the-leader pricing – pricing is based on the decisions of the largest firm,
- informal price agreements,
- price wars occasionally break out if one firm thinks it can effectively undercut the opposition.

Braun and Soskin (1999) investigated the transformation of the Florida (USA) theme park industry during the 1990s. Here Anheuser Busch carried out a series of acquisitions to complete a successful horizontal merger of the three major competitors to the market leader Walt Disney World. Busch then mobilized its financial resources to match Disney's $10 billion investment programme. Next the entry of Universal Studios with its considerable financial investment deterred other entrants to the market. Finally, aggressive pricing strategies consolidated the market share and drove out smaller competitors. In the 1980s, Walt Disney World operated like a dominant firm. The other firms matched Walt Disney World with a lag. However, the authors concluded that the late 1990s illustrate behaviour characteristic of an interdependent oligopoly. Price increases have been tempered, relative prices have converged and prices have become more stable.

Monopolistic competition

This is a common type of market structure, exhibiting some features of perfect competition and some features of monopoly. The competitive features are freedom of entry and exit, and the existence of a large number of firms. However, firms which are operating in essentially competitive environments may attempt to create market imperfections in order to have more control over pricing, market share and profits.

It is competition from other sellers with homogeneous products that forces market prices down, and thus firms will often concentrate on these two issues in order to exert more market power. The more inelastic a firm is able to make its demand curve, the more influence it will have on price, and thus firms will attempt to minimize competition by:

- product differentiation,
- acquisitions and mergers,
- cost and price leadership.

Product differentiation • • •

This entails an organization in making its product different from those of its competitors and exploiting unique selling points (USPs). The rationale for product differentiation is to make the demand for a goods or service less elastic, giving the producer more scope to increase prices and/or sales and profits. There are a number of routes to product differentiation.

The first is by advertising. One of the aims of persuasive advertising is to create and increase brand loyalty even if there are no major differences between a firm's product and that of its competitors. The second route to product differentiation is through adding value to a good or service. This may include, for example, making improvements to a good or service or adding value somewhere along the value chain. The value chain can be thought of as all the interconnecting activities that make up the whole consumer experience of a good or service. Table 6.2 demonstrates aspects of the value chain for Singapore Airlines' business class.

Exhibit 6.3 shows how Virgin trains are bringing product differentiation to their services. The point of adding value and differentiating product is that it enables firms to charge a premium price but still retain customers.

Table 6.2 Value chain for Singapore Airlines' business class

Pre-sales	Pre-check-in	Check-in	Flight	Arrival	Post-flight
Advertising	Valet parking	Dedicated check-in Express security/ passport route Dedicated lounge	Dedicated cabin Luxury meal Seat size Increased staff ratio	Rapid transit arranged to city centre	Frequent-flyer awards Complaints procedure

---

Exhibit 6.3   Seven types of Virgin

Richard Branson, who introduced new standards of service to his Virgin Airlines with his 'Upper Class' service, is now attempting a similar exercise on his trains. While rival rail networks still operate a two-class system, Virgin has introduced no less than seven different classes of ticket: These are:

- *First class (not pre-booked)*: here you may sit in a first-class compartment and enjoy free tea, coffee and alcoholic drinks.
- *Virgin business class* (*pre-booked*): with free drinks plus a free meal, parking and a London underground pass.
- *Virgin value first* (*pre-booked, off-peak trains only*): this also allows you to sit in first class but there is no free food or alcohol.
- *Standard full fare*: accommodation in standard compartment, free tea and coffee, and the possibility of upgrade to first (space permitting).

Then there are three types of bargain tickets:

- saver,
- supersaver,
- Virgin value.

These all come with restrictions relating to pre-booking times, period of travel and time of travel. They are also colour coded so that bargain passengers wait at a different colour-coded zones of the platform, and sit in colour-coded seats. The seats are in fact identical to each other.

Product differentiation is such a money spinner that even the Heathrow to Paddington rail link, owned by British Airports Authority, provides first and second class, although the journey takes only 15 minutes.

Source: The author.

Type of market	Number of firms	Entry barriers	Product differentiation	Firm's demand	Control over price
Perfect competition	Many	None	No	Perfectly elastic	None
Monopolistic competition	Many	None	Yes	Elastic	Limited
Oligopoly	Few	Some	Yes	Kinked demand	Some
Monopoly	One	Total	Unnecessary	Inelastic	Considerable

Figure 6.5 Market structure

Acquisitions and mergers ● ● ●

These are discussed in detail in Chapter 5, but they are an important consideration in pricing strategy as they can:

- reduce competition (and thus reduce downward pressure on prices),
- lead to economies of scale (which can underpin price leadership strategies).

Cost and price leadership ● ● ●

Another key strategic move to increase market share and profitability is through cost and price leadership. Cost leadership involves cutting costs through the supply chain – squeezing margins from suppliers, and economizing where possible in the production of goods or provision of services by stripping out unnecessary frills. The aim of cost leadership may be to increase margins but this is unlikely to be achieved since consumers are likely to resist lower quality of goods or services without any compensation in price.

Equally it is difficult to maintain cost leadership since other firms will attempt to achieve similar cost reductions. However, where cost leadership is translated into low prices it may be possible to increase market share. This can then lead to the creation of a virtuous circle where increased market share leads to economies of scale which enable lower costs and thus lower prices to be maintained ahead of rival firms. The no-frills airlines again provide good examples here. Virgin Blue (Australia), for example, has been competing strongly with the Australian flag carrier Qantas and by 2003 had captured 30 per cent of the domestic market. Similarly, the UK low-cost airline easyJet carried 1.7 million passengers in November 2003. This is comparable to passenger numbers for BA and demonstrates a rise of 15 per cent compared with the November 2002.

Figure 6.5 provides a summary of the main differences between different market types.

Pricing in the public sector

Prices of public sector goods and services will depend upon the market situation which prevails in a particular industry as well as the objectives set for a particular organization. These might be:

* profit maximization,
* break-even pricing,
* social cost/benefit pricing.

Profit maximization

In the case where public sector organizations have profit-maximizing aims, its pricing policy will follow the pattern set out earlier in this chapter. However public sector organizations are rarely allowed to exploit a monopoly situation if they have one.

Break-even pricing

Break-even pricing aims at a price which is just sufficient to cover production costs rather than one which might take advantage of market imperfections and maximize profit. In this case price will be set to produce a total revenue which covers total costs.

Social cost/benefit pricing

Where the aim of public provision is to take fuller account of public costs and benefits, the supply will be subsidized to produce a price either lower than market price (partial subsidy) or at zero price (total subsidy). More detailed analysis of this can be found in Chapter 7.

Pricing and the macroeconomy

The condition of the economy at large also has an influence on firms' pricing policy. If the demand in the economy is growing quickly, there may be temporary shortages of supply in the economy and firms will take advantage of boom conditions to increase prices and profits. Similarly, during a recession there may well be over-capacity in the economy and demand may be static or falling. These conditions will force firms to have much more competitive pricing policies to attract consumers.

Review of key terms

* Price taker: a firm in a perfectly competitive market which cannot directly influence price.
* Price maker: a firm in a monopoly market which sets its desired price.

- Price shaper: a firm in an oligopoly or imperfectly competitive market which may seek to influence price.
- Perfect competition: many buyers and sellers, homogeneous products, freedom of entry and exit to market.
- Monopoly: one seller, barriers to entry.
- Oligopoly: a small number of powerful sellers.
- Monopolistic competition: many buyers and sellers, freedom of entry and exit, products differentiated.
- Product differentiation: real or notional differences between products of competing firms.
- Price discrimination: selling the same product at different prices to different market segments.

Data Questions

Task 6.1   Ups and downs of cross-Channel prices

1994:   The Channel tunnel opens and the fares for Le Shuttle, the train that will ferry motorists and their cars under the Channel, have been set higher than expected. They range from £125 return for a carload in winter to a peak price of £310. Most are a little higher than the equivalent ferry fare.

There was an almost audible sigh of relief from the Channel ports as Christopher Garnett, Eurotunnel's commercial director, outlined the structure; at least the tunnel was not trying to undercut the ferries. Asked by the *Independent on Sunday* whether Eurotunnel would respond if the ferries cut their fares, Mr Garnett said: 'We would not be following. We're not going to get involved with price wars. We're not going to get involved in discounting.' Richard Hannah, an analyst with UBS and a close follower of Eurotunnel, is sceptical: 'I'm convinced there will have to be a price war because of the excess capacity created by the tunnel.' He said fares would have to come down sharply to generate the extra volumes needed to meet Eurotunnel's ambitious revenue targets. 'Even if Eurotunnel captured the entire existing cross-Channel business from the ferry companies, it would still not generate enough revenues even to cover its costs.' He argued that Eurotunnel had to create a fresh wave of demand for cross-Channel travel, and it could only do that by cutting prices.

Mr Garnett sees Le Shuttle's advantages over ferries as speed, convenience and reliability. But the other unknown quantity in the calculation is the response of the ferry companies and the ports. According to Chairman, Mr Dunlop, P&O has spent £400 million over the past 5 years modernizing its fleet. 'We've revolutionized the ferry industry in the last five years, creating an attractive product.' Certainly its newer vessels, such as the *Pride of Dover* and the *Pride of Calais*, are a far cry from the shabby, vomit-smelling, beer-soaked, cramped, crowded tubs that used to ply their trade across the Channel. 'The ferry crossing is now part of the holiday', said Mr Dunlop.

Source: Adapted from the *Independent on Sunday*, 16 January 1994.

1999: No one pays £310 to cross the channel any more. The opening of Eurotunnel gave rise to a period of intense competition and the 'Channel war' was a consumer's dream. The competition has seen the merger between the two ferry companies, P&O and Stena, but even so there continue to be good deals.

- Le Shuttle: A 35-minute crossing. A 5-day return costs £95 per car with four departures an hour during the day and three an hour at night. Few facilities but weatherproof.
- Sally Line: Ferry from Ramsgate to Ostend, from £25 for a car and two passengers. Smorgasbord restaurant, cafeteria facilities and a supervised crèche.
- P&O Stena Line: Car and passengers £95 for a 5-day return and £159 for a standard return. Restaurants, games arcade, cinema and club class available.
- Hoverspeed: Standard return on the Hovercraft for a car and passengers is £158. Crossing time is 35 minutes. Same price but 50-minute crossing on SeaCat.

2002: Prices seem to have crept back up again. The following are for a return car journey from Dover to Calais in summer 2002:

- P&O Stena Line from Dover to Calais: £234.
- SeaFrance from Dover to Calais: £209.
- Eurotunnel from Folkestone to Calais: £237.
- Hovercraft from Dover to Calais £278.

2003: The European commission launches a surprise investigation into cross-Channel ferry and rail prices and raided the offices of P&O and Eurotunnel in its hunt to uncover supporting evidence. The commission said that it suspected an illegal price-fixing cartel was in operation and that it was acting on complaints from British consumers, Amelia Torres, a commission spokeswoman said: 'Many consumers are concerned about the market and the commercial practices of firms who operate cross-Channel services and we have to take those concerns very seriously. We have a duty to investigate.'

The Dover–Calais ferry route is thought to be the busiest route in the world. It is dominated by the Anglo-French firm Eurotunnel which has a 50 per cent market share. P&O has about 25 per cent, SeaFrance 15 per cent, and Hoverspeed and Norfolk Line account for the rest.

Source: Adapted from *The Guardian*, 4 September 2003.

Recap Questions

1 What degree of competition exists in the cross-Channel market?
2 Explain why the Channel Tunnel's initial strategy was not price based.
3 What elements of product differentiation strategy are illustrated and what is the logic of these?
4 What have been the key factors affecting price in the cross-Channel market between 1994 and 2003? Explain this using economic theory and diagrams.
5 What pricing strategies would you recommend to P&O Stena Line to maximize revenue?
6 What is the economics behind price fixing?

Task 6.2   Researching prices and markets

Conduct local research in one of the following areas:

1 Air travel suppliers and prices.
2 Hotel accommodation suppliers and prices.
3 Restaurant suppliers and prices.
4 Package holiday suppliers and prices.
5 Cinema suppliers and prices.
6 CD suppliers and prices.
7 Other leisure markets in your locality.

Your research should concentrate on a specific product or service (for example return air fare from Auckland to New York) and identify the main suppliers, prices and product differences.

Recap Questions

1 Identify the market conditions which operate in your chosen market.
2 Account for the patterns of pricing which emerge from your research.
3 To what extent and why does your chosen market deviate from the model of perfect competition?
4 Is there any evidence of price discrimination or price leadership in your chosen market?
   – If so, explain the reasons and consequences.
   – If not, explain the reasons and consequences.
5 Compare and contrast your results with those of obtained in a different market.

Task 6.3   Go ploy to stop competition?

1998:   BA launches its new cut price airline 'Go' which operates out of London's fourth airport – Stanstead. The first destinations include Rome, Milan and Copenhagen from 5 June with introductory fares of £100 return as opposed to BA's standard return fare to Rome of around £300. Industry sources expect Go to maintain some £100 flights beyond the launch period as a loss leader to attract attention. In launching Go, BA is attempting to meet the challenge posed by a number of new cheap operators who have been highly successful in attracting passengers. These include Ryanair, Debonair and easyJet. These are so-called 'no-frill' airlines where passengers forgo free meals and drinks and are to be seated on a first-come first-served basis. Flights operate out of cheaper, secondary out-of-town airports and tickets are non-transferable and non-refundable. Go has initially avoided direct competition with these airlines by not duplicating their routes.

BA has assured its critics that Go is a completely separate business and it will not be cross-subsidized from the main airline. But opponents claim that Go represents a strategy to drive other no-frills airlines out of business and that in the long-term prices will rise again as the competition is reduced through predatory pricing.

US experience suggests that the period of low air fares sweeping the UK in the late 1990s may be short lived. No-frills flying was invented in the US by Peoples Express which has long since gone out of business as have most of its imitators as the big airlines have fought to maintain their domination in the market.

1999: Debonair, the UK-based 'low-cost' airline which was launched in 1996 went bankrupt.

2001: BA sells its budget airline Go to 3i, a venture capital company, for about £110 million. BA's Chief Executive Officer Rod Eddington said that Go was sold because it did not fit in with the main airline's strategy. He further stated that the deal 'represents an excellent return on our initial £25 million investment in the airline 3 years ago. Go is an excellent airline with a fine management and workforce.'

2002: easyJet takes over Go.

2003: Low-cost airline Ryanair announces plans to buy its smaller rival Buzz owned by KLM Royal Dutch Airlines. The price of the acquisition was €23.9 million (£15.6 million; $25.7 million). Ryanair chief executive Michael O'Leary said: 'there are a number of features of Buzz which makes this a favourable move at this time.' The deal would allow Ryanair to expand its services at Stanstead, where Buzz had operated 21 routes. Ryannair predicted it would be able double Buzz's passengers and turn around its performance. 'The management believe that by applying Ryanair's low-fares/low-cost formula, the traffic in Buzz can be increased this year from under 2 million to over 4 million passengers and the operating losses will be eliminated and profitability achieved.'

Recap Questions

1 What kind of market type is evident:
   (a) In the UK for airlines and how has the market changed?
   (b) In the country in which you are studying?
2 Are airlines price makers or price takers? Use diagrams to explain your answers.
3 Is it true that the continued prospects for low-fares are poor?
4 How does 'loss leadership' and 'cross-subsidization' affect prices. Are these activities beneficial to customers?
5 How was BA able to charge different fares for similar flights to Rome?
6 On what basis do airlines set fares?

Multiple choice

1 The demand curve for a firm under perfect competition is as follows:

   (a) Perfectly inelastic.
   (b) Upward sloping.
   (c) Perfectly elastic.
   (d) Of unit elasticity.

2 The kinked demand curve is a typical feature of the following:

   (a) Public sector markets.
   (b) Oligopoly.
   (c) Perfect competition.
   (d) Monopoly.

3 Which of the following is not a feature of perfect competition?

   (a) Barriers to entry for firms.
   (b) Perfect knowledge of products.
   (c) Identical products.
   (d) Many sellers.

4   **Which of the following is found under monopolistic competition but not under perfect competition?**

(a) Product differentiation.
(b) Many buyers.
(c) Freedom of entry for firms.
(d) Many sellers.

5   **Which of the following is not true?**

(a) Under price discrimination firms are able to increase their revenue in comparison to charging a single price.
(b) Yield management systems charge differing prices according to predicted demand levels.
(c) An oligopoly is a market dominated by a few large firms.
(d) A private sector monopoly will operate break-even pricing.

Review questions

1   What kind of market structures do the following operate in:
(a) Package tour operators?
(b) London five-star hotels?
(c) Brewers?
(d) McDonalds?
2   Explain the elasticity of demand of a kinked demand curve.
3   Why will a monopolist choose not to produce in the inelastic range of its demand curve?
4   Why are there so few examples of perfectly competitive markets?
5   Under what circumstances is price leadership likely to lead to increased profits?

Web sites of interest

British Airways: www.british-airways.com
Air Ticket Prices: http://www.cheapflights.co.uk/
EasyJet: www.easyjet.com
Learning help in economics and business studies: http://www.bized.ac.uk

Market intervention

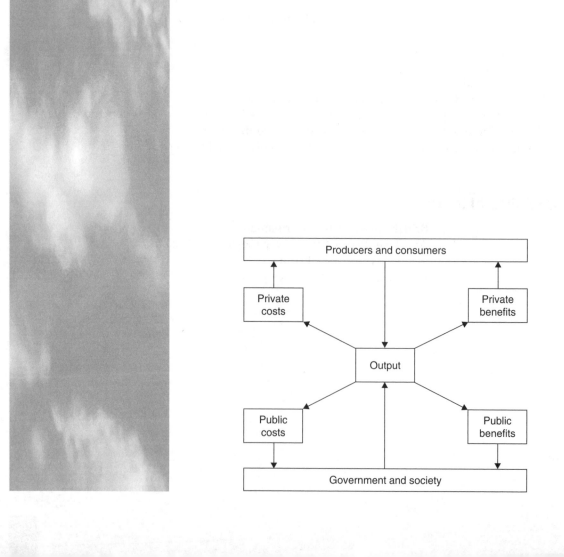

Objectives and learning outcomes

The price mechanism as described in Chapter 3 seems to offer a simple yet effective system of signalling consumer demands to producers. It is often contrasted with systems of state planning – particularly as practised in former communist eastern Europe. Many commentators noted that the Berlin Wall was built to stop people escaping from eastern Europe to western Europe, not the other way round. The economic landscape of eastern Europe was characterized by queues for goods and services, empty shops, shoddy goods and service sector workers who exhibited indifference to their customers. For example, Burns (1998) discusses some of the problems associated with developing a modern tourism industry in Romania. He finds that the main problem confronting tourism is the lack of a market ethos, and a prevailing view that service is demeaning to the server and concludes that a new customer-focused service sector needs to be developed. Free market economies, on the other hand, boast shops full of attractive consumer goods, few queues and a world of slick advertising and attention to service quality.

However, critical analysis of the market mechanism raises issues of concern. Sex tourists signal an effective demand for prostitution which suppliers satisfy as demonstrated in Exhibit 7.1. Similarly, the demand for snuff, and child pornography videos, and for addictive drugs is met by the operation of market forces. The market has also created the tower blocks of Benidorm.

The objectives of this chapter are first to examine whether leisure and tourism provision should be left to the free market, and second to consider reasons for, and forms of, market intervention.

After studying this chapter students will be able to:

- evaluate the benefits of the free market,
- evaluate the problems of the free market,
- understand the methods of market intervention,
- justify market intervention,
- understand recent developments in public sector provision.

The free market

The benefits of free markets

Adam Smith wrote in *The Wealth of Nations* of the main benefits of the free market (Smith, 1937). He drew attention to the fact that people exercising choice in the market in pursuit of their own self-interest led to the best economic outcome for society as a whole. The concept that 'the market knows best' was also a central plank of the economic philosophy of the Thatcher

Exhibit 7.1 Child sex tourism in Cambodia

There is growing interest in Cambodia as a vacation destination, but Cambodia also is a destination for thousands of men from around the world seeking sex with children. As other developing countries such as Thailand make progress in reducing sex tourism, opportunistic men simply travel to poorer, less developed neighbouring countries.

As one of the world's 20 poorest countries, Cambodia is ripe for such exploitation. Its 11.4 million people have an average income of only $300 annually. Its social, political and legal institutions still are recovering from the brutal legacy of the Khmer Rouge. Access to health care and education is very limited. Young girls are especially prone to drop out of school to help support their families.

At the same time, tourism is on the rise. Most visitors come to Cambodia for the rich heritage and natural beauty exemplified by Angkor Wat. The Cambodian government, which considers tourism to be a valuable part of its economic future, expects the number of foreign visitors to triple over the next 3 years.

Unfortunately, sex tourism also is on the rise in Cambodia. One-third of all sex workers in the country are estimated to be children, mostly ages 12–17, but some even younger. In a recent survey in conjunction with Cambodia's tourism ministry and its National Council for Children, World Vision found that 45 per cent of Cambodian travel agents said they had seen tour guides supply children to foreign visitors. More than 70 per cent of children surveyed around Angkor Wat and nearby towns said that tourists had approached them for sex.

Source: Laurence Gray, Director of Child Protection Programs in Cambodia for World Vision.

(UK) and Reagan (USA) administrations of the 1980s. Indeed, Mrs Thatcher's economic minister, Nigel Lawson, summed up this thinking as: 'The business of government is not the government of business.' The post-1980 period has seen free market economics gain favour in much of Europe and Australia. More significantly it has seen the collapse of communism in Soviet Russia and its replacement with economies in transition (from central planning to free markets).

In particular, free markets have the potential to deliver:

- economic efficiency,
- allocative efficiency,
- consumer sovereignty,
- economic growth.

Exhibit 7.2   Airlines continue to seeks cuts in costs in 2003

Toronto: Air Canada and its main pilots' union reached a 6-year cost-cutting deal. Air Canada had previously reached agreements with eight of its nine unions to cut 800 million Canadian dollars ($576 million) from its annual labour costs of $3 billion. However, the airline must still reach deals with creditors, bankers and other stakeholders to reduce its debt of $12 billion, cut its fleet and streamline operations.

Tokyo: Japan Airlines System, which last month widened its annual loss forecast by half, says it plans to rent out more aircraft to tour companies to increase earnings and may transfer part of its pension fund to the government to cut costs.

Hong Kong: Cathay Pacific Airways, Asia's sixth-largest airline is considering purchases of second-hand Boeing 747-400 aircraft as it adds more routes, reducing the expense of buying new planes that can cost as much as $211 million each.

Economic efficiency ● ● ●

Economic efficiency means having the maximum output for the minimum input. Profit maximization and competition between firms both result in firms choosing least-cost methods of production and economizing on inputs, as well as using the best technological mix of inputs. Exhibit 7.2 illustrates how competition in the market place stimulates organizations such as airlines into a drive for economic efficiency.

Allocative efficiency ● ● ●

Allocative efficiency is related to the concept of Pareto optimality and means that it is not possible to reallocate resources, for example by producing more of one thing and less of another, without making somebody worse off. It results first from economic efficiency and second from consumers maximizing their own satisfaction and implies maximum output from given inputs and maximum consumer satisfaction from that output.

Consumer sovereignty ● ● ●

Consumer sovereignty means that consumers are able to exercise power in the market place. It implies that production will be driven by consumer demand rather than by government decisions. In a free market system, firms which survive and grow will be those which make profits by being sensitive to consumer demand.

Economic growth • • •

Economic growth will be encouraged by the free market since those firms which are the most profitable will survive and flourish. Under conditions of competition, firms will compete to increase productivity and thus in the market system resources will be allocated away from unprofitable and inefficient firms towards those which are profitable and efficient, thus generating economic growth.

In summary, under a competitive free market system consumers will get the goods and services they want at the lowest possible prices.

Criticisms of the market solution

Criticisms of the free market focus on the following:

* the inappropriateness of the perfect market assumption,
* reservations about consumer sovereignty,
* externalities,
* public goods,
* realities of economic growth,
* equity.

Perfect market assumption • • •

For free markets to deliver economic and allocative efficiency, perfect markets as outlined in Chapter 3 are assumed, that is many buyers and sellers, homogeneous products, perfect knowledge, freedom of entry and exit in markets, and no government interference. The existence of market imperfections will reduce the efficiency of the free market system. The Thatcher (UK) and Reagan (USA) administrations in fact devoted considerable legislation to the removal of market imperfections, particularly in the labour markets. However, in practice markets are far from perfect. Omerod (1994, p. 48) pointed out that the competitive equilibrium model is 'a travesty of reality. The world does not consist, for example, of an enormous number of small firms, none of which have any degree of control over the market in which it is operating.' Instead, many markets are dominated by a few suppliers, and considerable product differentiation occurs by producers attempting to make their goods or services different from the competition in order to minimize price competition. These factors mean that consumers may not get the benefits of lowest prices afforded by perfect markets.

Consumer sovereignty • • •

There are a number of factors at work in market economies that undermine the concept of consumer sovereignty. The first is lack of information. In the complex world of competing goods and services – particularly for technical products – consumers may not have enough information about the range of goods available and may find it difficult to make comparisons beyond the superficial. Second, consumers are subject to persuasive advertising from producers, the aim of which is to interfere with the consumers' exercise of free choice.

Externalities, merit and demerit goods ● ● ●

It is also evident that free markets fail in their signalling function in some areas. For example, there are some missing markets. There is no market for the ozone layer. There is no market for peace and quiet. There is no market for views and landscapes. It is difficult therefore for people to register their preferences in these areas. Equally markets do not always consider the full range of costs and benefits associated with production, or consumption of certain goods and services. The selling of alcohol is associated with the private benefit of feeling happy but has the unwanted public cost of fighting and accidents. Missing markets and externalities are closely linked. Consider a plan for a development of holiday apartments on a piece of farmland adjacent to the sea. In a free market situation the developer will have to consider the costs of the land, materials and labour. However, the development will clearly have an impact on the landscape, the view and the tranquillity of the area. But no one owns these rights, so there is no market in them and there is no price associated with the using up of them to develop the site. In this case there is a clear difference between the private costs of development and the public or social costs of development.

In Figure 7.1, *MPC* is the marginal private costs of the development. This shows the additional private costs of supplying extra units and represents

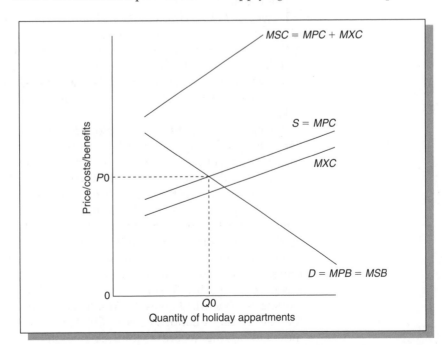

Figure 7.1
External costs and private costs: different equilibrium solutions (see text for details)

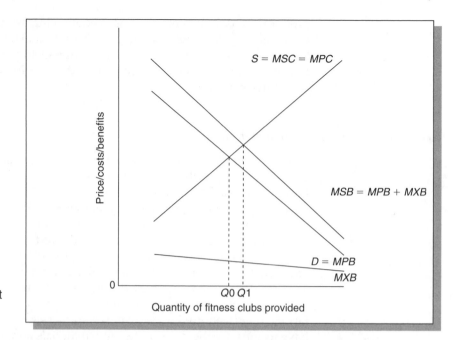

Figure 7.2
External benefits and
private benefits: different
equilibrium solutions
(see text for details)

the supply curve, S. The demand curve, D, shows the quantity demanded
at different prices and the marginal private benefit (MPB). In this case it is
assumed that there are no external benefits to consumption and thus this
curve also represents the marginal social benefit (MSB). A market equilibrium price is achieved at price $P0$ and the development will go ahead with
a quantity of $Q0$.

However, MXC represents marginal external costs, that is the costs in
terms of amenities lost such as views and tranquillity. Adding MXC to
MPC gives the marginal social cost curve (MSC). In this case it can be seen
that the external costs are such that no equilibrium is achieved in the market, since the MSCs exceed the MSBs at all prices. Thus we can see that the
free market overproduces goods and services which have significant external costs.

A similar argument may be deployed to demonstrate that the free market under-produces goods and services which provide external benefits to
society over and above the private benefits enjoyed by the consumer. In
Figure 7.2, MPB is derived from the use of fitness clubs and represents the
demand curve, D. S is the supply curve which shows the quantity supplied
at different prices and the MPCs. In this case it is assumed that there are no
external costs to provision and thus this curve also represents the MSC. A
market equilibrium quantity is achieved at $Q0$. MXB, however, represents
external benefits, that is the benefits to the community at large of the use of
fitness clubs which might include a fitter and more productive workforce,
less costs to the health service and a reduction in petty juvenile crime.
Adding MXB to MPB gives the MSB curve. In this case it can be seen that
the equilibrium quantity rises to $Q1$. Exhibit 7.3 demonstrates industry
moves to capture tax breaks for the fitness industry.

Exhibit 7.3   KPMG says tax breaks could boost health clubs sector

KPMG's head of leisure says that the introduction of US style tax breaks in the UK could provide a useful boost to the private health club industry.

In the US, the federal government is expected to enact the Workforce Health Improvement Programme (WHIP) bill, which seeks to encourage businesses to subsidize worker's exercise regimes by letting companies claim the contributions as income tax deductions. The International Health, Racquet & Sportsclub Association (IHRSA) is lobbying the government to implement the bill.

KPMG's director of leisure, Nick Pattie, feels that similar tax measures in the UK could help boost membership at private health and fitness sectors. He commented: 'A tax break for employees in the UK could be just the tonic to restore the health of the sector. Robust and increasing demand for private health clubs is firmly rooted in personal health. It is not a fashion fad, health club membership is considered by many to be a non-discretionary expenditure.'

Source: Adapted from *Health Club Management* (2003).

Goods which include substantial external costs are sometimes termed demerit goods. A demerit good is one which the government feels that people will over-consume and which therefore ought to be banned or taxed. Goods which include substantial social benefits are sometimes termed merit goods. A merit good is one which the government feels that people will under-consume and which therefore ought to be provided free or subsidized. Coalter (1998) examines the centrality of the merit good rationale to the public provision of leisure, suggesting that the leisure studies' defence of recreational welfare and leisure needs is not wholly coherent.

Public goods • • •

The market has an incentive to produce private goods or services because it can charge for them and make profits. It is very difficult to charge consumers for public goods and services and thus they are not provided in free markets. A public good is defined as a good or service which has features of non-rivalry and non-excludability and as a result would not be provided by the free market. Signposts to tourist attractions are an example of a public good since:

- they are non-excludable (you cannot exclude people who do not want to pay for them from seeing them); this is sometimes referred to as the free-rider problem;
- consumption is non-rival (if I use the sign it does not prevent anyone else from using it – unlike a tennis court).

Sable and Kling (2001) describe the 'double public good' model that can be applied to cultural heritage. They argue that social welfare is modelled on both public and private benefits of households' production of individual heritage experience. This in turn depends on the stock of historic assets (a public good) and access effort (a private good). The public benefit of private experience arises from 'shared experience' that fosters cultural identity and social understandings. They thus demonstrate the public good (that is merit aspects) of the public good (that is non-excludable) aspects of heritage.

Economic growth • • •

There is considerable debate as to whether the free market left alone will provide the fastest route to economic growth. It is true that the free market provides a kind of Darwinian natural selection process where profitable industries survive and unprofitable ones perish. However, the free market is also subject to economic upswings and downswings and does not include any inbuilt tendency to promote sustainable growth.

Equity • • •

Consumer sovereignty only exists for those who have the spending power to influence the market. Those with insufficient purchasing power to influence a market do not exercise any power over supply decisions. Therefore, production in unregulated free markets may favour the rich at the expense of the poor.

Market intervention

The following forms of market intervention are often proposed in order to address the problems inherent in a pure free market economy:

- central planning;
- control of monopolies and mergers;
- laws, planning controls and permits;
- taxes and subsidies;
- public provision.

Methods and benefits of market intervention

Central planning • • •

The most drastic solution to market failures is the adoption of state or central planning of production. In this model, production decisions are made by state planning teams rather than in response to consumer demand and profitability. This is the main way in which resources are allocated in China and Cuba; although both countries are increasingly liberating their markets.

Control of monopolies and mergers • • •

One of the aims of monopolies and mergers legislation is to protect the consumer from the disadvantages of the monopolization of an industry by a single firm. The key disadvantages are higher prices and the reduction in choice that may result from concentration of ownership in an industry. The key aspects of monopolies and mergers legislation are firstly the power to prevent mergers that could lead to market domination that is against the consumer interest and secondly to investigate firms where monopoly conditions appear to conflict with consumer interests.

One way to measure the degree of monopoly in an industry is to examine the concentration ratio. Thus the four firm concentration ratio shows the market share achieved by the largest four companies. In the UK package tour industry in 1998 the four firm concentration ratio was 85 per cent (Begg et al. 2002) indicating a high degree of market imperfection and potential monopoly power.

For the UK, the following milestones chart the development of government control over monopolies:

- *1948 UK Monopolies and Restrictive Practices Act*: This set up the Monopolies and Restrictive Practices Commission which could investigate any industry referred to it that had a market share of more than 30 per cent, and investigate whether the public interest was being served.
- *1956 UK Restrictive Trade Practices Act*: This banned formal restrictive practices (for example price agreements between firms) that were not in the public interest.
- *1965 UK Monopolies and Mergers Act*: This instigated a name change to the Monopolies and Mergers Commission and allowed examination of proposed mergers that might create a monopoly. Such mergers could be blocked.
- *1973 UK Fair Trading Act*: This reduced the definition of monopoly to 25 per cent of market share.
- *1980 UK Competition Act*: This widened the terms of reference of the Monopolies and Mergers Commission to include public corporations.
- *European Union Article 85*: This bans agreements and restrictive practices which prevent, restrict or distort competition within the European Union and affect trade between member states.
- *European Union Article 86*: This prohibits a firm from abusing a dominant position in the European Union which affects competition and trade between member states.
- *1990 European Union Merger Control Regulation*: This gave the European Union Commission (as opposed to national government regulators) responsibility for control over large-scale mergers which have a significant European Union dimension. The European Commission is able to fine firms up to 10 per cent of their turnover if they are found to be in contravention of Articles 85 or 86.

For example, the Commission exercised its powers to prevent mergers which would be detrimental to competition, by blocking the proposed take over in 1991 by Aerospatiale of France and Alenia of Italy, of the Canadian aircraft manufacturer de Havilland. It was argued that the proposed new company would force up prices of certain aircraft, where it would control 76 per cent of the world market and 75 per cent of the European Commission market. Investigations conducted by the UK Monopolies and Mergers Commission into firms in the leisure and tourism sector have included:

- P&O/Stena Sealink merger,
- the supply of package holidays,
- Isle of Wight ferry services,

Plate 7
Holidaymakers relaxing on a car ferry. But are they being ripped off by restrictive practices?
Source: The author

- the price of CDs,
- the brewing industry,
- proposed merger of BSkyB and Manchester United Football Club,
- vertical integration in the package tour industry,
- the exclusive broadcasting deal between BSkyB and the English football premier league clubs.

Szymanski (2000) examined the legal and economic reasoning that underlay the Restrictive Practices Court ruling allowing the UK Premier League's television deal with BSkyB. He is particularly intrigued by the qualified endorsement of the deal by the supporters which are also discussed. He suggests that future television deals will signal yet further increases in the price of watching football and continued limitations on the access to broadcast matches.

The main elements of the anti-trust (monopolies and mergers) legislation in the US are the:

- Sherman Act (1890),
- Clayton Act (1914),
- The Federal Trade Commission.

The Sherman Act has two main components. Section 1 forbids trade restraints that hurt competition and section 2 aims to curtail monopolization. The Clayton Act specifies actions that are illegal including price discrimination that hurts competition and exclusive dealing. The Federal Trade Commission enforces anti-trust legislation which examines the markets and investigates anti-competitive behaviour. In the USA, Eckard (2001) examined the creation of the first professional athletic labour market restriction in 1879. Here, professional baseball club owners agreed that each could reserve five players whom the others would not sign without permission, justifying the action by claiming that it was in the 'public interest'. Eckard found a lack of support for the public interest arguments proffered by owners and concludes that the more likely motive for the reserve rule was collusion to exploit the power of the clubs.

In Australia it is the Competition and Consumer Commission, an independent statutory authority, that administers legislation and informs government policy relating to competition and anti-trust law. The key pieces of anti-trust legislation are:

- the Trade Practices Act 1974,
- the Prices Surveillance Act 1983.

Exhibit 7.4 reports on the Australian Competition and Consumer Commission (ACCC) investigation into attempted resale price control.

There are also arguments for allowing large, potentially monopoly firms to prosper. These include competition with other large firms in the global

---

Exhibit 7.4   ACCC takes court action against Paraglider Company

The ACCC has issued legal proceedings against a supplier of para-gliders, High Adventure Pty Limited and its sole director Mr Lee Scott, alleging resale price maintenance in contravention of section 48* of the Trade Practices Act 1974. High Adventure Pty Limited is a supplier of Sky Paragliders' products in Australia. Sky.

The ACCC alleges that in July 2003, High Adventure made it known to Walkerjet, a retailer, that it would not supply Sky Paragliders' paragliders and/or accessories to Walkerjet unless it agreed not to sell or advertise Sky Paragliders' and/or accessories below the price specified by High Adventure.

On 12 July 2003 an e-mail was sent to a director of Walkerjet entitled: 'Dealer's price list for 2003 season'. Attached to this e-mail was a price list which specified 'Retail price in AUD' and terms for the supply of Sky Paragliders' paragliders and/or accessories. One of the terms stated that: 'Dealers can advertise that they sell the products but only with retail prices...'. The terms further stated: 'Failure of Compliance with above terms will result in immediate disqualifications.'

The ACCC is seeking declarations, a pecuniary penalty and injunctions restraining High Adventure from:

- making it known to any person that it will not supply goods to that person unless they agree not to sell or advertise the goods at prices less than those specified;
- offering to enter into an agreement with any person for the supply of goods requiring the person not to sell or advertise the goods at prices less than those specified;
- using in relation to goods it may supply to any person, a statement of prices that are likely to be understood as the prices below which the goods are not to be sold or advertised for sale.

The ACCC is also seeking an order that High Adventure Pty Limited offers to appoint Walkerjet as a dealer of Sky Paragliders' paragliders and accessories for a term of no less than 3 years. In addition, the ACCC is seeking declarations, injunctions and a pecuniary penalty against Mr Lee Scott. A directions hearing for the matter is listed for Tuesday, 27 January 2004 at 10.15 a.m. in the Federal Court, Melbourne.

*Section 48 of the Trade Practices Act 1974 prohibits 'resale price maintenance'. A company engages in resale price maintenance in part where it tries to stop a reseller from discounting a product or where it attempts to stop a reseller from advertising products below a specified price.

Source: Adapted from *Press Release, ACCC* (23 December 2003).

---

markets, the ability to engage in expensive research and development and the fact that competition is difficult where a natural monopoly exists. The latter is particularly true for firms that depend on an infrastructure that cannot feasibly be duplicated – for example a rail network.

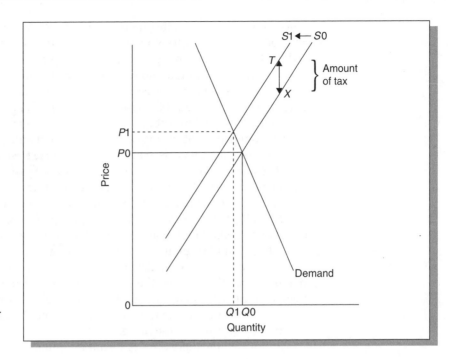

Figure 7.3
The effects of imposition of a tax on the market for cigarettes (see text for details)

Laws, planning controls and permits ● ● ●

Governments use laws, planning controls and permits to prevent the free market from operation in certain areas. For example, licensing laws limit the hours that licensed premises may open and who may be served with alcohol. Betting and gaming are regulated by the law. Similarly, some goods and services are banned outright. Possession of a whole range of drugs is illegal. Interestingly, legislating against something is not sufficient to prevent a market emerging and so black markets have arisen for the supply of drugs. Because of the risk involved in supplying drugs the market price reflects considerable profit. Planning control affects new buildings and change of use and is generally the function of local or state government.

Taxes and subsidies ● ● ●

Taxes and subsidies may be used to encourage the consumption of merit goods and discourage the consumption of demerit goods. Cigarette smoking, for example, is subject to large taxes although it is not entirely clear whether the main purpose of taxation is to collect revenue, or to cut consumption.

The effect on the market is illustrated in Figure 7.3. Originally, equilibrium price is established at $P0$ where demand equals supply at $Q0$. The effects of the imposition of a tax of TX is to shift the supply curve to the left, the vertical distance between the two supply curves representing the amount of the tax. Equilibrium price rises to *P*1 and cigarette consumption has been reduced to *Q*1. Notice that the demand curve has been drawn to reflect the relative demand inelasticity for cigarettes and thus the effect of a tax on quantity bought and sold is relatively modest.

If it were possible to measure marginal external costs of provision of a good or service, it would be possible to restore an optimum level of output in a market by the imposition of a tax. This is illustrated in Figure 7.4. The equilibrium price is at *P*0 with an equilibrium quantity of *Q*0. However, the existence of external costs marginal external cost establishes the marginal social cost curve to the left of the supply curve *S*, which only reflects marginal private costs. This would suggest an optimal price of *P*1 and quantity of *Q*1, but since the marginal external costs are purely national and do not actually affect the supply curve, overproduction of *Q*0–*Q*1 occurs. This could be remedied by the imposition of a tax which would shift the supply curve to *STX* and result in an equilibrium quantity of *Q*1.

An example of a tax on airlines to reduce the amount of noise pollution demonstrates that, whilst the problem can be addressed from an overall perspective (that is marginal social benefit equals marginal social cost), it is likely to be the government which benefits from the tax and not those who are directly affected by the noise.

Similarly, where there are significant marginal social benefits involved in the supply of a good or service, a subsidy could be used to ensure that the market equilibrium occurred where marginal social costs equal marginal social benefits, rather than where marginal private benefits equal marginal private costs. This is the economic justification for the subsidy of arts and recreation and such a policy results in more provision than would result from free market activity alone.

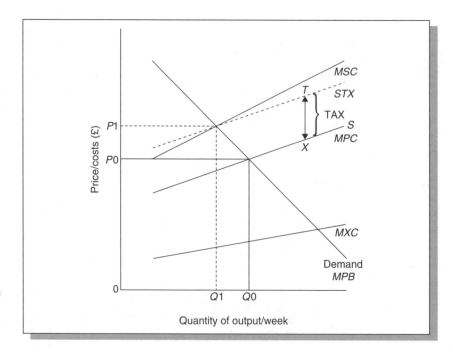

Figure 7.4
The use of taxation to restore optimal provision of goods with externalities (see text for details)

Public provision • • •

Public provision consists of supply through public corporations and local government ownership. The rationale for public ownership has included a mixture of political and economic aims. In the leisure and tourism sector in the UK the British Airports Authority and British Airways have both been privatized, although around the world there are still many examples of nationalized airlines, Air France being a prime example. There are many examples of public sector broadcasting (PSB) in evidence in Europe and O'Hagan and Jennings (2003) examine the key issues in the debate in Europe over public sector broadcasting. They consider the arguments for public sector broadcasting under five headings, namely diversity, democracy/equality, network externalities, innovation and investment and public broadcasting as 'insurance'. At a local level arts centres and leisure centres are commonly publicly owned.

Economic arguments for public ownership have included first:

- economies of scale,
- rationalization,
- avoidance of competitive costs.

These arguments all stem from government ownership of a whole industry. The resulting size of operation leads to economies of scale including bulk purchasing. Rationalization – making processes and products uniform and cutting waste – is also then possible, and competitive costs such as advertising can be eliminated. These arguments were powerful reasons for maintaining state monopolies in rail transport.

The second group of arguments in support of public ownership includes:

- control of monopoly power and excess prices,
- consideration of externalities,
- provision of merit and public goods,
- employment provision.

Under private ownership monopoly industries are able to charge high prices in the absence of competition, and profit maximization will encourage such industries to do so. State ownership enables non-profit-maximizing pricing strategies to be adopted. Price may be set, for example, to ensure that the industry breaks even to protect consumers from excess prices. In the case of an industry supplying merit goods or public goods, price may be set below market price where marginal social cost equals marginal social benefit. Such a pricing strategy would involve the industry making an accounting loss (since total private revenue would be less than total private costs) and thus require government subsidy. The use of public sector industries to provide employment would also be based on wider economic considerations, including social costs and benefits, rather than the narrow considerations of private costs and benefits. Exhibit 7.5 illustrates the range of leisure facilities offered by the City of Auckland, NZ showing which are private and which are public funded and which have mixed funding.

Exhibit 7.5   Spectrum of public support for leisure, Auckland, NZ

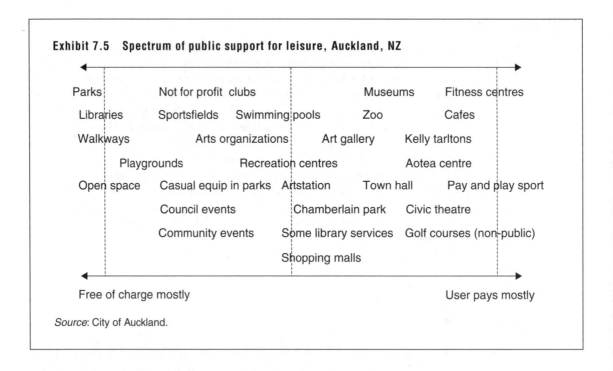

Source: City of Auckland.

Problems of market intervention

Resource allocation in disequilibrium ● ● ●

Where goods and services are provided free of charge – changing the guard at Buckingham Palace, roads, and children's playgrounds, for example – price is not able to bring demand and supply into equilibrium. The problem of excess demand often arises and therefore allocation of goods and services occurs in some other way. Queuing, first come first served, and ability to push are methods in which goods and services may then be allocated.

Public ownership: efficiency and culture ● ● ●

The profit motive engenders an organizational culture of efficiency and customer service. A criticism of public ownership is that lack of incentive leads to waste and poor service.

Side effects of subsidies and taxes ● ● ●

The provision of subsidies to industry has to be paid for. Subsidies are financed from increasing taxes or from reducing government spending elsewhere, or from government borrowing. Increasing the level of taxes can reduce incentives in the economy and it is rarely prudent to pay for current expenditure by borrowing since this merely postpones the raising of taxes.

Loss of consumer sovereignty • • •

In the extreme case of total state planning, consumer sovereignty is replaced by decision making by state officials, often leading to a mismatch between what consumers want and what the state provides. Government subsidies or ownership also reduce consumer sovereignty. Consumers' spending power is reduced by taxes, and government then makes decisions about how taxes will be spent. A key question here is whether the government is well qualified to choose, for example, what art should be produced.

Measurement of external costs and benefits • • •

Private costs and benefits are easily measured since they all have market prices. On the other hand it is very difficult to measure social costs and benefits which are not directly priced – what is the cost of the loss of a view for example?

Equity • • •

In order to subsidize recreation and leisure services, taxes need to be collected. This can lead to cross-subsidization of high-income earners (for example opera goers) by low-income earners.

Government interference and changing objectives • • •

A fundamental problem of state ownership of industry has been the lack of consistency of aims. As government policy and, indeed, as governments themselves change, so public corporations are given different aims. Governments sometimes interfere in purchasing decisions for political reasons. Public corporations are also hypersensitive to the condition of the general economy. Governments may interfere with public sector pay to control inflation, and investment funds may suddenly disappear when public sector borrowing becomes too high.

Trends in public sector provision

Central planning • • •

This has been abandoned by Eastern bloc countries and the two remaining significant examples of this – Cuba and China – are allowing the free market an increasing role in their economies.

Privatization • • •

Since the 1980s, the scale of public ownership has been drastically reduced. Government-owned companies have been privatized, their shares floated on the stock exchange and their aims have become those of profit maximization. Examples include Lufthansa in Germany and the railways in the UK. Those organizations remaining in the public sector have been subject to greater accountability. Exhibit 7.6 demonstrates privatization in Russia.

Service standards ● ● ●

These defined the rights, complaints procedures and compensation provision for customers.

Performance targets and indicators ● ● ●

Public sector organizations are increasingly required to define their provision in terms of measurable outcomes. These outcomes are often subject to interorganizational comparison – 'league tables' and targets for improvement from year to year.

Exhibit 7.6 Privatization of leisure in Russia

The city government of Moscow has extended its privatization programme by putting 200 hotels up for sale for an expected price of about $1 billion. The portfolio on offer is a mixed one. It includes the five-star National near to Red Square but also a number in a poor state of repair which require substantial refurbishment and in some cases reconstruction. The city has already been actively promoting joint ventures with foreign companies and currently has an equity stake in at least 80 hotels and restaurants.

The privatization will be subject to two conditions. First, the freeholds of the hotels, some of which are on prime sites will not be sold, but instead renewable leases of up to 49 years will be offered. Second, the city will retain a 25 per cent interest in the joint stock companies that are sold.

The main advantages to the city of Moscow are an immediate income from the asset sales and the inflow of foreign investment that is needed to bring the hotels up to international standards. Transfers of management expertise will also be beneficial as will the spreading of a service culture mentality from incoming multinational firms such as Hilton International and Marriott. Hotel management will be freed of the bureaucracy of local government ownership and control and uncertainties about finance and policy.

However, in the longer term, income will be lost to the city and profits of many cases will be repatriated to foreign multinational organizations. Employment prospects are mixed. Efficiency requirements will mean a loss of jobs and some jobs may be taken by foreign employees. However, the long-term development of the hotels may provide new jobs in the future. In terms of state planning, another small part of the economy will be lost to city control. Pricing policy, employment levels and the future development of these hotels will all be transferred to the free market.

Source: The author, from press cuttings (1997).

Contracting out ● ● ●

Exhibit 7.7 demonstrates how the provision of leisure (and other) services by local government has been subject to major reform, and Robinson and Taylor (2003) report on the results of a project from Sport England, which establishes performance indicators and national benchmarks for performance by local authority sports halls and swimming pools in England.

Exhibit 7.7   From compulsory competitive tendering to best value

Leisure centre management, in common with a range of local government services in the UK was subject to compulsory competitive tendering (CCT) in 1993. The idea of CCT was an attempt to bring competitive market forces into areas of provision which were previously provided by government employees. The Thatcher government was convinced that local government provision of many services was subject to waste and inefficiency and that wage rates paid were uncompetitive and that restrictive work practices had arisen.

Under CCT bids were invited, by a process of open tender, to manage centres in line with a detailed contract. The successful bid was the one with the lowest cost. This is not privatization, since the buildings and policy objectives remain in local government hands. In many cases the local authority's own Direct Service Organization (DSO) bids for contracts, and in some cases they are the only bidder. In reality DSO contracts still form the majority of CCT contracts.

There are several advantages claimed for CCT. First, since the lowest-cost bid wins the contract, there is an inbuilt pressure to deliver services more efficiently. Inputs are used more economically, and cost-saving practices and technologies are encouraged. Second, the actual management of a facility gains autonomy and is not subject to interference from the local authority. Third, standards and performance indicators have to be established in order to monitor the effectiveness of services provided by third parties. This encourages more emphasis on quality than might otherwise have occurred. Fourth, savings generated by lower costs of services subject to CCT can result in lower taxes or more expenditure on services elsewhere. Fifth, the bureaucracy of local government is reduced and thus it has more time to devote to its core services and policies. Finally, firms which are successful in CCT and which win multiple contracts can achieve economies of scale and develop their expertise.

However, there are also some robust criticisms of CCT. Perhaps one of the key points is the hidden costs of CCT. A range of extra costs arises out of the process which were not necessary under direct provision. These costs include contract specification, and negotiation, regular monitoring of performance and any legal costs arising from disputes. Second, the drive to reduce costs leads to a deterioration of working conditions and wages of those employed. Third, there arises an undue obsession with performance

---

targets, since these are the measures by which contractors will be judged. In reality a service is greater than a collection of performance targets and contains a range of intangibles. Fourth, there have been some conflicts of interest where persons with a direct link to councils have also acted on behalf of private sector tendering firms. Finally, services contracted to external suppliers must necessarily include a profit element that was not previously necessary. If the effects of CCT allow this profit to be met by increased efficiency of provision, there is a likely net gain, but it may be that the profit margin has to be met by shaving parts of the service.

Best value management replaced CCT legislation in January 2000. Best value requires local authorities to secure continuous improvements in the way functions are exercised. Reviews (local performance plans) must be carried out to:

1 Challenge why and how a service is being provided.
2 Invite comparisons with other councils' performance across a range of indicators.
3 Consult with local taxpayers, service users and the wider business community in the setting of new performance targets.
4 Embrace fair competition as a means of securing efficient and effective services.

Best value legislation includes powers for the Secretary of State to set performance standards for local authorities and to intervene if these standards are not met.

Review of key terms

- Consumer sovereignty: goods and services produced according to consumer demand.
- Economic efficiency: maximum output from minimum input.
- Allocative efficiency: maximum output from given inputs and maximum consumer satisfaction from that output.
- Externalities: costs or benefits which have social significance.
- Merit goods: goods with external benefits.
- Demerit goods: goods with external disbenefits.
- Public goods: goods which are non-excludable and non-rival.
- Concentration ratio: percentage of market share held by top companies.

Data Questions

Task 7.1   Michigan USA: show me the monet! Why not privatize the arts?

Since ancient times, the world's great aesthetes and philosophers have debated the seemingly simple question: 'What is art?' To some, it is a Mozart symphony or a painting by the French

Impressionists. To others, it may be Motor City Madman Ted Nugent singing 'Cat Scratch Fever.' Agreement over a definition of art can be surprisingly difficult to achieve.

People have widely divergent tastes and ideas about art that make Michigan's government subsidies for 'art' problematic at best and grossly unfair at worst. That is why the Governor should keep a 1991 pledge to end state funding for the arts.

Art subsidies are often sold to the public with the argument that providing government-approved artists with tax dollars will allow them to give their communities art and culture that would not exist without government support. But this argument relies on three dubious premises:

- Art and culture would or could not arise through entirely private efforts such as philanthropic grants, patron support or artists' own resources.
- A politically appointed arts elite can distribute the 'right' mix of theatre, paintings, music and dance to match the varying desires of different segments of the population.
- Government intervention will not break the all-important link of accountability between artists and art consumers.

And the best foreign film Oscar goes to America?   The European film industry is a good example of how government funding removes accountability from art and entertainment markets. Last year, 88 of the top 100 highest-grossing movies in Europe were American-made. The overwhelming majority of European movie-goers preferred dubbed or subtitled American films to those made in Europe. This is not to say that high-grossing films represent the pinnacle of art, either. After all, 'Ernest Goes to Camp' was popular among some at the box office, but you would be hard pressed to define it as path breaking artistry. Still, no one was forced to pay for its creation. State-subsidized art endeavors are a different story.

European governments provide lavish subsidies to their movie industries, which allows filmmakers to create products that they find valuable but which the public may not find valuable, artistically or otherwise. By contrast, American filmmakers work in a relatively undistorted marketplace where each ticket sold at the box office is a vote for a particular type of movie (and against other types). The final tally of these votes signals Hollywood to produce more or less of a certain movie form. The American public's tastes can, for example, be traced from periods such as the 1930s, when gangster films were popular, to the 1950s when science fiction movies reigned supreme, and so on. In addition, pop culture readily absorbs films that are both artistically acclaimed and successful commercially: Steven Spielberg's 'Schindler's List', Quentin Tarantino's 'Pulp Fiction' and Spike Lee's 'Do the Right Thing' come to mind.

The emperor's new clothes   Art subsidy supporters often argue that public funding of the arts is needed to support artists and art patrons who would otherwise not have the resources to enjoy art. The naked truth is that subsidy supporters have convinced themselves of this need when evidence suggests that government art subsidies flow from the poor and middle classes to wealthier citizens, and not vice versa. Consider just one example.

In 1998, the State of Michigan appropriated over $21 million for 'arts and cultural affairs'. The money was distributed to 38 of Michigan's 83 counties, according to Michigan Council for Arts and Cultural Affairs documents obtained by Michigan Privatization Report. Of the initial 38 grant recipients, the county of Alpena received the smallest grant of $2500. The largest grant, a hefty $12 944 237 (or 61 per cent of the total) went to Wayne County. Typically, every county eventually receives some of these funds through a 're-granting' program that allows initial grant recipients to dole out 'mini-grants' of up to $2000 to organizations that they believe are deserving.

One result of this grant process is that wealth is often taxed from lower-income Michigan workers and families and given for the enjoyment of higher-income workers and families. Wayne County, for example, has a population of 2 127 000 and a per capita income of $22 900. Alpena, in contrast, has a population of 30 638 and a per capita income of $20 000. As a ratio of grant funds to population, Wayne County will receive back from the state $6.09 per citizen while Alpena will get back only $0.80 per citizen.

The issue of fairness goes beyond number crunching. Supporters of government art subsidies should explain why it makes sense to tax people who do not voluntarily patronize the Detroit Symphony Orchestra (DSO) for the purposes of subsidizing those who do patronize the DSO. Would government grant makers indulge a crowd that wanted subsidies from symphony goers to pay for tickets to Ted Nugent's 'Whiplash Bash'?

Privatize the arts Art is highly personal and subjective. Forcing one person to subsidize another person's art is inherently unfair. Talented Michigan artists, like other professionals, should look to the private sector for income, not to government, for their sustenance. Every year, private philanthropists donate nearly $10 billion to further artists' visions of American culture. Artists whose work pleases their audiences will soon find voluntary support from such benevolent patrons.

Art and culture are too important to be left to the whims of politics. Michigan should rebuild the wall of separation between art and state.

Source: © The Mackinac Center for Public Policy Center (USA) (www.mackinac.org) reproduced with kind permission.

Recap Questions

1 What are the main arguments used by the author against subsidizing the arts?
2 Evaluate the case for and against subsidizing the arts under the following headings:
    (a) opportunity cost,
    (b) tax burden and borrowing,
    (c) merit goods and externalities,
    (d) consumer sovereignty,
    (e) equity.
3 Do you agree that 'Michigan should rebuild the wall of separation between art and state'?
4 Construct a graph to justify the subsidy of merit goods.
5 What recreation and leisure activities are currently subsidized in the country in which you are studying. What are the arguments for spreading or reducing such a subsidy?

Task 7.2   Regulating the railways

Since the railways were privatized in the UK, the government has faced two problems: first how to stop them exploiting their monopoly position; and, second, how to maintain a good level of service. Classical economic theory suggests that a private sector monopoly will increase prices and have little incentive to improve services – since the customer cannot go elsewhere.

The initial response to this was the provision of a rail regulator – OFFRAIL – to protect consumer interests. The regulator has now come up with a new plan to increase competition in the industry. Under the new scheme, rail companies will be able to offer services on tracks run by other companies. Railways have traditionally been thought of as natural monopolies where competition between different firms on the same lines is not possible. The idea of this scheme is to introduce competition and stimulate innovation, improve customer service and produce cheaper fares.

The regulator, Mr Swift, said: 'Passengers can reasonably expect to see the emergence of more attractive fares packages, higher frequency of service on popular routes and new direct services. It is my role to ensure that competition is in the public interest.'

The national secretary of the Save our Railways campaign group, Keith Bill, said: 'It will be cash from chaos, as companies take each other on, running services in direct competition on the most profitable routes. Commuters are losing out as companies switch their commuter trains to more lucrative routes like London to Birmingham and Gatwick. Mr Swift's proposals will turn these battles into full-scale rail wars, in which passengers will be the loser.'

Source: The author (1999), based on an article from *The Guardian*.

Recap Questions

1 What are the economic arguments in favour of privatization of the railways?
2 What are the economic arguments against privatization of the railways?
3 Evaluate the economic success of the privatization of the railways.
4 Why is rail transport thought to be a natural monopoly?
5 Why does the government intervene in the rail travel market but not in the air travel market?
6 Evaluate the likely success of this scheme in comparison with other methods for controlling monopolies.

Task 7.3 Tour operators' cover blown

In the UK, the Director General of Fair Trading, Mr John Bridgeman, is continuing talks with the major travel companies about the problems for consumers of vertical integration. Many consumers are unaware of the links between retail travel agents and tour operators, and may not be given the impartial advice they expect when entering the major agency chains.

However, in the meantime the government has now banned a widespread practice where travel agents insist that customers buy their insurance as part of a complete package or give discounts where customers take the insurance they offer. This follows a Monopolies and Merger Commission report on malpractice in the selling of insurance cover for travel. The Minister for Competition and Consumer Affairs, Mr Kim Howells, said: 'Consumers should not be forced to take out insurance which may not be competitively priced. Nor should they have to pay more for holidays because travel agents are discouraged by tour operators from offering discounts they would otherwise be prepared to offer.'

Customers who have bought insurance cover through travel agents can pay up to 60 per cent more than similar cover provided by direct insurers. For instance, cover for a 2-week break in Europe costs around £67 from Lunn Poly, while a comparable policy from an independent insurer costs just £26. The Monopolies and Merger Commission found that agents were taking advantage of their size on insurance sales. Commission on travel insurance earned the top four travel agents £186 million, a figure that was significantly more than the profits derived from selling holidays.

Source: The author (1999), from UK Monopolies and Merger Commission reports.

Recap Questions

1 Why and how does the government seek to intervene in the activities of tour operators and travel agents? What is the potential source of monopoly power and how might they act against the public interest?
2 One method of government control of the markets is by state ownership. Assess the economic arguments for public ownership of tour operators and travel agents.
3 Assess the degree of consumer sovereignty in relation to the main tour operators and travel agencies.

Multiple choice

1 **A merit good is one that:**

   (a) People should be rewarded with for good behaviour.
   (b) Is non-excludable.
   (c) Has external benefits.
   (d) Improves consumer sovereignty.

2 **The free market tends to:**

   (a) Overproduce merit goods.
   (b) Under-produce merit goods.
   (c) Produce goods and services inefficiently.
   (d) Limit consumer sovereignty.

3 **Which of the following is *not* an approach to preventing the abuse of monopoly power?**

   (a) Anti-trust laws.
   (b) Public ownership.
   (c) Subsidies.
   (d) Evaluation of mergers.

4 **Which of the following is *not* true of public goods?**

   (a) A public swimming pool is an example of one.
   (b) They are non-excludable.
   (c) Consumption of them is non-rival.
   (d) They tend not to be produced in a free market.

5 **Which of the following is *not* true of demerit goods?**

   (a) Cigarettes are an example of them.
   (b) They incur social as well as private costs.
   (c) They tend to be overproduced by the free market.
   (d) They are often subject to taxation.

Review questions

1 Why might leaving provision of the arts entirely to the private sector lead to suboptimal resource allocation? Use a diagram to show how provision of a public subsidy to the arts might restore optimal allocation and explain why achieving this aim might be difficult in practice.
2 Should children's playgrounds be provided free of charge?
3 Should opera be subsidized?
4 Should football admission be subsidized?
5 Should local authorities provide arts centres and what should their pricing policy be?
6 What problems arise from providing merit goods additional to those provided in the market?

Web sites of interest

Business organizations, tax, employment, government regulation, business incentives www.foxwilliams.co.uk/doingbus.htm
UK Office of Fair Trading www.oft.gov.uk/
Railway regulating body in the UK www.rail-reg.gov.uk/
UK Monopolies and Mergers Commission http://www.mmc.gov.uk/
The Australian Competition and Consumer Council www.accc.gov.au
Learning help in economics and business studies http://www.bized.ac.uk

Part Four

The External Operating Environment

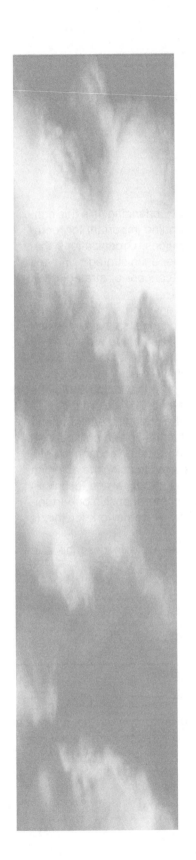

CHAPTER 8

The competitive, technological, political and socio-cultural environment

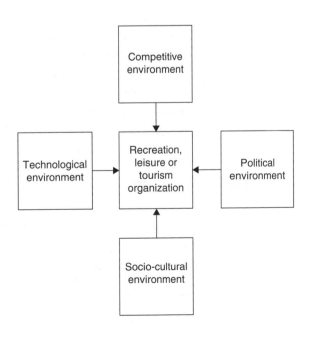

Objectives and learning outcomes

The environment in which organizations operate is often now characterized by the four 'D's:

- Difficult
- Dangerous
- Dynamic
- Diverse.

In other words, the environment is constantly changing. It is this constant change that makes environment scanning important for recreation, leisure, tourism and other organizations. Organizations that remain static in a dynamic environment experience strategic drift and are likely to fail. Figure 8.1 illustrates the concept of strategic drift which can explain such failure.

Between period $t0$ and $t1$, the operating environment is static, and the organization illustrated makes no policy change, so that by the end of the period, at $t1$, organizational policy at B is in tune with the environment at A. However, the period $t1$ to $t2$ represents a period of dynamic change in the operating environment. The organization, however, undertakes only marginal policy change so that by the end of the period it is experiencing strategic drift, represented by the distance CD.

Chapters 8 and 9 analyse the nature of the operating environment. This chapter considers the competitive, technological, political and socio-cultural environments. Chapter 9 considers the economic environment. These environments are often referred to using the acronym C-PEST (Competitive, Political, Economic, Socio-cultural and Technical) environment and their analysis enables a comprehensive opportunities and threats analysis to be undertaken. A framework for this is provided at the end of Chapter 9.

By studying this chapter students will be able to describe and analyse an organization's:

- competitive environment,
- technological environment,
- political environment,
- socio-cultural environment.

The competitive environment

In his book *Competitive Strategy* (1980), Porter proposes the following model ('the five forces') for investigating the competitive environment:

1 the threat of entrants,
2 the power of suppliers,
3 the power of consumers,
4 the threat of substitutes,
5 competitive rivalry.

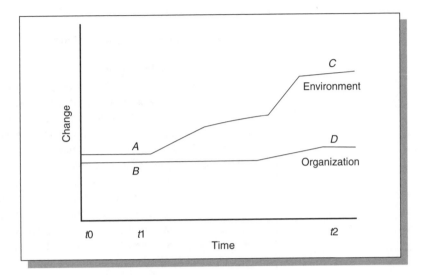

Figure 8.1
Strategic drift

The threat of entrants

The threat of new entrants into an industry will have a significant effect on a recreation, leisure or tourism organization. New entrants may stimulate more price competition or more investment in product differentiation as they attempt to win market share and profits and existing firms seek to defend market share and profits. Chapter 6 analysed these effects of competition on pricing policy and strategy.

The extent of the threat of new entrants will depend upon barriers to entry such as:

- economies of scale,
- capital and experience barriers to entry,
- advertising barriers to entry,
- availability of distribution channels (vertical integration),
- anticipated entry wars,
- natural monopoly conditions,
- product differentiation barriers.

Clearly barriers to entry will represent a hurdle to be surmounted for organizations wishing to enter an industry or defences to be maintained and strengthened in the case of established organizations. Exhibit 8.1 reports the threat of new entrants in the holiday industry.

Economies of scale • • •

Economies of scale, discussed in more detail in Chapter 5, result in reductions in average costs of production as the scale of production increases. Figure 8.2 illustrates the long-run average cost (LRAC) curve of an organization experiencing economies of scale.

163

Exhibit 8.1   Challenge to CenterParcs

CenterParcs brought the concept of woodland holiday villages to the UK and very successfully too. Their occupancy rates are over 90 per cent year round. The CenterParcs concept is based around an all-weather indoor leisure dome with restaurants, bars, shops, but most importantly a leisure pool and sports facilities. So whilst most UK holiday attractions are seasonal, CenterParcs, in beating the weather, is a year-round attraction.

No doubt the success of CenterParcs has attracted the rival Rank Leisure Group to imitate – it has introduced Oasis Holiday Villages. The first village in Whinfell, Cumbria, has close similarities with CenterParcs. It is set in a forest and up to 3500 guests stay in waterside villas and forest lodges. At the centre of things is an indoor waterworld, with shops, restaurants and sports facilities. Guests are encouraged to use the cycleways to move about the site.

The Managing Director of Rank said of similarities with CenterParcs, 'Although there will be some specific difference the two will be broadly similar'. But Sir Peter Moore, Managing Director of CenterParcs, retorted: 'It does not surprise us that Rank, no doubt prompted by our own success, are dipping a toe in the water but they would not find it easy. We are market leader and we intend to remain market leader'.

Source: The author (1999).

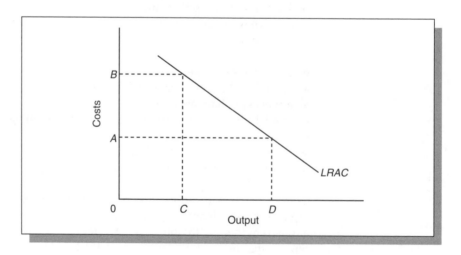

Figure 8.2
Economy of scale
barriers to entry

An established organization producing at level of output 0*D* will experience significant economies of scale with LRACs at 0*A*. A new entrant to the industry will initially produce a low level of output, for example at 0*C* and lack of scale economies will result in high average costs of 0*B*. The established organization can therefore often out-compete the new entrant by passing these lower costs on in the form of lower prices or use higher profit margins to finance more added value of the product.

Capital and experience barriers to entry • • •

For some areas of business the capital costs of entry are fairly modest. This is true, for example, for video rental stores, for dance and fitness classes, small hotels and guesthouses and for tour guiding. Entry into such areas is thus relatively easy. On the other hand there are substantial capital costs in entering the airline or theme park industry and thus entry barriers are stronger in such industries.

Similarly, an experience curve can be envisaged for the supply of complex goods and services. Established firms, having travelled along their experience curve, develop expertise that delivers lower costs and better service. Potential entrants will find themselves disadvantaged by being at the start of their experience curve.

Advertising barriers to entry • • •

Advertising may be used to create an artificial barrier to entry. Successful brands can be underpinned by extensive advertising which makes it difficult for newcomers to break into the market. For example, extensive advertising on lager brands has the effect of minimizing the threat of new entrants.

Availability of distribution channels • • •

Entry into some markets may be prevented or limited by access to distribution channels. There are many examples of this in the leisure and tourism sector. Many airlines would like to expand their operations into London Heathrow Airport but are unable to do so because take-off and landing slots are either unavailable or are at inconvenient times. British Airways (BA) is able to maintain some of its market power because of its allocation of slots. Exhibit 8.2 ascribes the lack of competition in domestic air travel to high costs and lack of access to distribution channels – in this case 'slots'.

One of the motives for vertical integration may be to discriminate against other suppliers by ownership of distribution channels, as discussed in Chapter 5. Thus Thomson's ownership of the Lunn Poly travel agency and MyTravel's ownership of Going Places retail travel may represent a strategy to prevent competitors from increasing their market share by preferential retail selling of a group's own products. Ownership of distribution channels has led to similar debates about fair access to markets in the film and cinema, and satellite television industries.

Anticipated entry wars • • •

Where entry into a market is likely to precipitate a strong reaction from established organizations, potential new entrants may be dissuaded from market entry. The example of SkyTrain in the 1970s is still a potent one. The

---

Exhibit 8.2   Grandfather rights keep the competition grounded

Potential new entrants to the airline business in the UK have to surmount a formidable hurdle in gaining access to take-off and landing slots at major airports. These landing rights give established airlines a big advantage over potential rivals. For example, there are around 430 000 slots at Heathrow, the world's busiest airport and BA owns the rights to a large percentage of these. Airlines are able to build up their holdings of slots by so-called grandfathering rights, a system under which its slots are automatically renewed the following year.

But BA is not alone in squeezing out competition through control of access through ownership of slots. Swiss holds 37 per cent of the slots at Zurich Airport, KLM has 39 per cent at Amsterdam, Austrian Airlines owns 43 per cent at Vienna, and Lufthansa has 55 per cent at Frankfurt Airport.

Even when slots are traded, new operators find it difficult to gain access to them since prime slots command premium prices, which means new entrants with limited capital are excluded.

Source: The author (1999).

---

arrival of this new service on UK/USA air routes led to price wars from BA and American carriers that were so intense that Laker Airways went out of business. The established companies had the financial muscle to cut prices deeper and for longer than Laker.

The arrival of Virgin Atlantic instigated similar entry wars that culminated in the infamous BA 'dirty tricks' campaign that allegedly poached Virgin customers by devious means. Exhibit 8.3 illustrates aspects of this entry war.

Natural monopoly conditions ● ● ●

A natural monopoly exists where it is not technically feasible or desirable to have many competing services. For example, it is only feasible to have one rail network or fixed telephone line network, and for smaller destinations one airport. Organizations operating in natural monopolies generally are less exposed to the threat of new entrants.

The power of suppliers

Supplier power is another important aspect of the competitive environment. Suppliers of an organization's inputs have a key impact on prices and quality and the greater the power of suppliers, the lower margins will be. Supplier power is increased by the degree of monopoly or oligopoly in

---

Exhibit 8.3 More BA 'dirty tricks' claims

Allegations of more 'dirty tricks' tactics have been made against BA. Virgin is currently engaged in a $1 billion lawsuit against BA in the USA, based on allegations of poaching passengers, and smears. One tactic used in the USA was to telephone Virgin passengers and offer them upgrades on BA flights. In the UK private detectives were hired to provide information for a disinformation campaign against Virgin.

New allegations involve American Airlines, Air France and Lufthansa whose passengers were poached by 'the ambush'. This involved business travellers arriving at Gatwick, who would be approached, often by young women, and offered a range of incentives to change their booking to BA. These teams, who were coordinated by radio handsets, were nicknamed 'Maude's marauders' after a Heathrow sales manager, Chris Maude. The reward for a successful maraud was a £5 gift voucher.

These allegations have called into question the notion of good faith and confidentiality, since many competing airlines have hired space on BA computers, and are now suspicious that BA may have used their passenger lists as a way of pirating passengers.

Sources: The author, from news cuttings (March 1994).

---

the supplying industry, and whether there are high costs of switching suppliers. Because of this airport operators are often able to exert considerable supplier power when negotiating with airlines. Supplier power is diminished where the organization buying inputs has large purchasing power.

In some cases, backward vertical integration is a route to avoiding supplier power by the take-over of the supplying organization. Thomson's ownership of its carrier Britannia and MyTravel's ownership of its airline (see Exhibit 8.4) mean that these organizations can dictate the level of service and its price. The latter is particularly important when demand is buoyant and airlines find their bargaining position enhanced.

The power of buyers

Where the buyer is a monopsonist (single buyer) or a near monopsonist, considerable power can be exerted over the selling organization. For example, in Spanish resorts where hoteliers have become dependent upon one or two UK tour operators, room rates are negotiated with very slim margins for the hoteliers.

Competition between suppliers is a key factor that increases buyer power. This is evident for air travel where there is intense competition on routes, for example London–New York fares are very competitive, but where a route is served by a single operator price per kilometre flown increases sharply.

The level of buyer knowledge is another important factor. In order to exercise buyer power, customers need information about goods and services on

Exhibit 8.4   MyTravel Company Structure, January 2004

	MyTravel UK	MyTravel Europe	MyTravel North America
Aviation	MyTravel Airways (UK) MyTravel Lite	MyTravel Airway (A/S)	Skyservice[+]
Tour Operating	Airtours Holidays Aspro Bridge Cresta Direct Holidays Escapades Manos Panorama Tradewinds	Always Bridge Gate Eleven Globetrotter Gullivers Saga Seereisen Skibby Spies Sunair Tjaereborg Travel Trend Trivsel	AlbaTours Alumni Holidays International Ship 'N' Shore Sunquest The Holiday Network
Distribution	Going Places Going Places Television Holidayline LateEscapes.com MyTravel.com Travelworld	Always Gate Eleven Globetrotter Gullivers MyTravel MyTravel.com MyTravel Reiswinkels Spies Saga Skibby Trivsel Tjaereborg	ABC Corporate Services Diplomat Tours DFW Tours FlyCheap Vacations Lifestyle Vacation Incentives MyTravelco.com MyTravel Retail Resort Escapes Travel 800
Other	Sun Cruises Hotel Division (Globales, Hotetur*, Aquasol*, Tenerife Sol*, Explorers, Sunwing) White Horse Insurance		

Notes: [+]Strategic Alliance *Joint Ventures and Part Owned.

Source: The author adapted from www.mytravelgroup.com/Group_Of_Companies.htm

offer and prices of competitors. In some areas of recreation, leisure and tourism this is difficult. However, the increasing use of the Internet offers consumers better knowledge in making price comparisons. The limitation to this however is the time cost of making comprehensive price comparisons.

Finally, the overall state of the market is important in determining the relative balance of buyer and supplier power. When the economy is growing strongly, there may be shortages of supply and supplier power becomes stronger. In conditions of recession there is often a shortage of customers and buyer power increases.

The threat of substitutes

Substitutes can take several forms. First a new product or service may make a current one obsolete. Word processors and CD players have made the typewriter and the music cassette obsolete. Second a substitute may result in a new product or service competing closely with existing ones. Third, to some extent all goods and services compete for consumers' limited incomes and thus new products even in distant markets may have some impact on a variety of unrelated organizations.

Organizations faced with the threat of substitutes may react in several ways. These include:

- price leadership strategies,
- differentiation strategies,
- withdrawal or diversification strategies,
- creating switching costs to prevent loss of customers.

The degree of competitive rivalry

Competitive rivalry within an industry is increased by the threat of new entrants and the threat of substitutes, but it is also influenced by current conditions in the industry. These include:

- whether competitors can cross-subsidize,
- degree of market leadership and number of competitors,
- changes in capacity,
- high storage costs/perishability.

Cross-subsidization occurs where an organization uses profits from one sector of its business to subsidize prices in another sector particularly where new competition is emerging. This can lead to intense competition in the markets for some goods and services. The motive behind cross-subsidization is to win market share by low prices, and to make life difficult for new entrants to a market.

The degree of market leadership and number of competitors also influences competitive rivalry. Clearly monopoly or near monopoly supply means little competitive rivalry. Oligopoly conditions can lead to competitive rivalry, but since, as Chapter 6 explains, rivalry reduces profits all round, organizations may choose to follow the lead of the dominant firms in such circumstances. Competitive conditions of supply are likely to lead to a state of constant rivalry. Firms may attempt to insulate themselves from such rivalry by differentiating their product from other products.

Where the supply of a good or service is subject to large increases in capacity, competitive rivalry is likely to become more intense. For example, the opening of the channel tunnel led to a sudden increase in the capacity for cross-channel traffic and was followed by an intense period of competitive rivalry.

Some goods and services have high storage costs or are highly perishable. Aircraft seats, hotel rooms, hire cars and theatre seats are highly perishable. There is always the prospect of intense last-minute competition to sell such services, but in reality competition here is carefully orchestrated so that an organization's main market is not disrupted. For example, tour operators want to encourage advance bookings at brochure prices and therefore do not make big advertising capital over the last-minute bargains that can be obtained.

The technological environment

Technological change offers two key opportunities for leisure and tourism organizations. First it can lead to cost reductions. The LRAC curve is constructed on the assumption that technology remains constant, and thus improved production technology will cause the LRAC curve of an organization to fall, as illustrated in Figure 8.3. LRAC1 represents the original LRAC curve. The use of improved production technology enables the curve to shift downwards to LRAC2. Average costs of producing level of output 0C now fall from 0A to 0B.

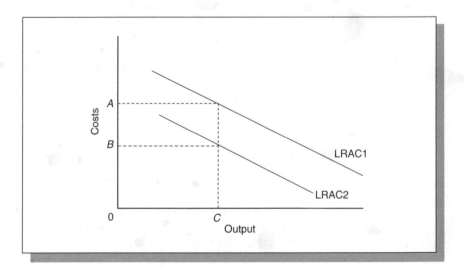

Figure 8.3
Shifting LRAC curve

Second, technology can provide new products and markets. Both of these routes can lead to an improvement in an organization's competitive edge, and can be the basis of price-based or differentiation strategies.

However, technological change also poses threats where existing products become obsolete in the face of new developments. Technological change is being delivered mainly at present by the increased processing power of microcomputers, the provision of high-capacity data links and the fall in price of hardware and software. Silicon chip developments lead to faster data processing. Fibreoptics and digital technology mean that data can be quickly transmitted globally at low cost, and these hardware developments mean that software of ever-increasing sophistication can be developed.

Multimedia continues to be a key driver of technological change and its components are illustrated in Figure 8.4. Thus at a simple level an organization's computer network on its own can perform word processing, accounting and other functions (circle A). Linked to other computers it can enable communications to take place inside the organization through its Intranet and it can communicate with the world outside through the Internet. For example, here it can access reservation systems, provide marketing and booking systems and access e-mail and Internet conferencing (circles A + B).

Linked to other media, at the simplest level text, images and video clips can be incorporated into software programs (circles A + C). At the most

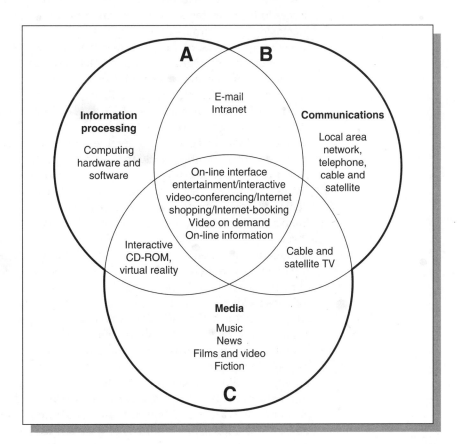

Figure 8.4
Multimedia

sophisticated level virtual reality can be set up. Linking personal computers (PCs) and media sources through data links provides access to the whole repertoire of computer applications (circles A + B + C). This includes, for example, downloading of music, video on demand, and Internet shopping. Home booking allows access to central reservation and booking systems from home, with the possibility of video clips of resorts and hotels.

The key drivers to multimedia technology include the falling price and rapidly increasing specification of PCs and the falling price and increasing availability of home broadband Internet connections.

Technological impacts may be analysed in the following areas:

- hospitality,
- tourism,
- leisure and recreation.

Hospitality

Technological developments include the following. First links into central reservation systems are important so that hotels can capture reservations generated from distant terminals. Most travel agents use one of the central reservation systems to book air travel, car hire and accommodation, and access to these systems represents an important marketing tool. However, increasingly consumers and suppliers are bypassing retailers and seeking direct bookings via the Internet, so a user-friendly real-time Internet booking system is important for hotels. Aksu and Tarcan (2002) found widespread use of Internet booking by five-star hotels in Turkey but reported that some uses (e.g. customer feedback) were not exploited. Additionally specialist Internet providers such as *lastminute.com* and *laterooms.com* specialize in selling unbooked rooms.

Second, there has been considerable progress in accounting packages. In management accounting, yield management packages are an important tool enabling hotels to maximize revenue by adjusting rates to best-fit changing market conditions. Yield management packages are able to compare likely demand with actual demand and capacity and suggest rates accordingly. In financial accounting, packages enable financial reporting to take place speedily and efficiently. Check-in time can be minimized by using credit card readers to automate registration and issue a high-technology key which can even be a credit card itself. High-technology keys reduce the possibility of theft since codes may be changed frequently at minimal cost. It is possible for a reservation system to use its database to provide personalized services such as provision of a particular newspaper. Computerized reservation systems can also reduce check-out time to a minimum.

Other computer-assisted management systems range from energy management systems to conference management systems and computer-intelligent buildings. A computer-intelligent building means that most of the functions of the building are computer-assisted, and so, for example, room cleaning schedules can be computer generated from information from guests' smart keys, pay rolling can be generated from reading employees' time sheets which themselves are based on electronic monitoring, and a wide range of on-screen services are available in rooms.

It is also vital for top hotels to ensure that their provision matches their customers' technology aspirations. This may include Plasma television screens, wireless connectivity and sophisticated music systems.

Exhibit 8.5 and Plate 8 show how technology has been used at the budget end of the hotel industry. Here its prime aim is to cut costs, enabling some French hotels to pursue an effective price-based strategy. The conference industry illustrates possible opportunities and threats posed by new technology. A recent study found that 36 per cent of hotel room sales was made to conference delegates, and there has been growth in the number of centres with capacities for in excess of 1000 delegates. However, firms such as Xerox are increasingly turning to video-conferencing as a way of reducing travel and hospitality costs, and saving expensive executive time. Some hotels are responding to this challenge and the Hilton National group, for example, has introduced video-conferencing in its key conference venues. However, with the growth of multimedia technologies it is possible that more conferencing will in future be office or home based, utilizing PCs. The implications of such a move would be a shift in conference spending away from airlines, hotels and local hospitality providers towards the providers of data links and other hardware and software companies.

Exhibit 8.5 Hi-tech hotels are revolutionizing budget accommodation in France – Rob Davidson

You are driving through France and decide to stop for the night. The question is: how do you break your journey without breaking the bank? The answer is the budget hotel where a clean, quiet room for up to three people sharing costs from £15 a night.

How are overheads kept so low? Most cost trimming is achieved by reducing services to a bare minimum. Hi-tech, manpower-saving devices also help to cut costs. A good example is automatic check-ins, which are placed at entrances for use when reception areas are unattended. La Réception Automatique works like a cash machine: you insert a credit card and 'converse' with the facility (in French, English or German) about the room you want, how long you plan to stay and whether you want breakfast. The machine then debits your card and issues a key and room number.

French technology is also applied in the automatic cleaning systems installed in the showers and lavatories of the hotels. Every time the facility is used, a powerful spray of a water–disinfectant mix ensures that it is left spotless for the next user.

The labour-saving devices and basic services mean that budget hotels can be run by just two people plus cleaning staff.

Source: The Independent.

Plate 8
Réception
Automatique, Hôtel
Première Classe,
France
Source: The author

Travel and tourism

Technological changes in transportation are likely to be extensions of exist-ing technologies in the form of larger jumbo jets, and faster trains for travel. Additionally some shortages of air space may be relieved by using information technology to create smaller air tunnels than the existing air corridors. So one of the key impacts of technology on this sector will be to continually open up the borders of the possible for travel as well as redu-cing travel time and cost. The flight of the first space tourist – Denis Tito – demonstrates possibilities for the future.

Buhalis (2003) offers a comprehensive review of the development of e-tourism. Booking and reservation systems are likely to become more sophisticated, globalized and more widely available. The increasing use of the Internet at one stage seemed to pose some threats to travel agents, but most of these have responded by introducing their own web sites for Internet bookings.

Leisure and recreation

The multimedia revolution offers the prospect of sophisticated home-based leisure and enhancement of attractions away from home. The reduction in price and wider availability of broadband for home use is likely to accelerate changes that are already in the pipeline. In the home, video on demand may spell the demise of the video rental store. Digitized movies will be stored in distant databases which can be accessed via a menu and decoding system using broadband. Interactive games which started life on floppy disks swiftly moved through CD-ROM and DVD-ROM technology and Exhibit 8.6 illustrates the development of interactive porn.

Exhibit 8.6   Sex comes on-line

1994:   Virtual Valerie was the cutting edge of technology for porn – a CD ROM game where 'Val obeys the user's every command'.

1999:   Karlin Lillingon of *The Guardian* gives an update on the techno-logical progress of porn: 'Not even the defence industry capitalizes on new technical developments as swiftly, and with as much innovation and pay-back, as the pornographers. They buy the best equipment, use some of the best Internet service companies in the business to give them ultra-fast connections directly to the Internet's backbone, and are always eager to test the newest applications – anything to push images as fast as pos-sible to the paying punters at the end of the mouse. From web video to live chat, on-line credit card transactions to image compression technologies, the on-line sex industry usually got there first and pioneered the format. As a result, the Internet has made silicone as ubiquitous as silicon. Sex is the web's killer application.

An IT applications engineer notes that pornography is one of the key industries involved in the purchase of computer equipment. The econom-ics of porn provide the motive for state-of-the-art expertise to provide competitive advantage. A third of web users surveyed reported that they had accessed a sex site. These billions of hits generate subscriptions and sales. For example, a Los Angeles-based web site called Danni's Hard Drive had a gross turnover of $2.7 million in 1997 resign to around $3.5 million in 1998. The site averages 5 million hits a day and has established a client base of over 22 000 paying subscribers. Access costs $14.95 per month which gains entry to photos, videos and six live real-time acts.

Industry analysts Forrester Research estimate that pornography pro-duced $137 million for US web sites in 1997, and $185 million in 1998. Forrester predicts that by 2001 revenue will have risen to $366 million. This makes pornography third in Internet sales after computers and travel. *Inter@ctive*, a magazine for the web industry, estimates that the supply of adult sites for 1997 was about 10 000.

The Hot and Heavy site boasts 'the hottest 3D virtual reality sex online', and entices its customers to 'use your mouse to move the hottest girls/couples in 3D'. But what of the future?

2002?:   Programmers predict that cybersex will take on new dimensions with developments in 'teledildonics'. Here cybersex moves from visual interaction nearer to virtual sex where visual interaction is merged with sensation.

2008?:   One cybersex futurologist predicts 'the ability to get and give virtual satisfaction through sensory interactivity'. This would involve donning a helmet to enter a virtual world and a suit to receive and transmits touch sensations. In fact a German research group have already produced a prototype of a full-body sensory suit for virtual sex.

Source: The author (1999).

Currently, the ultimate development goal of computer games appears to be virtual reality. Virtual reality is an extension of the technology of the flight simulator. It enables participants to enter a computer-generated three-dimensional environment and interact with the environment. Headsets, data gloves and data suits are the future passport to this virtual world where participants can travel from scene to scene and interact with virtual people and virtual objects. Virtual reality is also likely to affect leisure away from home. Sega has developed theme parks in Japan with interactive attractions which will let people shoot and steer their way through adventures. Disney utilizes virtual reality in its heritage theme park in Washington DC so that visitors can experience life as a civil war soldier, or as a slave. The future interpretation of heritage may well rely less on exhibits in glass cases and more on participation and interaction with virtual artefacts and virtual historical figures.

In recreation, technological developments in design and materials means a constant upgrading of sports equipment ensuring a healthy market for replacement goods. A similar situation arises in the music sector. Changing technologies for recorded music means that consumers often have bought the same music several times – on vinyl, tape and CD. However the huge growth in downloading of music from the Internet seems to be continuing threat for companies in this sector. The improvement in quality and rapid fall in costs of digital photography means that a new market opens up – but at the expense of other markets. In 2004, Eastman Kodak announced it was cutting 15 000 jobs because of the effects of digital photography on its core business.

The political environment

The political environment is shaped by those with political power, or the ability to influence events and Veal (2002) offers a comprehensive examination of policy in relation to leisure and tourism. A key player in this is the party in government for the immediate period until the next election in the case of democratically elected governments. Longer-term political trends are clearly difficult to predict since they depend largely upon which political party wins the next election. Although opinion polls give some indication of current party popularity they are likely to change considerably by the pre-election period and in any case do not have a good record of accuracy.

The government itself will be subject to its own operating environment and thus policy will be shaped by the economy, international relations and interest group activity. In addition radical political groupings which operate outside of mainstream politics – such as Al Qaeda – can have play a significant role in the political environment.

Given the range of possible directions of policy, scenario planning is likely to be used by organizations wishing to incorporate the political environment into their strategic planning. This involves analysing the impact of a range of possible political outcomes on an organization. Sources of information on changes in the political environment include:

- government reports,
- party manifestos,
- other interest groups,
- changes in the law.

Government reports

Government reports are a useful guide to policy. They set out detailed points which can affect specific organizations (e.g. the Taylor report on football) and give clues about the general direction of government policy. The following are examples of reports affecting the recreation, leisure and tourism sector.

The 1990 Taylor report (UK) • • •

The Taylor report on football concluded the public inquiry set up after the 1989 Hillsborough disaster. It recommendations included:

- halting the proposed national identity scheme for football spectators,
- football grounds to be converted to all-seat stadia by 1994 for top-division clubs and 1999 for the remainder of the league,
- making pitch invasions and the shouting of racial abuse a criminal offence.

1998: Low Pay Commission report on the minimum wage (UK) • • •

One of the manifesto commitments of the Labour Government, elected to power in 1997 was the introduction of a statutory minimum wage. Recreation, leisure and tourism is an industry where the introduction of a minimum wage has a significant effect since low wages are characteristic across much of the sector. Over a long period there have been two key interest groups fighting the battle for the minimum wage. On the one hand, the trade union movement has long supported a minimum wage since many of its members or potential members stand to gain by it. Opposed to this have been industrial groups such as the Confederation of British Industry (CBI). It was the responsibility of the Low Pay Commission to recommend a figure for the minimum wage. The eventual recommendation was for £3.60 an hour in 1999, rising to £3.70 in 2000. This represented a compromise between the Trade Union Congress (TUC), which lobbied strongly for a rate of more than £4.00 an hour, and the CBI submission which favoured a lower rate of £3.20.

The Tourism White Paper 2003 (Australia) ● ● ●

This White Paper sets out a foundation for the Australian tourism industry which:

- offers tourists uniquely Australian experiences of quality and value,
- welcomes more Australians undertaking travel in their own country,
- supports a diversity of sustainable and profitable enterprises that strive for satisfying customer needs,
- develops and grows high-yielding products and markets through development of innovative business strategies and high-yield niche markets,
- embraces innovation,
- attracts appropriate investment to support growth,
- supports a highly skilled workforce,
- is an integral part of the Australian social and economic fabric.

Party manifestos

These identify policies which political parties will follow if elected to government. They are generally available in the period preceding a general election, and reflect the main differences between political groupings shown in Exhibit 8.7.

Other interest groups

Some of the key interest groups that seek to influence recreation leisure and tourism include:

- Greenpeace,
- Tourism Concern,
- Friends of the Earth.

Exhibit 8.7   Key differences between political parties

Left-wing (e.g. Labour/ Democrat parties)	Right-wing (e.g. Conservative/ Republican parties)
• Need to control the free market	• Belief in supremacy of the free market
• Pro-trade unions	• Anti-trade unions
• Some state ownership of industry	• Private ownership of industry
• Progressive taxation	• Proportional taxation
• Regulation of industry	• Minimal state interference
• Higher government spending and taxes	• Low taxes and government spending
• Reduce inequality of incomes	• Inequality of income as incentive
• Pro-minimum wage	• Anti-minimum wage
• Provision of jobs a priority	• Control of inflation a priority
• Comprehensive welfare sate	• Minimal welfare state

Changes in the law

It is the introduction of new legislation where the political environment has most direct impact on recreation, leisure and tourism organizations. The following give examples of recent changes in the law and their impact on organizations.

The 1994 Sunday Trading Act (UK) • • •

The passing of this act made lawful what had already been widely practised. Although large stores have their opening hours restricted to 6 hours, the act enables leisure and travel retailers to trade lawfully. Do it yourself (DIY) stores had a long track record for Sunday opening, and the Sunday Trading Act has meant that a Sunday is now indistinguishable from any other day in many UK high streets. This act has led to a big rise in economic activity in recreation, leisure and tourism in the UK.

The 1998 Working Time Directive (European Community) • • •

The 1998 Working Time Directive gives an employee the right the refuse to work more than 48 hours per week, although the limit may be exceeded in a given week, provided the 48-hour limit is an average over a 17-week period. The directive states that no one can be dismissed or discriminated against for claiming their rights. The European Union (EU) is moving towards a reduction in working hours and for example France restricts working hours to 35 a week.

Proposals for health warnings on alcoholic drinks (Ireland) • • •

The Irish Minister for health is to consider legislation that would require drinks manufacturers to include government health warnings on all alcoholic drinks in the Republic of Ireland. This follows a recent, nationwide survey by the Irish Medical Times that found 71 per cent of doctors would back a proposal that all alcoholic drinks should carry a government health warning.

The socio-cultural environment

Socio-cultural factors include the make-up of society, for example in terms of its population structure, levels of education, social class and attitudes.

Demographics

Demography is the study of population, and population trends are important for the leisure and tourism sector for three key reasons. First the population is an important factor in determining demand. So, for example, the leisure requirements of a country are likely to change considerably as the average age of the population increases. Football pitches may need to give way to bowling greens. The location of leisure facilities similarly needs to be tailored to the migration trends of the population. Tourism marketing also needs to be informed by relevant population data. The dramatic growth in extended winter sun breaks reflects the demands of an ageing population. Second the population provides the labour force. Where there is a constant stream of school leavers entering the job market, recruitment and training are relatively straightforward. But when the proportion of the population in the working age group is shrinking, firms have to operate more worker-centred policies. Third an ageing population is likely to have a less progressive culture and adapt to change less easily. It is therefore useful to have information about trends in the total population and its structure in terms of age, sex, geographical and socio-economic distribution.

Population: growth and age distribution • • •

The rate of growth of the population is determined by the birth rate, the death rate and net migration. The birth and death rates are generally expressed as crude rates, for example:

Crude birth rate = Number of births per thousand population.

The UK, USA and Spain in common with many developed countries, have relatively stable populations and Figure 10.1(c) illustrates this. This is because the birth rate and the death rate for these countries have both stabilized at similar levels. Birth rates are linked with economic development and high per capita income countries tend to have low rates since women are more likely to want to be active in the labour market, the cost of upkeep of children is high, and birth control is widely practised. High birth rates in low per capita income countries need less explanation. In these countries there are fewer factors reducing the higher crude birth rate that is natural in humans. Children are seen as natural, as extra help and as an insurance in old age, and birth control is less widely adopted. Figure 8.5

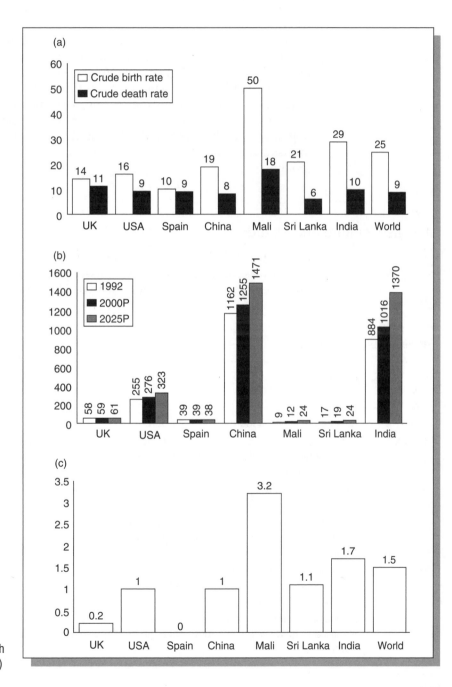

Figure 8.5
Population growth for selected countries. (a) Crude birth and death rates (per thousand per year 1992); (b) total populations in millions (P = projections); (c) average percentage yearly population growth (projection: 1992–2000)

illustrates the consequences of this for population sizes and growth rates in different countries.

Economic development tends to a lowering of death rates (which are partially determined by nutrition, hygiene and medical technology) earlier than birth rates, which are dependent on attitudes. Thus many countries are still witnessing rapid population growth. The population of India is forecast to grow by more than a third over the next 30 years, whilst that of Mali will more than double. The one important exception to this is China, where a strict one-child policy is enforced.

Examples of differing age structure of the population are offered by Nigeria and Italy. In Nigeria, for example, 44 per cent of the population is under 15 years old and 3 per cent is 65 years or older. Italy's population, on the other hand, is only 14 per cent children and 18 per cent older adults. Countries which are still experiencing rapid population growth have a much lower average age of their population. Differing age groups of the population can be identified as having distinct demands for leisure and tourism. Table 8.1 illustrates characteristics and demands of distinct age groups.

Lifestyles, culture and attitudes

In the UK by 1990 two-thirds of households were owner occupiers. The increase in home ownership has encouraged the growth of home-improvement leisure activities such as DIY and gardening. Television

Table 8.1 Age characteristics

Life stage	Characteristics	Leisure income	Leisure time
Child	Leisure decisions generally taken by parent	Low	High
Single	High propensity for leisure pursuits and travel. Independence asserted, budget travel popular, social aspects sought	Medium	Medium
Partnered	High leisure and tourism propensities underpinned by high income and free time	High	Medium
Full nest	Children become key preoccupation. Leisure and tourism must meet children's requirements. Costs per person important	Medium	Low
Empty nest	Children have left home. Opportunities for leisure and tourism increase. Exotic destinations and meaning of life sought	High	Medium
Old age	May lack partner, may suffer from infirmity. Safer leisure and travel pursuits sought, package holidays popular	Low	High

continues to exert a big influence on people's lives and 98 per cent of households have television sets. The total hours of television viewing have changed very little over the last 10 years. However, there is a marked division between social classes in their viewing habits. By 1999 over half of households had access to a car and the extension of the motorway network has extended the distance that can be reached within 3 hours of home. Out-of-town shopping and browsing has become a key leisure pursuit. Visitor attractions have benefited from increased mobility, and some parts of the countryside are becoming overwhelmed by their urban visitors.

Culture refers to the dominant beliefs, values and attitudes of society, or a sub grouping in society. Changing beliefs, values and attitudes affect the way in which people perceive, demand and use leisure and tourism products, for example:

- The mass availability of visual and music media has led to a large upward revision of what is ordinary. This leads to an ever-desperate search for the extraordinary in leisure and tourism pursuits.
- Culture is organic. For example, materialism has replaced religion; feminism has made inroads into sexism; hedonism has become a dominant form of social behaviour. Leisure and tourism accommodate these changes with Sunday betting, women-only swimming sessions and sex tourism in Bangkok.
- The population is becoming less culturally homogeneous and more culturally fragmented. Subcultures have particular leisure and tourism demands.
- Advertising is promoting leisure and tourism fantasies.
- Crime is increasing, as is fear of crime.
- Women have become more significant in leisure and tourism provision and Exhibit 8.8 explores the attitudes and lifestyles of young, single employed women.

Exhibit 8.8   Women with attitude

The Centre for Micro-social Change at the University of Essex has used information from the British Household Panel Study to explore the attitudes and lifestyles of single women between the ages of 25 and 44 in professional and managerial occupations. Between 1966 and 1996 the percentage of women of working age in employment rose from 42.2 per cent to 67 per cent and women form a growing percentage of the rise in numbers of single-person households. These are forecast to rise by 3.4 million between 1996 and 2016. The Household Panel Study is based on a national sample of more than 5500 households. Findings include that single professional women aged 25–44.

- Lead active social lives. They regularly go to the cinema and theatre and maintain frequent contact with friends.
- Have a high propensity to engage in weekly active sports (66 per cent compared with less that 50 per cent of other women).
- Tend to be satisfied with their social lives (72 per cent to compared with only 50 per cent of other women.
- Are less concerned about the environment (50 per cent fewer express anxiety about the ozone layer than other women).
- Are less likely to own video recorders, dishwashers and microwave ovens.
- Are more likely to eat out rather than buy convenience food.
- Have greater concerns about health.
- Owns fewer PCs (only 16 per cent compared with 55 per cent of others).

Visiting Professor Richard Scase and researcher Jonathan Scales conclude: 'The number of single professional and managerial women aged 25–44 is rapidly increasing and their work patterns and lifestyles will have a growing impact on demands for leisure, retailing and housing. Their attitudes are likely to affect the nature of corporate cultures and political debate and the issues that concern them are very different from those that have preoccupied traditional feminism'.

Source: Research findings from The Centre for Micro-social Change at the University of Essex.

Review of key terms

- Environment scanning: monitoring of operating environment.
- Strategic drift: failure of business strategy to keep abreast of environment change.
- Operating environment: competitive and PEST environment.
- PEST: political, economic, socio-cultural and technical environment.
- Barriers to entry: factors making entry into industry difficult.
- Monopsonist: single buyer.
- Cross-subsidization: using profits from one division to subsidize prices in another division.
- Fibreoptics: high-capacity data transmission lines using optical fibre rather than copper wire.
- CRS: computerized reservation system.
- Multimedia: combination of media sources (e.g. video), computing and communications.
- Computer-intelligent building: building use monitored and controlled by computer (e.g. security, temperature, staff location and room use).
- Digitalization: transforming images and sound to digital code for ease of storage and transmission.
- Internet provider: company which provides Internet access to PC user.
- Broadband: wide bandwidth providing faster data transmission for the Internet (cf. narrowband).

- Political power: the ability to influence events.
- Scenario planning: developing plans to cope with different views of future.
- Crude birth rate: number of births per thousand population.
- Ageing population: average age of population increasing.

Data Questions

Task 8.1   Skywars

1995:   A 14-day advanced purchase excursion fare (APEX) return flight between London Heathrow and Glasgow costs £138. It is about the same distance as Los Angeles–San Francisco which costs only £51. That is not the worst comparison. Stanstead to Aberdeen is the same distance as Chicago to Kansas but at £192 costs 3 times as much. Why? Some of the difference lies in costs. It costs more to run an airline in the UK than in the USA. But the main difference must lie in the competitive environment. People's Express, the now-defunct US carrier, started the ball rolling with its $49 New York–Miami fare. Recently there has been a huge growth in imitators of this service on the busy short-haul routes such as Los Angeles–San Francisco and Washington–New York. They offer no frills but low fares. You might have to lug your own bags to the far side of the runway (cheap aircraft parking), pack your own sandwiches and fly a propeller museum piece, but you will not have to dig too deep into your pocket. Competition in Britain's domestic air travel market is much more limited. Since the collapse of Dan-Air in 1992 there are only three major players: BA, British Midland and Air UK. A major problem for potential entrants is the UK's crowded skies and airports. There are few slots available for competitors at London.

1999:   London to Glasgow from £68 return (British Midland and easyJet) London to Inverness from £68 return (easyJet). 'Frills included' boasts British Midland in a swipe at its rival easyJet. Suddenly the UK skies are criss-crossed with competing airlines – KLM UK, Ryanair, Debonair, BA, easyJet, Go, Virgin Express and British Midland. They are still airborne despite doubts that they could ever start up or that they would not last. But although passenger numbers are booming profits are not. The new entrants have mainly logged losses. Sir Michael Bishop, Managing Director of British Midland, predicts that not all the current airlines can survive. He points to cut-throat competition which has forced prices down to uneconomic levels, unsustainable losses being borne by some airlines and rising airport charges. He also notes that few of the budget airlines that started in the USA have survived bankruptcy or take-over. Several factors have helped the new airlines to gain a competitive advantage over their older-established competitors. For example, some of the new entrants managed to secure cheap use of secondary airports such as Stanstead, but these are now coming up for renegotiation, and slots at main airports remain heavily oversubscribed. Their cost-cutting 'no frills' have been undermined by the established carriers competing on price but maintaining frills. Sir Michael sums up the prospects saying: 'There will be some natural consolidation at some stage. The same thing has happened in the US, where there was a huge initial launch of low-cost airlines but then many disappeared. Five went bust last year.' He singled out Debonair as a likely victim.

1999:   Debonair goes out of business.

185

2003: The great Ryanair seat sale: Fly for just 1 penny plus taxes.
2004: The future holiday forum publishes its report on predications for the travel industry. These include that 'within two decades a long weekend in New York will cost just £50 and a week in Australia could be as little as £99'.

Source: The author from cuttings (1995, 1999, 2004).

Recap Questions

1 Analyse the changes in the competitive environment of UK air travel using Porter's five forces analysis.
2 Examine the possible responses of BA to new entrants under the following headings:
   (a) Price leadership strategies,
   (b) Differentiation strategies,
   (c) Withdrawal or diversification strategies,
   (d) Creation of switching costs.
3 How have new entrants managed to penetrate the entry barriers found in the airline business?
4 Evaluate the future the competitive environment of air travel.

Task 8.2   Internetting the market

1994: If you need to buy a book you will have to visit a bookshop or telephone one that does mail order.
1995: Amazon.com started the Internet market in book sales.
1997: Amazon becomes the third largest bookseller in the USA, as sales reach $148 million.
1998: WH Smith (UK) acquires for £9.4 million bookshop.co.uk, Europe's largest on-line retail site, selling more than 1.4 million book titles and 50 000 CDs, videos and computer games. This is seen by analysts as a defensive/offensive move against Amazon as well as a way to capture a growing market. In 1997 Internet sales in the UK were worth about £200 000, and are forecast to increase to £800 000 by 2000.
2002: In just 8 years Jeff Bezos has made Amazon the world's leading online sales operation – it is even showing a profit.
2004: WH Smith issued a severe profits warning. Beverley Hodson, the Managing Director of the retail business, is leaving immediately, after the alert on profits wiped almost 20 per cent off the company's stock market value.

Analysts say that the growth of on-line sales is not necessarily at the expense of high-street booksellers – but rather that it is generating extra sales. The reasons for this are several. First, on-line bookstores offer substantial discounts which can be as high as 40 per cent. Second, interactive screens entice potential purchasers with lists of bestsellers, recommendations tailored to personal interests, reviews of books extracts and interviews with the authors.

On-line selling costs are cheaper not only because of cheaper premises costs and lower staff costs but also because of minimal stock costs – Internet bookstores only take the stock when a customer has ordered a book. The publishing houses are already moving towards smaller print runs and this could lead eventually printing on demand which would further reduce costs of returns and holding stocks.

However despite all these benefits Internet bookstores are slow to move into profits: in 1997, Amazon reported losses of $28.6 million and only moved into profit in 2002.

Recap Questions

1 Account for the differences in fortunes between Amazon and WH Smith.
2 What are the benefits of on-line sales to consumers and retailers?
3 Conduct an opportunities and threats analysis on a named bookseller that operates high-street outlets.
4 Evaluate the impact of on-line sales elsewhere in the leisure and tourism sector.

Task 8.3   Grey expectations

Whilst global greening is still in its infancy, global greying gathers momentum.

Almost everywhere in the world, from Japan to Taiwan, in Singapore, western Europe and the USA, populations are getting older. In the western European Organization of Economic Co-operation and Development (OECD) countries, the population of over-65s will grow from a figure of 50 million in 1990 to over 70 million by 2030 – a rise of 40 per cent. With the number of people of working age falling there will be only roughly three workers per retiree compared with five at present. Within these countries, the effects of ageing will be felt most acutely in Germany, with ageing in the UK being more moderate. Since these predictions can be made with some certainty, we ought to look to the possible consequences: tax and benefit systems may need reviewing. Savings and investment patterns may alter. There will certainly be changes in demand. The market research group Mintel has identified 'third-age consumers' as a significant and distinctive market for leisure, holidays and health care. Another commentator, Ms Frankie Cadwell of a New York advertising firm, Cadwell Davies Partners, expresses surprise that European companies have been much slower to address the needs of this market than their US counterparts. Her firm specializes in selling to the over-50s.

Finally, older populations may be less innovative, more conservative, and have a less adaptive labour force. If this is so, there may be some shift in competitive advantage towards those newly industrializing economies where the average age is lower, such as China, Brazil and India.

Source: The author, from news cuttings.

Recap Questions

1 To what extent is it true that population trends can be predicted with certainty?
2 'Economists predict that demographic restructuring could alter patterns of consumption, production, employment, savings, investment and innovation'. Use these headings to predict how a named recreation, leisure or tourism organization might be affected by demographic change.
3 Why might ageing lead to a competitive disadvantage, and which countries are likely to be affected by this?

Multiple choice questions

1 Which of the following is not one of Porter's five competitive forces?

 (a) The power of suppliers.
 (b) The power of buyers.
 (c) The power of buyers.
 (d) The power of negotiators.

2 Which of the following does not represent a barrier to entry for new firms in an industry?

 (a) Perfect competition.
 (b) Natural monopoly conditions.
 (c) Economies of scale.
 (d) Capital requirements.

3 Which of the following is not true?

 (a) An ageing population can be caused when the birth rate exceeds the death rate.
 (b) Italy has an ageing population.
 (c) An ageing population tends to be more conservative and less risk-taking.
 (d) Ageing populations are typical in less economically developed countries.

4 Which of the following is not generally true of left-wing governments?

 (a) They favour minimum wage legislation.
 (b) They favour minimal state interference.
 (c) They wish to reduce inequality of income.
 (d) They wish to provide a comprehensive welfare state.

5 Which of the following statements is not true?

 (a) Technological advances tend to reduce an organization's long-run average cost curve.
 (b) Technological advances can bring opportunities and threats for leisure organizations.
 (c) Airport operators often have strong supplier power.
 (d) Horizontal integration can secure distribution channels.

Review questions

1 How does strategic drift occur?
2 Which sectors of the recreation, leisure and tourism industry are currently secure from new entrants?
3 Where is supplier power high in the leisure and tourism industry?
4 What are barriers to entry? Identify entry barriers for airlines and hotels.

5 What factors tend to create a high degree of competitive rivalry?

6 What effects might the 1998 Working Time Directive and the 1999 Minimum Wage Act have on the leisure and tourism sector?

7 Why is the population of the Italy ageing? What are the consequences of this for leisure and tourism organizations?

8 How are changes in lifestyles and attitudes affecting leisure and tourism?

9 Explain how video-conferencing makes use of multimedia technology.

10 Is home-based reservation an opportunity or a threat?

Web sites of interest

Leisure opportunities: daily news www.leisureopportunities.co.uk

Marriott International: http://www.marriott.com

Trump Hotels & Casinos Resorts Inc.: http://www.trump.com

Virgin Atlantic: http://www.bized.ac.uk/compfact/vaa/vaaindex.htm

Political parties around the world: http://www.psr.keele.ac.uk/parties.htm

Political parties around the world: http://www.agora.stm.it/politic/

The UK Labour Party: www.labour.org.uk

The UK Conservative Party: www.tory.org.uk

The UK Liberal Party: www.libparty.demon.co.uk

The economic environment

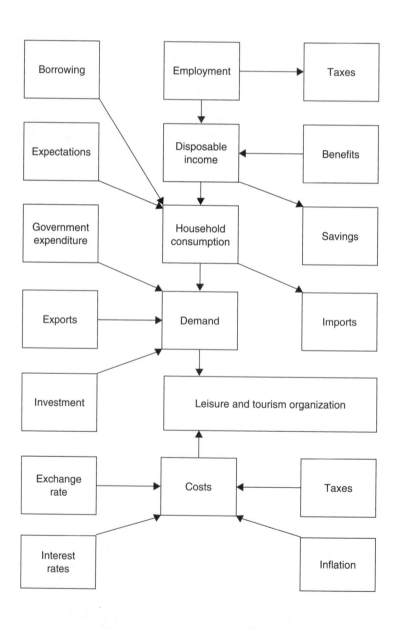

Objectives and learning outcomes

National economies are characterized by upswings and downswings. The UK, for example, witnessed the boom years of the mid-1980s – characterized by rising profits – as well as the profound recession of the early 1990s – characterized by rising bankruptcies. The period 1994–2004 saw the UK economy performing well witnessing an unusually stable period of modest economic growth. On the other hand the economy of China has demonstrated rapid economic growth in the decade 1994–2002, whilst the Japanese economy has languished in a prolonged recession.

Figure 9.1 charts the path of the UK economy over recent years. It is clearly important for organizations to monitor their economic environment carefully. Managers who read the rapid growth of the UK economy between points *A* and *B* as being normal and sustainable may well have instigated optimistic and expansionary strategic plans. These plans may have proved ruinous as the economy nose-dived between points *B* and *C*. This squeezed organizations from two directions as sales revenue fell, and increasing interest rates added to costs. Additionally the fact that the UK economy has delivered stable economic growth 1994–2004 is not a guarantee of benign economic conditions into the future.

Exhibit 9.1 illustrates the effects of changes in the economy on recreation, leisure and tourism attractions in the UK. This chapter considers the variables in the economy that affect leisure and tourism organizations and the causes of changes in these variables. It also peers tentatively into the future and summarizes the features of an opportunities and threats analysis.

By studying this chapter students will be able to:

- identify the key variables in the economy which affect leisure and tourism organizations;

- identify and utilize information sources;

- analyse the impact of changes in economic variables on leisure and tourism organizations;

- explain the interrelationship between key economic variables;

- understand and analyse the causes of change in the economic environment;

- understand and evaluate government economic policy and the significance of the budget;

- understand the global economic environment;

- utilize economic forecasts with due caution;

- conduct an opportunities and threats analysis.

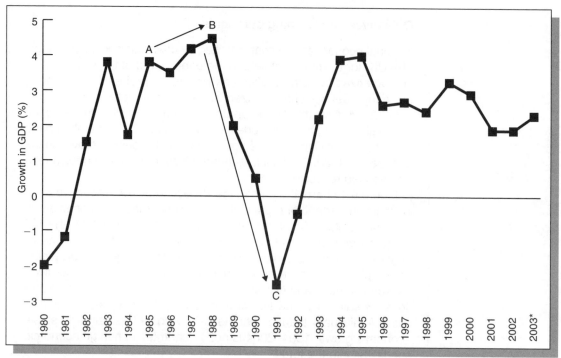

Figure 9.1 UK economic growth
Source: Office for National Statistics, Economic Trends.
*Estimate.

Exhibit 9.1   Leisure ups and downs

1991: The Tower of London and other leading attractions are suffering in the recession, the English Tourist Board reported. The tower was visited by 1.9 million people last year (1991), 16 per cent fewer than in 1990.

Source: *The Independent* (10 August 1992).

1991: Tussauds Group had a tough trading year. The Gulf War, and the recession affected visits to tourist attractions and the spending of those who did visit was less than 1990 levels. For the group as a whole, attendances were therefore lower than in the previous year, and profits down 44 per cent to £8 million.

Source: *Pearson PLC: Annual Report* (1991).

1993: Attendances, turnover and operating profits of the Tussauds Group reached new heights in 1993. Operating profits reached £14.1 million, an increase of 34 per cent. Attendances at Alton towers reached an all time high and there were improved attendances at Madame Tussauds in London. With continuing improvement in the UK economy, trading prospects for 1994 and beyond are encouraging.

Source: *Pearson Group Annual Report* (1993).

1999: In the UK, bookings for winter 1998–1999 are currently 6 per cent ahead of the previous year. To date the overall bookings taken in the UK for the next summer is 5 per cent ahead of the position achieved at the same time last year.

Source: *Airtours Annual Report* (1999).

2001: London continues to be one of the most popular cities for overseas tourists with 11.5 million visitors in 2001, although there was a drop of 13 per cent between 2000 and 2001, and a 15 per cent drop in overseas visitor spending. The weak global economy and the effect of the Foot and Mouth outbreak were partially responsible, but there was also the impact of the September 11 terrorist attacks.

Source: National Statistics web site: www.statistics.gov.uk

2002: Last year (2002) was a good year for the (UK) leisure industry, seeing the strongest growth – 4.8 per cent in real terms reaching £187 billion in value – since 1998. ... Household demand has been very strong in the UK despite slowing growth in the GDP and reduced share prices. In this sense the UK economy stands out from other industrial economies, except for the US and France.

Source: Gratton and Kokolakakis (2003).

2002–2007: Overall the (UK) leisure economy will grow by 15 per cent in real terms over the period 2002–07

Source: Gratton and Kokolakakis (2003).

What are the key variables?

The economic environment affects organizations in the leisure and tourism sector in two main ways. First changes in the economic environment can affect the demand for an organization's products and second changes may affect an organization's costs. Additionally background factors such as share and property prices may affect organizations. These three areas will be discussed in turn.

The economic environment and demand

The key macroeconomic factors affecting demand for recreation leisure and tourism industries are:

- household consumption,
- export and import demand,
- government expenditure,
- investment.

Plate 9
What economic factors
are keeping the tourists
at home?
Source: The author

Household consumption

Household consumption can be defined as the total expenditure on goods
and services for immediate consumption. Thus the level of household consumption is a key element in determining the demand for goods and services in the leisure and tourism sector. However, care needs to be taken in
interpreting household consumption statistics. Table 9.1 shows two series for
household consumption. One column shows household consumption at
current prices (sometimes referred to as 'money household consumption'),
whilst the bottom row shows household consumption at 2000, or constant
prices (sometimes referred to as 'real household consumption'). Notice that
the data for household consumption at current prices rises even through
the recession of the early 1990s. An organization basing its business planning on such data would draw false and overly optimistic conclusions
about the state of the economy. This is because household consumption at
current prices includes the effects of inflation on household consumption.
However, household consumption at constant prices has had the inflationary
element removed and is therefore a more useful guide.

Real household consumption = money household consumption
− inflation

It can be seen from Table 9.1 that household consumption at constant
prices rose strongly between 1987 and 1989 and then fell in 1991. This burst
of activity, followed by an abrupt halt, encouraged some organizations
to expand recklessly only to suffer difficulties when the recession started
to bite.

Table 9.1 UK Household final consumption expenditure (£ million)

Year	Constant 2000 prices	Current prices
1987	415 718	251 390
1988	447 123	283 965
1989	462 441	311 437
1990	466 093	337 646
1991	458 583	359 616
1992	460 894	379 758
1993	472 833	401 970
1994	486 600	422 397
1995	494 324	443 367
1996	512 918	474 311
1997	531 882	503 813
1998	552 186	536 933
1999	577 665	570 440
2000	603 349	603 349
2001	622 136	635 704
2002	644 441	666 877
2003*	667 579	690 821

Source: Adapted from National Statistics
web site: www.statistics.gov.uk
*Estimate.

To understand fully the movements in household consumption we need to consider its determinants. The main determinants of household consumption include:

- real household's disposable income,
- employment,
- benefits and taxes,
- borrowing and savings,
- expectations.

Real household's disposable income ● ● ●

The main determinant of consumers' expenditure is the amount of income earned. Figures for national income can be an important source here, but real household's disposable income provides a more useful guide. To understand real household's disposable income we need to consider the meaning of the terms 'real' and 'disposable'. First, we are generally more interested in real income rather than money income since the former has had the effects of inflation removed. Therefore:

Real income = money income − inflation

Table 9.2 UK real households disposable income, constant 2000 prices (£ million)

Year	£ million	Year	£ million
1987	436 399	1996	571 440
1988	460 195	1997	595 043
1989	481 799	1998	596 745
1990	498 632	1999	616 235
1991	508 686	2000	654 649
1992	522 915	2001	685 263
1993	537 310	2002	695 183
1994	545 269	2003*	715 444
1995	557 940		

Source: Adapted from National Statistics
web site: www.statistics.gov.uk
*Estimate.

Second, disposable income can be defined as the amount of income left after deduction of direct taxes (such as income tax and national insurance contributions), and the addition of state benefits (such as child benefit and unemployment benefit). In other words, it is the amount of income available for spending:

$$\text{Real household's disposable income} = \text{real household's income} - \text{taxes} + \text{benefits}$$

Table 9.2 records recent data for real households' disposable income.

Employment and wages • • •

The change in the income component of real household's income is determined by the level of employment and the amount of wages and salaries earned. As the level of employment in the economy grows, so generally does the level of income. Table 9.3 shows recent fluctuations in the level of UK unemployment. It can be seen that unemployment levels in 1987 and again in 1993 exceeded 10 per cent of the workforce – over 3 million people. Such high levels of unemployment depress levels of income and this in turn feeds into lower levels of household consumption and less sales. The level of unemployment has several effects on firms in the recreation, leisure and tourism sector. High unemployment has a detrimental effect on household spending and confidence. Ironically, it provides individuals with more leisure time, but with reduced spending power to enter leisure markets. The extent of membership and power of trade unions also affects wage rates.

Table 9.3 Unemployment rate: UK, aged 16 and over in (per cent)

Year	Per cent	Year	Per cent
1987	10.8	1996	8.3
1988	8.8	1997	7.2
1989	7.3	1998	6.2
1990	6.9	1999	6.1
1991	8.4	2000	5.6
1992	9.8	2001	4.9
1993	10.5	2002	5.2
1994	9.8	2003*	5.0
1995	8.8		

Source: Adapted from National Statistics web site: www.statistics.gov.uk
*Estimate.

Table 9.4 Income tax rates (in per cent), 2003

Brazil	20
China	5–45
Denmark	41–60
Hong Kong	15
The Netherlands	36–60
Russia	13
Saudi Arabia	2.5
UK	0–40
USA	0–38.6

Source: Adapted from www.worldwide-tax.com

Taxes and benefits

Changes in taxes and benefits can cause significant changes to the disposable element of disposable income. For example, deductions for income tax in the UK range for 25 per cent of 40 per cent of income. In Canada, income is subject to both federal (national) and provincial (local) tax. Table 9.4 illustrates differing rates of income tax from around the world ranging from 2.5 per cent in Saudi Arabia to 60 per cent in Denmark. On the other hand most countries also operate systems of benefits which can add to disposable income. These may include tax credits for low income earners, and credits for dependent children.

In addition to household disposable income the amount consumers actually spend depends on the following factors:

- borrowing, saving and interest rates;
- expectations.

Exhibit 9.2   UK consumer debt hits record high

A report released by Market analysts Datamonitor shows that the average unsecured debt of UK borrowers has risen by more than £1000 over the past five years to 2003. Unsecured borrowing (that is debt which is not secured against an asset such as property) is made using credit cards, store cards, overdrafts and personal loans currently averages £3383 per person. This represents a significant rise from the 1998 level of £2231. Borrowing on credit cards has grown at the quickest pace, and now stands at £1062 per person, more than double what it was in 1998.

A number of factors have stimulated the surge in consumer debt. Interest rates in 2003 were at their lowest level for 50 years, house prices continue to rise making households feel richer and the economy has enjoyed several years of stability.

Source: The author, from press cuttings (2003).

Borrowing, saving and interest rates • • •

Borrowing enables households to spend in excess of their current disposable income. The level of borrowing depends on several factors including the ease of obtaining credit, future income and interest rates. Many organizations offer in-house credit facilities in order to increase the demand for their products.

Interest rates have an important effect on household consumption. In general, lower interest rates tend to stimulate household consumption for two reasons. First, at lower interest rates borrowing becomes cheaper and thus more credit is credit taken out. At the same time households with mortgages find their monthly repayments falling thus leaving more money available for spending. Exhibit 9.2 illustrates the record level of debt held by UK households. Second, low interest rates make savings less attractive and savings may tend to fall. The level of savings is also affected by culture, habit, and income.

Table 9.5 illustrates recent changes in interest rates. It can be seen that in recent years interest rates peaked at 15 per cent 1989 and troughed at 3.5 per cent in 1993. The impact of these changes on household consumption can be traced in Table 9.1. The growth in household consumption slowed dramatically in 1990 and went into reverse in 1991, whilst some growth was recorded again from 1993. The term 'interest rates' can be misleading since there are many interest rates in the economy. The bank base rate which is quoted in Table 9.5 is the rate to which many other interest rates are referenced. Taking 1993 as an example, bank base rate averaged 5.5 per cent. Rates paid to savers in building society ordinary share accounts would be around 2 per cent. Mortgage rates would be around 8 per cent, whilst interest charges on credit cards would be about 23 per cent. A change in the bank base rate will trigger a change in the whole structure of interest rates. The reasons behind changes in interest rates are discussed later in this chapter.

Table 9.5 UK bank base rate

Year (Oct)	Interest rate (%)	Year (Oct)	Interest rate (%)
1987	9.50	1996	6.00
1988	12.00	1997	7.00
1989	15.00	1998	7.25
1990	14.00	1999	5.25
1991	10.50	2000	6.00
1992	8.00	2001	4.50
1993	6.00	2002	4.00
1994	5.75	2003	3.50
1995	6.75		

Source: Adapted from National Statistics
web site: www.statistics.gov.uk

Expectations • • •

Expectations (or business confidence) refers to the degree of optimism or pessimism with which consumers and business people view the future. Expectations have a profound effect on the economy because they tend to deliver self-fulfilling prophecies. When consumers feel optimistic about the economy they tend to spend more and they thus cause the economy to grow. Conversely, when they feel pessimistic about the economy they tend to spend less and thus they may prolong the recession that is causing their pessimism. Expectations tend to be influenced by recent experience, by the mass media, by asset prices (particularly property prices) and by the level of unemployment. Measuring expectations is often done by way of surveys, as illustrated in Exhibit 9.3.

Export and import demand

Not all of household consumption results in demand for the gods and services of domestic firms. Some household consumption is spent on imports. For the recreation, leisure and tourism sector this can be a significant amount. The demand for imports is affected by overseas costs, quality and uniqueness and the exchange rate. On the other hand some demand for the goods and services of domestic firms arises from overseas customers in the form of imports. The demand for exports is similarly affected by relative costs, quality and uniqueness, the exchange rate and the prosperity of overseas economies. Exhibit 9.4 illustrates a period of economic recession for the 'tiger economies' of Asia which has had impacts for example on tourist destinations that are dependent on Japanese tourists.

Thus uniqueness in terms of cultural heritage, nature, landscape or climate can be important in determining tourism demand to various countries. Equally low production costs and a favourable exchange rate mean that

---

Exhibit 9.3   Changing expectations

1994: The most pessimistic level of confidence since April 1990 was revealed by a Gallup survey conducted in March 1994. 42 per cent of those questioned felt that their financial position would deteriorate over the next year.

Source: The author, from Gallup data.

1998: The Dun & Bradstreet survey on business confidence questioned 1400 finance and managing directors in June 1998. It showed business confidence has hit its lowest level since the end of the last recession. Senior analyst Mr Philip Mellor said: 'As more firms expect further increases in interest rates, so gloom has spread from exporters into the domestic economy. For the first time in years the survey has shown a severe drop in confidence among the service, retail and wholesale sectors.'

Source: The author, from Dun & Bradstreet survey.

2003: The Confederation of British Industry today scaled issued downbeat forecasts for economic growth predicting that the economy will grow by only 1.8 per cent in 2003. The CBI chief economic adviser, Ian McCafferty. The CBI said 'We were expecting the route to recovery to be long and difficult but, even so, the first 6 months of the year have been disappointing. It is clearly going to be a long haul, and this means that UK growth will remain lacklustre for some time yet.'

Source: The author, from CBI survey.

2004: According to a survey by the Woolwich bank millions of people still believe that the housing boom will continue. The Woolwich found that 53 per cent of people expect house prices to increase significantly in 2004. Of that number, 34 per cent believe they will rise by up to 10 per cent, while the rest expect an increase of more than 10 per cent.

Source: The author, from Woolwich survey.

China, Thailand and Vietnam are significant suppliers of leisure goods such as PCs, hi-fi, cameras and sports equipment.

Government expenditure

Leisure and tourism organizations which are sensitive to changes in government expenditure are those which depend upon government for their income. Examples of these include arts organizations including museums, community sports organizations and national and local tourist marketing organizations. The level and detail of government expenditure tend to reflect two things. These are the state of government finance and the political party in power.

Exhibit 9.4 Prospects uncertain for global economy

While 1997 saw the global economy performing well across the continents, 1998 saw the world edge nearer to a global recession. Japan and the tiger economies of Asia, for years the envy of the world, finally saw their economies suffer major downturns.

The domino effect was started when Thailand devalued its currency in 1997 and, one by one, neighbouring countries and trading partners have dragged one another down. By 1998 Japan, the world's second largest economy, was in recession. Elsewhere, Russia has defaulted on its debts and Brazil suffered a major devaluation in its currency.

The effects of this on the leisure and tourism industry have been mixed. In the countries suffering from recession, domestic demand for leisure and tourism has diminished considerably as real disposable incomes have fallen. For some countries, devaluation has caused an increase in the inflow of tourists who seek better value for money. Leisure and tourism outside of these countries is affected mainly by the Japanese recession. Japan traditionally has been a high-spending country on tourism abroad. So destinations which have previously been dependent on visitors from Japan have been affected.

More serious consequences would result were the economic effects of economic problems in Asia, Russia and South America to cause a recession in Europe and the USA. The leisure and tourism industries would be early casualties of a global recession.

Source: The author (1999).

When government finances are in deficit its is often 'soft' areas of expenditure such as the arts that are cut in order to reduce public spending. This is because its is very difficult to reduce core areas of government spending such as education and social security. A change in government can also change the economic fortunes of leisure organizations that are dependent on government subsidy. Right wing governments generally attempt to reduce public spending, whilst left wing governments are more likely to support leisure organizations that bring benefits to the community. Exhibit 9.5 illustrates a package of government support for the visual arts that will benefit the Australian state of Tasmania.

Investment

Some organizations do not supply goods and services to consumers, but specialize in supplying capital goods to other firms. Thus the aircraft manufacturer Boeing, selling to airlines and tour operators, finds demand for its products is sensitive to the level of investment in the economy.

> **Exhibit 9.5   Visual Arts and Craft Strategy funding for Tasmania, Australia**
>
> The Australian Government Minister for the Arts and Sport (Senator Kemp) and the Minister for the Arts in Tasmania have announced funding for Tasmania through the Visual Arts and Craft Strategy. 'The Australian and Tasmanian Governments have worked together to increase the viability and vitality of Australia's contemporary visual arts and craft sector,' Senator Kemp said.
>
> The Visual Arts and Craft Strategy is a comprehensive major new 4-year investment by the Australian, State and Territory Governments of at least $39 million which is designed to strengthen and sustain Australia's visual arts and craft sector. Australian Government funding of $19.5 million over 4 years matched dollar-for-dollar by State and Territory Governments will increase funding for Australia's contemporary visual arts and craft sector by at least 33 per cent.
>
> Through the Strategy, Tasmania will receive a 4-year funding package totalling nearly $1.2 million. This will give an immediate funding increase of $184 000 to Tasmania's visual artists, craft practitioners, organizations and activities. New funding will be increased over current levels by more than $370 000 from 2005–06.
>
> *Source*: The author, adapted from press release (2003).

The economic environment and costs

The key macroeconomic factors affecting costs of recreation, leisure and tourism goods and services are:

- interest rates,
- inflation,
- the exchange rate,
- indirect taxes.

The effects of changes in interest rates have been discussed above with reference to household consumption. However, interest rates also affect firms' costs, particularly those with significant borrowings.

Inflation can be defined as a general rise in the level of prices in an economy. Leisure organizations operating in high inflation economies will face regular increases in their input prices – particularly labour and raw material costs.

The exchange rate is the price of the domestic currency in terms of foreign currencies. Where imports form a substantial component of a good or service, changes in the exchange rate can have an effect on production costs. A fall in the exchange rate of the US dollar against foreign currencies will make imports into the US more expensive. This would affect retailers of

---

Exhibit 9.6   UK Government announces new tax on air travel

This will be set at £5 for departures to anywhere within the UK and the European Union and £10 for departures to other destinations. The new duty will come into force next October (1994) and will raise some £330 million in a full year.

Source: Ministerial Budget speech to the UK House of Commons (1993).

---

recreation and leisure equipment and clothing much of which is imported from the Far East.

Indirect taxes are taxes paid indirectly to the government. They are paid first to a third party – generally a retailer. In the US, Sales Tax and in the European Community, Value Added Tax are each examples of indirect taxes. Any increase in indirect taxes will generally cause an increase in prices. Exhibit 9.6 records the introduction of a tax on air travel which was announced by the UK government in 1993 budget. There was considerable protest from the airline industry over this new tax. In particular they argued that, since surface transport is not subject to such a tax, it may cause a loss of passengers. This is particularly likely on routes such as London to Paris, where the rail service Eurostar offers a close substitute to air travel.

Economic cycles and government policy

Economic cycles

The economic environment is rarely stable. Rather, as indicated in Figure 9.1, economies are subject to economic cycles demonstrating upswings and downswings in economic activity. Sometimes the downswings are pro-longed causing deep recessions such as the great depression of the 1920s and the Japanese recession of the late 1990s. Equally the upswings may cause an economy to become overheated causing high or hyper-inflation and an unsustainable boom in imports. Figure 9.2 summarizes they key characteristics of upswings and downswings.

The economist John Maynard Keynes was important in bringing an understanding to the analysis of economic cycles. First, he analysed their causes. In particular he demonstrated the circular flow of income. This showed for example how a downswing could occur. If unemployment rose, households would have less income and their expenditure would fall. This would mean less demand for goods and services so firms would cut back production and employ less factors of production causing unemployment to rise further and the cycle to repeat in a downward direction.

Second, he argued that there is no reason that economies should be nat-urally stable in a virtuous state of growth or that full employment was the norm. Instead, he showed how economies might get stuck in a recession with persistent and high levels of unemployment. Third, he showed how

	Upswing/boom	Downswing/recession
Unemployment	Falling	Rising
Profits	Rising	Falling
Household spending	Rising	Falling
Consumer borrowing	Rising	Falling
Imports	Rising	Falling
Inflation	Rising	Falling
Expectations	Optimistic	Pessimistic
Economic growth	High	Low/negative
Can lead to ...	Hyper-inflation	Recession

Figure 9.2
Characteristic of
economic cycles

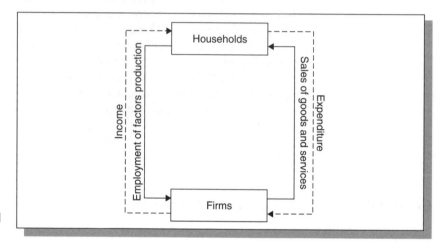

Figure 9.3
The circular flow of national
income and expenditure

governments could intervene in the economy with a view of making economic cycles less pronounced and attempting to generate full employment.

Much of the period after 1940 has been characterized by government attempts to manage the macroeconomy. Crudely speaking in Keynesian terms the government would attempt to stimulate the economy to offset a slump and to cool-down the economy to counter a boom. It would do this by adjusting its own spending and attempting to influence household spending. However, Keynesian policies were criticized in the 1970s with the onset of stagflation (high inflation and high unemployment). Opponents of Keynesianism argued against government intervention arguing instead that only a return to free markets (less trade union power, lower taxes, more competition and less state ownership) could deliver economic growth without inflation.

Government economic policy

It is impossible to understand changes in the external economic environment without consideration of the government's role in the economy. This in turn can be understood in terms of aims and policies.

The following aims are followed by most governments:

- low inflation,
- low unemployment,
- balance between government spending and income over the medium term (balanced budget),
- balance between overseas earnings and expenditure (balanced trade),
- economic growth.

However, different governments have different priorities among these objectives. Right wing (Conservative/Republican) governments, for example put control of inflation and a balanced budget at the top of the list. Left wing (Labour, Liberal and Democrat) governments generally have full employment as their top priority. It must also be recognized that these aims are sometimes conflicting (in particular full employment often goes hand in hand with higher inflation. Also, as elections occur, policy aims are often distorted towards short-term reductions in taxation.

Economic policy refers to a set of measures designed to affect the economy. Classic Keynesian policies can be divided into:

- *Fiscal policy*: This uses changes in the level of taxation or government spending to influence the economy.
- *Monetary policy*: This uses changes in interest rates, and thus the cost of borrowing, to influence the economy.

A Keynesian recipe for managing a recession would utilize each of these. Fiscal policy would be expansionary with a reduction in taxes (to stimulate household expenditure) and an increase in government spending. Monetary policy would reduce interest rates to stimulate spending. However, an increase in spending and a reduction in taxes meant that the government budget would fall into deficit which could cause other economic problems – particularly inflation.

UK economic environment and government policy 1985 – present

An analysis of the UK economic environment over the past two decades gives a useful insight into the cyclical nature of the economy showing changes in key economic indicators as well as government tactics to manage the economy.

Table 9.6 shows changes in the main indicators for the UK economy since 1985, and four distinct phases can be identified.

1985–1988: Boom ● ● ●

It can be seen that the UK economy grew strongly in the period 1985–88, and unemployment which was at a high level of over 3 million fell. This was despite the fact that monetary policy was generally quite tight during

Table 9.6 The UK economy: selected indicators

	1985	1986	1987	1988	1989	1990	1991	1992	1993	1994	1995	1996	1997	1998	1999	2000	2001	2002
Growth (percentage change)	3.8	3.6	4.4	4.5	1.9	0.6	−2.5	−0.5	2.0	3.9	4.0	2.6	2.7	2.7	3.8	2.3	1.3	2.4
Inflation (percentage change)	6.1	3.4	4.1	4.9	7.8	9.5	5.9	3.9	1.9	2.5	3.5	2.4	3.1	3.4	1.5	3.0	1.8	1.7
Current balance (£ billion)	−0.6	−3.6	−7.5	−19.8	−26.3	−22.2	−10.7	−13.0	−11.9	−6.7	−9.0	−7.0	−0.9	−3.7	−20.9	−19.5	−18.0	−19.0
Unemployment (million)	3.2	3.2	2.9	2.4	1.8	1.6	2.2	2.7	2.8	2.5	2.3	2.1	2.0	1.8	1.8	1.6	1.4	1.5
Rate of interest (%)	15	13	11	13	15	14	10.5	7.0	5.4	6.25	6.5	6.0	7.25	6.2	6.0	5.8	4.0	3.9
Public sector net cash requirement (£ billion)	7.4	2.4	−1	−12	−9	−2	13	37	46	39	35	25	12	−7	−15	−19	−16	6
£/$	1.3	1.5	1.6	1.8	1.6	1.8	1.8	1.8	1.5	1.5	1.6	1.6	1.6	1.6	1.6	1.5	1.4	1.5
£/Euro	1.7	1.5	1.4	1.5	1.5	1.4	1.4	1.3	1.2	1.3	1.2	1.2	1.4	1.5	1.5	1.6	1.6	1.6

Note: 1 Rate of interest: 3-month interbank.
Sources: Adapted from Office for National Statistics, *Economic Trends* and *Barclays Bank Review.*

this period. The purpose of tight monetary policy and high interest rates was to suppress inflation. The rationale behind this policy was first that high interest rates reduced consumer demand by making credit expensive, and second that import prices were kept low as high interest rates stimulated the demand for sterling and kept the exchange rate high. However, the government reduced interest rates in 1987 and also relaxed fiscal policy. The 1987 budget cut the basic rate of income tax to 27 per cent and the 1988 budget made a further cut in income tax to 25 per cent and scrapped higher rates of income tax from 60 to 40 per cent. The result of this loosening of monetary and fiscal policy was that economic growth became unsustainable. By 1989 inflation had risen rapidly to nearly 8 per cent, and the UK's overseas trading account showed a deficit of £26 billion.

1989–1992: Bust ● ● ●

The rapid deterioration in inflation and foreign currency earnings meant that the government had to apply the brakes to the economy. Monetary policy was designated for this task, and interest rates were progressively increased to 15 per cent in 1989. The government used the famous phrase, 'if it's not hurting it's not working' to explain the policy. What this meant was that interest rates were going to be used by the government to slow down household consumption – mainly by making credit expensive – and that rates would continue to rise until household consumption was curbed.

Eventually the government's policy did work, but perhaps too successfully, since the economy slowed down and went into reverse, economic growth being a negative figure for both 1991 and 1992. As the recession took hold, unemployment rose quickly to reach 2.8 million by 1993. During this period government policy got into a mess. The recession, and the consequent rise in unemployment, meant less tax receipts for the government and more spending on state benefits. Thus the public sector net cash requirement increased sharply and the government had to borrow £37 billion in 1992. The high government borrowing meant that it was difficult to stimulate the economy by reducing taxes. At the same time, the government had taken sterling (£) into the exchange rate mechanism (ERM) of the European monetary system (EMS). Monetary policy was used to maintain sterling's agreed rate of exchange against European currencies. High interest rates were used to make sterling an attractive currency and thus maintain its value. Thus the recession was prolonged by high interest rates, and tax cuts could not be used to stimulate consumer spending because of high government borrowing.

1992–1994: a lucky escape ● ● ●

Despite all the government's efforts (interest rates were raised from 10 to 15 per cent in one day), sterling was forced to leave the ERM in September 1992. This enabled the government to relax its monetary policy and interest rates were lowered in a series of moves from 10.5 per cent in 1991 to 7 per cent in 1992. This allowed the economy to recover, led by a rise in household consumption. However, government borrowing was still high, reflecting the effects of the recession in reducing government tax income and increasing benefit payments and in 1993 the government had to borrow £46 billion. The budgets of 1993 and 1994 thus contained a series of measures to increase taxes to reduce government borrowing. They also maintained tight control on government expenditure.

1994–2005: sustainable growth? • • •

The period between 1994 and 2005 has been a period of modest economic growth and stability in the British economy. Unusually there have been no significant crises in any of the main economic indicators. The economy has entered a period of low inflation. The economic policy of the incoming Labour government in 1997 was to keep to existing public spending plans and to set up an independent monetary policy committee of the Bank of England whose task is to use interest rates to keep inflation at 2.5 per cent. This led to rises in interest rates in 1997 and 1998. The 1998 rises coincided with worries about a world recession and caused alarm amongst some policy analysts. But rates were reduced rapidly again in 1999 as inflation steadied. So as this text went to press in Spring 2004, the economic picture was one of:

- low inflation,
- falling unemployment,
- modest economic growth,
- low interest rates,
- modest government budget deficit.

The future

An eminent professor of economics, the Lord Maurice Peston of Mile End, cautioned against blind faith in economic forecasting, suggesting that random typing of a monkey at a keyboard would result in equally useful forecasts as those produced by complex mathematical models. However, economic forecasts are an essential part of business planning, but must be used with extreme caution, and the assumptions upon which they are made must be constantly monitored. Many forecasts now include a pessimistic outlook, an optimistic outlook and a middle range forecast.

Opportunities and threats analysis

An opportunities and threats analysis examines an organization's operating environment. The operating environment can be audited using the framework established in this and the previous chapter and this is illustrated in Table 9.7.

Once the key opportunities and threats have been established for an organization, its strategic plan can be updated to show how opportunities can be exploited and threats can be countered.

Table 9.7 Opportunities and threats analysis

Environment	Opportunities	Threats
Competitive		
Threat of entrants		
Power of buyers		
Power of suppliers		
Threat of substitutes		
Competitive rivalry		
PEST		
Political		
Economic		
Sociocultural		
Technological		

Review of key terms

- Real household consumption: money household consumption − inflation.
- Disposable income: income − direct taxes + government benefits.
- Recession: two consecutive quarters of falling output.
- Public sector net cash requirement: government spending − taxes.
- Gross domestic product (GDP): total value of output of an economy in a year.
- Economic cycle: up and down movement of economic activity.
- Fiscal policy: use of tax and government spending levels to influence the economy.
- Monetary policy: use of interest rates to influence the economy.

Data Questions

Task 9.1   Prospects for the US Economy: 2004 and beyond

The US recovery gained considerable momentum in late 2003. Real GDP growth reached over 5 per cent in the 3 months to September 2003. It looks as though record low interest rates, a number of tax-cut programmes and a post-Iraq war improvement in business and consumer confidence have made their mark on the US economy. The upturn in economic activity has primarily been driven by stronger consumer spending. Here, low interest rates and rising house prices have led to unprecedented levels of refinancing activity and equity withdrawal in the housing sector. Many households also received tax rebate cheques in the summer of 2003 and monetary and fiscal policy look set to support domestic demand in the short term.

Full-year economic growth is likely to be around 2.7 per cent for 2003 rising to 3.7 per cent in 2004. Rising employment and relatively loose monetary and fiscal policy are likely to support a growth in disposable income growth and spending. Export growth should also increase in line with the recovery in global demand and a weaker dollar, but a strong demand for imports of consumer and capital goods imports means that the contribution to growth from net trade will turn increasingly negative from 2004 on.

Loose monetary and fiscal policy should continue to support consumer spending in the short term. The US Federal Reserve Bank has indicated that interest rates will remain low for the 'foreseeable future'. Interest rates are unlikely to rise until the middle of next 2004 and even then the increases will only be gradual. Lower income tax rates and more rebate cheques – the next batch are due in spring 2004 – will also help to support consumer spending and there has been a small improvement in employment. Recent trends in business investment have also been encouraging.

In terms of sustainability, 3 years low growth, successive tax-cut programmes and higher defence spending have resulted in the sharpest deterioration in the budget position in 30 years. The Office of Management and Budget (OMB) forecast that the federal budget deficit will reach 4.2 per cent of GDP this year. In 2000 the government ran a healthy budget surplus and if state budgets are included the overall figure would probably be closer to 6.0 per cent. 'It unrealistic to expect any corrective action in a pre-election year. Presidential elections are due in November 2004 and George W Bush will be keen to avoid the same fate as his father, who failed to secure a second term in office having 'won the war, but lost the economy' according to Royal Bank of Scotland economists.

Export growth is likely to improve only slowly despite a weaker dollar, as the global recovery will take time to build. However, inflationary pressures remain subdued. Consumer price inflation declined to an annual rate of 2.2 per cent in August from 2.6 per cent at the beginning of the year. Core inflation, which excludes food and energy prices, has eased even further, falling to 1.3 per cent from 1.9 per cent over the same period. It is likely that the Fed will leave interest rates as they are at 1.0 per cent, until the middle of next 2004, despite growing signs of recovery.

Source: Adapted from Royal Bank of Scotland US Quarterly Update October 2003: www.rbs.co.uk

Recap Questions

1 Explain the significance of the term 'loose monetary and fiscal policy'.
2 What are the main factors causing an improvement in the growth of the US economy towards 2004?
3 Why may the growth in the US economy not be sustainable?
4 What is 'real GDP growth'?
5 Nike imports most of its footwear from overseas, particularly the Far East and sells to the domestic US, market and overseas markets. What are the implications of the above forecast for Nike's business prospects in 2004?
6 What are the arguments for and against increasing interest rates and raising taxes? How likely are either of these possibilities?
7 What is the current state of the US economy? Explain any changes from those forecast.

Task 9.2 The UK recession 1990–92

A widely used definition of a recession, adopted in this article, is that of 'two or more consecutive quarters of falling output'. The latest recession was spread over seven quarters. Recessions can be caused by many different factors. The 1990–92 recession in the UK followed a period of unsustainably fast growth during the late 1980s. The anatomy of the 1990–92 recession was as follows: manufacturing output fell by 7.5 per cent and output in the services sector fell by 2 per cent. The services sector includes retailing and wholesaling, hotels and catering transport and communications, and business and financial services. The services sector amounted to over 60 per cent of GDP in 1990, whereas manufacturing only accounted for about 25 per cent, so its impact on total GDP is significant. Consumers' expenditure fell steeply in the 1990–92 recession. Households built up debt rapidly during the boom years of the late 1980s; this led to a sharp retrenchment in their spending in 1990 and 1991 as they acted to reduce their debt in the face of high interest rates. The initial impetus to recovery came mainly from consumer spending and exports. The substantial cut in interest rates over the past 3 years, and strong growth in real personal disposable income, boosted personal sector spending power. By the third quarter of 1993 most of the fall in consumer spending during the recession had been reversed. As the recovery becomes more firmly established, businesses are likely to increase their spending as they become more confident that the pick-up in demand is sustained. The improvement in company finances and a modest increase in capacity utilization will also encourage investment in new and replacement stocks. These developments will help to broaden the recovery and strengthen growth.

Source: Adapted from HM Treasury: *Economic Briefing* (February 1994).

Recap Questions

1 What evidence is there to support the assertion of 'unsustainably fast growth during the late 1980s'?
2 Why did 'unsustainably fast growth during the late 1980s' lead to a recession?
3 'The initial impetus to recovery came mainly from consumer spending …' Explain this statement by reference to the determinants of consumer spending.
4 'As the recovery becomes more firmly established, businesses are likely to increase their spending … and a modest increase in capacity utilization will also encourage investment in new and replacement stocks'. Explain which industries in the leisure and tourism sector are likely to benefit from this and what other factors are likely to encourage investment.

Task 9.3   Scenario planning

Organizations increasingly use the method of scenario planning to anticipate changes in the external environment. This enables them to plan considered responses.

Recap Questions

1 Choose two firms in the leisure and tourism sector and analyse how they might be affected by the following scenarios:
   (a) A rise in interest rates.
   (b) A fall in unemployment.
   (c) A fall in the exchange rate.
   (d) A rise in inflation.
2 Which two of these represent the most likely scenario for the next 2 years? Explain your reasoning.

Multiple choice

1 **Which of the following is unlikely to cause a fall in household consumption?**

   (a) A rise in unemployment.
   (b) An increase in interest rates.
   (c) Pessimistic expectations about the economy.
   (d) A fall in income tax.

2 **Which of the following is true of real household's disposable income?**

   (a) It equals real household's income − direct taxes + benefits.
   (b) It equals real household's income − benefits + direct taxes.
   (c) It is directly determined by the level of real exports.
   (d) It equals real households income − borrowing + savings.

3 **Generally an increase in interest rates will**

   (a) Reduce savings.
   (b) Increase consumption.
   (c) Decrease consumption.
   (d) Reduce an organization's costs.

4 **Which of the following is unlikely during an economic boom or upswing?**

   (a) Unemployment is falling.
   (b) Household consumption is rising.
   (c) Imports are falling.
   (d) Expectations are optimistic.

5 **Which of the following is false?**

   (a) Fiscal policy involves changes to interest rates.
   (b) Real income: money income – inflation.
   (c) Keynesian policy seeks to stimulate the economy during an downswing.
   (d) Public sector net cash requirement will rise if taxes fall and government spending rises.

Review questions

1 Households' consumption at current prices rises from £100 billion in year 1 to £110 billion in year 2. Over the same period inflation is 10 per cent. What is the level of households' consumption at constant (year 1) prices in year 2?
2 What is the definition and what are the characteristics of a recession?
3 What is the definition and what are the characteristics of a recovery?
4 Distinguish between fiscal and monetary policy.
5 What type of fiscal and monetary policy could be used to stimulate the economy in a recession?
6 What is the relationship between public sector net cash requirement, taxation and government revenue?

7 What is the present outlook for the UK economy?
8 Explain the significance of the following to a named leisure or tourism sector organization:
  (a) Interest rates.
  (b) Exchange rates.
  (c) Real disposable income.
  (d) Expectations.

Web sites of interest

Economic model of the economy www.bized.ac.uk
USA: statistics http://www.stat.usa.gov/
Global economic outlook www.merrilllynch.com
Organization for Economic Development and Cooperation: statistics and commentary www.oecd.org
European Union: statistics http://europa.eu.int
Australian Bureau of statistics http://www.abs.gov.au
Brazil: statistics http://ibge.gov.br
Canada: statistics http://www.statcan.ca
New Zealand: statistics http://www.stats.govt.nz/statsweb.nsf
Office for National Statistics http://www.statistics.gov.uk

Part Five

Investment

Investment in the private sector

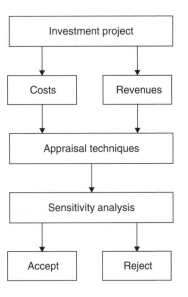

Objectives and learning outcomes

With hindsight it is not difficult to analyse the factors that have made some investment projects in the recreation, leisure and tourism sector such successes and others such dismal failures. The failures include projects (The Millennium Dome, London), transport systems (United Airlines) and electronic games (Sega Saturn). The successes include projects as diverse as films (*Lord of the Rings*), visitor attractions (Port Aventura, Spain), and electronic games (Sony PlayStation).

However, at the planning stage, it is much more difficult to forecast the success of investments, largely because of the uncertainty surrounding the future. This chapter seeks to define the meaning of investment, consider how potential investment projects are appraised and stress the shortcomings of quantitative techniques.

By studying this chapter students will be able to:

- define and distinguish between different types of investment;

- analyse the factors which affect an investment decision;

- utilize techniques for investment appraisal;

- understand the uncertainty surrounding investment appraisal;

- analyse the effects of investment on the economy;

- evaluate government policy with regard to investment.

Definition and examples

In general usage people use the term 'investment' to include bank and building society deposits and the purchase of stocks and shares. Economists are more specific in their use of the term. Investment may be defined as expenditure on capital goods and working capital. Capital goods can be contrasted with consumer goods. The latter are produced because of the direct satisfaction they yield (e.g. food, CDs and clothes), whilst the former are produced because they improve efficiency of production.

Fixed capital goods therefore consist of buildings, plant and machinery, and in the leisure and tourism sector examples include hotel buildings, computer reservation and booking systems, aircraft, and golf-ball making machinery. The total expenditure on such items is recorded as 'gross domestic fixed capital formation' in government statistics.

Working capital consists of stocks of raw materials, semi-manufactured goods and manufactured goods which have not yet been sold. Manufacturers monitor stocks of unsold products closely and these tend to be the key signals in a market economy to reduce or increase production. Working capital is an essential part of production, although 'just-in-time' production techniques have reduced the need for large stocks of raw materials and

Table 10.1 UK Gross Fixed Capital Formation £ million (at constant 2000 prices)

Year	£ million	Year	£ million
1987	103 137	1995	120 389
1988	118 455	1996	127 238
1989	125 542	1997	135 876
1990	122 326	1998	153 148
1991	112 250	1999	155 576
1992	111 273	2000	161 210
1993	111 613	2001	167 032
1994	116 814	2002	170 004

Source: Adapted from National Statistics web site: www.statistics.gov.uk

components to be held in factories. Expenditure on these items is recorded in government statistics as 'increase in stocks and work in progress'.

Table 10.1 shows recent changes in gross domestic fixed capital formation. This refers to the total amount of investment in new capital goods. The term 'gross' means that it covers all capital investment including the replacement of worn-out machines. The term 'net' would cover only investment over and above the replacement of worn-out machines.

$$\text{Net investment} = \text{gross investment} - \text{depreciation}$$

Table 10.1 shows a considerable fall in investment from 1990 to 1993. Some important factors affecting the level of investment include:

- households' consumption,
- expectations,
- amount of spare capacity,
- interest rates.

It is therefore changes in the above factors that should be examined for an explanation of the fall in investment evident from Table 10.1 in 1990. In fact, all four factors contributed to the fall in investment. High interest rates had the double effect of reducing households' consumption and increasing the cost of borrowing for investment projects. The fall in households' consumption meant that suppliers were left with spare capacity in the form of empty planes, unused accommodation and idle machinery and thus there was little need for additional or replacement investment. Finally, as the recession deepened, people's expectations became more pessimistic and investment depends on optimistic expectations about future levels of income and expenditure.

It should be noted that lower interest rates will not necessarily, single-handedly, stimulate investment demand in a recession since there may already be spare capacity in the organization and expectations may remain pessimistic. Thus there was no immediate recovery of investment in 1992 when interest rates fell.

Investment can also be divided into gross investment and net investment. Gross investment includes all investment, including that which is for replacement of worn-out machinery, whilst net investment only includes investment that adds to a country's capital stock.

Factors affecting investment

Investment in the private sector is undertaken to increase profitability. Since we assume that the motive of private sector organizations is the maximization of profits, such organizations will seek to invest in those projects which yield the highest return. Investment projects will incur planning, construction and running costs and yield revenue when in operation. Thus the profitability of an investment project can be analysed by investigating its costs and revenue.

Exhibit 10.1 illustrates some of the barriers to tourism investment in Australia identified in the 2003 government White Paper on tourism strategy where low rates of return, cyclical markets and government red tape are seen as key obstacles to increasing investment in this sector.

Cost of investment

The main costs of an investment will be:

- planning costs,
- costs of capital goods,
- cost of financing investment,
- running costs of the investment.

Exhibit 10.1   Barriers to tourism investment in Australia

'Attracting investment into tourism is impeded by a number of factors, including:

- a history of low rates of return amongst some segments of the tourism industry
- lack of basic information to help potential investors determine rates of return on investment
- the inherent cyclical and/or seasonal nature of tourism which makes it difficult to meet consistent yield expectations, and
- the complexities of dealing with multi-level government project approval processes.'

Source: Commonwealth of Australia (2003).

Planning costs • • •

The planning costs of an investment include consultancy costs for technical feasibility, market research, competitor scanning, financial appraisal and overall project planning. For large-scale projects, planning costs can be considerable and add to the overall project timetable. The British Airports Authority (BAA) has been planning a substantial investment in a new passenger terminal – terminal 5 – at London Heathrow Airport (Plate 10). Table 10.2 shows the original timetable for the project as envisaged in 1992. It can be seen that the planning, consultation and enquiry phase represents an equivalent 5-year period to the construction phase, doubling the project timetable to 10 years. In the event this timetable underestimated the planning stages of the project and the UK government did not give the go ahead until 2001 – 4 years later than expected. This added significantly to the costs of the project which are discussed in Exhibit 10.2.

Plate 10
Terminal 5 at Heathrow
Airport, London
Source: By kind
permission of British
Airports Authority

Table 10.2   Terminal 5 timetable

Year	Projected stage
1992	Local consultations
1992	Submission of planning application
1994	Start of public planning inquiry
1995	End of public planning inquiry
1997	Government decision expected
	Subject to planning approval being granted
1997	Start of construction
2001	Completion of phase 1 construction
2002	Opening of phase 1
2016	Terminal reaches maximum capacity

Source: BAA (1992).

Exhibit 10.2   High costs of terminal failure

1999: If things had gone according to plan, BAA's Terminal 5 (T5) would by now be a busy construction site of cranes, half-completed buildings, and road links. The fact that the site is still occupied by the Perry Oaks Sludge Works demonstrates how far the project has slipped behind schedule. The year 2001 was to have seen the completion of phase 1 of the project, but it will now be the year when the government gives its final decision on whether the project is allowed to go ahead. This will push back the opening of phase 1 from 2002 to 2006, if the project is allowed. The main delay to the project has been the public enquiry which in the event has taken 3 years to hear the evidence of the BAA, local authorities, environmental campaigners and other interest groups. The overall project has an estimated cost of Euros 2.6 billion. But the delays to the project mean that the planning and preparation costs, which have to be paid even if the project is eventually rejected, have now reached Euros 360 million. These costs have been needed to pay for legal teams at the public enquiry, design costs of the building and the cost of land purchase.

2001: On 20 November 2001, the Government announced its decision to approve the building of Heathrow's Terminal 5 after a planning process which has cost nearly $120 million over 14 years. The cost of this process has been met mostly by BAA and British Airways, the two main proponents of the Terminal's development. The new terminal is expected to be completed in 2007 and project itself will cost around $3 billion.

Source: The author, from press reports and briefings (1999, 2004).

Costs of capital goods • • •

The capital costs of an investment are the costs of buildings, plant and machinery. In some cases these are known costs, since there is a market in commonly purchased capital goods such as computer systems, vehicles and standard buildings. For more complex investments capital costs can only be estimated in the planning stage and for large construction projects, estimates of costs are notoriously unreliable. The original estimate for building and equipping the Channel Tunnel was £5 billion but by 1993 the figure had been revised to £10 billion. Such escalations in costs are typical of large construction projects. In the case of the Channel Tunnel, factors such as price increases in materials, increased wages, unforeseen technical difficulties in boring the tunnel, specification changes to improve safety, and legal disputes over costs between Eurotunnel and the construction company Trans-Manche Link (TML) have all added to the increased costs.

Cost of financing investment • • •

Finance for investment projects may be found internally out of a company's profits, or externally from the capital markets, for example, through banks or share issues.

External funding by loans carries costs in terms of interest rates that have to be paid for the duration of a loan. These interest rates may be fixed or variable. External funding by share issue incurs issue costs but the costs of funding (i.e. the dividend payments to shareholders) are then tied into future profits.

It might appear that internally generated funds do not carry any special costs, since a company does not have to pay interest on its own funds. However, there is an opportunity cost of using internal funds. That is the cost in terms of other uses to which the funds could have been put. A company could put funds on deposit in the money markets and gain interest on such deposits. Thus, even where internal funds are used for investment, a notional interest rate will be used to represent their opportunity cost. In general, higher interest rates will act as a disincentive to investment.

Running costs of the investment • • •

The running costs of an investment will include all the other costs of operating the project. These include labour costs, maintenance costs and raw material costs. New technology which reduces running and production costs can be an important cause of investment.

Revenue from investment

Total revenue from sales resulting from an investment project can be calculated by multiplying the selling price by the quantity sold and thus the main factors affecting the revenue obtained from an investment are:

- price of output,
- quantity of output sold,
- other factors.

Price of output • • •

The price of the output of an investment project will largely depend on demand and the competition in the market under consideration. This is discussed fully in Chapter 6, and in general the less competition, the more power a supplier will have to set price. Where a monopoly or near-monopoly exists, price can be producer determined (but quantity sold will reflect demand). However, potential competitors will move quickly to produce near substitutes where possible, particularly if a premium price is being charged. Where a few producers exist in a market (oligopoly or monopolistic competition), the impact of a new entrant will change the actions of those already in the market and thus lead to unpredictability. In a perfectly competitive market prices will be driven down to reflect the lowest average costs in the industry. Thus, although a company may have market intelligence about current prices in the market where its investment is to take place, any estimate of prices in future years is likely to be very uncertain. Channel Tunnel prices, for example, have changed considerably between the planning stage and the present. This reflects the changing marketing strategies of competing ferry and airline companies.

Quantity of output sold ● ● ●

Quantity sold will be closely related to price charged. However, it will also be related to factors including consumers' income, competitive prices and advertising. Figure 10.1 shows forecasts of passenger demand for airports in the south-east of England. These were part of the feasibility study for London Heathrow's Terminal 5. Clearly there are a range of factors, for example environmental pressures, taxes, fuel costs, and other unforeseen shocks which might cause the forecasts to be wrong.

The Tourism Forecasting Council (1998) has developed the Tourist Accommodation Regional Demand, Investment and Supply (TARDIS) model. This is a tool to measure the interaction between the demand for

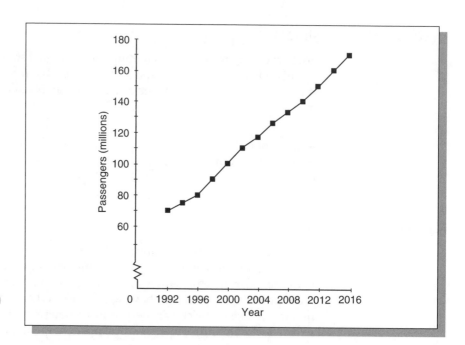

Figure 10.1
Passenger demand forecasts for airports in the South-east
Source: BAA

and the supply of tourist accommodation to help determine the viability of proposed investment.

Other factors • • •

Government policy may affect the revenue that derives from an investment project in several ways. First, government taxation policy may affect prices (sales taxes), or spending power (income tax) or profits (corporation tax). Second, government legislation may affect the demand for goods, and finally monopolies and mergers legislation may have an impact upon prices that can be charged.

Expectations play a key part in investment decisions. Expectations reflect views about how successful the economy will be in future years. Where investors have a pessimistic view about the future economy they will generally defer investment decisions.

Property development is a prominent feature of much leisure and tourism investment. Whilst rental income is a part of the anticipated revenue from such developments, capital appreciation can also be an important factor. Thus, such developments are often sensitive to expectations about future prices of property.

Above all, the factors surrounding an investment decision are subject to a great deal of uncertainty. Few of the factors have known values. Current interest rates are known, and where an investment obtains funds at fixed rates, this provides a predictable element. However, where funds are obtained at variable interest rates, considerable uncertainty will exist. Similar uncertainty surrounds the final costs of complex capital projects, price of output and demand for the final good or service. These are all subject to changes in the competitive and political, economic, socio-cultural and technological (CPEST) environments.

Knowles and Egan (2000) review the impact of the combined effects of global recession and the terrorist attacks of 11 September 2001 on the international hotel industry. They argue that those hotel companies heavily dependant on the US market, particularly four- and five-star properties located in the major gateway cities, will see significant falls. First, in revenue per available room (revPAR) and second, in occupancy. From an investment point of view Knowles and Egan argue that the major firms, which had announced significant expansion plans prior to September, are likely to be extremely cautious in their implementation. They also note that a key factor that affects the international hotel industry is consumer confidence and that UK surveys during October 2001 recorded a decline in confidence, particularly with regard to peoples' willingness to travel.

Appraisal techniques

Having identified the factors affecting the profitability of an investment, these can be used in a variety of quantitative methods to aid decision-making.

Investment appraisal reports may appear very authoritative, neatly summarizing projects in figures. However, in view of the uncertainties discussed in the previous section, care should be taken to examine the assumption on which appraisals are made. The main appraisal techniques are:

- payback method,
- average rate of return,
- net present value,
- internal rate of return.

Payback method

This method compares investment projects by measuring the length of time it takes to repay the original investment from the revenues earned. It therefore favours projects which have the earliest payback. The key problems with this method are first that earnings that an investment may make after the payback period are not taken into account, and second revenues are not discounted so earnings within the payback period are given equal weight irrespective of the year they appear in. On the other hand, the sooner the payback, the less a project will be subject to uncertainties, and some companies may see speed of return as a priority over total return. Table 10.3 shows an example of this method and it can be seen that in this example the payback period is 3 years, when the cumulative cash flow reaches zero.

Average rate of return

This method calculates the total earnings from an investment and divides this by the number of years of the project's life. This figure is then expressed as a percentage of the capital costs of the project. For example, if an investment project had a total cost of £100 000 and earned a total of £150 000 over 5 years, the annual earnings would be £10 000, which represents an annual average rate of return of £10 000/£100 000 or 10 per cent on the capital employed. This method also fails to discount future earnings.

Table 10.3 Payback method of investment appraisal (£ million)

Year	0	1	2	3	4
Costs	2.4	0.4	0.4	0.4	0.2
Revenue	0	1.0	1.2	1.4	1.4
Cash flow	−2.4	0.6	0.8	1.0	1.2
Cumulative cash flow	−2.4	−1.8	−1.0	0.0	1.2

Net present value

The net present value method takes into account the fact that future earnings have a lower value than current earnings. For example, £100 today could be invested at a rate of interest of 10 per cent to give £110 in a year's time. Working this backwards, £100 in a year's time is only worth £90.91 today at a rate of interest of 10 per cent. In other words, it has been discounted at a rate of 10 per cent to find its present discounted value (PDV). Discount tables exist to assist such calculations but there is also a formula for calculating PDV:

$$PDV = R_t/(1 + i)_t$$

where R = return, t = year and i = rate of interest or discount rate (expressed as decimal).

Row 1 of Table 10.4 shows the net revenues of a project with an initial capital cost of £16 million in years 1–4, and row 2 shows these figures discounted to their present values using a discount rate of 10 per cent. The net unadjusted revenues sum to £19 million and thus the project appears to show a net surplus of £3 million. However, the net present value technique compares costs and revenues discounted to their net present values. The total net revenue falls to £14.55 million when discounted to present value, and the project shows the following net present value:

Costs at present value: £16.00 million.
Revenue at present value: £14.55 million.
Net present value: –£1.45 million.

This negative figure indicates an unprofitable investment.

Internal rate of return

The internal rate of return method also uses discounted cash flow. It calculates the discount rate that would equate the net present value of future earnings of an investment to its initial cost. This rate is called the internal rate of return. An investment will be profitable if its internal rate of return exceeds the rate of interest that has to be paid for borrowing funds for the investment, allowing a margin for risk. A feasibility study into a fixed

Table 10.4   Discounted cash flow method of investment appraisal (£ million)

Year	0	1	2	3	4
Net revenue		2.0	5.0	6.0	6.0
PDV of net revenues		1.82	4.13	4.5	4.1

Note: Discount rate = 10 per cent.

channel link by Coopers and Lybrand and Setec Economie in 1979 concluded that the internal rate of return on the project would be between 11 and 18 per cent. When comparing investment projects those with the highest internal rate of return will be selected.

Changes in the level of investment

Changes in the level of investment will be caused by changes in the costs and predicted revenues of investments. These factors are summarized in Table 10.5.

The fall in investment in 1990 shown in Table 10.1 can be attributed to high interest rates making the cost of borrowing funds to invest high, falling consumers' expenditure, and poor expectations about the economy in the medium term. Falling demand leaves production or service capacity under-utilized and thus there is little need for new investment.

The accelerator principle

Investment activity in economies tends to be volatile, that is subject to considerable fluctuations. One of the explanations of this is the accelerator principle.

When demand for consumer goods and services is relatively stable in an economy, much of the demand for capital goods will take the form of replacing worn-out plant and machinery. However, if demand for final goods rises and there is no spare capacity in an industry, then new machinery will have to be purchased. Thus the demand for capital goods will significantly increase to include new machines as well as replacement machines.

Table 10.5 Factors causing changes in investment

	Investment conditions	
	Good	**Poor**
Rate of interest	Low	High
Capital costs predictable?	Yes	No
Project duration	Short	Long
Price of output	Predictable	Uncertain
Market for product	Rising	Uncertain
Competition in proposed market	Limited	Competitive
Political stability	Stable	Unstable
Expectations about economy	Optimistic	Pessimistic
Sensitivity of project to shocks	Low	High
Spare capacity	Low	High

Similarly, if the demand for final goods in an economy falls, firms will find they have over-capacity and too many machines. They will reduce the stock of machines to the new lower levels needed by not replacing worn-out machines, so the demand for capital goods will fall. Thus a rise in the demand for final goods will cause an accelerated rise in the demand for capital goods, and a fall in the demand for final goods will cause an accelerated fall in the demand for capital goods. The accelerator theory helps to explain the sudden fall in investment in 1990, in response to a fall in consumer demand.

Risk and sensitivity analysis

Sensitivity analysis is a technique for incorporating risk assessment in investment appraisal. It works by highlighting the key assumptions upon which investment appraisal figures were based. For example, revenue forecasts for an investment might be based upon:

- sales of 100 000 units per year,
- market growth of 3 per cent per year,
- price of £3 per unit,
- exchange rate of £1 = $1.5.

Sensitivity analysis would calculate the effects on an investment appraisal of changes in these assumptions. Such analysis would demonstrate the effects of, for example:

- sales of 80 000 units per year,
- market growth of 1 per cent per year,
- price of £2.50 per unit,
- exchange rate of £1 = $1.75.

and thus illustrate a project's sensitivity to a variety of scenarios.

Sources of funds

The main sources of funds for private sector investment include:

- retained profits,
- new share issues (see Chapter 2),
- loans,
- government assistance (see Chapter 11).

The differences between large and small enterprises becomes apparent when considering alternative sources of finance. Generally, large organizations will have easier access to investment funds. Bank loans are likely to be at lower rates and access to equity finance via shareholders can reduce costs and risks of investment. Smaller organizations will generally find it more difficult and expensive to access investment funds. For example, Brooker

(2002) argues that financing the smaller end of the hotel sector is made difficult by city attitudes and the capital intensity of the business in the UK. He considers the capital-intensive nature of the hotel industry and how various capital markets work in relation to the hotel sector. He argues that the franchising can offer a route to securing investment funds for the small business.

Government policy

In general, right-wing governments interfere as little as possible in free markets, while left-wing governments are often prepared to offer financial assistance where a project provides employment in areas of high unemployment, or where there are wider community benefits.

Review of key terms

- Investment: expenditure on capital goods and working capital.
- Fixed capital: durable capital goods such as buildings and machinery.
- Working capital: finance of work in progress such as raw material stocks, partially finished and unsold goods.
- Net investment: gross investment − depreciation.
- Payback method: appraisal technique to see how quickly an investment repays its costs.
- Average rate of return: appraisal technique where the average annual returns are expressed as a percentage of the original capital costs.
- Net present value: appraisal technique where all future revenues are recalculated to their present value so that a comparison can be made with the project costs.
- Internal rate of return: the rate of return of a project on capital employed, calculated by finding the rate that discounts future earnings to equal the capital costs.
- Accelerator theory: explanation why changes in consumer demand lead to larger changes in demand for investment goods.
- Sensitivity analysis: investigation of sensitivity of an investment project to changes in forecasts.

Data Questions

Task 10.1   The A380: superjumbo or white elephant?

In Toulouse, France sits a vast 12-hectare factory that is to assemble the biggest airliner in history – the Airbus A380. By 2005 the first planes will be assembled with a capacity to produce around half a dozen a month.

The A380 is a double-decker superjumbo which can carry up to 550 people, compared with the 424 in Boeing's 747 and 365 seats in its 777. It represents a massive investment of $10.7 billion (excluding the factory buildings) and cannot but bring back memories of another major European aircraft collaboration – Concorde – which represented a massive loss-making exercise.

Airbus predicts that the project will break even when between 200 and 250 planes, at $260 million each, are sold. In 2003 Airbus had 103 orders from 10 customers, and about 100 further 'options'. But the project also contains some substantial downside risks:

1 The project has half its costs in euros and its revenues in dollars. Because of this Airbus has had to hedge ahead a massive $40 billion to cover currency movements.
2 Although Boeing – Airbus's main competitor has no similar aircraft scheduled for production it will probably compete very strongly on price to keep its orders for its existing range of planes.
3 Part of the projections include a total €1.5 billion worth of cuts to the company's €15 billion cost base.
4 Because break even for the A380 years away, its development must be funded through current revenues. Airbus has a target of 300 aircraft deliveries for 2003 and has said that a significant fall-off in deliveries – say to about 270 – would jeopardize revenues and the financing of the A380.
5 A falling market has intensified competition with Boeing.
6 The fallout of September 11, and the effects of the Iraq war on passenger numbers. Airbus believes the resumption of close to 5 per cent per annum air travel growth will resume after a period of uncertainty.
7 Boeing's 'spoiler' campaign in announcing the 747× (stretched to take 522 passengers) to take on the A380.
8 The future shape of air travel. If markets are fragmenting carriers may target regional airports direct rather than 'hubs' suiting the long range, lower capacity 777.
9 The massive growth of low-cost airlines focused on short-haul traffic. Estimates are that low cost airlines will account for 25 per cent of the market. Currently eight of 10 low-cost airlines chose the Boeing 737 because of lower operating and maintenance costs.

Source: The author, from press cuttings (2004).

Recap Questions

1 What factors caused Concorde to be such a loss-making investment?
2 Identify the key costs and revenue factors affecting the A380 and analyse their likely impacts on its financial success.
3 Identify and analyse the key sensitivity factors affecting this project.
4 Explain using the accelerator principle why the demand for aircraft is so volatile.
5 Identify and explain the key factors that would make the A380 project a financial success.

Task 10.2   Reverberations from the Asian economic crisis

The domino effect of the slump in the Asian economies was demonstrated in 1998 by the sacking of 760 staff of Hong Kong's Cathay Pacific Airways. This represented about 5 per cent of its total workforce of 15 000. Speaking in 1998, David Turnbull, Managing Director of Cathay Pacific, said 'Just 6 months ago I would never have thought we would be forced to resort to such painful measures'. The cuts are the most dramatic in the history of Cathay Pacific and follow a recent announcement to reduce the workforce in building maintenance and other services by 550. Mr Turnbull underlined the urgency of the crisis by his comments on December 1997 figures for the airline which he described as 'truly appalling' when turnover fell by more than 25 per cent. The airline reported that 1997 had been a very bad year and that the prospects for 1998 showed few signs for improvement.

Other airlines operating in the region have been similarly affected. Philippine Airlines has an order for 15 new aircraft which were scheduled to be delivered in 1998 – this contract has been put under review. The Australian airline Qantas has reduced its services to Indonesia, Thailand and Malaysia. Similarly, Garuda, the state-owned airline of Indonesia has been unable to meet a payment for planes leased from Airbus.

The worry in Europe and America is that as airlines hit by the Asian economic crisis seek to reduce capacity this will have a severe knock-on effect leading to cuts in the production of aircraft – particularly by Boeing and Airbus. However, a spokesperson from British Aerospace was confident that a contract to supply 20 Hawk jets to Indonesia would survive the economic crisis.

Source: The author (1999).

Recap Questions

1 Compare and contrast the findings of tasks 10.1 and 10.2. What lessons should be learned from these cases?
2 What determines the demand for aircraft? Is this demand likely to be stable?
3 How does the globalization of the economy affect the sales of aircraft?
4 The article suggests that 1998 would also be a difficult year for airlines. By reference to the data in Table 9.6, evaluate the likely prospects for demand for aircraft in 1998 and 1999 from UK airlines.

Task 10.3   City: black hole – Jeremy Warner

There was a depressing familiarity about last week's news that Eurotunnel has lost another round of its battle to keep the lid on the costs of the Channel Tunnel. Unless it can reverse the order on appeal, Eurotunnel is going to have to pay the Channel Tunnel contractors a lot more to complete the project than previously thought – making yet another refinancing of the venture look almost inevitable. You do not need much experience of the construction industry to know that in all building projects the customer inevitably ends up paying considerably more than anticipated. At the risk of embarrassing Warburg Securities, however, I am going to quote from a City circular issued by the firm as part of the marketing effort for Eurotunnel shares when they were first sold to the public in the autumn of 1987. 'We believe,' the circular said, 'The balance of probability is that Eurotunnel will be completed both on time – May 1993 – and to budget.' The projected cost of the Channel Tunnel was then £4.8 billion. After numerous upgradings, that figure had risen to more than £8 billion by last November. It's a racing certainty that by the time the tunnel opens (late, naturally) the final tally is not going to be far south of £10 billion – or roughly double the original estimate.

So were investors and bankers conned? Sir Alastair Morton, Chief Executive, and all the others involved in raising finance for Eurotunnel, no doubt were convinced that what they were saying was true. A part of this was to boast how the contracts had been deliberately designed to thwart the contractor's natural tendency to inflate his price. It's all proved so much hogwash and one suspects that deep down everyone must have guessed there wasn't a hope in hell of bringing the project in on budget. The imperative was to make sure it was built, a noble enough aim in itself, but hardly the first priority of the investor. It's possible the tunnel will still yield an adequate return, but it's looking increasingly less likely. The inflated cost of the tunnel is only part of the problem. The greater imponderable is revenues once the system is up and running. It's hard to see why Eurotunnel's revenue predictions should be any more believable than its estimate of costs.

Source: *Independent on Sunday* (5 April 1992).

Recap Questions

1 What would be an 'adequate return' for the channel tunnel project? How would this be calculated?
2 Why are construction costs difficult to predict?
3 What impact does the late opening of the channel tunnel have on profit forecasts?
4 Why is this article sceptical about revenue predictions?
5 Evaluate the success of the Channel Tunnel.

Multiple choice

1 **Net investment equals the following:**

  (a) Gross investment plus depreciation.
  (b) Gross investment minus depreciation.
  (c) All investment in a given year.
  (d) Money investment minus inflation.

2 **All other things remaining equal which of the following will cause an increase in investment?**

  (a) A fall in interest rates.
  (b) A rise in interest rates.
  (c) A fall in demand.
  (d) Pessimistic expectations.

3 **The accelerator principle explains the following:**

  (a) The positive relationship between investment and the rate of interest.
  (b) The negative relationship between investment and the rate of interest.
  (c) The relationship between gross and net investment.
  (d) Fluctuations in the level of investment.

4 **Which of the following is true?**

  (a) Net present value analysis translates future earnings to a lower present value.
  (b) The average rate of return = total earnings/the rate of interest.

(c) Payback method of investment includes credit cards and direct debits.

(d) All of the above.

5 Which of the following is false?

(a) An aeroplane is fixed capital.

(b) Stocks of goods represent working capital.

(c) The existence of spare capacity in an industry will stimulate new investment.

(d) Investment financed from retained profits is cost free.

Review questions

1 Distinguish between net investment and gross investment.
2 How important is the rate of interest in affecting the decision to invest in a project?
3 Distinguish between the short-term and long-term effects of investment to an economy.
4 Evaluate the payback method of investment appraisal.
5 What is a project's internal rate of return?
6 Distinguish between working capital and fixed capital.
7 Why is sensitivity analysis used?

Web sites of interest

UK share prices: http://www.moneyworld.co.uk/stocks/
Railtrack: www.railtrack.co.uk
British Airways, investor information: http://www.british-airways.com/inside/ir/index.shtml
Granada Group: plc http://www.granada.co.uk
Marriott International: http://www.marriott.com
McDonald's Corp.: http://www.mcdonalds.com
Nintendo of America Inc.: http://www.nintendo.com
Scottish and Newcastle, plc: http://www.scottish-newcastle.com
Sony Corporation: http://www.sony.com
Time Warner Corporation: http://www.timewarner.com
Trump Hotels and Casinos Resorts Inc.: http://www.trump.com
Wilson Sporting Goods Co.: http://www.wilsonsports.com/
Virgin Atlantic: http://www.bized.ac.uk/compfact/vaa/vaa/index.htm
Learning help in economics and business studies: http://www.bized.ac.com

Investment in the public sector

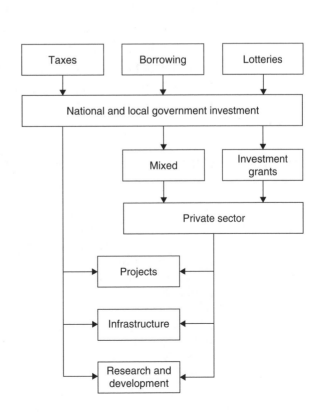

Objectives and learning outcomes

Transport is essential to many recreation, leisure and tourism activities. Provision of transport infrastructure for example roads, railways and airports requires considerable investment expenditure. It is very noticeable around the world that different governments have different approaches to investment. Taking the railways as an example, France has a very sophisticated system of national rail. At the heart of its system is the Train à Grande Vitesse (TGV) (high-speed train). In order to run the TGV new, straight track had to be laid – a massive investment and in France this has been undertaken by the government. The story in the UK is quite different. The railway system was privatized in the 1990s and has since suffered from under-investment and a poor record of safety or reliability.

Those who support public sector investment readily look to the failings of the UK privatized rail system to make their point. Opponents of public sector investment point to previous symbols of policy failure such as Concorde as representing the worst aspects of public sector investment – consuming ever-increasing sums of taxpayers' money and never achieving viable commercial sales.

By studying this chapter students will be able to:

- identify the sources of public sector investment,
- identify different types of public sector investment,
- describe different methods of public sector investment,
- appraise public sector investment projects,
- identify public sector incentives for private sector investment,
- understand private public partnership agreements,
- identify sources of funds for public sector investment.

Sources, types, methods and aims of public sector investment

Sources

Public sector investment can be financed from different sources. At the national level, government channels leisure and tourism investment through public corporations, quangos such as Sports Councils and government departments (for example the Department of Culture, Media and Sport in the UK). In Australia the following government departments impact of public sector investment relevant to recreation, leisure and tourism:

- the Department of Transport and Regional Services;
- the Department of Industry, Tourism and Resources;
- the Department of Communications, Information Technology and the Arts;
- the Department of Environment and Heritage.

Local government is the other major source of public sector investment. For European countries there is also a supranational level of government and here the European Union (EU) is a key source of investment funds, particularly through the European Regional Development Fund.

Types

Public sector investment may also be classified according to type. First public sector investment may be in buildings and land, for example parks, leisure centres and museums. Second public sector investment includes plant and machinery such as playground apparatus, computerized booking systems and canal lock equipment. Third public sector investment may be made in infrastructure. Infrastructure, or social overhead capital, is the construction needed to support economic development, for example, roads, railways and airports, water and sewerage, power and telecommunications.

Public investment on infrastructure has been relatively higher in France than that in the UK and Exhibit 11.1 reports on the completion of a cornerstone in French public investment strategy. Infrastructure development is a key part of tourism destination development, as it has to precede specific project development such as hotels, leisure sites and restaurants. Finally public sector investment may be spent on research and development, as illustrated in Exhibit 11.2.

Methods and aims

The main methods of public sector investment are first via projects which are wholly public sector-financed, second via projects which are jointly financed by the public and private sectors and finally via projects which are private sector investments but which are eligible for public sector investment incentive grants.

Exhibit 11.1   'The train arriving at runway 3 ...'

Passengers landing at Charles de Gaulle airport used to be faced by a messy onward journey into France. Now, a TGV high-speed station has been opened. The £300 million glass and steel construction links four methods of transport: air, road, *metro* and high-speed rail. The TGV route is able to bypass Paris so that passengers can, for example, be in Lyons within 2 hours without having to change trains. Announced by the French government in 1987, the project was co-funded between French Railways (SNCF) and Aeroports de Paris (ADP). Further development of the site is to include banks, restaurants, shops and a Sheraton hotel.

Source: The author, from news cuttings (November 1994).

Exhibit 11.2 Framework programme 5: EU-funded research and development in the new millennium

The fifth framework programme has a budget of £15 billion and offers a strategic plan for the EU's research and development (R&D) over a 5-year period from 1999. Edith Cresson, the European Commissioner-in-charge of research and innovation, explained that the new programme is radically different from the previous one. 'We are moving from research based on performance for its own sake to research which focuses on the social and economic problems which face society today.' The programme is divided into five thematic areas most of which include possible tourism and leisure. These are:

1 Quality of life and management of living resources.
2 User-friendly information society.
3 Competitive and sustainable growth.
4 Energy, environment and sustainable development.
5 Human potential and the socio-economic base.

R&D projects in leisure and tourism which have been funded by EU funds include:

● ESCAPE – project to investigate pollution of coastal waters.
● A project to restore the stonework of European historic buildings by using laser techniques.
● TOURFOR – a project to use environmental management systems to limit environmental damage of tourism and recreation in forest areas.
● BRAIN – a project to develop mathematical models to improve sound-proofing in aircraft cabins.

Source: The author, from *RTD Information*.

The aims of public sector investment include provision of goods and services which have significant public benefits, but which might not be profitable enough to attract private sector investment. O'Hagan and Jennings (2003) discuss some of the key issues in the current debate in Europe over public sector broadcasting (PSB) and examine the arguments for PSB. They find these to be classified under five headings, namely diversity, democracy/equality, network externalities, innovation and investment and public broadcasting as 'insurance'. They also examine the issues surrounding the licence fee as an instrument for funding PSB. These include the determination of the level of the fee, collection costs and evasion and the fairness of the instrument.

Public sector investment may also be focused on projects aimed at the economic development or regeneration of a particular area. Exhibit 11.3 reports on the contribution of mixed public and private sector investment in the arts to the economy of Edinburgh.

Exhibit 11.3   Lights up for Edinburgh's new theatre

In 1992 Lothian and Edinburgh Enterprise Limited – part of the Scottish Development Board – backed a £21 million project to turn a bingo hall into a theatre. It is a mixed investment where £6.6 million has come from the private sector and no revenue subsidy will be needed in its operation. The result is a multi-use theatre with the largest stage in the UK. The theatre represents a major project in Edinburgh's economic revival. It is estimated that 16 000 extra tourists will be attracted to the city, boosting the city's tourism income by £7 million to £257 million.

Source: The author, from news cuttings.

Investment appraisal in the public sector

Cost–benefit analysis

Investment appraisal for private sector projects is relatively straightforward, as described in the previous chapter. If a project yields the required return on capital employed then the investment will go ahead. The different nature of the public sector makes investment appraisal more complex in this sector. Some parts of the public sector are run on private sector lines. In these cases an investment is required to earn a specified rate of return on capital employed and thus the investment decision is fairly clear-cut. However, many public sector investments are made for reasons of wider public benefits and thus private sector methods of appraisal are inappropriate. In such cases cost–benefit analysis provides a more useful method of project appraisal.

Cost–benefit analysis is described in detail in Chapter 17; however, its essential details are that all the costs and benefits of a project are identified and weighed up, including social as well as private ones. Table 11.1 shows an example of possible private and social costs and benefits for a canal restoration scheme. Private sector investment appraisal of such a scheme would calculate the private costs of the project, and the private benefits. These would be discounted to net present value (as explained in Chapter 10) and since the private costs would almost certainly exceed the private benefits, the investment would not proceed. However, cost–benefit analysis would analyse the wider costs and benefits. Some extra costs such as noise and congestion associated with the construction phase might be identified. Social benefits of the scheme would include lives saved through improved canal safety, greater public well-being caused by improved aesthetics from the project, and the effects on the local economy of new industries and employment attracted to the area because of the project. The total figures would be subjected to discounting to calculate net present value and it might well be the case that total public and private benefits would exceed costs. Thus there may well be an argument for public sector investment in the project.

Table 11.1 Cost–benefit analysis of canal restoration scheme

Costs	Benefits
Private costs	*Private benefits*
Construction costs of project, e.g.	Revenue from project, e.g.
• Materials	• Craft licences and charges
• Labour	• Fishing licences
• Professional fees	• Rentals from renovated buildings
Social costs	*Social benefits*
Inconvenience costs to local residents of construction	Drownings avoided through improved canal safety
	New jobs created by project
	Improved aesthetics of area

Newman et al. (2003) note that arts projects have become an important part of community development strategies but that project are expected to have positive and measurable impacts on local social capital. They show that funding organizations routinely demand evidence for this, and that formal cost benefit evaluations of projects are frequently a condition of investment. However, they further note that quantifying the impact of the arts in terms of 'social gain' presents considerable difficulties. These problems are not just methodological. They also raise the question of the extent to which creative processes can (or should) be managed and controlled. In other words cost–benefit accounting may be incompatible with the creative arts.

Pitegoff and Smith (2003) carried out an investigation into US State Destination Boards which have traditionally operated Welcome Centres at key vehicular entrance points to their states. These are often viewed as cost centres. However, they note that if visitors modify trips in the state as a result of their Welcome Centre experience so as to make an incremental economic contribution to the State, then what has been perceived as a cost centre may actually be a profit centre for the State. In other words a wider public cost–benefit analysis rather than a strict accounting of the direct costs and revenues of the operation of these Welcome Centres can provide an economic argument for their continued existence.

Other factors affecting public investment

Whilst cost–benefit analysis is used for appraising some major public sector investment projects, its use is far from widespread. Public sector investment decisions are often determined by the priorities of the political party in power at a national or local level. Decisions will also be affected by interest group activity, and the general economic environment.

Public expenditure at a local level often comes under direct and indirect control from central government since. Task 11.1 of the data questions at the end of this chapter illustrates how a move to the left in the Labour party on Birmingham council (UK) led to a reversal of its public investment policy. 'City boosterism' had been the philosophy behind a massive investment in leisure, sports and arts facilities, designed to bring visitors and jobs to an area suffering from the effects of deindustrialization. The new leadership has returned to a more conventional policy of investment in schools and housing.

Investment incentives for tourism and leisure projects

Most governments offer incentives for to encourage private sector investment particularly:

- in areas of high unemployment,
- where there are clear social benefits offered by a scheme,
- where structural changes in the economy have led to geographic areas of economic decline (e.g. inner city decline, rural decline, etc.).

These incentives can include:

- matched funding,
- tax relief,
- subsidized loans,
- simplified planning procedures.

Exhibit 11.4 describes the steps taken by the European Commission to improve transport links in Europe, and the limited funding it has at its disposal.

Exhibit 11.5 reports on public sector support for investment projects in recreation, leisure and tourism in the UK.

Exhibit 11.4 Trans-European Networks

Piece by piece, the transport system for Europe is dropping into place and 1998 saw the opening of Europe's longest suspension bridge, a 10-mile road and rail link between Denmark and Sweden. The link is part of an £400 billion project called TENs or Trans-European Networks planned up to 2010. But with EU funding for this network limited to £5 billion between 1998 and 2003, the Transport Commissioner, Mr Neil Kinnock, describes the role of the EU as one of pump priming, rather than full underwriter of costs. So EU expenditure is primarily targeted at feasibility and planning studies and securing funds from other sources. These sources include the governments of EU member states and lenders such as the European Investment Bank and the European Investment Fund. Mr Kinnock has also stressed a greater role for private sector funding, saying, 'we know

---

that the conventional source of infrastructure investment – the public sector – is not going to be able to meet all the costs'. By 2015 the TENs' plan will improve rapid road and rail links across the EU and into the new member states of Eastern Europe. The key TENs scheduled for completion by 2005 include:

- The Madrid–Barcelona–Montpellier high-speed rail link, connecting to the TGV network (£16 billion).
- The Paris–Luxembourg–Strasbourg–Mannheim high-speed rail link (£4.5 billion).
- The London–Paris–Brussels–Amsterdam–Cologne high-speed rail link (£19 billion).
- The Greek motorway network (£10 billion).

Source: The author (1999).

Exhibit 11.5 Public sector leisure investment initiatives in the UK

The following examples show support from a number of different public sector sources for leisure and tourism investment projects:

- Somerset District Council has opened a visitor centre on the River Parrett at Langport with financial help from the Rural Development Corporation.
- Tourism in Thanet has won funds from the European Regional Development Fund, and the UK Government Single-Regeneration budget to support investment in local hotels and attractions.
- The Imperial War Museum is to build a 6000 square foot site in Manchester with a budget of £28.5 million. This is a mixed private sector/public sector initiative with £12.5 million coming from the private sector (Peel Holdings), £8.2 million from the European Regional Development Fund, and £2.5 million each from English Partnerships, Trafford Council and the Imperial War Museum.
- The Manchester Museum, the Manchester City Art Gallery and the Manchester Museum of Science and Industry share a £4.5 million grant from the European Regional Development Fund.

Source: The author (1999).

Sources of funds

Sources of funds for public investment include:

- operating profits,
- taxation,
- borrowing,

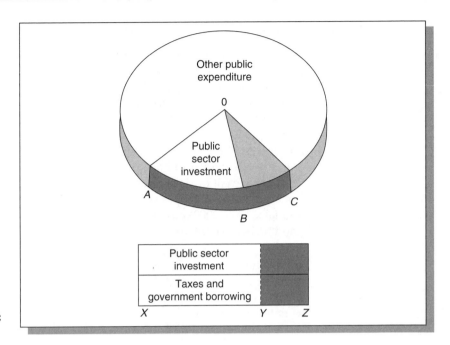

Figure 11.1
Opportunity cost of public
sector investment

- National Lotteries,
- Public Private Partnerships (PPPs).

Operating profits, taxation and borrowing

Operating profits are rare in public sector organizations since, as discussed in Chapter 2, they are run for motives other than profit. Thus public sector investment is mainly financed from taxation receipts and government borrowing. This is a key reason why public sector investment is often under attack from opposition parties and from the government's own Treasury department.

Because of the impact on public finances, the opportunity costs of public sector investment are immediately apparent. Thus the opportunity cost of more public investment is higher taxes, or less government expenditure elsewhere, as illustrated in Figure 11.1. The circle represents total government spending and no increases in taxes or government borrowing are assumed. An increase in public sector investment from $A0B$ to $A0C$ can only be accommodated by a fall in other government expenditure of $B0C$. Alternatively, it is assumed below that other government expenditure remains unchanged. In this case an increase in public sector investment from XY to XZ can only be financed through an increase in taxes or government borrowing of YZ.

Second, when the economy is performing badly, investment is often a target of government policy. If government borrowing is running too high, cutting social security payments or pensions has readily identifiable victims. Cutting investment generally results only in some improvement not taking place and therefore its consequences are more blurred.

National Lotteries

In some countries, National Lotteries offer significant income sources for public sector investment. For example, the first estimates for the costs of the Sydney Opera House (Plate 11) were $7 million. An appeal fund raised about $900 000 but the rest of the $102 million that the Opera House ended up costing came from the profits of a series of lotteries. The building was completely paid for by July 1975. Today the NSW Government contributes about 30 per cent of the annual cost of maintaining and operating the complex.

In the UK, whilst public spending has generally been squeezed by the Treasury, recreation, leisure and tourism are key beneficiaries of the National Lottery. Twenty-eight per cent of the lottery revenue (estimated at £5 billion annually 1998–2002) goes to five major causes, four of which benefit leisure and tourism. These are:

- charities,
- the arts,
- sports,
- national heritage,
- the Millennium Fund.

Projects in the arts which have benefited from the National Lottery include first, the South Bank arts complex in London. The National Theatre has recently completed a major refurbishment of its foyer area with the help of lottery funds. Second, the lottery has provided investment funds for the Tate Gallery's new Bankside museum for modern art. The estimated cost of conversion of a disused power station in east London for this project was £80 million. The English National Opera is also seeking funds to renovate the London Coliseum.

Plate 11
Public Sector
Investment: Sydney
Opera House
Source: The author

The Sports Council has set up a lottery board to distribute its share of funds. Projects of between £5000 and £5 million can be considered for a grant of up to 65 per cent. Large projects include a new national stadium at Wembley and local council sports facilities.

The National Heritage memorial fund has responsibility for channelling funds into areas such as museum collections, historic buildings and monuments, landscapes, libraries and industrial heritage.

Other examples of contributions of lottery funding to leisure and tourism investment projects include the following which were announced in 1999:

- The Natural History Museum Earth Galleries (£6 million from Heritage Lottery Fund).
- National Trust renovation of Paul McCartney's Teenage Liverpool home (£47 500 from Heritage Lottery Fund).
- Redevelopment of Royal Naval Museum, Portsmouth (Heritage Lottery Fund).
- The National Space Science Centre, Leicester (£23 million from the Millennium Commission).

Public Private Partnerships (PPP)

A PPP is where governments contract a private company to finance, design, construct, operate and maintain a project in return for future income. Projects include examples such as railways, leisure centres and concert halls. The finance for such schemes may involve investment companies or fund managers for insurance or pension bodies providing the initial investment in return for future revenue which may be generated through a variety of schemes that may include tolls, rentals or 'shadow payments' where the government pays a fee for each customer of the project. Through PPPs different combinations of public–private investment are possible. But the basic idea is that public payment for the project is not required up-front – but is made as the project comes into use. Of course there is potential conflict in PPPs. The public sector is seeking a community benefit – better services and facilities delivered sooner at least cost to the community, whilst the private sector wants a profit. Long-term mutual benefit depends on how well the private sector manages the risk transferred to it and on the public sector's success in managing the contracts over the duration of the project.

The public sector investment debate

Public investment has been subject to considerable debate and the arguments against public investment include the following:

1 The public sector is not a good interpreter of people's wants and thus often invests in 'white elephants'.
2 The public sector is not good at ensuring efficient use of funds and tends to allow waste.

3 Public sector investment causes an increase in taxation or public borrowing.

4 Public sector investment 'crowds out' private sector investment.

In the UK in the 1980s, the Thatcher government therefore removed a large slice of investment from the public sector through its privatization programme. It then concentrated its efforts on creating an 'enterprise economy' which it hoped would stimulate private sector investment by reducing income and corporation tax and making the labour market more flexible. The privatization of the public sector has been carried out with similar enthusiasm in parts of Europe – and of course particularly in ex-communist states.

However, many countries in the world still favour a substantial public sector and the arguments favouring public sector investment include the following:

1 There is insufficient incentive for the private sector to invest in public goods (see Chapter 7).

2 The private sector under invests in goods which have mainly social benefits.

3 The private sector may not be able to undertake the finance or risk for very large projects.

4 Public sector investment can help regenerate parts of the economy which have suffered from restructuring.

5 Public sector investments can generate jobs when unemployment is high.

Thus, where the market is used as the main determinant of investment, infrastructure projects with important public and merit angles will tend to be overlooked, despite the fact that the future capacity of the economy may depend on them. This has led to calls to distinguish between capital spending and current spending in government public sector accounts since the former will involve future benefits.

Review of key terms

- Infrastructure: construction needed to support economic development.
- Cost–benefit analysis: full analysis of public and private costs and benefits of project.
- 'City boosterism': investment in projects to regenerate city centres in economic decline.
- European Regional Development Fund: EU fund for projects and infrastructure to bring jobs to designated areas.
- Opportunity costs of public sector investment = alternative uses the funds could have been used for.
- PPPs: where governments contract a private company to finance, design, construct, operate and maintain a project in return for future income.

Data Questions

Task 11.1   Rattled of Symphony Hall: Birmingham's bid for new greatness included balletic endeavour, Olympic attempts and brave new temples of culture. Then the city council changed its tune – Nick Cohen

When Simon Rattle raised his baton on 15 April 1991 to lead the City of Birmingham Symphony Orchestra into the first chords of Stravinsky's *Firebird*, the idea that a funding crisis could bring the most acclaimed conductor in the country close to resigning would have seemed preposterous. At the opening night of the Birmingham Symphony Hall the evidence of the city's bold, almost reckless commitment to economic regeneration through the spending of millions on culture, tourism and service industries could not have been more obvious to the 2200 guests.

The symphony hall, everyone agreed, was one of the finest in the world. Labour-controlled Birmingham City Council had, with the support of local Conservatives, uncomplainingly paid the bulk of the £30 million cost. No expense had been spared. Next door, in Centenary Square, a £150 million convention centre, which was confidently expected to attract business tourists from around the world, was all but complete. Behind the centre a new 13 000-seat indoor athletics stadium which, city planners assured the voters, would help make Birmingham the UK sporting capital, was ready to receive athletes. The policy of growth through prestige developments was outlined in a council development plan published shortly after the hall opened. 'To a large degree the prosperity of the whole city will depend on the city centre,' it said. 'Entertainment, culture, leisure and recreation have an increasingly valuable role. Indeed, [they] represent the very essence of a large metropolitan international centre.' In the 1970s, the essence of Birmingham was making things people wanted to buy.

But the recession of the early 1980s wiped out 110 000 jobs in a city of 1 million people. In desperation at first, then with an increasingly evangelical conviction, Birmingham's councillors turned to American models of urban regeneration pioneered in the rust-belt cities of Baltimore and Detroit. Civic boosterism is the jargon label – the belief that eye catching developments in the city centre could replace the lost manufacturing jobs by attracting high-spending tourists, conventioning businessmen and sports fans. There were early warning signs that the policy was not working. Two Olympic bids failed in the 1980s and a Super Prix car race collapsed. But it seemed almost bad taste at the time to mention these setbacks as the right-wing Labour council and their allies in business and the council bureaucracy exuberantly proclaimed that Birmingham 'was ready to compete with Barcelona and Lyon's'.

Birmingham's boosterism in the 1980s has been followed by a profound shift in the city away from prestige projects to a kind of left-wing, back-to basics policy. Last year, Theresa Stewart, a 63-year-old grandmother and veteran left-winger, beat the right-wing candidates for the Labour leadership on a policy of stopping the search for prestige. Ever since, there has been a changed atmosphere in the city. Education, housing, social services were the priority, not tourists, theatre-goers and conventions. 'For 10 years I was told the council was developing municipal socialism,' she said after winning office. 'It's been more like municipal stupidity.' Ed Smith, the orchestra's general manager, recognizes the shift in emphasis. 'Not a day goes by without money worries', he said.

Other attractions are also in trouble. Councillor Stewart has said she would 'not spend £10 on another Olympic bid'. Stand outside the gleaming concert hall and strike out in any direction and in 15 minutes you will hit Birmingham's inner city – a ring of misery running clockwise from Handsworth through New Town, Aston, Small Heath and Sparkbrook to Ladywood. The statistics give a prosaic idea of the poverty. In the nine inner-Birmingham wards, 31 per cent of adults are out of work. Almost four out of 10 of the city's population receive state benefits. In the New Town district, to take just one example, the number of single-parent families is three times the national average and two out of three residents do not have a single O-level or General Certificate of Secondary Education (GCSE). If the symphony hall, convention centre and the rest were really to be the source of regeneration, then these are the people who should have benefited from the trickle-down effect. They have not. Most of the jobs created were menial, part time and low paid. The council recognized the problem and devised a training programme to prepare the unemployed for full-time work in the convention centre. The result was pitiable. Just 19 inner-city residents got jobs.

More significantly, money was diverted from the core services the poor depend on to fund the building boom. An analysis by the University of Central England (formerly Birmingham Polytechnic) estimated that £123 million was taken from Birmingham City Council's housing budget and that spending on school buildings fell by 60 per cent while the lavish city centre developments were being built. Most notoriously of all, the council took more and more from the budget for education, leaving Birmingham with some of the worst schools in the country. In 1991 Birmingham was spending £46 million less than the amount recommended by central government. Birmingham city centre may look marvellous, but it is a gleaming heart surrounded by a decaying body. Councillor Stewart cannot knock down the convention centre, much as she may like to, and the symphony hall and indoor arena will remain. But it is clear that from now on the council's priorities will be housing and education. An extra £43 million will be pumped into schools this year and the money will have to come from somewhere.

Source: *The Independent* (9 March 1994).

Recap Questions

1 What was the economic rationale behind 'city boosterism'?
2 What factors would you take into account in conducting a cost–benefit analysis on investment in 'city boosterism'?
3 What factors caused a change in Birmingham's investment strategy?
4 What were the opportunity costs of 'city boosterism' in Birmingham?

Task 11.2 Public spaces: lost Victorian heritage

1832: The Whig government conceives the idea of 'public walks'.

1837: Joseph Hume MP tables a parliamentary motion calling for the provision of open spaces to be financed from the public purse for the enjoyment of the public.

1840: The Arboretum in Rosehill, Derby, is opened to fanfares and fireworks. Joseph Strutt commends the park as offering local workers 'the opportunity of enjoying, with their families, exercise and recreation in the fresh air and in public walks and grounds'. The Arboretum is planted with 913 types of trees and shrubs and more than 100 types of rose.

1979: Mrs Thatcher comes to power. Public sector spending cut.

1998: Patrick Weir of the *Guardian* surveys the sorry state of the park. He reports: 'The Lodge House, at the Rosehill Street entrance, serves bleak notice of what lies beyond: a crumbling, boarded up edifice, it would look more at home on a Hammer Horror set. Once in the park, signs of decay are all too evident. Public monuments are in disrepair, the bandstand is burned down, statues are missing and the centrepiece fountain is fenced off. Trees remain untrimmed, while graffiti, litter and dog dirt scar the environment. Gangs congregating at night render the park even less inviting.'

1999: Derby City Council awaits the result of a bid to the Heritage Lottery for £3 million. The council has made provision to access an initial £200 000 of lottery funds by providing £43 000 in matched funds, but it is not confident of finding the next tranche of £750 000 necessary to release the rest of the lottery's £3 million.

Steve Jardine, of the DERBYES! Campaign, hopes that residents, local businesses and grant-providing trusts can help. He said: 'The council can't do everything. People must be more proactive. It's a case of priorities and how much we value our parks. They are the lungs of the city, and, as recognized by the Victorians, areas where people can relax and play.'

Source: The author based on article in *The Guardian*.

Recap Questions

1 What differing government attitudes to public sector investment does this article demonstrate?
2 What are the arguments for and against leaving provision of parks and gardens to the private sector?
3 Given the shortage of local council funds – suggest ways in which improvements in this park could be financed.
4 Explain the meaning of the terms *opportunity cost, crowding out, merit goods* and *public goods* in relation to this article.

Task 11.3   Three trains and a bridge

Railtrack, UK: Railtrack, the privatized owner of the UK rail infrastructure, announced in 1998 plans to spend £17 billion over the next decade on investment in the railways. Sir Robert Horton, Railtrack's Chairman described Railtrack's plan as 'a blueprint to regenerate the railways'. However, other commentators saw the proposed investment in a different light.

The rail regulator Mr John Swift criticized Railtrack for a failure to invest adequately in the industry and announced he would be carrying out a detailed investigation into the sufficiency of Railtrack's plan. He said of Railtrack: 'Its statement contains very few commitments to deliver significant improvements across the rail network which passengers can recognize. I therefore intend to find out from train operators and funders of the railway whether Railtrack's statement meets their reasonable needs as required by its licence. I must be satisfied that Railtrack has sought to identify these requirements and reflect them in practical plans to improve the railway.'

Mr David Bertram, chairman of the central rail users' consultative committee, added to the criticisms saying: 'We had hoped for something more ambitious. The £4 million a day due to be spent by Railtrack may well not be sufficient, and the easing of congestion at many key points is only at the planning stage, with no firm dates yet.'

The London Underground, UK: The London Underground is to remain in public ownership but will receive a substantial injection of private finance. It is to benefit from a £7-billion programme of private sector investment to be carried out over 15 years. Future plans for the Underground had included privatization but the government has opted for a private–public partnership.

Skye bridge, UK: Skye bridge spans the sea between the Isle of Skye and the Scottish mainland and was built under the private finance initiative (PFI). Under this programme public schemes are funded by private money. A private sector consortia designed, built and financed the bridge and shouldered risks such as construction delays. In return the government entered into a contract to pay for yearly use of the bridge.

The Madrid–Seville high-speed train, Spain: The Spanish Ministry of Transport paid for the pts 450 billion construction costs of the high-speed train from Madrid to Seville which opened in 1992. It has been such a success that it later authorized the construction of the extension from Madrid to the French frontier to link with the Train à Grande Vitesse (TGV) system.

Source: The author (1999).

Recap Questions

1 What different types of investment are demonstrated in this article?
2 In each case what is the main determinant of the level of investment?
3 What are the benefits and drawbacks of investment in transport schemes under regimes of:
    – Private sector?
    – Private/public sector partnerships?
    – Public sector?
4 What factors would be taken into account in a cost–benefit analysis of the Madrid–Seville high-speed train?

Multiple choice

1 **Which of the following is not a social benefit of a canal restoration scheme?**

(a) Improved aesthetics.
(b) Revenue from boat licences.
(c) New jobs created by the project.
(d) Drownings avoided through improved safety.

2 **Public sector investment is most appropriate where:**

(a) Social and private benefits exceed social and private costs.
(b) Private benefits exceed private costs.
(c) A project would not otherwise be undertaken.
(d) A project has the support of local residents.

3 **Under a PPP scheme:**

(a) The public sector partner provides the initial investment funds.
(b) The private sector partner receives revenues for use of the facility.
(c) Both the public and private partners will necessary benefit.
(d) Consumers are guaranteed low prices.

4 **Which of the following statements is not true?**

(a) Public sector investment may 'crowd out' private sector investment.
(b) Because the public sector is not a good interpreter of people's wants it often invests in 'white elephants'.

(c) Public sector investment is inadvisable when unemployment is high.

(d) The private sector may not be able to undertake the finance or risk for very large projects.

5 **Which of these is not an opportunity cost of public investment?**

(a) Extra taxes paid by households.

(b) Other possible government projects.

(c) Interest paid on borrowings to finance the project.

(d) Regeneration effects of the project.

Review questions

1 Under what circumstances would investment grants be available for the construction of a theme park?

2 What is cost–benefit analysis and why is it sometimes difficult to calculate?

3 Compare the sources of funds for public investment projects with sources available in the private sector.

4 What specific leisure and tourism projects might benefit from the National Lottery?

5 Compare the factors determining an investment decision in the public sector with those in the private sector.

Web sites of interest

English Sports Council: http://www.english.sports.gov.uk/

Forestry Commission: http://www.forestry.gov.uk/

Help for National Lottery Bids: www.havering.gov.uk/decs/lottery.htm

Department for Culture, Media and Sport: http://www.culture.gov.uk

British Tourist Authority: www.visitbritain.com

Railtrack: www.railtrack.co.uk

Learning help in economics and business studies: http://bized.ac.uk

Part Six

Economic Impacts

Income, employment and prices

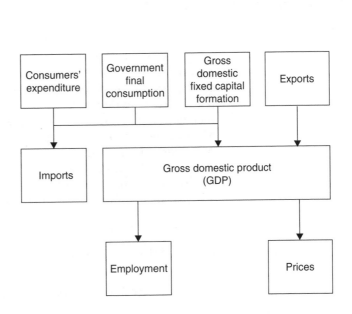

Objectives and learning outcomes

Chapter 9 looked at the effects of the economic environment on recreation, leisure and tourism organizations. The aim of this chapter is to examine the other side of this question, and ask how the leisure and tourism sector contributes to the general level of economic activity. In particular it will examine the contribution of leisure and tourism to national output, national income and national expenditure, to the level of employment and consider the question of inflation. The issue of economic growth will be covered in Chapter 13, and international impact of leisure and tourism will be addressed in Chapter 14.

By studying this chapter students should be able to:

- distinguish between microeconomics and macroeconomics;
- measure the total level of economic activity in an economy;
- distinguish between changes in real and money gross national product (GNP);
- measure the contribution to GNP;
- understand the contribution to employment;
- understand the contribution to tax revenue;
- utilize simple economic models of the macroeconomy;
- understand and apply the multiplier principle;
- measure inflation in the recreation, leisure and tourism sector;
- interpret government policy in this area.

Gross national product and the level of recreation, leisure and tourism activity

Macroeconomics

Chapters 2–7 dealt mainly with microeconomic issues. These were issues concerning the actions of individuals (demand) and firms (supply) and their interaction to determine prices in specific markets (e.g. the market for television sets and the market for air travel). Chapters 12–15 look mainly at macroeconomic issues. These are issues that affect the whole economy. Macroeconomics deals with aggregates. Thus it adds together the spending of individuals to calculate consumers' expenditure, or aggregate demand. It adds together the output of individual organizations to measure national output or product. Similarly, the general price level and rate of inflation are investigated rather than prices in individual markets.

A simple macroeconomic model

Figure 12.1 illustrates a simple model of the national economy. The economy is divided into two sectors, households and firms. Households own

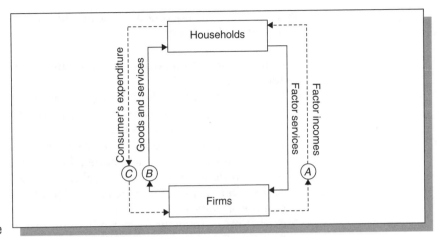

Figure 12.1
The circular flow of income

factors of production whilst firms utilize factors of production to produce goods and services. It is assumed in this initial model that all the output of firms is sold, and all income is spent. Additionally, there is no government activity, no savings or investment, and no international trade.

There are two flows in this system. First, 'real' flows are designated by unbroken lines. These represent the flow of factors of production (land, labour and capital) from households to firms, and the flow of goods and services, made from these factors of production, from firms to households. Second, 'money' flows are designated by broken lines. These represent factor rewards and payments for goods and services. For example, if a member of a household works for a firm it supplies the factor of labour and receives the reward of wages in payment. This payment can then be used to purchase goods and services from firms.

In this simple model of the economy firms buy factors of production to make goods and services, and households sell factors of production to buy goods and services.

Gross and net national income

The model can be used to illustrate the concept of national income. National income is a measure of the total level of economic activity which takes place in an economy over a year. In Figure 12.1, if the total flow of money at point A was measured over a year, this would represent the level of national income. The same picture can be viewed from different angles. The total value of goods and services passing point B over a year would represent national output or national product, and the total amount of expenditure passing point C over a year would represent national expenditure. This gives an important accounting identity:

National income = National product = National expenditure

The key rule in deciding how an item should be treated for national income calculation is whether it represents income earned by or output (or expenditure on that output) produced by, factors of production of the country under consideration. There are three methods of measuring gross domestic product (GDP).

- In the income method incomes accruing to factors of production are added up.
- In the expenditure method the total spending on final output under different headings is measured. Some goods will be semi-finished or finished but not yet sold, so these are added as 'increase in stocks and works in progress'. Exported goods have been produced but not bought domestically so their value is added. Imports have been bought but not produced domestically, so their value is deducted. Finally, taxes artificially inflate prices and subsidies undervalue the underlying production costs, so these are deducted and added respectively to move from market prices to factor costs. An item for residual error is included. So the formula for measuring GDP by the expenditure method is:

  Consumers' expenditure
  +Government final consumption
  +Gross domestic fixed capital formation
  +Value of increase in stocks and works in progress
  +Exports of goods and services
  −Imports of goods and services
  −Residual error
  =GDP (at market prices)
  −Expenditure taxes
  +Subsidies
  =GDP (at factor cost)

- Under the output method the outputs of different sectors of the economy are valued, taking care to avoid double-counting.

From gross domestic product to national income ● ● ●

GDP values the flow of goods and services produced domestically. But some income arises from investments and possessions owned abroad and thus an adjustment for net property income from abroad is made to GDP to calculate GNP. Finally, some investment spending occurs to replace worn-out machinery. Net national product NNP or national income deducts this amount (capital depreciation). These final calculations are summarized below:

  GDP
  +Net property income from abroad
  =GNP
  −Capital consumption
  =NNP (national income)

Real and money national income ● ● ●

When national income figures are compared over two different time periods, the effects of inflation can be misleading. Money national income or national income at current prices includes the effects of inflation. Real national income or national income at constant prices has had the effects of inflation removed.

Recreation, leisure and tourism contribution to gross national product

Importance • • •

Table 12.1 gives an indication of the importance of the leisure and tourism sector to the UK economy. From the data it can be seen that 18.2 per cent of average expenditure in 2000–01 was on leisure items. Table 12.1 also shows the difficulties in defining leisure and measuring its specific impacts on the national economy. The Office for National Statistics has two categories – leisure goods and leisure services. However, clearly some aspects of 'food', 'alcoholic drink', 'motoring', 'clothing and footwear' and other headings will include leisure expenditure. Care therefore needs to be exercised in

Table 12.1   Average household expenditure, UK, 2000–01

Housing (net)	63.90
Fuel and power	11.90
Food and non-alcoholic drinks	61.90
Alcoholic drinks	15.00
Clothing and footwear	22.00
Household goods	32.60
Household services	22.00
Personal goods and services	14.70
Fares and other travel costs	9.50
Leisure goods	19.70
Books, maps, diaries, address books and sheet music	1.70
Magazines and periodicals	1.00
Television, video, computers and audio equipment	8.80
Sports and camping equipment	0.90
Toys and hobbies	2.10
Photography and camcorders, including developing	1.10
Horticultural goods, plants and flowers	2.20
Leisure services	50.60
Cinema and theatre	1.20
Sports admissions and subscriptions	3.30
Television, video, satellite rental, television licences and Internet	4.40
Miscellaneous entertainments	1.40
Educational and training expenses	6.50
Holiday abroad	12.50
Other incidental holiday expenses	6.80
Gambling payments	3.90
Cash gifts and donations	8.10
Miscellaneous	0.70
All expenditure groups	385.70

Source: Adapted from Office of National Statistics Family Spending 2000–01.

interpreting the contribution of leisure to national income using Table 12.1 alone. Additionally, we must note that the table records UK household expenditure, but as the earlier section on GNP calculation explained, exports of leisure goods and services need to be added to this figure and imports deducted. Similarly, some leisure activity does not involve an activity which is bought and sold in the market. Neither informal sports games nor do it yourself (DIY) labour are measured in GNP statistics because of this, although both result in services enjoyed and value added. Therefore traditional GNP figures often under value the true contribution of recreation, leisure and tourism to national economies.

Satellite accounts • • •

It has been seen that it is not always easy to isolate spending on recreation, leisure and tourism from other expenditure in national economic accounts. Taking tourism as an example, tourism is not an industry in the traditional sense. Traditional industries are classified according to the goods and services that they produce (e.g. restaurant and café meals). However, classifying a good or service as a tourism good or service depends on the status of the customer (i.e. those restaurant and café meals consumed by tourists). Nearly all of the broad industry groups are involved to a greater or lesser extent in providing goods and services directly to tourists. While all the products that are produced and consumed in meeting tourism demand are counted in national economic accounts, the specific contribution of tourism is not readily apparent.

Because of this many countries now compile Tourism Satellite Accounts (TSA). TSAs partition industries into tourism and non-tourism activities so that the direct contribution of tourism to the economy can be measured on a consistent basis with more traditional industries such as manufacturing, agriculture and retail trade. TSAs are generally prepared using tourism surveys to impute tourism values to broader economic activities. Typically TSAs are compiled using a combination of visitors expenditure data from surveys conducted on tourists and industry data from national economic accounts. However, it should be noted that TSA estimates of tourism's value relates only to the direct impact of tourism. TSAs ignore tourism's indirect contribution to the economy (this is discussed later in this chapter under the heading of the multiplier). Recent examples in the literature of measurement of economics impacts include West and Gamage's (2001) article which uses an input–output model to assess the economic impacts of tourism on the economy of Victoria in Australia.

Exhibit 12.1 describes the contribution of tourism to the economy of Australia based on figures from its TSA.

Employment

Riley et al. (2002) examine tourism employment in a holistic way. They consider behavioural and economic perspectives to address questions that

---

Exhibit 12.1   Tourism and the Australian economy

Tourism is a significant factor in the Australian economy as it stimulates a wide range of industries. Tourism GDP is the total market value of Australian produced goods and services consumed by tourists after deducting the cost of goods and services used up in the process of production. The tourism industry share of GDP was 4.7 per cent in 2000–01. This is significantly higher than in 1997–98 (4.5 per cent) or than in 1999–2000 (4.4 per cent). The international visitors' share of Tourism GDP rose by 1.7 per cent to reach 24.0 per cent in 2000–01, reflecting the impact of the Sydney Olympic and Paralympic Games.

Tourism gross value added measures the value of tourism gross output at factor prices (i.e. product taxes such as the GST are excluded) by all industries which supply tourism products. This measure also excludes the value of the inputs used in producing these tourism products. Tourism gross value added grew from $22.4 billion in 1997–98 to $26.3 billion in 2000–01. Tourism's share of total industry gross value added was 4.3 per cent in 2000–01. When compared to other traditional industry groupings the gross value added of tourism ranks twelfth. Its value exceeds that of groupings such as government administration and defence; agriculture, forestry and fishing; communication services and electricity, gas and water supply. The industries which accounted for the largest shares of tourism gross value added were: air and water transport (15 per cent); accommodation (11 per cent); cafes, restaurants and takeaway food outlets (9 per cent) and the other retail trade industry (9 per cent).

Sources: Adapted from Tourism Indicators, Australia, 2002 and Australian National Accounts: TSA – 2000–01.

---

are salient to manpower planning, education planning and tourism management. The demand for labour is a derived demand. Labour is demanded when a good or service is demanded. PricewaterhouseCoopers (2002) analysed hotel employment trends in the UK where they noted that following spectacular job gains in the UK in the mid to late 1990s, during 2000 and 2001 UK hotel employment was hurt by a combination of factors that included foot-and-mouth disease and the global economic slowdown. The article confirms that hotel occupancy is the primary driving force behind hotel employment trends. Employment in the leisure and tourism sector is thus directly related to expenditure on goods and services offered by the sector. Figure 12.2 shows the possible outcomes of leisure and tourism spending.

Some expenditure will be on imported goods or services and will therefore create employment overseas. Domestic recreation, leisure and tourism goods and services will be supplied as a result of domestic expenditure and exports. The resulting derived demand for labour will also depend upon the price of labour relative to other factors of production and the possible

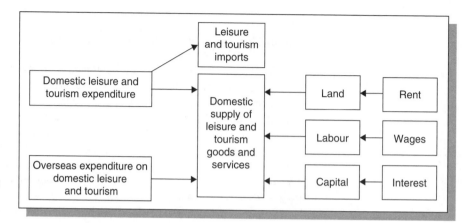

Figure 12.2
Demand for labour in leisure and tourism sector

Table 12.2 Employment in tourism-related industries, Great Britain ('000)

Year	Hotels and other tourist accommodation	Restaurants, cafes, etc.	Bars, public houses and nightclubs	Travel agents and tour operators	Libraries, museums and other cultural activities
1992	311.0	303.0	414.2	69.2	74.8
1996	399.1	487.9	506.4	104.0	73.9
2000	406.2	555.2	576.1	131.4	88.9
2002	418.0	545.4	535.9	133.6	81.4

Source: Adapted from Office of National Statistics, Annual Abstract of Statistics.

---

technical mix of factors of production able to provide the goods or services. For example, if the price of labour rises, producers will attempt to use more machinery (capital) where this is technically possible. It is generally the case that the recreation, leisure and tourism share of total employment is higher than its share of industry gross value added. This is because this sector tends to be more labour intensive, on average, than other forms of economic activity.

Table 12.2 shows recent employment trends in tourism-related industries in Great Britain. It demonstrates a rise in employment in each of the component sectors and an overall contribution to national employment of 2.1 millions (about 10 per cent of the workforce). This represents an increase of about 27 per cent in the period 1992–2002. However, in some areas of Great Britain leisure and tourism is of particular significance and is one of the main sources of economic activity. For example, a 1993 survey by PA Cambridge Economic Consultants Ltd and the Southern Tourist Board found that approximately 20 per cent of the workforce of the Isle of Wight was employed in the tourist industry and 24 per cent of its GDP was generated by tourism. Additionally, Thomas and Townsend (2001) examine evidence on tourism employment in the UK and find that the 1990s shows

Table 12.3 Employees by sector, Great Britain (millions)

	1980	1985	1990	1995	2000	2003
Services	14.9	15.1	17.1	17.4	19.4	20.2
Manufacturing	6.4	5.0	4.7	4.0	3.9	3.4

Source: Adapted from Office of National Statistics, Monthly Trends.

major departures from patterns of change of the 1980s and from other sectors in the 1990s. In the 1990s they note that the tourism sector no longer seemed to exhibit the exceptionally rapid growth that had been almost an article of faith for those who build economic development strategies around tourism.

In Australia, there were about 551 000 persons in tourism generated employment in 2000–01, the number of tourism employed persons grew by 7.4 per cent between 1997–98 and 2000–01 and the tourism share of total employed persons in 2001 was 6.0 per cent. Retail trade generated the most tourism employment, whilst the three areas of retail trade, accommodation, and cafes and restaurants accounted for more than half of the employment generated by tourism.

In the USA, data from the Quarterly Census of Employment and Wages (Bureau of Labour Statistics) (2004) shows that for the economy as a whole arts, entertainment, and recreation represents about 1.4 per cent of all employment and accommodation and food services makes up about 8.0 per cent of all employment. Estimates for leisure and hospitality show annual average employment at 9 732 000 in 1993, rising to 11 969 000 by 2002.

It is more difficult to extract employment in leisure manufacturing from published data, as many of the industrial classifications used by governments include leisure and non-leisure items. Table 12.3 shows the employment totals for the services and manufacturers sectors in Great Britain. It shows a picture common in many post-industrial nations. Whilst employment in the services sector has grown in importance, manufacturing employment has shown a long-term decline. This is known as deindustrialization. This is caused by three factors. First, technological progress enables productivity increases in manufacturing and thus the ratio of labour input to output declines. Second, manufacturing has been subject to intense competition from low-labour cost countries such as China and Vietnam, so many manufactured goods are now imported. Third, as incomes increase expenditure on services increases by a greater proportion (services demonstrate high-income elasticity of demand). Although in many cases new service sector jobs have made up for lob losses in manufactures there are some concerns that wage levels for these emerging industries are less than those of the declining industries. Smeral (2003) discusses why in general, tourism grows faster than the economy as a whole. He notes structural changes in demand and the differentials between productivity in tourism and manufacturing. He also notes that the demand factor explains why tourism's income elasticity is above 1.

Wages

Wages in any particular labour market will be determined by the demand and supply of labour but will also be influenced by Trade Union activity and minimum wage legislation. In this regard Waddoups (2001) has investigated the situation of a significant union presence in the hotel-casino industry in Las Vegas, Nevada, USA, juxtaposed to the near absence of union representation in Reno. Results of the analysis show a significantly higher incidence of poverty-level wages among hotel-casino workers in Reno compared to workers in similar occupations in Las Vegas. The supply of labour to some parts of the recreation leisure and tourism (e.g. hotels and catering) sector is largely unskilled and this exerts a downward pressure on wages. Similarly more women than men are employed in this sector and the lower wages of the sector therefore reflect the lower wages paid to women than men in general.

This is illustrated in Table 12.4 which shows comparative annual salaries of selected industries in the state of New York. These figures should be viewed with some care as it is not always easy to classify jobs accurately to the leisure sector (e.g. does an accountant for a leisure organization appear under professional and business services or leisure). However, the figures show that salaries in the leisure and hospitality industries are significantly lower than those in other sectors. The authors of this and similar reports note that the salary levels in the new service sector jobs are rarely as high as those in the old manufacturing sector jobs that they replace.

Workers in the hotel and catering sector are amongst the key beneficiaries of minimum wage legislation where it exists.

Table 12.4 Annual average salaries for industries in New York state, 2002

Industry	Salary ($)
Educational and health services	34 613
Leisure and hospitality	21 184
Retail trade	24 985
Other services	26 307
Government	42 947
Construction	47 721
Financial activities	103 744
Natural resources and mining	26 190
Transportation and utilities	43 410
Wholesale trade	55 917
Manufacturer of non-durable goods	42 763
Professional and business services	58 626
Information	66 569
Manufacturer of durable goods	48 924

Source: Adapted from Economic Policy Institute,
www.fiscalpolicy.org/jan21economicupdate~jobquality.pdf

Taxation

Recreation, leisure and tourism activities also offer an important stream of taxation revenue. A World Travel and Tourism Council (WTTC) Research Report has forecast that travel and tourism's global direct, indirect and personal tax contribution will exceed $802.6 billion in 1998. This contribution is projected to grow to $1765.3 billion by 2010. The industry's indirect tax contribution has been estimated at 10.6 per cent of total tax revenues worldwide. Estimates for each of the 24 Organisation for Economic Co-operation and Documentation (OECD) counties put the Travel and Tourism indirect contribution between 9 per cent and 24 per cent. As an example tourism tax revenues to the Province of Ontario, Canada represent 3.7 per cent of its total tax revenue. Whilst most of the tourism taxation revenues arise from income, sales and profits taxes there are some specific taxes on tourism such as air travel taxes, departure taxes (see Plate 12), overnight stay taxes and environment taxes. Exhibit 12.2 details some of the special tourism taxes in Florida, USA and their contribution to state tax revenues.

Plate 12
Tourism's contribution to
tax revenue
Source: The author

Exhibit 12.2 Tourist and Convention Development Tax in Miami-Dade County, Florida

Tourist and Convention Development Taxes fall within three main categories:

1 Tourist and Convention Development Taxes on Transient Rentals (bed taxes). In total, there is a 6 per cent tax collected on the rental amount from any person who rents, leases or lets for consideration any living quarter accommodations in a hotel, apartment hotel, motel, resort motel, apartment motel, rooming house, mobile home park, recreational vehicle park, single family dwelling, beach house, cottage, condominium or any other sleeping accommodations rented for a period of 6 months or less.
2 Tourist Development Surtax (TDS) on Sales of Food and Beverages in Hotels/Motels. A 2 per cent Food and Beverage Tax is collected on the sale of all food and beverages (alcoholic and non-alcoholic) by restaurants, coffee shops, snack bars, wet bars, nightclubs, banquet halls, catering or room services, and any other food and beverage facilities in or on the property of a hotel or motel.
3 Homeless and Domestic Violence Tax on Sale of Food and Beverages. A 1 per cent Homeless and Domestic Violence Tax is collected on all food and beverage sales by establishments that are licensed by the State of Florida to sell alcoholic beverages for consumption on the premises, except for hotels and motels. Only businesses that make over $400 000 in gross receipts annually are obligated to collect this tax.

Tourism-related taxes contributed nearly $4 million into Miami-Dade's economy in November 2003, an increase of more than a half-million dollars from the same month the previous year.

Sources: Miami-Dade County Tax Collector, and Miami Today.

Multipliers

The analysis of data in the previous sections has looked at tourism, recreation and leisure contributions to national income and the economy at a single point in time. This is termed as 'static' analysis. However, consideration of Figure 12.1 shows that tourism and leisure expenditure, like any other form of expenditure, also has 'dynamic' or 'multiplier' (Archer, 1982) effects due to the circular flow of income and expenditure in the economy. The initial effects of expenditure will generate income but there will be further effects as that income generates expenditure and so on.

Figure 12.3 illustrates the circular flow of income and expenditure derived from Figure 12.1. Assume now that there is an investment into this closed system of £100 000 on a new leisure complex. Firms will hire factors of production to the value of £100 000 and therefore national income, measured at point *A*, will rise by £100 000. However, the effects of the

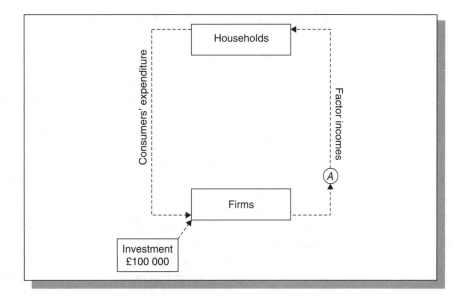

Figure 12.3
Investment and the
circular flow of income

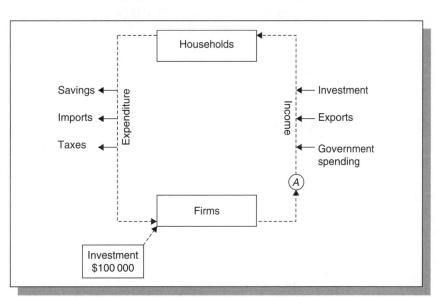

Figure 12.4
Circular flow with
injections and leakages

investment do not stop there. The workers who earned money from building the complex will spend their money in shops and bars, etc. Thus the incomes of shop and bar owners will rise. They in turn will spend their incomes. In other words, a circular flow of income and expenditure will take place. The investment expenditure sets in motion a dynamic process, and the total extra income passing point *A* will exceed the initial £100 000. This is known as the multiplier effect.

In the closed system illustrated by Figure 12.3, the effect would be perpetual and infinite, with the extra expenditure circulating round and round the system. In the real world however there are points at which money can leave and enter the system. This is illustrated in Figure 12.4.

The key leakages or withdrawals from the economy are savings, imports and taxes. Savings represents funds retained by households and firms. Imports result in expenditure flowing overseas, and taxes represent money taken out of the circular flow of income by the government in the form of income tax, value-added tax (VAT) and corporation tax, for example.

On the other hand there are also injections or flows into the circular flow of income. These are investment, exports resulting in money from overseas entering the circular flow, and government spending including for example pensions and unemployment benefit. Clearly there are often strong relationships between specific leakages and injections. To keep the model simple, injections and leakages are located neatly around the system but in reality they occur in many different places.

The existence of leakages means that money is flowing out of the economy during each cycle. So, in the example of the £100 000 investment in a leisure complex, perhaps £10 000 might be saved by workers, £5000 spend on imported goods, and £10 000 taken in taxation. Thus the initial effect on national income measured at point A in Figure 12.4 is £100 000. Out of this, £25 000 will be lost in leakages from the economy, leaving £75 000 to recirculate, adding another £75 000 to national income at point A. This process then continues, but with each cycle becoming smaller. It should be seen that the size of the multiplier effect will depend upon the amount of the original injection under examination and the leakages from the economy.

The Keynesian multiplier

The Keynesian multiplier can now be formally analysed. The multiplier (k) shows the amount by which a change in expenditure (ΔEXP) in an economy leads to a change in national income (ΔY).

$$\Delta EXP \times k = \Delta Y$$

Thus if an increase in investment on a leisure complex of £100 000 led to a final increase in national income of £400 000, then the multiplier would have a value of 4.

The multiplier can be illustrated by reference to Table 12.5 and Figure 12.5.

Investment in the leisure complex of £100 000 is made and national income at point A is raised by £100 000. In round 2, leakages consist of £10 000 in savings, £10 000 in taxes and £5000 in imports, leaving £75 000 in domestic expenditure to recirculate round the circular flow. An extra £75 000 is therefore added to national income at point A. In round 3, leakages consist of £7500 in savings, £7500 in taxes and £3750 in imports, leaving £56 250 in domestic expenditure. This process continues, and the leakages reduce the value of extra domestic expenditure and national income at every round. In fact, the extra amounts of national income tend towards zero. If the additions to national income in column 6, for years $1 - n$ (where n: the year in which the effect has dwindled to near zero) were added up, they would sum to £400 000, thus giving a value for the multiplier of 4.

Table 12.5 Multiplier rounds

Round	ΔS	ΔT	ΔM	ΔEXP	ΔY
1				100 000	100 000
2	10 000	10 000	5 000	75 000	75 000
3	7 500	7 500	3 750	56 250	56 250
4	5 625	5 625	2 812.50	42 187.50	42 187.50
5	4 218.75	4 218.75	2 109.36	31 640.63	31 640.63
6	3 164.06	3 164.06	1 582.03	23 730.47	23 730.47
7	2 373.05	2 373.05	1 186.02	17 797.85	17 797.85
8	1 779.76	1 779.76	889.89	13 348.39	13 348.39
$9 - n$	...	...	...	...	...
Total				400 000	400 000

Note: Rounds $9 - n$ represent the remaining multiplier rounds. *S*: Savings; *T*: taxes; *M*: imports; *EXP*: expenditure; *Y*: income; Δ: change in.

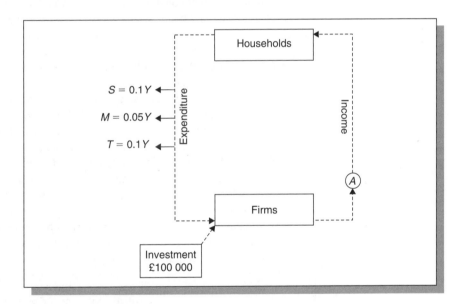

Figure 12.5
The multiplier round
S: savings, *M*: imports,
T: taxes and *Y*: income

There is also a formula for calculating the multiplier:

$$k = 1/MPL$$

where MPL = the marginal propensity to leak (the proportion of extra income that leaks out of the economy).

$$MPL = MPS + MPM + MPT$$

where MPS: marginal propensity to save (the proportion of extra income saved), MPM: marginal propensity to spend on imports (the proportion of extra income spent on imports) and MPT: marginal propensity to be taxed (the proportion of extra income taken in taxes).

In the above example, $MPS = 0.1Y$, $MPM = 0.05Y$ and $MPT = 0.1Y$, where Y = income. Therefore:

$$k = 1/(0.1 + 0.05 + 0.1)$$
$$k = 1/0.25$$
$$k = 4$$

Tourism multipliers

Considerable research has been done into the impact of tourism and leisure expenditure using multiplier techniques. Salma (2002) explains the meaning of the indirect effects of tourism and measures these effects for the Australian economy and this is illustrated in Exhibit 12.3.

Exhibit 12.3   Indicators of direct, indirect and total contribution of tourism to the economy of Australia

'The economic contribution of tourism has two elements: direct and indirect. The direct contribution is solely concerned with the immediate effect of expenditure made by visitors. For example, when a tourist uses a taxi service, the direct output effect includes only the service of the taxi driver and the direct employment effect includes the proportion of the driver's employment that is spent driving tourists.

   The taxi driver, however, buys fuel from a petrol station, machinery parts from a garage, meals while on duty from a food outlet and so on. Petrol stations, garages and food outlets all hire staff and produce output to serve the taxi drivers, who in turn serve customers, some of whom are tourists. The food outlet in turn engages food manufacturers, electricity companies, delivery services and many other industries to provide the necessary inputs required to prepare the snacks it sells. Similarly, many industries are involved in supplying the necessary inputs to the petrol stations and the garages. The chain effects on output and jobs started by the initial taxi service demand of the tourist comprise what is termed tourism's indirect effects on output and employment.'

	Direct contribution	Indirect contribution	Total contribution
Tourism gross value added (AUS $ million)	26 284	26 772	53 056
Per cent	4.3	4.4	8.7
Tourism GDP ($ million)	31 814	27 287	59 101
Per cent	4.7	4.1	8.8
Tourism employment ('000 jobs)	551	397	948
Per cent	6.0	4.3	10.4

Source: Adapted from Salma (2002), indirect economic contribution of tourism to Australia (www.abs.gov.au).

The aim of this approach is to assess the full impact of the sector on incomes, output and employment at national, regional and local levels. However, Leiper (1999) argues that recent studies grossly overestimate tourism's contribution to employment in Australia which he estimates to be around 200 000. Impacts and multipliers are clearly an important issue for governments in assessing the contribution of such developments to economic activity. The main multipliers developed for impact analysis are:

- the output multiplier,
- the income multiplier,
- the employment multiplier,
- the government revenue multiplier.

Taking the case of the tourism income multiplier (TIM), values vary according to leakages, as summarized in Table 12.6, and actual results include Canada ($TIM = 2.5$), UK ($TIM = 1.8$), Iceland ($TIM = 0.6$) and Edinburgh ($TIM = 0.4$). Exhibit 12.4 discusses tourism multipliers in Scotland.

Table 12.6 Multiplier and expenditure impacts

Value of multiplier	Leakages from the economy	Impact of expenditure on income
High	Low	High
Low	High	Low

Exhibit 12.4 Small is beautiful

The Scottish Office has been studying the relationship between size of tourism establishments and effects on local income and spending. Its findings are that smaller organizations are more beneficial to local economies because the centralized buying activities of large organizations take spending take spending out of the local area.

The Scottish Tourism Multiplier Study on Edinburgh made the following findings. In 1990, it is estimated that domestic and overseas tourists spent £276 million in Edinburgh. For every £1000 spent by UK-resident tourists in Edinburgh, approximately £346 in income is generated locally and £127 in income is generated in the rest of Scotland. It takes about £27 000 of spending by domestic tourists to create one new job in the city.

Source: Scottish Office.

Leisure and tourism inflation

Inflation can be defined as a rise in the general level of prices or a fall in the purchasing power of money. It is measured by the retail price index (RPI). If one country has a faster rate of inflation than that of other countries, it can cause a decline in international competitiveness. This is likely to affect firms producing leisure products for the export market, and countries which rely on tourism. It is less likely to affect firms in leisure services since customers rarely have the option to seek lower prices overseas for these.

Constructing a tourism destination price index

It is possible to construct a tourism destination price index (TDPI) using a similar methodology to that used to construct the general RPI. Table 12.7 gives an example of such an index. The steps are as follows (with rows and columns referring to Table 12.7):

- First it is necessary to define the population for whom the index is intended. This might be a specific index for golfers or skiers.
- Next an expenditure survey must be conducted to establish the spending patterns of the target population, ensuring that a representatve sample of the target population is surveyed.
- From this two important findings should emerge – first a 'basket of goods' (and services) that lists the items bought by tourists can be compiled (column 1), and second the relative importance of each item can be gauged from the expenditure survey and each item given a weighting accordingly. For example, if an expenditure survey in Japan showed

Table 12.7 Tourism price index, example (Japanese yen)

Item	Weight (W)	1996 Price (P)	P × W	1997 Price (P)	P × W	1998 Price (P)	P × W
Wine (25 cl)	0.4	200	80	220	88	250	100
Beer (0.5 l)	4.0	190	760	195	780	200	800
Three-course meal	11.6	800	9280	880	10 208	950	11 020
...	...	...	...	...	...	...	...
...	...	...	...	...	...	...	...
Total			50 107		52 612		56 119
Index multiple				0.0019957291			
Index			100		105		112

Notes: Item = row 1, column 1; the dots in rows 6 and 7 denote the rest of the basket of goods.

10 times more beer to be consumed than wine, then beer would be assigned a weighting 10 times more than that for wine (column 2). Thus, if beer and wine both rose in price by 20 per cent, the effect of wine on the TDPI would be less than the beer effect.

- A survey of the prices of the basket of goods is then conducted (column 3).
- Expenditure on each item is determined by multiplying its price by its weighting (column 4).
- The total expenditure on the basket of goods is recorded (row 8).
- This amount is then converted to a index number with base 100, by using a multiplier (row 9), and this becomes the base year reading. (e.g., if the expenditure total is £50, a multiplier of 2 is needed to convert the result to 100.)
- The basket of goods is priced at regular intervals (columns 5 and 7), with expenditure totals (row 8) being converted to an index number (row 10) using the multiplier established in the base year (row 9).

The index resulting from this exercise (Table 12.7) gives a picture of tourism inflation in the local currency. It is possible to adjust the index to reflect exchange rate conditions in different countries. Thus, whilst Table 12.7 measures tourism inflation for a Japanese visitor to a Japanese destination, Table 12.8 shows how the index can be adapted for a British visitor.

Table 12.8 uses the expenditure data from row 8 of Table 12.7. This is then converted to an equivalent in the currency under consideration (sterling in this example). A new index multiple is calculated to convert the raw expenditure figure to an index number with base 100. Comparison of the two tables shows the importance of considering exchange rate fluctuations when comparing prices between tourist destinations.

It must be remembered that any tourism price index represents an average picture, and individuals will be affected differently according to their particular expenditure patterns. Care must also be exercised in the collecting of data. There must be consistency of sources, otherwise the index will be distorted by changes in prices which result for example, by moving from a local store to a supermarket.

Table 12.9 shows the relative dollar prices of commonly consumed leisure goods and services in different countries.

Table 12.8 Tourism price index (exchange rate-adjusted)

	1996	1997	1998
Total (yen)	50 107	52 612	56 119
£1 = ? yen	198	240	251
Total (£s)	253.06	219.22	223.53
Index multiple		0.39516	
Index	100	86.54	88.33

Table 12.9 International price comparisons for leisure goods and services ($) (2000)

Item	Japan	Russia	Denmark	Argentina	UK	USA	Brazil	Ecuador	Zimbabwe
Chocolate (100 g)	1.86	0.94	1.26	1.82	1.07	1.25	0.76	0.46	0.99
Whisky (75 cl)	19.00	29.75	30.05	15.84	21.33	19.38	17.87	19.88	11.97
White wine (75 cl)	16.56	16.66	6.89	8.69	8.66	10.98	7.60	7.39	7.05
Cigarettes (20)	2.51	1.44	4.65	1.60	6.04	3.12	0.92	0.72	1.08
Compact disk (CD) (one)	23.13	22.81	19.76	21.41	23.09	16.44	11.47	16.17	16.96
CD Player	234.90	148.74	223.16	236.57	165.66	116.44	152.91	180.38	278.37
Gasoline (1 l)	0.97	0.31	1.09	1.00	1.22	0.37	0.68	0.44	0.36
Dinner at restaurant*	58.12	51.12	48.46	40.02	38.32	35.67	24.35	15.75	14.50
Drink at bar (double)	11.77	11.20	8.98	10.42	5.82	6.33	4.53	4.88	1.48

Source: Adapted from ECA International Survey.

Government policy

Income and employment

Governments throughout the world see recreation leisure and tourism as a source of employment, particularly where structural changes in the economy have led to job losses. Government policies to promote employment may include the following:

- Demand management: Where there is unemployment throughout the economy, some economists advocate government stimulation of aggregate demand so as to induce more production and thus employment. Aggregate demand may be stimulated through tax cuts, increased government spending and interest rate cuts. The major drawback to such a policy is its tendency to encourage inflation.
- Export-led policies: Overseas expenditure on leisure and tourism products can contribute to employment. Government policy here includes expenditure on overseas marketing to promote tourist demand for leisure, recreation and tourism services. A low-exchange rate also assists exports of services and leisure goods.
- Project assistance: The government also considers direct assistance with projects on an individual basis, particularly where a project can be shown to bring employment to areas of high unemployment (see Chapter 11). For example, there was considerable competition between

France and the UK over inducements offered to lure EuroDisney to each country. The European Union (EU) also has a regional fund which can be a source of financial assistance.

Inflation

Governments of countries with comparatively high rates of inflation may utilize counter-inflationary policy. However, it is important first to diagnose the cause of inflation.

Causes of inflation • • •

The causes of inflation can be divided into the categories of cost-push, demand-pull, monetary, taxation and expectations.

Cost-push inflation occurs when increased production costs are passed on as price rises. These can include first wage increases which outstrip productivity increases. Second increased raw material prices can be important. If raw materials are imported, a fall in the exchange rate can increase their local currency price. Demand-pull inflation tends to occur when an economy is growing too fast. It arises because the aggregate demand in the economy exceeds the aggregate supply in the economy and therefore prices are bid up. For example, labour may become scarce, putting an upward pressure on wages.

Too rapid an increase in the money supply of an economy can cause an increase on consumer credit which can stimulate demand-pull inflation and accommodate cost-push inflation. Increases in indirect taxes such as sales taxes will have an effect on prices, whilst if people expect inflation to rise, they will often seek to protect their living standards by higher-wage demands. These of course will then cause the very inflation that people are seeking to avoid.

Counter-inflationary policy • • •

Government counter-inflationary policy will affect the economic environment of leisure and tourism organizations. Cost-push inflation may be tackled by a high-exchange rate policy. Whilst this may be good for tackling inflation, it makes firms' exports less competitive. Wage rises may be tackled by government-imposed incomes policy to curb pay increases. This may cause a deterioration in industrial relations. Deflationary policy may be used to tackle demand-pull inflation. This may entail increasing interest rates to curb consumer borrowing, or increased taxes to reduce consumer spending. Either way, whilst inflation may be tackled, firms will suffer a general contraction in demand. High-interest rates are sometimes also used to curb overexpansion of the money supply by reducing the demand for borrowing. Indeed many Central Banks now set national interest rates at a level to control inflation.

Review of key terms

- Macroeconomics: the study of the national economy.
- National income: a measure of the total level of economic activity which takes place in an economy over a year.
- GDP: gross domestic product.
- GNP: gross national product.
- NNP: net national product (national income).
- Money national income: national income calculated at current prices.
- Real national income: national income calculated at constant prices (inflationary element removed).
- TIM (Tourism Income Multiplier): exaggerated effect of a change in tourism expenditure on an area's income.
- TDPI: tourism destination price index.
- Basket of goods: typical items bought by a defined group.
- Cost-push inflation: inflation caused by changes in input prices.
- Demand-pull inflation: inflation caused by excess of aggregate demand over aggregate supply.
- Demand management: government policy to influence total demand in an economy.

Data Questions

Task 12.1

Table 12.10 shows inflation rates for selected countries.

Table 12.10 Inflation rates

	2001	2002	2003	2004
Japan	−0.7	−0.9	−0.3	−0.6
UK	2.1	2.2	2.8	2.5
Turkey	54.0	45.0	26.0	13.0
Thailand	1.5	0.6	1.4	0.1
USA	1.3	2.2	1.7	1.6

Source: Adapted from IMF, World Economic Outlook.

Recap Questions

1. If entrance to Disneyland cost $20 at the beginning of 2004 and its price has kept pace with inflation, what would a ticket cost at the beginning of 2005?
2. Why might the RPI for a country not be a good guide to tourism prices?
3. What other information would you seek before deciding on which countries might be good or bad value to visit?

4 Account for the differing rates of inflation between countries.
5 Describe and account for the possible causes of the different inflationary conditions in Japan and Turkey.
6 What likely consequences are there of inflation in Japan and Turkey?

Task 12.2 Local reflections on the Channel Tunnel

The Channel Tunnel is dug, equipped and running. How does local opinion see its effects? John Ovenden, Labour leader, and Allison Wainman, Liberal Democrat leader on Kent County Council, made a joint statement reflecting on possible impacts, on the official tunnel opening.

'For Kent, the tunnel is a mixed blessing. There is no doubt that many people in Kent have paid and will continue to pay a high price in terms of the environmental effect of the project. 'Equally, traditional cross-Channel operators, who provide many jobs for Kent people, face a real challenge, although there is every sign that they are responding positively. 'However, we are determined to maximize the benefits for Kent of the tunnel. By opening up transport corridors at the heart of Europe, it represents an opportunity too good to be missed at a time when the country is well placed to take advantage. For too long, parts of the county have been in the economic doldrums.'

It is certainly true that Kent has had its fair share of economic misery in recent years. Agricultural employment in the county, renowned for hop growing and orchards, has suffered a steady long-term decline in the face of mechanization. It is easy to forget that Kent once had a coal industry which closed in the face of cheap imports in the 1980s. Defence cuts and the peace dividend have been responsible for the decline of Chatham whose prosperity has rested on its naval dockyards. Such is the level of unemployment in north and east Kent that they have gained assisted-area status. Thanet is eligible for assistance from the EU on account of its 17 per cent unemployment rate.

Consultants estimate that nearly 2000 jobs will have been created by the Channel Tunnel by 1996. However, it is also estimated that about 15 000 people are employed in jobs related to port activities in Kent and that a net loss of 3000 of these jobs will result from the impact of the tunnel on ferry services by 1996. More difficult to estimate is the employment effects of the tunnel on the tourism industry. The county is second only to London as a destination for overseas visitors, who spent £132 million in 1992. It is likely that the tunnel will boost this figure.

Source: The author, from news cuttings.

Recap Questions

1 What general employment conditions are described in the article for Kent?
2 Describe the employment effects of the Channel Tunnel using the following headings:
   (a) Direct (employment provided by the project itself).
   (b) Displacement (employment lost because of the project's effects).
   (c) Indirect (employment gained or lost by the project's effects).
3 What are the likely multiplier effects on Kent of:
   (a) the construction phase of the tunnel?
   (b) the operation phase of the tunnel?

Task 12.3

Table 12.11 shows the economic impact of tourism on the Province of Ontario, Canada.

Table 12.11   Tourism and the economy of Ontario

Total tourism receipts ($ billion)	Can $19.4 (US $12.5)
As a per cent of provincial GDP	4.4 per cent
Tourism value added ($ billion)	Can $7.4 (US $4.8)
As a per cent of provincial GDP	1.7 per cent
Tourism employment ('000 of jobs)	261.7
As a per cent of provincial employment	4.4 per cent
Tourism labour income ($ billion)	Can $5.6 (US $3.0)
As a per cent of provincial labour income	2.3 per cent
Provincial tourism tax revenues ($ billion)	Can $1.8 (US $1.2)
As a per cent of provincial tax revenues, 2001/2002	3.7 per cent
Municipal tourism tax Revenues ($ billion)	Can $0.6 (US $0.4)
Federal tourism tax Revenues ($ billion)	Can $2.4 (US $1.6)
Tourism's foreign earnings ($ billion)	Can $7.3 (US $4.7)
As a per cent of ontario's total exports	3.2 per cent
Ontarians' total spending on tourism ($ billion)	Can $16.9 (US $10.9)
As a per cent of total personal spending	6.8 per cent
As a per cent of personal disposable income	6.2 per cent

Source: Ministry of Tourism, Ontario (2004).

Recap Questions

1 Describe and explain in economic terms the economic impact of tourism on Ontario.
2 This data does not include the indirect effects of tourism. Explain what these are using multiplier analysis.
3 How could the provincial government seek to increase the economic impacts of tourism on Ontario?
4 What is GDP? How is it measured? What problems arise from attempting to measure the economic impact of tourism on an economy and how can these be addressed?

Multiple choice

1 **Which of the following is not true?**

   (a) National income = national expenditure.
   (b) Real and money will be the same where there is no inflation.
   (c) Employment in the services sector is falling in most developed economies.

(d) Minimum wages have little effect on those working in the hospitality industry.

2 **Tourism Satellite Accounts:**

(a) Are useful because otherwise the contribution of tourism to GNP is under estimated.
(b) Are necessary because the contribution of tourism to GNP is often over estimated.
(c) Measure the contribution of Space Tourism to the economy.
(d) Are needed to discount the effects of inflation on tourism's value to GNP.

3 **A survey on a tourism destination found that for every £1 spent, 25 penny leaked out of the economy of the destination in the form of savings, taxes and imported goods. The value of the destination income multiplier would be**

(a) 4.00
(b) 0.75
(c) 0.25
(d) 2.50

4 **Which of the following is classified as a leakage in the circular flow of income?**

(a) Savings
(b) Investment
(c) Inflation
(d) Exports

5 **Which of the following is not true?**

(a) Cost-push inflation occurs when increased production costs are passed on as price rises
(b) Inflation can be defined as a rise in the general level of prices
(c) Inflation causes a rise in the purchasing power of money
(d) Most Central Banks set interest rates to control the level of inflation

Review questions

1 Distinguish between changes in money and real GNP.
2 What are the main leakages and injections into the circular flow of income?
3 What is meant by the TIM and what determines its size?
4 Outline the main steps involved in constructing a tourism price index.
5 What government polices have
  (a) Encouraged?
  (b) Discouraged employment in the leisure and tourism sector?
6 Why is it difficult to measure the impact of recreation, leisure and tourism to the economy?

Web sites of interest

USA statistics www.stat-usa.gov/
New Zealand statistics www.stats.govt.nz/statsweb.nsf
Australian Bureau of Statistics www.abs.gov.au
Brazil statistics www.ibge.gov.br
Canada statistics www.statcan.ca
UK statistics www.emap.com
World Bank www.worldbank.org
International Monetary Fund www.imf.org
Learning help in economics and business studies www.bized.ac.uk

Economic development and regeneration

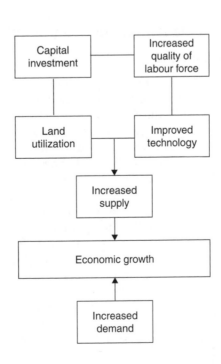

Objectives and learning outcomes

The objective of this chapter is to examine how recreation, leisure and tourism can contribute to the long-term growth of economies and to the regeneration of areas affected by structural change. First, general aspects of economic growth will be discussed. Second, case studies will demonstrate how leisure and tourism have contributed to economic growth in developed countries such as France, Japan and Spain. Third, the special problems of growth and development in less-developed countries will be examined. Case studies of China and Vietnam will be used to illustrate the role of leisure and tourism in such development. There is clearly much further scope for tourism development in less-developed countries which had only about a quarter share of world tourism receipts in the 1990s. Fourth, the chapter will consider the issue of regeneration. Issues surrounding the costs of economic growth and development will be examined in Chapters 16 and 17. By studying this chapter students should be able to:

- define and explain economic growth,
- review critically the concept of economic growth,
- understand the determinants of economic growth,
- evaluate appropriate growth strategies for developed and developing countries (DCs),
- evaluate the role of the sector in regeneration strategies,
- evaluate the contribution of the sector to growth.

Meaning and measurement of economic growth

Meaning and measurement

Economic growth is defined as the increase in real output per capita of a country. There are thus three elements involved in its measurement. First, the change in output of an economy needs to be measured. The most commonly used measure of output is gross national product (GNP). However, as explained in Chapter 12, money GNP, or GNP at current prices, can overestimate changes in a country's output. This is because they include increases due to higher prices (inflation) as well as higher output. Therefore real GNP figures are used to calculate growth. Second, the GNP figures need to be adapted to take account of increases in population. Dividing real GNP by the population gives real GNP per capita. Figure 13.1 illustrates some comparative data for international growth rates.

It can be seen that the economy of China has exhibited remarkable growth of 10 per cent per annum, due largely to its economic reforms which have allowed foreign investment and private enterprise. By contrast the rate of growth in Japan has been comparatively modest. A number of countries have witnessed negative economic growth – meaning their output is shrinking each year. These include two economies in transition (the

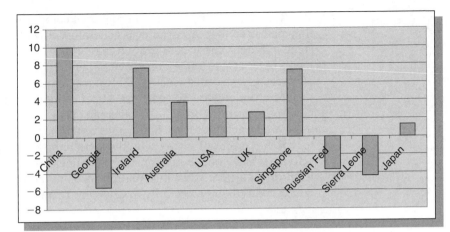

Figure 13.1
Growth rates (per cent change in real GDP) for selected countries 1990–2001
Source: Adapted from IMF. www.worldbank.org/data

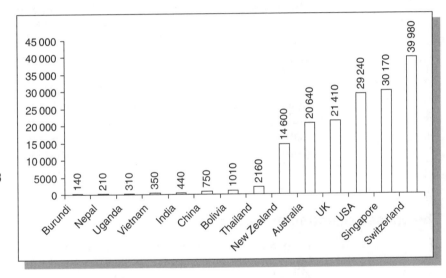

Figure 13.2
GNP per capita ($US), selected countries, 1998
Source: Adapted from World Bank.
www.worldbank.org/depweb/english/modules/economic/gnp/data.html

Russian Federation and Georgia where economic reforms and the transition to the market economy has caused economic problems) and Sierra Leone.

Problems of measurement

Figure 13.2 records per capita GNP data for various countries and demonstrates the huge international inequalities that are apparent. However, there are several problems involved in the measurement of GNP and thus economic growth. First, there are the problems associated with collecting national income data, as discussed in Chapter 12. Data collection is a particular problem in countries which do not have a highly developed statistical branch of government. Less-developed countries also have a bigger subsistence sector where goods and services are produced for self-consumption and therefore do not enter the market or appear on national income statistics. Second, in making international comparisons, country information measured in local currency is generally converted to dollar units. Thus some apparent changes in growth may in fact stem from currency movements against the dollar. Third, over a period of time the labour force may work fewer hours in a week. GNP figures do not reflect this and they may therefore underestimate some aspects of economic improvement. Fourth, GNP per capita figures are an average. They may disguise the fact that there are large differences in incomes of the population, or that some sectors of the community may actually be becoming poorer. Finally, economic activity which contributes to GNP has some unwanted side-effects in the form of pollution. GNP information takes no account of these, a matter which is discussed more fully in Chapters 16 and 17.

Rationale for growth

The rationale for the pursuit of growth is that people become better off in an economic sense. There are more goods and services produced to meet people's material wants. This may result in some combination of more employment, more public services, less taxes, more leisure time or more consumption. How the benefits of growth are actually distributed depends on the workings of the economic system and government policy. In less-developed countries the results of economic growth are generally much more profound, bringing social and environmental changes with material prosperity. Distribution of benefits is often less even. 'Those with land to sell, housing to rent, hotels to run, and labour, goods and services to sell favour it. The landless poor are generally less impressed.'

The causes of economic growth

Economic growth is promoted by an increase in the quality or quantity of inputs into the economy. It can therefore be examined under the headings of land, labour, capital and technology.

Land

Different countries have not only differing amounts of land but also different types of land. Resources may include mineral and agricultural ones, and in the leisure and tourism sector, climate, scenery, coasts and countryside are important resources. It is by the exploitation of such resources that countries can use their comparative advantage against other possible tourist destinations. The success of the French tourism industry is largely dependent on the country's natural endowments which allow skiing and beach and countryside leisure developments. Similarly, specific land resources can be identified as attractions for other destinations, including:

- Nepal: Everest.
- Caribbean: Coral Reef, climate.

- USA: Grand Canyon, Niagara Falls, Death Valley.
- Kenya: game parks.
- The Gambia: beaches and climate.

Labour

The labour force can be analysed in terms of its quantity and quality. The importance of the quantity of the labour force depends largely upon its relationship with other factors of production, land and capital. Where labour is a scarce factor of production, growth may be achieved by increasing the supply of labour, for example by encouraging immigration. However, in many economies labour is in over abundant supply. This means that the productivity of labour is low. This is particularly true in less-developed countries in the agricultural sector where land is overcrowded. On the other hand the low wages that result from an abundant labour force can in some cases be a source of economic growth. Wages in China and Vietnam, for example, are very low by international standards, and this has partially accounted for the inflow of foreign investment and the growth of China's industrial sector. The production of leisure goods such as audio equipment and toys is an important part of this industrial growth.

It is the quality of the labour force that is important in increasing productivity and improvements in quality stem from education and training programmes. Exhibit 13.1 illustrates steps being taken to improve the training of tourism workers in Tibet.

Exhibit 13.1   Training for tourism in Tibet

Nearly 30 administrators from Tibet's tourist industry attended a seminar in Beijing for developing tourism in the region.

Topics such as trends in China's tourism industry, and the special nature of Tibetan tourism were discussed with representatives from different areas in Tibet. The seminar is an example of China's wish to encourage tourism to help in the economic develop of its western regions and its efforts to train more qualified personnel for the emerging tourist industry of Tibet.

The China National Tourism Administration (CNTA) has taken several steps to encourage better training. These include the compilation of special textbooks for Tibet tourism professionals, and the development of tourism courses at Tibet University. CNTA has also provided books and computers for Tibet.

Li Yuezhong, an official with CNTA said that tourism will drive Tibet's economy in the future, so it is essential to train the autonomous region's tourism professionals. Over 600 000 tourists visited Tibet in 2001 with the number expected to reach 900 000 in 2002 including 120 000 visitors from overseas.

Source: Adapted from People's Daily Online
http://english.peopledaily.com.cn/

Finally, it is differences in cultural aspects of countries' populations that is an important motivation for tourism.

Capital

Capital, in the form of plant and machinery, results from investment and a distinction must be made between gross investment and net investment. Net investment refers just to investment which increases a nation's capital stock and therefore does not include replacement investment.

$$\text{Net investment} = \text{Gross investment} - \text{Depreciation}$$

Investment in new plant, machines and other capital enables labour productivity and GNP to rise. This can be an important source of economic growth for developing countries as labour moves from a relatively unmechanized agricultural sector to a mechanized industrial sector. The quality of investment is also an important issue. Investment in inappropriate machinery will have little effect on productivity and growth. Investment in infrastructure is important to develop industry in the leisure and tourism sector. This includes airports, ports and motorways, which allow access. Jamieson (2001) outlines eight key measures for creating a favourable atmosphere for investment in tourism infrastructure. These are:

1 Create a clear picture of the role of tourism in solving social, economic and environmental problems.
2 Creation of tourism investment information centres.
3 Encourage cooperation and integrated tourism development planning.
4 Creation of a positive investment climate.
5 Creation of special tourism investment zones.
6 Support human resource development.
7 Create opportunities for strategic product development.
8 Adopt innovative means of delivering quality infrastructure development.

A nation's cultural heritage includes investments made in previous generations and preserved for enjoyment today and therefore cultural capital is an important resource. For example, a third dimension to France's tourism attraction is its rich and well-preserved historical built environment. Other examples of cultural heritage capital include:

- China: the Great Wall and the Forbidden City.
- Rome: the Sistine Chapel and the Coliseum.
- Egypt: the Pyramids.
- Peru: Macchu Picchu.

Technology

Improved technology can increase growth by reducing production costs and creating new products for the market. The leisure products industry has particularly benefited from new product technology with camcorders,

---

Exhibit 13.2   Space tourism

1999:   As the search for the exotic becomes more difficult on earth, attention has turned to space to satisfy the demands of the most adventurous tourists. Buzz Aldrin a former Apollo astronaut, is one of a number of people employed to develop and promote space tourism.

A Japanese firm is developing plans for a hotel on the moon and a firm of architects, Wimberly Arson Tong and Goo, are planning a hotel in space which is scheduled to be orbiting 200 miles above the earth by 2017.

A UK firm called Space Adventures are already accepting deposits for space flights. It is estimated that the flights will cost around £60 000, and a deposit of £4000 secures a place on the waiting list.

2001:   A Soyuz U successfully launched Soyuz TM-32 carrying tourist Dennis Tito to the International Space Station (ISS) from Baikonur Cosmodrome, pad LC 1, at 0737 UTC (12:37 a.m. PDT) April 28. The Soyuz TM-32, flying on autopilot, docked with ISS at 1258 UTC (1:58 a.m. PDT) on April 30. Tito is reported to have paid US $20 million for his trip.

Source: The author (1999, 2001).

---

personal stereos, CDs, PCs and the electronic games market. So research and development (R&D) can be an important stimulus for economic growth. Exhibit 13.2 demonstrates the potential of technology to change the frontiers of tourism.

Promoting growth

Growth-promotion policies tend to be split into those that require government intervention and those that rely on liberalizing the free market.

Intervention

Interventionists believe the government should play a key role in funding appropriate education and training, R&D and investing in projects and infrastructure. They also note that the volatility of interest rates and exchange rates in the free market inhibits growth and so argue that government should manage the economy to provide a stable environment. Government intervention can also promote balanced growth where aggregate demand expands at a similar rate to aggregate supply, thereby avoiding the problems of inflation or unemployment associated with unbalanced growth.

Free market

The free market approach blames government intervention for lower growth. It is claimed that government spending programmes 'crowd out' funds, leaving less available and at higher interest rates for the private sector. Similarly, it is claimed that high taxes act as a disincentive for firms to invest. Supporters of market liberalization argue that profit is the best incentive for investment and that free trade and the actions of the price mechanism will ensure that investment and other resources are attracted to high-growth areas of the economy. Such policies are often referred to as 'supply side' policies. Supply side policies include:

- reducing government expenditure to release resources for the private sector,
- reducing taxes to increase incentives,
- reducing trade union power to encourage flexible labour markets,
- reducing welfare payments to encourage individual enterprise,
- encouraging risk and entrepreneurship and privatization,
- encouraging competition through deregulation,
- reducing red tape.

Leisure and tourism development in developed countries

The following case studies illustrate the role of different factors in the economic growth of Spain and Japan.

Leisure and tourism development in Spain

Leisure and tourism development has clearly made an important contribution to raising Spain's GNP per capita to levels approaching its European Union (EU) partners. Table 13.1 shows the continued growth of international tourist arrivals to Spain to reach second place in the table of international arrivals in 2002 earning US $33.6 billion.

The rapid growth of Spain's tourism industry can be attributed to a number of causes. First, its natural resources – particularly of coastline, beaches and climate. However, many countries enjoy similar natural features but have not enjoyed such growth. It is Spain's proximity to the fast growing economies of western Europe that provided the demand, with tourists from the UK, Germany and France being the most numerous. Accessibility in terms of air transport and motorway developments has also played a part. In recent years Spain has proved to be even more accessible

Table 13.1 International tourism arrivals to Spain (million)

1990	1995	1998	1999	2000	2001	2002
34.0	34.9	43.4	46.8	48.2	49.5	51.7

Source: Adapted from World Tourism Organization (WTO) statistics.

as low-cost air travel has developed rapidly in its main supplier country – the UK. This has led to a trend toward taking more frequent breaks, is establishing major cities as tourist destinations, and is contributing to the deseasonalization of tourism. Spain has also proved to be resilient to recent tourism shocks (9/11 and the Iraq war).

The success of tourism in Spain has itself stimulated investment. Earlier investment was often subsidized by overseas aid. For example, German investment in Gran Canaria was encouraged by the German government as a result of the 1968 Strauss Act which granted tax concessions for investments in underdeveloped countries. To these factors must be added the low-wage costs which have enabled Spain to compete successfully with France and the active encouragement of government.

There is a government ministry with direct responsibility for tourism, the Ministry of Transport, Tourism and Communications, and tourism has been represented at ministerial level in Spain since 1951. Government has provided direct investment (for example, in the *paradores* – the chain of state-run hotels often using renovated buildings of historical interest), as well as subsidies and infrastructure improvements (for example, to develop ski resorts). The government also funds the Institute of Tourism of Spain which promotes Spain abroad. Since joining the EU in 1986, Spain has benefited from European Regional Development Fund grants for infrastructure, particularly for providing better road access in the northern coastal region.

Tourism has been an important driving element of Spanish economic growth in the period 1995–2002, contributing more than 10 per cent of gross domestic product (GDP) annually with peaks in 2000 and 2001 in which it contributed more than 12 percentage points to the GDP. In 2002, foreign tourism brought more than €40 000 million to the Spanish balance of payments. Payments related to outbound tourism (tourism carried out by Spaniards outside of Spain) rose to €11 000 million. The difference between both shows a tourism credit balance of €29 000 million on the Spanish economy, equivalent to 4.3 per cent of the GDP. Tourism has also played an important role in the generation of employment in Spain since activities in tourism industries tend to be labour intensive. Here, the so-called 'characteristic' industries of tourism (hotels and other accommodations, restaurants, transport, travel agencies, etc.) generate more than 1½ million jobs, which is almost 10 per cent of the Spanish total employment.

The main problems that have arisen from Spain's reliance on tourism are first its dependence on economic prosperity in countries such as the UK, Germany and France. Spain is highly dependent on spending by German and UK tourists, who accounted for a combined 48.4 per cent of total visitors in 2003. However, the two countries displayed differing trends, with the number of German visitors falling and the number of UK tourists rising year-on-year over the 1999–2003 period. Earlier, recessions in those countries in the early 1980s and early 1990s caused tourism expenditure to fall in Spain.

Second, tourism employment tends to be low skilled and seasonal, and finally the dash for tourism growth in the 1960s and 1970s caused environmental degradation which threatens the continued prosperity of some of the earlier resort developments. However, by the late 1990s, tourism in

Spain had recovered in line with the economies of Europe, and there have been successful programmes to rescue resorts such as Benidorm, Torremolinos and Magaluf from earlier planning mistakes.

Balaguer and Cantavella-Jordá (2002) have examined the role of tourism in Spain's long-run economic development. They confirmed a tourism-led growth hypothesis through cointegration and causality testing. The results of this indicate that during the last three decades, economic growth in Spain has been influenced by the persistent expansion of international tourism. They find that the increase of this activity has produced multiplier effects over time. External competitiveness is proved in the model to be a fundamental variable for Spanish economic growth. From their empirical analysis the authors infer that there is a positive effect on income that government policy may bring about – through ensuring adequacy of supply as well as by the promotion of tourist activity.

The sectors which benefit from tourism include:

- Accommodation where receipts are predicted to amount to €10 592.2 million in 2003, up by 17.7 per cent on 1999. The economic slowdown and the competitiveness of new, cheaper sun and sand destinations on the Mediterranean were the major constraints on growth.
- The car rental market which is expected to reach a value of €995 million in 2003, up by 3.6 per cent on 2002.
- Tourist attractions which are predicted to earn €1373 million in 2003, up by 46.8 per cent on 1999.

Leisure and tourism development in Japan

Japan's post-war economic development was largely driven by the export of manufactured goods. These included a comprehensive range of leisure goods. Indeed, it was the quality and innovative nature of much of these products that made them so successful. The product list includes recreational cars and motor cycles, jet-skis, audio and video equipment, sports equipment and musical instruments.

Following the wave of manufacturing investment there has been a movement towards investment in leisure projects. This has been encouraged by the government with the passing of the Comprehensive Resort Region Provision Act in 1987 which provides tax relief and infrastructure support for resort construction projects. One of the aims of this is to create more balance in Japan's growth. Japanese economic growth has relied heavily on exports and these are subject to external factors such as overseas recessions and exchange rate movements. Investment in domestic leisure provision stimulates domestic demand and provides development in rural areas.

Projects have included golf courses, ski facilities, marinas and amusement parks along with hotel and infrastructure development. Ironically, Japanese workers have generally elected not to take the benefits of economic growth in increased leisure time. Their working year is around 200 hours more than in comparable industrialized countries. Japan's persistent surplus on the current account of its balance of payments accounts for two other important features in its leisure and tourism activities. First, Japan runs the world's biggest tourism account deficit, with tourism expenditure overseas exceeding tourism receipts by US $35 566 million in 1995. Second, Japan is very active in overseas investment. Some of this has involved aid to developing countries (for example, loans for resort infrastructure in Thailand). The majority is in the form of private investment. It is estimated for example that Japanese companies own 150 golf courses overseas. In contrast to many developing countries, Japan is able to build on its strong economic base. High GNP enables high savings which can finance more investment which further contributes to GNP. However, in 1998 Japan suffered from a severe economic recession with GNP declining by 2.6 per cent so that economic growth has averaged a very poor 1.7 per cent in 1990–2001.

Economic growth in developing countries

Stages of development

The World Bank classifies countries according to the following criteria.

Advanced economies • • •

The World Bank classifies 29 economies as advanced ones. This group contains the following subgroups:

- Major advanced economies, often referred to as the Group of Seven (G-7): these are the seven largest in terms of GDP – the USA, Japan, Germany, France, Italy, the UK and Canada.
- The EU (15 countries) and the European area (12 countries).
- The newly industrialized Asian economies.

Countries in transition • • •

The group of countries in transition (28 countries) is divided into two regional subgroups:

- central and eastern Europe,
- the Commonwealth of Independent States and Mongolia.

Developing countries • • •

The group of developing countries (125 countries) includes all countries that are not classified as advanced economies or as countries in transition. The developing countries are also classified according to two analytical criteria and into other groups.

- The first criterion, by source of export earnings, distinguishes between the categories of fuel, non-fuel and non-fuel primary products.
- The second criterion, focuses on net creditor and net debtor countries, which are differentiated on the basis of two additional-financial criteria: by official external financing and by experience with debt servicing.
- The other groups of developing countries constitute the heavily indebted poor countries (HIPCs) and Middle East and North Africa (MENA) countries. The first group comprises the countries (except Nigeria) considered by the International Monetary Fund (IMF) and the World Bank for their debt initiative, known as the HIPCs. The second group includes the MENA a group, whose composition straddles the Africa and Middle East and Europe regions. It is defined as the Arab League countries plus the Islamic Republic of Iran.

The major point of differentiation between advanced and developing countries is their GNP per head. There are a number of explanations for the low incomes of developing countries and several strategies for promoting economic growth. For some of these countries, promotion of the recreation, leisure and/or tourism will be an appropriate strategy.

Characteristics

The low standards of living enjoyed by developing countries are characterized not just by low per capita GNP but by a range of other indicators. These include high levels of mortality, and low levels of literacy, medical care and food consumption. The economic circumstances of developing countries vary widely but barriers to economic growth in developing countries may include:

- High-population growth: this may lead to overpopulation of land, the splitting of land into non-viable subunits and low-labour productivity.
- Low-incomes: this leads to low savings, leading to low investment, leading to low incomes (low rate of capital formation).
- An undeveloped-financial sector: this can mean that there is an absence of banks or a lack of trust in banks. Savings in this case are kept as cash or kind and not re-circulated into the economy as investment. This also means that access to cheap loans is difficult so that moneylenders are able to charge high rates of interest. This may mean that it is difficult to escape poverty, or that cheap funds for investment in machinery are not available.
- Absence of welfare system: this can lead to overpopulation where children are seen as a financial insurance for old age.
- Low levels of training and education: this may be where there is a direct opportunity cost in lost agricultural labour where children stay on in school. Additionally there is a shortage of state funding for education.
- Existence of a large subsistence sector: this can mean that taxation is difficult.

- Few resources.
- Dependence on raw material exports.
- Employment centred on the agricultural sector of economy.
- Traditional (non-entrepreneurial) culture.
- Foreign currency shortages.
- Poor terms of trade (exports cheap, imports expensive).
- International debt.

Development strategies

Strategies to promote faster economic growth in developing countries generally involve investment in the agricultural, manufacturing or service sectors of the economy in order to improve labour productivity. This then raises the two key considerations for development. First, given the low rates of GNP per head, where will investment funds be obtained from? Second, what specific projects are most appropriate? The main sources of investment funds are:

- domestic savings (but these are often low because of low incomes),
- government investment funded through taxes or borrowing (but governments often have a low-tax base because of low incomes and subsistence economies and high-foreign debt repayments),
- private foreign investment,
- overseas aid.

The main strategies for development include:

- import substitution (producing goods that are currently imported),
- export-led growth (producing goods and services where a local cost or other advantage can be established) – leisure and tourism can be important elements in this strategy,
- population control,
- education and training projects,
- infrastructure projects.

Plate 13 depicts continued tourism development in Koh Phi Phi, Thailand. Here, tourism development is characterized by small and medium sized enterprise development with modest capital requirements and strong local multiplier effects.

These strategies may take place under a planning environment which can be either market- or government-led. However, the history of development projects includes a number of projects that have been inappropriate for the circumstances of the particular developing country. This particularly applies to technologies which require expert foreign management and costly imports, and projects which are labour saving in countries with high unemployment. The following case studies show the contribution of the leisure and tourism sector to economic development in China and Vietnam, illustrating different development strategies.

Plate 13
Unloading building
materials for beach
accommodation, Koh Phi
Phi, Thailand
Source: The author

Leisure and tourism development in China

The characteristics of the Chinese economy are atypical of many developing countries, yet its population of over 1 billion and rapid rate of development will ensure its growing importance over the next few decades. It is atypical first because of its communist government and second because, despite its low per capita GNP and large agricultural sector, it has relatively high-literacy, low-mortality rates and its economic growth has recently been spectacular, averaging 7.8 per cent between 1985 and 1994 and exceeding 10 per cent since 1994. Its population growth is slowing rapidly with a one-child policy. Table 13.2 shows the increasing importance of Chinese tourism.

It is expanding first, because of China's open-door policy, which has replaced a long period of mistrust of foreigners and barriers to tourism. Second, China is rich in cultural capital, and third, its low-wage economy makes tourism relatively cheap. However, investment in infrastructure and accommodation is crucial to tourism development and to counter the low, level of investment associated with its low per capita GNP, China has encouraged private foreign investment in the form of joint ventures. This has been important in the accommodation sector for the development of hotels. In Beijing, for example, the Hotel Beijing-Toronto was financed with Canadian capital, is run by Japanese management and profits are shared with China. China's growth is fuelled primarily by its growth in exports. Here China exploits its international advantage in wage costs. Exports cover a range of goods and include audio equipment, toys and sports goods from the leisure sector. The movement of labour from China's agricultural sector to the manufacturing and service sector has enabled labour productivity to increase.

Table 13.2   International tourist arrivals and receipts

	Arrivals (million)			Receipts (US dollars billion)	
	2002	**Change 2001–02**		**2002**	**Change 2001–02**
France	77.0	2.4	USA	66.5	−7.4
Spain	51.7	3.3	Spain	33.6	2.2
USA	41.9	−6.7	France	32.3	7.8
Italy	39.8	0.6	Italy	26.9	4.3
China	36.8	11.0	China	20.4	14.6
UK	24.2	5.9	Germany	19.2	4.0

Source: Adapted from WTO Tourism Highlights 2003.

Table 13.3   Total visitors to Vietnam, 1990–2003 (million)

1990	1991	1992	1993	1994	1995	1996	1997	1998	1999	2000	2001	2002	2003
0.2	0.2	0.4	0.7	1.0	1.3	1.6	1.7	1.5	1.8	2.1	2.3	2.6	2.4

Source: Adapted from www.vietnamtourism.com

Tourism in Vietnam

In 1975, the communist government of Vietnam emerged victorious from a long war with the USA. Vietnam entered a period of centrally planned economic development and international isolation, limiting its trade and tourism exchanges to those with the former USSR and its allies.

A change in direction was heralded in 1986 when strict central planning was relaxed in favour of free enterprise. Additionally the period of international isolation finished as restrictions on foreign investment and ownership were lifted. Tourism was a key beneficiary of this change in policy direction. Vietnam is well endowed in many of the basic tourism factors of production – unspoiled beaches, interesting landscapes and cultural heritage. To this can be added a cheap and plentiful labour supply.

After 1986, capital, the missing ingredient for economic development was now supplied by foreign investors. Between 1988 and 1995, almost $2 billion was invested in over 100 hotel projects including those involving multinational hotel chains such as the Hyatt and Marriot (USA), Omni (Hong Kong) and Hotel Metropole (France). Tourism to Vietnam boomed with arrivals rising from 300 000 in 1991 to over 1.3 million by 1995 (Table 13.3). By 1995, tourism earnings were estimated at over $400 million making a strong contribution to Vietnam's GNP. However, as a result of the Asian economic crisis, the number of foreign visitors declined in 1998. But by 2000, 130 000 jobs were provided directly by tourism as well as those in businesses related to the tourism industry. The industry's contribution to the country's GDP had reached 5.8 per cent. By 2002, the country could boast 1940 hotels, nearly 670 guesthouses, bungalows and villas and 11 tourist villages.

There are two major problems facing Vietnam in its progress towards economic growth. First is the problem of foreign debt. Vietnam owes over $26 billion in foreign debt and the World Bank classifies Vietnam as a severely indebted low-income country. This hampers the development process as Vietnam has to use a high proportion of its national income to repay interest and capital on its foreign debt. The second problem is one of multinational ownership. The lack of domestic capital has mean that much of Vietnamese investment in tourism has been supplied by multinational corporations. This enables tourism capacity to grow in the short run faster than otherwise might be the case. But multinational investment means that the multiplier effect of tourism to Vietnam is reduced with a high proportion of tourism expenditure being exported back to shareholders of the multinationals in the form of profits. Both of these factors limit the ability of low-income countries such as Vietnam to enjoy the full benefits of the expansion of tourism. Additionally Vietnam suffers from poor basic infrastructure (road networks, airports and communications).

The year 2002 was a good year for tourism industry. It attracted a record 2.6 million foreign tourists as well as 13 million domestic holiday-makers. This was an increase of over 11 per cent over the previous year and earned US $1.52 billion in revenues. But the Sars outbreak in early 2003 result in a big setback to the tourism industry and the number of incoming tourists was only one-third of the figure that was recorded over the same period in 2002, although the 22nd Southeast Asian Games which were held in Vietnam increased the volume of tourists towards the end of the year. Additionally in 2003, the Vietnam National Administration of Tourism (VNAT) announced that the Vietnamese Government would invest an additional VND450 billion (nearly US $30 million) in the tourism industry. The move demonstrates the government's strategy to harness the tourism industry to spearhead economic development and help to develop other industries. One important effect of the increased investment is that it acts as a catalyst attracting more projects from domestic and foreign investors. Previous government investment into the local tourism (US $17.7 billion in 2001 and US $24 billion in 2002) focused on localities such as Quang Ninh, Ninh Binh, Nha Trang, Khanh Hoa, Thua Thien-Hue, Hai Phong and Ho Chi Minh City and attracted other capital sources into tourism projects. For example, Quang Ninh attracted a combined domestic and foreign investment of nearly US $56.6 million in its tourist resorts, especially in the province's United Nations Educational Scientific and Cultural Organizations (UNESCO)-recognized World Cultural Heritage of Ha Long Bay.

Regeneration

As well as being a source for national growth strategies, recreation, leisure and tourism are also used in regeneration schemes. Regeneration is the term used to describe the process of economic redevelopment generally in an area that has suffered decline because of structural changes in the economy. It can be applied both to urban and rural contexts.

Keynes noted that full employment is not a necessary equilibrium position in a market economy. The same idea may be applied to the level of economic activity in any particular localized area. Market economies are by their nature dynamic and markets are constantly signalling and causing change. But there is no reason that a decline in one aspect of a local economy should be automatically offset by a growth in another aspect. A local area will suffer economic decline where the rate of loss of existing jobs exceeds the rate of creation of new jobs. If this pattern is sustained a point will be reached where an area becomes 'depressed' or 'deprived'. The economic indicators of localized economic depression include the level of unemployment and per capita incomes.

Just like at the national level a recession can turn into a long depression without intervention, a similar process may occur at a localized level. Typically the sequence of events illustrated in Figure 13.3 occurs and the circular effect shows how the multiplier process can exacerbate the situation.

Regeneration is therefore generally about replacing the gap left by declining industries by implanting new centres of economic activity.

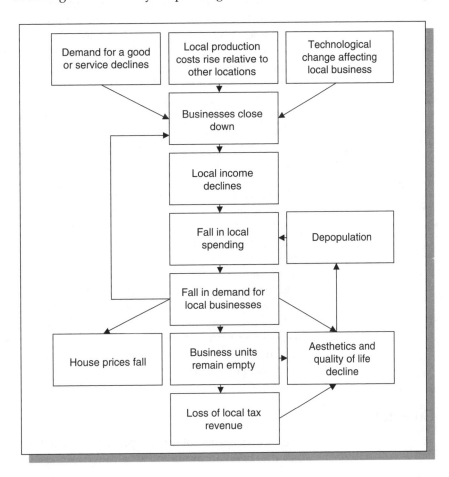

Figure 13.3
Local economic decline

Leisure, recreation and tourism projects can provide a popular focus for this. There is generally a threefold impact of regeneration. First, local jobs are provided at the construction stage of new projects. Next, local jobs are generated when the new projects are commissioned. Third, leisure projects often attract spending from outside the local area. Where regeneration is successful the whole multiplier process swings into reverse and increased spending attracts further investment.

Urban regeneration

Smith (2003) examines the role of the cultural industries in urban regeneration. Examples here include the Guggenheim Museum in Bilbao, northern Spain which has led to an increase in tourism to this area where traditional industries such as steel and shipbuilding were in decline. Similarly, Glasgow in the UK achieved the status of European City of Culture in 1990, enhancing its external image, and attracting tourism and inward investment. Mega events are also used to kick-start local economies. Examples here include the hosting of Expo and in 1998 the Lisbon Expo was projected to attract over 8 million visitors and generate additional income to the city of $900 million. In London, the Millennium Dome was generally seen to be a failure in direct revenue terms. However, it brought a new underground rail line to a depressed area of southeast London and its surrounding area of the Greenwich peninsula is exhibiting signs of regeneration with new housing, leisure and tourism developments. Elsewhere in the UK Sheffield an area once renowned for its steel industry, launched a cultural industries strategy in the 1990s and established a 'Cultural Industries Quarter' based around television, pop music and film. It also hosted the World student games in 1991.

The hosting of the Olympic Games is also seen as an opportunity to re-invigorate urban economies and regeneration of the Lea Valley and Eastern Gateway is an important consideration in the bid to host the 2012 games to London (see Exhibit 13.3). In respect of the Sydney Olympics in 2000, consultants Jones Lang LaSalle and LaSalle carried out an economic impact analysis. They reported that the games increased the international profile of Sydney, encouraged tourism and hotel development and acted as a catalyst for a range of residential, retail and business developments, as well as improving transport infrastructure. One of the sites – Homebush – now host to a leading sporting venue and popular residential community – was previously part swamp and part munitions dump.

However, it is also often reported that local communities may fail to benefit fully from regeneration activities – either through having no interest or access to new projects or by being uprooted by new schemes, or by loosing their traditional retailers, or where the new jobs go to those from outside the local community.

Rural regeneration

The rural economy of the UK presents a mixed picture. The rural economy has not been immune from a range of restructuring processes which

---

Exhibit 13.3   The London Olympics 2012

London 2012 would be much more than just a celebration of sport, culture and the Olympic ideals.

It would form part of the most extensive transformation of the city for generations. And its legacy would transform one of the most underdeveloped areas of the country for generations to come. The key catalyst would be the development of the 500-acre Olympic Park and the resulting transformation of the Lower Lea Valley. The Park, containing the main sporting facilities, would be set in 1500 landscaped acres stretching from Hackney Marshes down to the Thames – one of the biggest new city centre parks in Europe for 200 years.

It would also feature a revitalized network of waterways serving new communities and businesses that will be the start of a regeneration stretching out from the Valley through East London and beyond. Each of the Games venues has been conceived to meet long-term needs. And the Olympic Village would also have a designated post-Games use as housing. All development would form part of an enormous and tangible legacy, ranging from sport and venues through to infrastructure and environment.

Thousands of jobs would be created in construction, thousands more as the redevelopment moved ahead and created new businesses and communities. London 2012 would change the face of the capital forever.

Source: www.london2012.org

---

include European policy reforms, changes in economy and society, international trade patterns, development of new technologies, environmental pressures, the buying power and patterns of large supermarkets and the perception of agriculture by potential workers. The effects of all these have been exacerbated by recent farming and food crises.

Farming is still an important industry though it accounts for only about 4 per cent of GDP in rural areas. It supplies much of the food of the UK and provides direct employment for around 600 000 people (although this includes seasonal and part-time workers). It is estimated that it contributes about £7 billion each year to the UK economy. But farm incomes have fallen by around 60 per cent over the past 5 years and farming is going through its most difficult period over the last 50 years. The crisis in farming affects many related businesses as well as the prosperity of market towns. It is likely to deteriorate further as the period 2002–07 brings further reforms to the Common Agricultural Policy so that farm production subsidies are likely to be progressively reduced.

Despite this employment and self-employment are generally higher in rural areas than in urban areas and unemployment is lower. Against this average earnings are lower and rural jobs are more likely to be casual or seasonal, than jobs in urban areas. The nature of employment is changing, with fewer jobs in primary industries such as farming, and other jobs moving to edge of town locations. Home-based working is on the increase.

Against this context, Sharpley (2003) notes that the UK Rural White Paper published in 2000 firmly established tourism as a vehicle for the social and economic regeneration of the British countryside. He further notes that the Foot and Mouth crisis in 2001 served to demonstrate both the interdependence of various elements of the rural economy and the fragility (or lack of sustainability) of the tourism and leisure industry in particular. He therefore points to the pressing need for the effective and integrated management of the countryside as a resource for tourism and leisure.

In terms of the significance of leisure to the UK rural economy it can be noted that total spending by all visitors to the countryside was estimated to be around £11.5 billion in 1998. Of this 77 per cent is associated with day visitors from home, 17 per cent with UK holiday-makers and 6 per cent with overseas tourists. Total employment directly supported by recreation and leisure visitor activity in the countryside is estimated to amount to some 290 000 jobs in 1998 and a further 50 000 indirectly in other sectors of the rural economy.

It is because of the decline in the role of farming and the potential of recreation leisure and tourism to provide an alternative source of income and employment that this sector is seen as important in rural regeneration. Schemes that have been successful include the Eden project in Cornwall (see Exhibit 13.4) and the Tate Gallery in St Ives.

However, it would be naïve to presume that in the UK rural prosperity depends on either farming or tourism. There is an increasing movement of the population into rural areas, particularly in the south of England and increasing use of the Internet means that business opportunities are no longer confined to urban areas.

Exhibit 13.4   The Eden project

The Eden project cost £86 million and this was raised by a public/private sector partnership bringing together public sector regeneration and lottery funds (£43 million was provided by the Millennium Commission) with private sector loan finance and sponsorship. In terms of employment the project's first 34 staff were all recruited locally and by its opening in 2001, it employed a full-time equivalent staff of 200 people – the majority from the local area. The project's construction partner, McAlpine JV also worked positively to follow this ideal – out of the 300 workers employed on the site, approximately 85 per cent were local. Due to its success the project currently (2004) employs 600 local full-time staff and contributes an estimated £300 million incrementally to the Cornish economy. It is expected to accumulate £2 billion in its first decade. Additionally, the project has worked closely to co-ordinate the facilitation of local supplier networks. For example, bread, dairy products, meat and vegetables for the catering facilities are all sourced locally.

Source: Various.

Review of key terms

- Economic growth: the increase in real output per capita.
- Per capita: per person.
- Net investment: gross investment − depreciation.
- Productivity: output per employee.
- DC: developing country.
- Import substitution: producing goods that are currently imported.
- Infrastructure: social capital such as roads and railways.
- Joint venture: overseas and domestic investment partnership.

Data Questions

Task 13.1   Tourism and economic development in India

Tourism can provide an important route for economic growth in India. It has been estimated that international tourism has an income multiplier of 0.93, which suggests that a large proportion of spending by international tourists is retained in the country. The effects on employment are also significant. Estimates here suggest that an increase in international tourism expenditure of Rs. 1 million results in the creation of 173 new jobs.

But tourism to India has shown only modest growth in recent years. Arrivals have risen from 1.28 million in 1981 to 2.12 million in 1995. However, when set against the expansion of tourism at the global level, it can be seen that India's share of tourism has in fact fallen. So whilst in 1981 tourist arrivals to India represented 0.44 per cent of total world arrivals of 288.8 million, by 1995 world arrivals had risen to 563.6 million and India's share of these arrivals had fallen to 0.38 per cent. The same picture of relative decline can be traced through data for tourism receipts. In 1981, India's share of world tourism receipts stood at 1.14 per cent. This figure had fallen to 0.69 per cent by 1995.

It is also noted that the tourism performance of India compares unfavourably with its neighbours in the region – particularly Hong Kong, Thailand and Singapore. The main reasons proposed for India's poor relative performance is that tourism has had a low priority in the government's national development plans. The fact that India was largely closed to inward investment until the 1990s is cited as one key problem inhibiting development of a tourism infrastructure. An inappropriate civil aviation policy is cited as another major problem area. Attention has also been drawn to areas such as marketing, and manpower development, neither of which have been given sufficient support by the government.

Suggestions for improving India's performance in international tourism include the following:

1 Greater power and financial resources to the Department of Tourism to coordinate tourism development policy.
2 Policies to improve the level of investment in tourism infrastructure (both private and public sectors).
3 Development of a more competitive and liberalized civil aviation sector.

Source: The author, based on: Raguraman, K. (1998), Troubled passage to India, *Tourism Management*, **19**(6), pp. 533–543.

Recap Questions

1 What factors inhibit economic growth in India?
2 Why has India's share of international tourism declined?
3 Distinguish between an income and employment multiplier. Suggest reasons why these multipliers are relatively high for India.
4 What factors determine the level of public sector and private sector investment in India?
5 Evaluate the case for and against encouraging greater foreign private sector investment in India.
6 Evaluate the case for and against greater public sector planning of tourism in India.

Task 13.2   Development of sustainable rural tourism in Bulgaria

The following are extracts from Ilieva's (1998) strengths, weaknesses, opportunities, threats (SWOT) analysis of the potential for rural tourism in Bulgaria:

Strengths:
• Natural and anthropological potential.

Weaknesses:
• Superstructure: in many cases facilities do not meet the requirements of the modern tourist.
• Infrastructure: outdated traffic and telecommunications systems.

Opportunities:
• National advertising budget: financial resources for national tourist advertising.
• Educational programmes: there are five higher education institutions and many colleges where tourism students are being taught.

Threats:
• Macroeconomic frame: the slow pace of reforms, the unstable economic, political and legal situation ... hamper the development of tourism.

Source: Ilieva, L. (1998) Development of sustainable rural tourism in Bulgaria. In D. Hall and L. O'Hanlon, *Rural Tourism Management: Sustainable Options Conference Proceedings*, SAC, Ayr.

Recap Questions

1 What other factors affecting Bulgaria should be included in a SWOT analysis?
2 Evaluate the potential for tourism to contribute to Bulgaria's rural economic development in view of its SWOTs.

Task 13.3   Leisure and tourism development in France

Leisure and tourism is central to French economic prosperity. France is the world's most popular international tourist destination and tourism makes an important contribution to its balance of payments, as illustrated by Table 13.2. France has a diverse and well-balanced tourism industry. Winter sports tourism attracted between 1.5 and 2 million arrivals in 1997 excluding day trips. Disneyland Paris is now the leading short-break destination in Europe and visitors have risen from 9.8 million in 1991 to 11.7 million in 1996. The Eiffel Tower attracted 5.5 million visitors in 1996. However, the capacity of tourism capacity to France has only risen slightly from 17.163 million beds in 1994 to 17.307 million in 1997 (all accommodation including hotels and campsites).

As well as being the premier international destination, France is the premier destination for its own residents. Tourism in France accounted for about €86 billion of expenditure in 1997, representing around 7 per cent of GNP and 9.7 per cent of total employment, but 56 per cent of this expenditure was by French domestic tourism. One reason for this is that, in contrast to Japanese workers, French workers receive a minimum of 5 weeks' paid leave and this represents considerable potential domestic demand. As well as tourism services, France exports leisure goods – particularly skiing and camping equipment, and has domestic air and ferry capacity in the form of Air France and Brittany Ferries. The latter was set up specifically to promote tourism to Brittany so as to promote that region's economic development. The demand for tourist facilities stimulates considerable private investment in hotels and other provision, but there is also a history of state encouragement. In terms of infrastructure, for example, France has a well-developed system of roads and railways. Recent investment in the high-speed train (TGV) has resulted in links between Paris and Lyons, Lille, Nantes and Bordeaux.

The Maison de France, mainly financed from public funds, was set up in 1987 to promote French tourism products. It is estimated that every euro spent by the Maison de France generates €15 in tourism receipts and its main activities include information, advertising, sales promotion and public relations. Maison de France has 33 offices abroad, but government funding fell from 72 per cent in 1987 to 38 per cent in 1997. There have been two major government-assisted regional development schemes based on tourism. First the Languedoc-Roussillon project. This was supported by more than €1 billion of state funding and commenced in 1963. It stimulated private investment and increased tourist visits to the area from 500 000 in 1964 to over 3.5 million by the late 1980s and it has been estimated that 30 000 new jobs were created in the region between 1965 and 1980. The second government initiative was the Aquitaine scheme which planned a big increase in tourism capacity on the Atlantic coast south of La Rochelle.

Recap Questions

1 What special features does France have that put it top of the international arrivals table?
2 What factors may account for the fact that France has more international tourist arrivals than the USA but lower receipts? How could this issue be addressed?
3 What are the key economic impacts of recreation, leisure and tourism on the economy of France?
4 What are the arguments for and against state intervention against the free market as effective means of encouraging economic growth through leisure and tourism in France?

Multiple choice

1 **Which of the following is false for real per capita growth in GNP?**

(a) It takes into account the total population.
(b) It takes into account inflation.
(c) It falls if the rate of growth of the population exceeds the rate of growth of the economy.
(d) It is always greater than zero.

2 **Which of the following is false?**

(a) A large subsistence sector will mean that the value of GNP is underestimated.
(b) Reducing taxation is a 'supply side' policy for stimulating economic growth.
(c) HIPCs are high-investment poor countries.
(d) Iraq is a MENA country.

3 **Which of the following is not a policy designed to improve economic growth in developing countries?**

(a) Import substitution.
(b) Export-led growth.
(c) Investment in infrastructure projects.
(d) Import-led growth.

4 **Which of the following is not a typical feature of developing countries?**

(a) High level of savings.
(b) Dependence on raw material exports.
(c) Employment centred on the agricultural sector of economy.
(d) International debt.

5 **Which of the following is true of regeneration projects?**

(a) They always favour poor people.
(b) They are designed to counter structural changes in a locality.
(c) They are most successful when they have a low-multiplier value.
(d) They often cause local investment to fall.

Review questions

1 What is real GNP per capita?
2 What are the key determinants of economic growth?
3 What is balanced growth?
4 What factors led to the importance of leisure and tourism in the economy of Spain?
5 What are the advantages and problems of joint ventures for the Chinese economy?
6 Why is China successful in exporting toys?
7 Compare private foreign investment with government investment in a hotel as alternative development strategies.

Web sites of interest

USA: statistics http://www.stat-usa.gov/
New Zealand: statistics http://www.stats.govt.nz/statsweb.nsf
Australian Bureau of Statistics http://www.abs.gov.au
Brazil: statistics http://www.ibge.gov.br
Canada: statistics http://www.statcan.ca
World Bank http://www.worldbank.org
International Monetary Fund http://www.imf.org
World Tourism Organisation www.world-tourism.org
Guardian Newspaper www.society.guardian.co.uk/regeneration

Part Seven

The Global Economy

The balance of payments and exchange rates

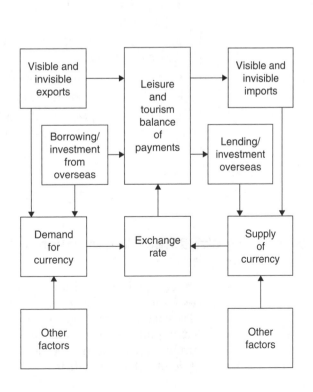

Objectives and learning outcomes

As well as measuring the contribution of the recreation, leisure and tourism sector to the level of national income we can consider its contribution at the international level to a country's balance of payments. The balance of payments records export earnings and import expenditure. Exchange rates are an important part of the picture. The exchange rate of a country's currency is inextricably linked with the balance of payments. Changes in a country's balance of payments may cause changes in the demand and supply for its currency and thus movements in its exchange rate. These currency movements may subsequently cause changes in the patterns of exports and imports which can cause feed-back to the balance of payments. The balance of payments is also one of the key macroeconomic variables which government policy-makers monitor closely. If the balance of payments should move into an unsustainable deficit, government policy would be changed to address the problem, causing repercussions throughout the rest of the economy.

After studying this chapter students will be able to:

- understand the arguments for free trade, the role of the World Trade Organization (WTO) and General Agreement on Trade in Services (GATS);
- understand the balance of payments accounts;
- analyse the contribution of the sector to net export earnings;
- describe and explain comparative data for balance of payments accounts;
- understand the significance of exchange rates to recreation, leisure and tourism organizations;
- distinguish between spot and forward rates of exchange;
- analyse exchange rate movements;
- understand government and European Community (EC) policy in trade and international payments.

Free trade, the World Trade Organization and General Agreement on Trade in Services

The economist David Ricardo was instrumental in developing the idea that free trade could bring greater economic benefits to those involved. The essentials of his argument ('The theory of comparative advantage') were that different countries had different resource mixes and therefore differing costs for producing a range of goods and services. It therefore paid countries not to attempt to be self-sufficient in producing a complete range of goods and services but to specialize in those where its production costs were lowest and their production efficiency highest. They would then trade with other countries to meet their full range of demands. Ricardo argued that specialization and trade would lead to an increase in total output compared to a position of no specialization and trade, based upon greater efficiency of production.

Some countries are more efficient at producing across a whole range of goods and services than others (e.g. the USA) and in this sense they are said to possess an 'absolute advantage' in production. However it will still benefit such countries to specialize in producing those goods and services which is the very best at producing (where it has a 'comparative advantage' over other countries) and trading where its comparative advantage is less strong. This is really an example of playing to your own strengths and specializing.

Once countries specialize their production in particular areas additional benefits of economies of scale and acquired expertise are likely to arise. Consumers benefit from free trade in terms of wider choice and lower prices.

The WTO is the international agency that promotes free trade and its GATS is an important treaty that seeks to operationalize this aim. Free trade liberalization under GATS is based on three specific pillars:

1 *Market access*: Foreign owned companies have free access to domestic markets.
2 *Most favoured nation status*: Concessions granted to any one country must also be made available on a non-discriminatory basis to all other signatories of the agreement.
3 *National treatment*: Foreign investors must be treated on an equal basis with domestic investors, domestic investors must not receive any favourable treatment that could be conceived as protectionist.

Diamantis and Fayed (2002) consider two main issues relating to GATS namely its impact on the labour market and on its relevance to developing countries.

However in the real world practical issues arise that can militate against the benefits of free trade. First there are extra costs involved in currency conversion and risk. Second, transport costs can add to production costs. Third, extra costs are involved in adapting goods and services for local markets. Fourth many countries seek to protect their home markets by protectionist policies. Fifth most countries wish to maintain some balance of production in key strategic goods and services so as not to expose themselves to over-dependence on foreign countries. Sixth, although overall there are significant gains to be made from trade, which particular countries benefit most will depend on the terms of trade.

Trade and trading blocs

A trading bloc is a group of countries who join together to liberalize trade between member states. There are four major trading blocs in the world.

The European Union

The European Union (EU) has become the most powerful trading bloc in the world with a gross domestic product (GDP) now exceeding that of the US. The EU continues to liberalize trade within community countries. The Single European Act, which came into effect in 1992, defines the single market as 'an area without internal frontiers in which the free movement of goods, persons, services and capital is ensured in accordance with the provisions of this treaty'. Some of the specific outcomes of this act which impinge on the leisure and tourism sector include the dismantling of EU internal border checks (some exceptions remain), and more competition in air and shipping services. On 1 January 1999 11 EU countries fixed the exchange rate between their currencies in a landmark step towards full introduction of the Euro which occurred in January 2002. The EU members are:

Austria	Greece	Poland
Belgium	Hungary	Portugal
Cyprus	Ireland	Slovak Republic
Czech Republic	Italy	Slovenia
Denmark	Latvia	Spain
Estonia	Lithuania	Sweden
Finland	Luxembourg	UK
France	Malta	
Germany	The Netherlands	

Bulgaria and Romania will become members in 2007 (provisional date).

North American Free Trade Agreement

The US has linked with Canada and Mexico to form a free trade zone, the North American Free Trade Agreement (NAFTA). It hopes to extend NAFTA to the rest of Latin America to create a Free Trade Area of the Americas. The US is already negotiating with Chile to join NAFTA, but that has caused controversy with some other South American countries. The NAFTA agreement covers environmental and labour issues as well as trade and investment. Its members are:

Canada
Mexico
United States

The Asia-Pacific Economic Cooperation forum

The Asia-Pacific Economic Cooperation (APEC) forum is a loose grouping of the countries bordering the Pacific Ocean who have pledged to facilitate free trade. Its 21 members account for 45 per cent of world trade. Progress on free trade initiatives was seriously dented by the Asian crisis, which affected the economies of the fast-growing newly industrialized countries like South Korea and Indonesia. Its members are:

Australia	Japan	Philippines
Brunei	South Korea	Russia
Canada	Malaysia	Singapore
Chile	Mexico	Taiwan
China	New Zealand	Thailand
Hong Kong	Papua New Guinea	United States
Indonesia	Peru	Vietnam

The Cairns group

The Cairns group of agricultural exporting nations was formed in 1986 to lobby at world trade talks in order to free up trade in agricultural products. Highly efficient agricultural producers, including those in both developed and developing countries, want to ensure that their products are not excluded from markets in Europe and Asia. Its members are:

Argentina	Columbia	Paraguay
Australia	Fiji	Philippines
Brazil	Indonesia	South Africa
Canada	Malaysia	Thailand
Chile	New Zealand	Uruguay

The terms of trade

The terms of trade measures the relative prices of what a country exports in relation to the prices of its imports. It is expressed by the formula:

$$\frac{\text{The average price of exports}}{\text{The average price of imports}}$$

If the terms of trade rise (i.e. export prices rise faster than import prices) the terms of trade are said to improve. This is because more imports can now be bought with a given amount of exports. Changes in the terms of trade are brought about by changes in the demand and supply of exports and imports and movements in exchange rates.

A persistent argument put forward by developing countries is that they face unfavourable terms of trade in comparison with developed countries. This is because the raw materials and commodities which are characteristic of the exports of developing countries generally command much lower prices than the manufactured and services exports characteristic of developed countries' exports.

The balance of payments

The balance of payments is an account which shows a country's financial transactions with the rest of the world. It records inflows and outflows of

Table 14.1 UK balance of payments (£ million)

Date	Current account	Capital account	Financial account	Net errors and omissions
1996	−7001	1260	3959	1782
1998	−3796	516	2219	1061
2000	−19 539	1527	24 944	−6932
2002	−18 965	1045	3536	14 384

Source: Adapted from ONS *The Pink Book*.

currency. Although the accounting conventions of presenting these accounts differ from country to country there are some basic similarities in that the balance of payments has three main components – a current, a capital and a financial account. The main difference between these parts is that the current account measures the value of goods and services traded, whilst the capital account measures flows of capital, for example investments and the financial account measures financial transactions involving the claims on, and liabilities to, non-residents. In addition there is a net errors and omissions item which arises because, due to inaccurate data collection, the figures do not always add up as they should. Table 14.1 shows recent balance of payments data for the UK.

The balance of payments account always balances in an accounting sense. Every expenditure of foreign currency must be offset by a receipt, otherwise the expenditure could not take place. For poorer countries (as with poorer people), this means that expenditure (on imports) cannot exceed earnings (from exports) because they simply run out of (foreign) currency. However for countries with a developed financial sector, current import expenditure may exceed current export income. This can be financed perhaps by borrowings, or perhaps by selling assets. In such a case, although the account would balance in an accounting sense, it would show structural imbalance. This is because such a position could not be sustainable over a long period. Sources of borrowing would dry up and there is only a finite stock of assets to be sold. The implications of such a structural deficit are discussed below in the section on government policy. In the UK balance of payments account for 2002 shown in Table 14.1, it can be seen that the four parts of the balance of payments sum to zero:

$$-18965 + 1045 + 3536 + 14384 = 0$$

The current account

The current account records payments for trade in goods and services and is thus divided into two parts – visible and invisible trade.

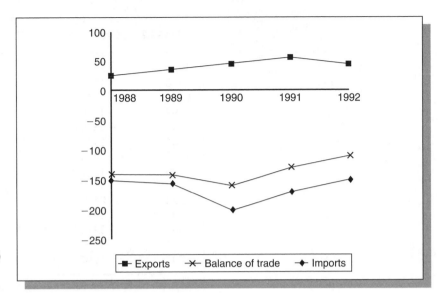

Figure 14.1
Value of foreign trade in
sports footwear (£ million)
Source: Adapted from
CSO; *The Pink Book 1994*

Visibles ● ● ●

Visibles represents exports and imports in goods and is divided into the following sections:

- food, beverages and tobacco;
- basic materials;
- fuels;
- semi-manufactures;
- manufacture;
- others.

The leisure sector is represented in this part of the account, for example, by trade in alcoholic beverages, electrical goods, sports equipment and sports wear. Figure 14.1 shows the balance of trade in sports footwear, whilst Table 14.2 shows the UK total visible trade balance over recent years. The information for sports footwear demonstrates similar characteristics to that for UK visible trade as a whole. First it exhibits a deficit, with imports exceeding imports. This has been caused by uncompetitive UK exchange rates and cheap overseas production costs – particularly labour costs. Countries such as South Korea, Indonesia and the Philippines, for example, account for more than 50 per cent of the value of imports for trainers.

Second the information shows the deficit peaking in 1989 and then again in 2002. This demonstrates the relationship between growth in the economy as a whole and the balance of payments. During the late 1980s the UK experienced a period of rapid growth followed by a sharp recession, but the period 1992–2002 witnessed sustained growth. For the UK as in most countries there is a strong link between economic growth and import demand.

Table 14.2 UK trade in goods (£million)

1989	−24 724
1990	−18 707
1991	−10 223
1992	−13 050
1993	−13 066
1994	−11 126
1995	−12 023
1996	−13 722
1997	−12 342
1998	−21 813
1999	−29 051
2000	−32 976
2001	−40 620
2002	−46 455

Source: Adapted from ONS *The Pink Book*.

Invisibles • • •

Invisibles records the trade in services or intangibles under the following headings:

- government,
- sea transport,
- civil aviation,
- travel,
- financial and other services,
- interest, profits and dividends,
- private transfers.

The key items of relevance to the leisure and tourism sector are civil aviation and travel. Also of significant are interest, profit and dividends, which records payments relating to overseas business investments. For example, profits returned to the French-owned Brittany Ferries from its activities in the UK would represent an invisible trading debit under this section.

Table 14.3 shows how tourism makes an important contribution to Australia's export earnings. For example, in 2000–01, international visitors consumed $17.1 billion worth of goods and services produced by the Australian economy. This represented 11.2 per cent of total exports of goods and services. But although Australia's tourism exports grew quite strongly since 1997–98, so has her exports of other goods and services. This has resulted in a slight decline in the tourism share of total exports since 1998–99. However the data in Table 14.4 also shows that exports of tourism characteristic products compare favourably with other Australian 'traditional' export products. For example, exports of tourism products are higher than coal, iron, steel and non-ferrous metals, although they are lower than

Table 14.3 Exports of tourism products and services, Australia

	1997–98	1998–99	1999–00	2000–01
International visitor consumption (million dollars)	12 792	13 446	14 611	17 100
Total exports (million dollars)	113 744	112 025	125 972	153 140
Tourism share of exports (%)	11.2	12.0	11.6	11.2
Growth in international visitor consumption (%)	–	5.1	8.7	17.0
Growth in total exports (%)	–	–1.5	12.4	21.6

Source: Adapted from Australian National Accounts: Tourism Satellite Account 2000–01.

Table 14.4 Selected exported commodities, as a percentage of Australia's total exports

Coal	8.4	8.3	6.6	7.1
Iron, steel, non-ferrous metals	6.3	6.2	7.0	6.6
Food and live animals	14.1	13.8	13.4	13.1
Tourism products	11.2	12.0	11.6	11.2

Source: Adapted from Australian National Accounts: Tourism Satellite Account 2000–01.

Exhibit 14.1 They came, they saw … but did not spend much

The following extract from the *International Tourism Reports* comments on East European tourists to Paris:

'Paris has long represented a dream destination for many East Europeans. When they were suddenly free to travel after so many years of isolation from the western world it was natural that the French capital would be their first goal. It should nevertheless be pointed out that most East Europeans travelling to France in the early 1990s slept in their coaches travelling to and from and at their destinations and took much of their food with them. As a result their contribution to the country's international tourism receipts was minimal.'

Source: *International Tourism Reports*, 1998, Vol. 3, Travel and Tourism Intelligence, London.

food and live animals. This is true for many developed countries where earnings from invisibles can offset deficits on the visible account. Note that the value of tourism earnings depends not just upon the number of visitors but also their average expenditure and Exhibit 14.1 illustrates this point.

Exhibit 14.2   Football kicks off into the red

From 1998 the UK Office for National Statistics will include football trans-fer market dealings in the balance of payments statistics. This is largely due to the big increase in value of international signings to premiership clubs which are in excess of £70 million for 1998. They will either be included as erratic items if clubs record them as intangible assets or invis-ibles if they are treated as providers of a service.

Official figure for the 1998 balance of payments showed an overall deficit of around £2 billion on the current account, largely due to the strength of the pound making imports more competitive and the Asian cri-sis suppressing demand for UK exports. The inclusion of football transfers will add to the deficit given a net excess in value of imports over exports of footballers.

Reporting for *The Guardian* newspaper, Mark Atkinson and Mark Milner said, 'The level of recent deals is equivalent to the UK's annual imports from Trinidad (Aston Villa got Dwight Yorke cheap when they bought him from there for £120 000 9 years ago) or double the annual imports of lemons. Given the performances of some signings from abroad, that is enough said about lemons'.

Source: The author based on report in *The Guardian* (1998).

Table 14.5   US international travel and tourism balance of trade, 1992–2002

	1992	1994	1996	1998	2000	2002
Receipts/exports (million dollars)	71 360	75 414	90 231	91 423	103 087	83 593
Payments/imports (million dollars)	49 155	56 844	63 887	76 454	88 979	78 013
Balance (million dollars)	22 205	18 570	26 344	14 969	14 108	5 580
% Change	17	−17	16	−38	−1	−20

Source: Adapted from Office of Travel and Tourism Industries http://tinet.ita.doc.gov

Exhibit 14.2 shows how football signings add to the UK balance of pay-ments deficit.

Tourism is a net earner to the balance of payments of some countries and for example Blazevic and Jelusic (2002) discuss the importance of tourism to the Croatian balance of payments. France and Spain boast large tourism surpluses, and tourism surpluses are rising rapidly for Turkey and China. On the other hand, Germany and Japan both have significant deficits in their tourism payments accounts, and the UK has a steadily deteriorating deficit. Table 14.5 shows how international tourism contributes positively

---

Exhibit 14.3   Tourism key to Cuban economic recovery

Cuba's GNP fell by around 35 per cent between 1989 and 1993 mainly as a result of the ending of its special relationship with the former Soviet bloc. In 1989 the top four export earners for Cuba were sugar, nickel, shellfish and tobacco. However, by 1994, sugar exports were in decline having been hit by a combination of poor harvests and the loss of guaranteed prices in the USSR.

Tourism, for many years spurned by the Castro government, has proved to be a source of economic recovery. Presenting the 1997 budget, Mr José Luis Rodriguez said that a lack of foreign currency was the biggest obstacle to sustained economic growth. Exports had increased by 33 per cent in 1996 headed by tourism which had surpassed sugar as the main export earner. But imports had risen by a similar amount leading to a trade deficit of over $1.2 billion. He said that prospects for continued success in export earnings from tourism and nickel were good.

Source: The author, from press cuttings.

---

to the balance of payments of the USA, although it is notable that expenditure on foreign tourism is rising faster than receipts from tourism.

The capital and financial account

Whilst the current account of the balance of payments records the export and import of goods and services, this part of the account deals mainly with movements of capital. Such capital movements can be considered under the headings of investment, lending and borrowing, and official reserves activity.

Investment • • •

This can be further subdivided into direct investment and portfolio investment. Direct investment is the direct purchase of firms or land or buildings abroad. Portfolio investment is the purchase of securities or shares abroad. Such activity leads to an outflow of funds, but a potential future inflow of profits or dividends under invisibles in the current account. Conversely, disinvestment or overseas inward investment causes an inflow of capital.

Lending and borrowing • • •

This records international loans. A loan to an overseas company will lead to an outflow of capital but future inflows of interest payments in the invisible part of the current account.

Official reserves activity • • •

Government use of official reserves of foreign currencies is recorded here. An increase in reserves leads to a corresponding outflow of capital from the balance of payments account.

The balance of leisure and tourism payments

The complex effects of leisure and tourism activities on a country's balance of payments are illustrated in Table 14.6 by an example of international currency flows associated with Disneyland Paris.

Overall we can predict that the economic impact of Disneyland, Paris would make a positive contribution to the balance of payments of France. However, potential earnings can be diminished in several ways. First, consider the element of overseas ownership. The greater the share of overseas ownership, the more profit is exported in the form of dividends to overseas shareholders. Second the role of overseas banks is significant. A high initial loan from foreign banks results in significant capital and interest repayments flowing overseas. Third, the degree of import content of goods

Table 14.6 The balance of Disneyland Paris payments for France

	Exports/credits	Imports/debits
Current account		
Visible trade	Exports of Disneyland Paris merchandise	Purchase of overseas equipment
		Merchandise imported from USA and Far East for sale
		Imported foods for catering
Invisible trade	Admission charges paid by overseas residents	Royalties and management fees paid to US parent company
	Souvenirs bought by overseas residents	Dividends paid to overseas shareholders
	Meals bought by overseas residents	Interest paid on loans to overseas banks
		Overseas marketing
		Private transfers by overseas workers employed
Capital and Financial Account		
Investment in France by overseas residents	Direct investment from the US parent company of 49 per cent of Disneyland Paris	Sales of Disneyland Paris shares by overseas residents to French residents
	Purchase of Disneyland Paris shares by overseas residents	
Investment overseas by French residents Banking transactions	Borrowings from overseas banks	Capital repayments to overseas banks

sold must be considered. Tourists buying Disney *Dumbo* video tapes are making more of a contribution to the US balance of payments than the French one. Fourth some projects employ a high proportion of foreign nationals who repatriate some of their earnings. Finally the construction of a project may entail the use of overseas contractors and importation of equipment. A further example of potential leakages is demonstrated in Plate 14. Tourism represents a key export earner for Thailand but some expenditure leaks out of the economy to purchase imports to satisfy the demands of international tourists – in this case an Italian coffee making machine.

Trends and comparisons

Table 14.7 shows recent changes in the totals and components of the US balance of payments. The current balance recorded a record deficit in 2002

Plate 14
Tourism leakages: An Italian Coffee machine unloaded on a Thailand beach
Source: The author

Table 14.7 US balance of payments (dollars billion)

	Year			
	2002	**2001**	**2000**	**1999**
Current account	−480.9	−393.7	−411.5	−290.8
Capital account	−1.3	−1.1	−0.8	−4.8
Financial account	528.0	415.6	456.3	236.6
Total	45.9	20.8	44.1	−59.1
Balancing item	−45.9	−20.8	−44.1	59.1

Source: Adapted from US Bureau of Economic Analysis.

Table 14.8   The effects of currency movements on prices

		Local currency price	Purchase price: £1 = $1.50	Purchase price: £1 = $2.00
Visible import	Apple Music iPod	$300	£200	£150
Invisible import	Hotel for week in Miami	$600	£400	£300
Visible export	Litre of Scotch whiskey (before tax)	£5	$7.50	$10.00
Invisible export	Night at Heathrow hotel	£100	$150	$200

of nearly £481 billion. Other categories confirm that central bank buying (included in the finance account) remains a big factor in financing the current account deficit.

Government policy

In the short-term a balance of payments deficit on current account is not necessarily a problem. It can be offset by borrowing from overseas, or overseas inward investment, or selling of assets overseas. There are, however, limits to borrowing and the selling of assets abroad, and so an acute long-term current account deficit will require government intervention. This may take the form of:

● devaluation or currency depreciation,
● deflation,
● protectionism.

Each of these will affect leisure and tourism organizations.

Devaluation or currency depreciation ● ● ●

This is a policy of allowing a country's currency to fall in value or depreciate under a system of floating exchange rates, or moving to a lower rate under a fixed exchange rate system. The aim is to stimulate exports by making their foreign currency price cheaper and to curb imports by increasing their price in the domestic currency. An example of the effects of devaluation is shown in Table 14.8. Here the dollar falls against sterling from £1 = $1.50 to £1 = $2.00. This should stimulate demand for US exports in the UK (in this case the £ price of iPods and US hotel accommodation goes down) and reduce US demand for UK exports (the dollar price of Scotch whiskey and UK hotel accommodation goes up).

Success of the policy will depend upon demand elasticities. For example, devaluation will only increase total foreign currency earnings from exports if demand is elastic, so that the fall in the foreign currency price per unit is compensated for by a larger proportionate rise in demand.

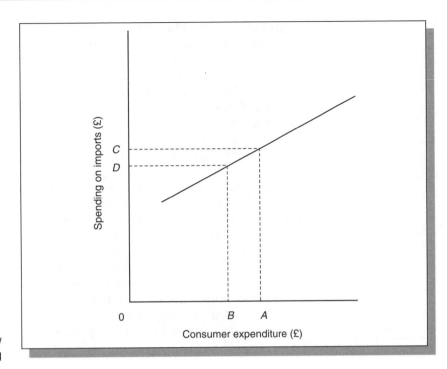

Figure 14.2
The effects of deflationary
policy on export spending

Deflation • • •

A deflationary policy involves the government reducing spending power
in the economy. The rationale is that, since imports form a significant proportion of consumer expenditure, a reduction in spending power will in
turn reduce imports. Figure 14.2 shows the relationship between imports
and the overall level of consumer spending in an economy.

Deflation is achieved through increasing interest rates or increasing
taxes. If deflationary policy reduced consumer expenditure from $0A$ to $0B$,
then import spending would fall from $0C$ to $0D$.

Protectionism • • •

This entails direct controls on imported goods, including taxes on imports
(tariffs) and limits on import volumes and values (quotas). The threat of
retaliation and the rules of international treaties such as the EU and GATT
(which exists to reduce protectionism) make protectionism a difficult option.

Exchange rates

Significance of exchange rates

The exchange rate is the price of one currency expressed in terms of
another currency. Exchange rates are important to leisure and tourism
organizations for a number of reasons. Firms selling or manufacturing

goods may import either the finished good or the raw materials to make the finished good. For example, ski equipment is mainly imported into the UK and a fall in the value of sterling against the currency of the exporting country will mean a rise in the sterling cost of equipment.

The purchase of tourism facilities abroad is classed as an invisible import and so a fall in the value of the domestic currency will increase the local price of such services. A fall in the value of domestic currency will however reduce the foreign currency price of visible exports and invisible exports, including inbound tourism.

Organizations selling imported goods and services may favour a higher exchange rate, whereas those exporting goods and services may favour a lower one. Exhibit 14.4 links a fall in the value of the rand to tourism growth in South Africa. Above all, stability of the exchange rate is crucial for organizations whose operations involve significant foreign currency transactions. This was a key argument for the creation of a single EU currency – the Euro. However exchange rates are only part of the equation determining export competitiveness and Dwyer et al. (2002) outline a method that allows the various determinants of tourism price competitiveness, such as exchange rate and price changes, to be highlighted and their influence on the indices to be identified.

Determination of floating exchange rates

A floating exchange rate is one which is determined in the market without government intervention. Here the exchange rate is determined, like most prices, by the forces of demand and supply. For example on the foreign exchange markets the £ sterling is demanded by holders of foreign currency wishing to buy sterling and sterling is supplied by holders of sterling wishing to buy foreign currency. Using the Australian dollar to stand for

---

Exhibit 14.4   Rand continues to fall

The South African rand fell by more than 5 per cent in 1 day in 1998, after speculators started to sell the currency in large amounts. This followed the realization that intervention to support the rand on the foreign exchange markets was being financed from South Africa's own limited foreign exchange reserves rather than by the USA and Britain. The clear signal was that the rand would fall further – prompting the rash of sales. Here speculators sell in order to repurchase in the future at a lower price.

While the continued weakness of the rand is good for exports in general and for tourism in particular it makes imports more expensive and can therefore lead to a worsening balance of payments in the short-term. This is because it can take some time for consumers to adjust their spending patterns as prices change.

Source: The author (1999).

all foreign currencies, we can identify the main determinants of the demand for and supply of sterling as follows:

Demand for sterling (supply of Australian dollar) • • •

- Demand for UK visible exports.
- Demand for UK invisible exports.
- Demand for funds for direct and portfolio investment in the UK.
- Demand for funds for overseas deposits in sterling bank accounts.
- Speculation.
- Government intervention.

Supply of sterling (demand for Australian dollar) • • •

- Demand for Australian visible exports.
- Demand for Australian invisible exports.
- Demand for funds for direct and portfolio investment in Australia.
- Deposits for funds for deposits in Australian bank accounts.
- Speculation.
- Government intervention.

Figure 14.3 shows typical demand and supply curves for sterling against the Australian dollar. The demand for pounds is represented by the demand curve $D0$, and $S0$ shows the supply of pounds. The equilibrium

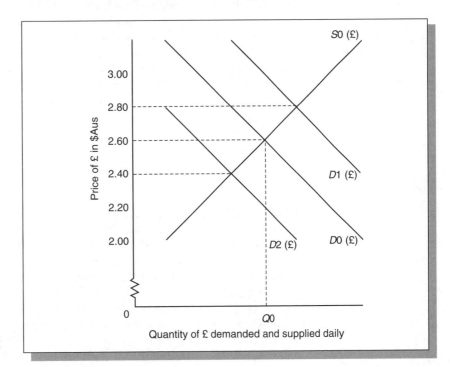

Figure 14.3
The price of sterling in Australian dollar (see text for details)

exchange rate is at £1 = AUS $2.60, where the number of pounds being offered on the foreign exchange market is equal to the number of pounds demanded (0Q0).

Should any of the determinants of the demand or supply of sterling change, the demand and/or supply curves will shift position and a new equilibrium price will be achieved. The price of sterling will rise if the demand curve for sterling shifts to the right. In Figure 14.3 a shift of the demand curve from D0 to D1 causes the exchange rate to rise to AUS $2.80. This could be caused for example by a significant increase in the value of UK exports, or a rise in UK interest rates causing foreign currency holders to switch their deposits into sterling accounts to earn higher interest rates.

A leftward shift of the supply curve for sterling would have a similar effect on the exchange rate. The price of sterling will fall if the demand curve for sterling shifts to the left. In Figure 14.3 a shift of the demand curve from D0 to D2 causes the exchange rate to fall to AUS $2.40. This could be caused for example by a significant fall in the value of UK exports, or a fall in UK interest rates causing foreign currency holders to switch their deposits out of sterling accounts to earn higher interest rates abroad. A rightward shift of the supply curve for sterling would have a similar effect on the exchange rate.

Determination of fixed exchange rates

A fixed exchange rate system is where the price of one currency is fixed in terms of another currency. For example for a period before full monetary union and the introduction of the Euro most EU member states fixed their currencies at an agreed rate. Similarly some countries peg their exchange rate to the US dollar. The idea behind fixed exchange rates is to avoid the sudden changes to trading conditions that can accompany large and sudden fluctuations in exchange rates. However a key problem is maintaining a fixed rate. This generally involves substantial intervention by the government directly to buy or sell its own currency or indirectly by changing interest rates to make its currency more or less attractive as a medium for international savings.

The Euro

The (then) 11 EU countries fixed their exchange rates on 1 January 1999 in the final preparations for the introduction of the Euro – the single European currency. The Euro was introduced fully in 2002, although the UK, Norway and Denmark retained their national currencies. The Maastricht Treaty, signed in 1992, laid the foundations for the Euro and set the economic conditions necessary for member states to join. These were known as the convergence criteria. In 1994, the European Monetary Institute was set up. This is the institution that has the responsibility for the introduction and the managing of the Euro. In effect it is a European central bank. The introduction of the Euro was held up because too few countries had met economic convergence criteria, but by 1998, the 11 founder members had all met the criteria.

The main advantages of joining the Euro for member countries are a reduction in the transaction costs of trading: a reduction in foreign currency risk and greater competition that comes from easier price comparisons across the Eurozone. The main drawback is the acceptance of a single interest rate across member states. This may be inappropriate if member states are experiencing differing economic conditions. For example high unemployment would generally dictate a fall in interest rates whilst high inflation would call for a rise in interest rates. Many EU consumers also felt that the introduction of the Euro was seen by producers as an opportunity to raise prices.

Spot and forward foreign exchange markets

The spot market is the immediate market in foreign currency and represents the current market rate. Payment is made today and the transaction takes place today at today's rate. There is a margin making dealers' selling prices slightly more than buying prices. However some organizations seek protection from exchange rate fluctuations, particularly if they need to quote for contract prices involving a large foreign currency consideration. The forward market exists to satisfy demand for a guaranteed future exchange rate. Payment is made today but the transaction is made in the future (e.g. 3 months) at a rate agreed today.

Exchange rate trends and government policy

In theory a floating exchange rate should provide an automatic adjustment mechanism to changes in a country's trading position. A deficit would cause the exchange rate to fall thus stimulating the demand for exports and reducing import demand as relative prices changed. In practice there are many factors that mean that this self-adjusting role of the exchange rate rarely happens. For example, where demand or supply are particularly inelastic exchange rate-induced price changes may have a limited effect on sales. At the same time speculation and interest rate effects can each cause currencies to rise or fall to levels that do not reflect a country's balance of payments position.

In the past governments have often intervened in the market (a process called dirty floating) in an attempt to influence the exchange rate. Policy instruments to affect the exchange rate consist of interest rates and direct buying and selling of currency by the Central Bank. Raising interest rates will generally increase the demand for a currency as savings are moved from overseas banks to domestic banks to benefit from higher interest rates.

The government faces a dilemma in its exchange rate policy as in many other policy areas. A lower exchange rate makes export prices competitive and discourages imports, whilst a high exchange rate, by cutting import prices, helps to combat inflation.

Review of key terms

- Terms of trade: relative prices of imports and exports.
- Balance of payments: record of one country's financial transactions with the rest of the world.
- Exchange rate: price of one currency in terms of another.
- Current account: value of trade in goods and services.
- Visible trade: trade in goods.
- Invisible trade: trade in services.
- Devaluation or currency depreciation: movement to a lower exchange rate.
- Deflationary policy: government policy to reduce economic activity.
- Protectionism: policy to control imports.
- GATS: General Agreement on Trade in Services.
- Floating exchange rate: one which is determined in the market without government intervention.
- Fixed exchange rate: constant rate of exchange maintained by market intervention.
- Spot market: the immediate market in foreign currency.
- Forward market: futures market for currency.

Data Questions

Task 14.1

Table 14.9 shows the exchange rate between the South African rand and the US dollar 1997–2002

Table 14.9   Exchange rate of South African rand to US dollar

Year	1997	1998	1999	2000	2001	2002	2002
Rand/dollar	4.60	5.54	6.12	6.95	8.60	10.52	7.56

Source: Adapted from Federal Reserve Bank of US http://www.federalreserve.gov

Recap Questions

1 Comment on the changes shown in the data.
2 Draw a demand and supply graph to illustrate the likely causes of the change in the exchange rate.
3 What are the likely impacts of these changes on inbound and outbound tourist statistics for South Africa?
4 What steps could the government of South Africa take to support the exchange rate of the rand?

Task 14.2   Twenty Euros for a can of Coke? You must be kidding

The 11 European Member States of Austria, Belgium, Finland, France, Germany, Ireland, Italy, Luxembourg, the Netherlands, Portugal and Spain were all in the first wave of the Euro zone. On 1 January 1999 exchange rates between their currencies were fixed and the Euro became legal currency. From 1 January 2002 Euro notes and coins replaced those of domestic currencies and all transactions have been in Euros. The agreement of European Monetary Union (EMU) was ratified by the Treaty of Maastricht and the Exchange Rate Mechanism (ERM) provided a practical rehearsal. The European Central Bank in Frankfurt was established in 1998 to regulate the new currency. Jacque Santer, the former President of the European Commission, cited the following benefits of the Euro in a speech in Chicago in May 1998:

1 '...The future Euro zone is roughly comparable in size and economic weight to the United States. It will have nearly 300 million inhabitants, and account for almost 20 per cent of the world GDP and of world trade, comparable to the United States.'
2 '...The Euro zone will have a high degree of stability. The European Central Bank, whose independence has constitutional rank, will guarantee price stability, defined in operation terms as inflation between 0 and 2 per cent.'
3 '...It will continue to spur economic growth, and will therefore indirectly stimulate job creation.'
4 '...The Euro will also have a profound microeconomic effect on the functioning of Europe's internal market. By removing transaction costs and completely eliminating currency fluctuations and currency risk, trade, investment and travel in the Euro zone will be greatly facilitated, and prices driven downwards through greater competition.'
5 '...In the financial sector, the potentially positive impact of the Euro is especially large.'
6 '...The big unknown is the Euro's international impact. Will it become a truly international currency, performing the role of the unit of account, means of payment and reserve currency?'

Willem Buiter, Professor of International Macroeconomics at the University of Cambridge, gave a more measured support for the Euro at a speech in London in December 1998:
'EMU will succeed in generating greater Euroland-wide prosperity than would have been likely under any alternative monetary arrangement. As regards macroeconomic stability it will make a modest positive contribution, provided the national countries redesign their automatic fiscal stabilizers to generate more strongly anti-cyclical deficits. Lower transaction costs and greater price transparency will help complete the single market, limit price discrimination and other restrictive practices. These are worthy and worthwhile gains, but it is unlikely to add up to a hill of beans.'
Those opposed to EMU draw attention to the following questions:

• Would joining EMU create better conditions for firms making long-term decisions to invest in an EMU country?
• How would being part of the single currency affect trade?
• Are business cycles compatible so that those economies in the EMU zone can prosper under a single Euro interest rate?
• If economic problems or currency problems do emerge, is there sufficient flexibility to deal with them.
• Will joining the EMU help to promote higher growth, stability and a lasting increase in jobs.

Sources:

The European Commission (web site: http://europa.eu.int/euro/html/)

The Bank of England (web site: http://www.bankofengland.co.uk)

Newspapers: *The Guardian* and *The Daily Telegraph*.

Recap Questions

1 Explain the meaning and importance of the following terms to a named leisure or tourism organization: *macroeconomic stability, single Euro interest rate, anti-cyclical deficits, restrictive practices*.
2 Evaluate the impact of the Euro on consumers of leisure and tourism goods and services.
3 Evaluate the impact of the Euro on producers of leisure and tourism goods and services.
4 Evaluate the decision of the UK and Denmark to opt out of the initial Euro zone.

Task 14.3   Made in China

In 1998 as the crisis in the Asian economies grew, South Korea, Thailand and Indonesia all suffered severe currency falls. China's exports were threatened by this crisis and there were calls by its manufacturers to devalue its currency to boost competitiveness. In the event, the government kept the Yuan fixed at 8.28 to the US dollar.

In 2002 with the Yuan still valued at $8.28 its trading partners such as Japan and the US are urging China to let its currency appreciate. Why? This is because of the incredible success of Chinese exports. China supplies the world with cheap goods including cameras, televisions, bicycles, CD and DVD players and its exports increased by 20 per cent in 2002, while its economy expanded by nearly 10 per cent. In China itself, overproduction has helped push industrial prices down by 7 per cent over the past 5 years and retail prices by 10 per cent.

To most world consumers Chinese goods are a big bonus as they see prices falling and competition rising. But some economists have argued that a deflationary China poses a real threat to the world. Morgan Stanley economist Stephen S. Roach recently wrote that 'China's prices are becoming global prices.' One effect of this is that prices have collapsed for many consumer-electronics firms and leisure goods producers. Even where producers in advanced developed countries do not compete directly with Chinese goods they worry that Chinese manufacturers are rapidly moving up the chain of expertise into semiconductors, telecom equipment, and other sophisticated digital devices. This will result in the loss of jobs. The Japanese are relocating car production to China and an influx of cheap Chinese consumer goods has worried Japanese producers.

Chinese prices are also causing imbalances in the developing world. Mexico is seeing whole industries relocate to China mainland and new manufacturing investment is weak in most of Southeast Asia.

So some economists suggest revaluation of the Yuan to make China's products more expensive and curb its exports. A move to floating China's currency might result in a stronger Yuan (although some analysts say that because of China's huge bad loan problem a floating Yuan would be weaker than it is now.) However the exchange rate is only part of China's trade advantage. The supply of $100-a-month Chinese labour seems inexhaustible. And according to the Bank of China the $50 billion of annual foreign investment into China is upgrading Chinese industry and raising productivity by 4 per cent annually.

Mark L. Clifford writing in *Business Week* concludes, "China's export juggernaut will certainly mean plenty of disruption for the global economy. But do not look for quick solutions. China deflation will not go away until the flood of workers from farms to factories slows–a process that will take decades".

Source: Adapted from news cuttings, 2002.

Recap Questions

1 In what ways does the above article demonstrate Ricardo's explanation of the gains from trade?
2 In what ways does China's export success represent a threat to leisure goods' producers?
3 What factors make Chinese exports of leisure goods so competitive?
4 How is the exchange rate of the Yuan currently determined?
5 Draw a diagram to explain the possible changes to the exchange rate if the Yuan were to be allowed to float?
6 What are the benefits and drawbacks to China of a stronger Yuan?

Multiple choice

1 **The terms of trade will improve if.**

   (a) The price of exports rises faster than the price of imports.
   (b) The price of imports rises faster than the price of exports.
   (c) Export earnings are greater than import expenditure.
   (d) Import expenditure is greater than export earnings.

2 **Which of the following is not a benefit of specialization and trade?**

   (a) Self-sufficiency.
   (b) Economies of scale.
   (c) A rise in total output.
   (d) Acquired expertise.

3 **The exchange rate for US dollar falls. Which of these will be a direct consequence to 'Leisurewear', a US organization which imports raw materials and exports finished products?**

   (a) Import costs will fall.
   (b) Import costs will rise.
   (c) Import costs will remain unchanged.
   (d) US labour costs will fall

4 **In 1995 the estimated tourism balance of payments for the UK was as follows:**

Overseas tourism spending in UK £104 60 million	UK tourism spending overseas £142 00 million.

   Which of the following statements are true?
   (i) There was a deficit of tourism payments of £3740 million.

(ii) There was a surplus of tourism payments of £3740 million.

(iii) UK GNP rose by £24 660 million.

(iv) PSBR was reduced by £3740 million.

(a) (i) only.

(b) (ii) only.

(c) (i) and (iii) only.

(d) (iii) and (iv) only.

5 Which of the following is true?

(a) A rise interest rates will tend to make the exchange rate fall.

(b) Tourism is classified as an invisible trade item.

(c) A fall in the exchange rate will tend to reduce inbound tourism.

(d) The purchase of an overseas leisure company represents an outflow under the current account.

Review questions

1 Illustrate which parts of the balance of payments account are affected by the activities of a named organization in the leisure and tourism sector.

2 Under what circumstances would a fall in the value of the Euro (a) increase and (b) decrease earnings of US dollar for Greece?

3 How might persistent current account deficits affect organizations in the leisure and tourism sector?

4 Explain how a fall in the value of the domestic currency would affect three different organizations in the leisure and tourism sector?

5 Explain what factors have caused fluctuations in exchange rates over the past few years?

Web sites of interest

USA: statistics http://www.stat-usa.gov/

New Zealand: statistics http://www.stats.govt.nz/statsweb.nsf

Australian Bureau of Statistics http://www.abs.gov.au

Brazil: statistics http://www.ibge.gov.br

Canada: statistics http://www.statcan.ca

The Euro (EU site): http://europa.eu.int/euro/

Euro help for firms: http://www.euro.gov.uk/

Learning help in economics and business studies: http://bized.ac.uk

Globalization

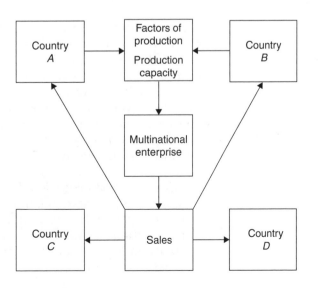

Objectives and learning outcomes

A significant trend in the last 25 years is the globalization of the eco-nomic environment. This means that goods and services are increas-ingly being produced and sold across national economic boundaries. This chapter investigates the rise of globalization and the multi-national enterprise (MNE) and analyses the motives for multinational operations as well as the effects of MNEs on consumers, parent coun-tries and host countries. It also considers the relationship between MNEs and governments in parent and host economies. The signifi-cance of MNEs cannot be underestimated since it has been estimated that the 200 largest MNEs have a combined sales equal to about one-third of the world's gross domestic product (GDP).

By studying this chapter students should be able to:

- explain the meaning of globalization;
- explain the meaning of an MNE;
- understand the motives for extending operations overseas;
- analyse the effects of MNEs;
- evaluate government policy relating to MNEs.

Globalization

Robertson (1992: 8) describes globalization as

'the compression of the world and the intensification of conscious-ness of the world as a whole … concrete global interdependence and consciousness of the global whole in the twentieth century.'

Under globalization people around the world are more connected to each other than ever before in a variety of ways. Information and money flow more quickly than ever and between more people and at greater distances. Goods and services produced in one part of the world are increasingly available to the rest of the world. International travel is more frequent. International communication is commonplace. In fact globalization has a variety of dimensions including cultural, political and environmental ones. This chapter will concentrate on the economic dimensions of the term. In this sense Friedman (1999: 7–8) offers the following definition:

'[T]he inexorable integration of markets, nation-states, and technolo-gies to a degree never witnessed before – in a way that is enabling individuals, corporations and nation-states to reach around the world farther, faster, deeper and cheaper than ever before … the spread of free-market capitalism to virtually every country in the world.'

Economic globalization represents a development of markets and expansion of global linkages. It would be possible to identify four main stages of this development from subsistence (little market interaction) to the development of local and regional markets through to the importance of national and finally to the ready access to international markets. It refers to the increasing integration of economies around the world. This integration is evident mainly through trade and financial flows but it also includes the movement of people (labour) and knowledge (technology) across international borders.

- *Trade*: International trade has risen dramatically over the past 25 years. This has lead to a big increase in the range of leisure goods and services available as global markets offer greater opportunity for consumers to tap into more and larger markets around the world. Trade has increased as transport has become cheaper and faster so that resource differentials in different countries can be exploited. Markets promote efficiency through competition and the division of labour encouraging greater specialization that allows people and economies to focus on what they do best, but at the same time entailing more trade. The strongest rise has been in the export of manufactured goods whilst the share of primary commodities in world exports, such as food and raw material, has declined. The increase in world trade has also hastened the structural changes in economies. Advanced industrial economies have witnessed rapid de-industrialization as manufacturing has become relocated in newly industrialized developing countries, particularly in Asia.
- *Capital movements*: This aspect relates to funds to finance investment and there were rapid increases in private capital flows, particularly to developing countries during much of the 1990s and direct foreign investment is the most important category.
- *Movement of people*: This has been one of the less spectacular aspects of globalization. Given the vast differentials in wages and living conditions it might be expected that more workers would move from one country to another to exploit better employment opportunities. However whilst trade and capital movements have been liberalized, labour migration has not. Most countries still operate restrictive immigration policies. In the period 1965–90, the proportion of labour forces round the world that was foreign born increased by about one-half but most migration occurs between developing countries.
- *The spread of knowledge (and technology)*: Knowledge, information and technology transfer is a significant, aspect of globalization. It can occur at two levels. For example, countries may benefit from technical innovation from direct foreign investment. However knowledge about management techniques, export markets production methods and economic policies is also much more readily available and at comparatively low cost to companies and individuals who wish to benefit from it.

The rise of globalization has been facilitated by technological advances. In particular there has been a revolution in communications based on information technology and the Internet and a steady increase in the efficiency

Table 15.1   Global significance of tourism (2001)

Total tourism receipts ($ billion)	US $3012.9
As a per cent of world GDP	9.5%
Tourism value-added ($ billion)	US $1201.3
As a per cent of world GDP	3.8%
Tourism employment ('000s of jobs)	69 212.0
As a per cent of world employment	2.8%
Capital investment in tourism ($ billion)	US $631.9
As a per cent of world capital investment	9.4%
Tourism foreign earnings ($ billion)	US $496.7
As a per cent of world exports	6.3%
Consumer spending on tourism ($ billion)	US $1960.8
As a per cent of total personal spending	10.0%

Source: Adapted from World Trade Organization (WTO) data.

of transportation. These have made it easier, cheaper and quicker to complete international transactions – both trade and financial flows.

Globalization is seen by some as a power for good whilst others see it as laden with threats. Those who advocate its benefits refer to improved communications, a more open world, the advent of new, better and cheaper products, the reduction in barriers to trade and its contribution to faster economic growth. For this group globalization offers significant opportunities for world development and they see the major problem that it is not progressing evenly. They note that some countries have been integrated into the global economy more quickly than others and that these are seeing faster growth and reduced poverty. For example, free-trade policies have brought dynamism and greater prosperity to much of East Asia, transforming it from one of the poorest areas of the world 40 years ago.

However, to others, globalization is a pejorative term sometimes used as shorthand for the ills of capitalism. Here concerns are expressed about the deterioration in the well-being of particular groups (these range from whole countries, to workers in developed countries who have seen their jobs exported, to workers in developing countries who work under conditions of exploitation), the sovereignty and identity of countries, the disparities of wealth and opportunities among countries and people, the health of the environment and the greater exposure it brings countries to sudden and profound economic shocks.

Tourism is a particularly significant aspect of globalization (Mules, 2001). Its supply and demand is global and its operation creates and recreates new identities at the consumer, organizational and national levels. Above all it is a very significant economic activity in global terms as Table 15.1 and Plate 15 illustrate. Sugiyarto et al. (2003) examined the economic impact of globalization and tourism in Indonesia and found that tourism growth amplifies the positive effects of globalization and lessens its adverse effects. Production increases and welfare improves, while adverse effects on government deficits and the trade balance are reduced.

Plate 15
Same (but different
greeting): MacDonald's,
Thailand
Source: The author

Globalization is sometimes thought of as a synonym for global business. However at the same time that businesses have organized themselves at a global level so have other agencies – some representing governments and some representing non-governmental interests. The United Nations and its variety of subsidiary offices are a good example of the former. Greenpeace, Friends of the Earth, the WorldWide Fund for Nature, are examples of the latter.

Meaning and extent of multinational enterprise

An MNE is one which has production or service capacity located in more than one country. The MNE has a headquarters in a parent country and extends its operations into one or more host countries. The headquarter countries for many of the key MNEs in travel and tourism are the USA, the UK, France, Germany, Japan and Hong Kong. The main ways in which multinational operations are extended are by investment in new or 'greenfield' capacity, by taking an equity stake in a foreign company (i.e. buying up shares) or by operating a franchise or alliance with a foreign company. Coca-Cola is a good example of a global corporation as illustrated in Exhibit 15.1.

Motives for going multinational

The general motive for companies going multinational is profit maximization. In this respect investment overseas can be viewed in a similar way to any investment. The criterion for profit maximization for an investment is

Exhibit 15.1   The global thing

Coca-Cola is the world's largest beverage company, with four of the world's top five soft-drink brands. The company was created in the US and its first international bottling plants opened in 1906 in Canada, Cuba and Panama. Today, it produces nearly 400 brands in over 200 countries. More than 70 per cent of its income comes from outside the US.

Worldwide Net Operating Revenues (% of total)	
Latin America	10
Corporate	1
North America	30
Africa	4
Asia	24
Europe/Eurasia/Middle East	31

For example:

Asia: Net operating revenues in Coca-Cola's Asia strategic business unit were $5.1 billion in 2003, with unit case volume increasing 4 per cent in 2003 compared with 2002. Results were particularly strong in China, India and Thailand where core carbonated soft drinks – particularly single-serve packages – performed well. Results in Japan and Philippines were less than expected.

Thailand: In Thailand products of the Coca-Cola Company were first produced in 1949 and the company now employs 9000 people. It operates seven bottling facilities including a state-of-the-art plant that opened in 1997 in Korat. Additionally Coca-Cola has two licensed bottling partners in Thailand: Thai Pure Drinks, which operates in most of the country, and Haad Thip Public Company Limited, which serves the south. The company has a 49 per cent share in Thai Pure Drinks.

Africa: The Coca-Cola Company and its 40 bottling partners constitute the largest single private employer in Africa. Coca-Cola was first bottled in Africa in 1929 and today the Company markets more than 80 brands, with local beverages such as Sparletta, Hawai and Splash complementing core brands including Coca-Cola, Fanta and Sprite.

Source: Adapted from Annual Report (2003).

that the rate of return should be better than other possible uses for the capital that is to be employed. The rate of return will be related to the cost of, and the revenue derived from, the investment. Thus motives for overseas investment will include cost reductions or increased sales resulting from production or service provision overseas.

Companies involved in manufacturing leisure as well as other goods now have much weaker ties with any particular region or national economy. The increase in international trade has made the market place more competitive and companies much more aware of the need for achieving price leadership or adding value to their products in order to achieve market share and profitability. Thus firms are more ready to transfer production to another location should circumstances favour this. Service sector companies that wish to extend their services to overseas markets generally have little option other than to invest in capacity overseas.

Specific motives for multinational expansion can include the following:

- lower labour costs;
- lower other costs;
- exploiting 'national diamonds';
- marketing advantages;
- scale economies, integration and competition;
- extension of product life cycles;
- tariff avoidance;
- incentives in host economies.

Labour costs • • •

In order to achieve price leadership, firms are constantly attempting to lower their costs below those of their rivals. One of the key factor costs that can be reduced by globalization is labour costs. Countries such as China, Malaysia, Vietnam and Thailand are popular destinations for production plants for MNEs because of their cheap labour rates. As well as cheap rates, labour and health and safety legislation is much less onerous on organizations in these countries. Union power is also very limited. Thus in the audio products industry, Motorola, a Swiss Company, has an assembly plant in China for some of its car stereo range which it sells in the UK. Similarly, the Japanese Sony Company has products assembled in Malaysia. It is not uncommon for UK publishers to have books printed in Singapore and Hong Kong. A similar trend towards investment in tourism destinations can be observed with countries such as Turkey offering lower wage rates than those found in Spain and France.

Other costs • • •

MNEs have access to international capital markets, so local interest rates are rarely a consideration. Land costs and planning regulations, though, can be an important factor, particularly in 'greenfield' developments. The rate of exchange between the parent and the host economy will also be significant.

'National diamonds' • • •

Porter (1990) investigated the source of different countries' competitive advantage in the production of goods and services. He suggested an important factor which he calls the 'national diamond' effect. Why should the Japanese, for example, be so competitive in the production of cars when they have few local raw materials and relatively high wages? Porter's answer is that intense competition and demanding consumers in the home market are key factors which cause firms to improve technology, quality and marketing. In other words, the product is polished and reworked into a national diamond. This then enables such companies to compete successfully in overseas markets where local products are comparatively uncompetitive since they have not been similarly honed.

Marketing advantages

Some companies have an internationally renowned corporate image which can be exploited by extending operations overseas. Examples here include Holiday Inn (hotels), McDonald's (fast food) and Disney (entertainment). The name is important for two reasons. First it guarantees a standard. This may encourage use, for example, by tourists in foreign destinations who may want their hotel room to represent 'a slice of home', or who are sceptical about using unknown hotels. Second, foreign branded names, particularly US ones, are popular status symbols in some less-developed countries. The queues around McDonald's in Beijing and Moscow are testimony to this.

Scale economies, integration and competition

Multinational expansion may be a way of extending profits through vertical integration. For example, tour operators and airlines invest in accommodation overseas to extend their profits. Similarly, a strong incentive for horizontal integration may be the reduction in competition that occurs from buying foreign competitors. There are also considerable economies of scale to be achieved through transnational ownership. Economies of scale are discussed more fully in Chapter 5, and include bulk purchasing, advertising economies and utilization of specialist inputs from different geographical areas.

Extension of product life cycles

Product life cycle refers to the different stages in the marketing of a product. Products which have reached the mature end of their product life cycle in their initial market and are thus suffering a decline in sales may be revived by launching them in overseas markets – particularly in less-developed economies.

Tariff avoidance

Where the exports of a country are affected by tariffs, companies affected may elect to set up production within the tariff area. This is perhaps one of the reasons why the UK has attracted so much investment from Japanese

MNEs in the past decade. Such companies can thereby market freely into the European Community (EC) without tariff barriers.

Incentives in host economies ● ● ●

Investment and running cost can often be reduced by operating overseas and taking advantage of government incentive packages.

Multinational enterprises in leisure and tourism

Examples of significant MNEs in leisure and tourism include:

Airlines	Electronics	Entertainment	Consumer products
AMR (American)	Hitachi	Walt Disney	Coca-Cola
UAL (United)	Matsushita	Time Warner	McDonald's
British Airways	Sony	News	Nike
(BA)		Corporation	
Delta		Viacom	
Lufthansa		Seagram	

Air travel

There is a growing tendency for global strategies in major airline companies. The two main directions to this strategy are horizontal globalization and diversification. Horizontal globalization involves extending service networks worldwide. The motives for this include the general benefits of horizontal integration as discussed in Chapter 5, but increased market share is clearly a key motive. For example, whilst BA's turnover is highest in Europe there is significant potential growth in passengers in the Americas, Southern and Pacific regions.

Hence BA's global strategy has involved investment in foreign airlines to provide global representation and extend BA's passenger base. An added advantage is that allied airlines can use code sharing. Under code sharing, connecting flights of an airline group can share a common flight number. So a passenger flying from the UK to Perth, Australia will see the flight as one BA flight number rather than a BA flight and a Qantas transfer. Exhibit 15.2 records the announcement of BA's 'Oneworld' alliance. Most of the world's major airlines have entered similar global alliances and Figure 15.1 shows some of the major airline partnerships. Fayed and Westlake (2002) examine the impacts of globalization and GATS on air transport industries and note the trends towards the privatization of airline companies in the context of the development of so-called global 'alliances' or 'partnerships' and liberalization at regional level and within trade groups such as the European Union (EU).

There is also an incentive for airlines to diversify into complementary activities. The logic behind this is that the airlines have customers who are likely to require related travel services – primarily car hire and accommodation. Thus

---

Exhibit 15.2   Oneworld

British Airways announced its new global partnership in 1998. BA's Oneworld is an alliance between BA, American Airlines, Canadian Airlines International, Cathy Pacific and Qantas. The heart of this alliance is a 'code-sharing' agreement where one airline sells a ticket on another carrier's flight, but issues a ticket carrying its own two-letter code. Oneworld is taking its activities further by joint marketing activities and the pooling of the frequent-flyer programmes of it members. Such agreements help airlines to extend their marketing and fill empty seats.

The popularity of alliances is the fact that there are financial and political difficulties which face airlines attempting traditional take-overs and mergers. Alliances allow airlines many of the benefits of merger without the related problems.

The main advantage is to establish a global network where passengers can be sold tickets in any part of the world to travel between any airports in the world. This helps to reduce passenger wastage when customers are forced to change carriers to reach destinations outside the network of their initial carrier.

Oneworld employs 220 000 staff and serves 632 destinations in 138 countries. It operates 1524 aircraft, accounts for an aircraft departure on average every 14 seconds and carries 174 million passengers each year.

Source: The author (1999).

Star Alliance	Air Canada, Air New Zealand, ANA, Asiana Airlines, Austrian, bmi, LOT Polish Airlines, Lufthansa, Mexicana, Scandinavian Airlines, Singapore Airlines, Spanair, Thai Airways International, United and VARIG
Oneworld	BA, Aer Lingus, American Airlines, Cathay Pacific, Iberia, Lan Chile, and Qantas.
Sky Team	Aeromexico, Air France, Alitalia, TSN, Delta and Korean Air.

Figure 15.1   World airline partnerships

it is not uncommon for airlines to have alliances with or equity stake in or ownership of car hire companies and hotel operators.

Shipping

Ferry and cruise operations tend to be multinational in their operations. Many UK, US and Scandinavian cruise companies operate in the Caribbean. Typically such ships are registered not in the country of their parent firm but in countries which offer flags of convenience, such as Panama and the Bahamas. In doing this, shipping companies can benefit from less stringent shipping regulations and lower taxes. The crewing of such ships is often provided from low-wage countries to cut costs, whilst the officers tend to be recruited from parent countries. Purchases of ship's stores and refittings can be done in ports which offer lowest costs.

Hotels and hospitality

Major MNEs in the hotel sector include US corporations such as Starwood, and Marriott International and UK companies such as the InterContinental Hotels (ICH) Group (formerly Bass plc).

Bass expanded significantly into a global hotel presence during the late 1980s. It bought the Holiday Inn chain outside North America in 1988 and the remainder in 1990 and 1993. Holiday Inn worldwide has more than 1770 hotels and 338 000 guest rooms making it the single largest hotel brand in the world. Throughout 1993, 159 hotels were added and joint venture agreements signed in Mexico, Indonesia, and India, with development agreements in Germany and South Africa. Approximately 90 per cent of Holiday Inn hotels are owned by franchisees. Hotel owners select the Holiday Inn name because they want access to the global marketing power a strong brand name and an advanced hotel reservation system.

In 1998 Bass paid nearly £1.8 billion for the ICH chain. This added 117 hotels with 44 000 rooms and a handful of mid-range Forum hotels to its global hotel portfolio. Globalization is able to bring important cost savings to hotel chains. For example, Bass was able to develop a single reservation system covering both Holiday Inns and InterContinental. MNE hotels are also able to exploit their international brand names and can often take advantage of cheap land prices at an early stage of the development of a tourist destination. The move towards globalization is driven by economies of scale, marketing benefits and the good growth prospects for international tourism.

With its acquisition of ICH, Bass achieved good coverage across price ranges and is able to offer four-star hotels in addition to its mid-market Holiday Inns. It also added to its geographic coverage in Europe and Asia.

In 2001 Bass plc changed its name to Six Continents plc and in 2002 Six Continents announced the separation of the group into Mitchels and Butlers plc and the ICH Group plc. By 2004 the ICH Group PLC owned a portfolio of well-recognized brands, including InterContinental, Crowne Plaza, Staybridge Suites, Candlewood Suites, Holiday Inn and Express by Holiday Inn. With more than 3300 owned, leased, managed and franchised hotels and approximately 520 000 guest rooms across nearly 100 countries and territories, the hotel group is the most global hotel business and the second largest in the world by number of rooms.

Effects of multinationals on host economies

The effects of MNEs on host economies are mixed. The main benefits can include:

- extra investment and related effects (growth, exports and employment);
- technology and skills transfer.

However some of the problems that can arise from MNE activities include:

- leakages from the economy;
- prices and bargaining power;
- exporting of externalities;
- threat to local competition;
- power to pull out;
- enclaves and dual development;
- resource grabbing;
- labour exploitation.

Benefits of multinationals to host country

Extra investment • • •

The key benefit to host economies is the introduction of new investment. Such investment will represent investment which is extra to that which a host economy is able to generate itself and is important because capital tends to be scarce in developing countries and such capital shortages can retard economic development. In terms of the benefits of globalization to developing countries, it is those countries which have encouraged direct foreign investment that have seen dramatic increases in living standards over recent years. This is particularly true for China and countries in Southeast Asia. The effects of such investment will be the primary effects (resulting from construction of facilities, etc.) and the secondary effects (resulting from running of the facilities). As discussed in Chapter 12, the investment will give rise to extra income and growth in the economy and the associated benefits in terms of employment and foreign currency earnings.

Technology and skills transfer • • •

It may be that the use of skilled labour and advanced technology introduced to an area by MNEs transfers to the local economy by way of demonstration effects. This depends partly upon the training and level of skilled employment offered by the MNE.

Problems of multinationals for host country

Leakages from the economy • • •

MNE investment in an economy will generally generate more leakages than investment funded locally. This is because MNEs will remit profits to the parent company, often employ more foreign staff and sometimes use more imported inputs.

Prices and bargaining power • • •

MNEs which represent monopoly or near-monopoly purchasers of a local input (for example, hotel rooms) will be able to negotiate low prices with suppliers and thus reduce the impact of foreign expenditure in a local host area.

Exporting of externalities • • •

It is sometimes alleged that the reaction of MNEs to environmental pressures and legislation in parent countries is to set up overseas in order to avoid extra compliance costs. In this view, externalities of production are simply exported, often to less-developed countries which are sometimes keen to accept such externalities in order to retain international competitiveness.

Threat to local competition • • •

The low-cost, high-technology and high-quality goods and services associated with MNEs may make it difficult for new local firms to enter the industry. This is illustrated in Figure 15.2. LRAC represents a typical long-run average cost curve (LRAC) is associated with the production of a particular product. It is downward sloping, reflecting the considerable economies of scale that are derived from large-scale production. Because of its size and international buying power, an MNE is likely to enjoy low average costs of 0C at a large global level of output 0B. New domestic firms

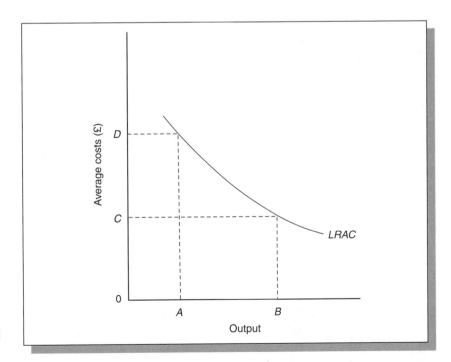

Figure 15.2
Costs for MNEs and local firms. LRAC

trying to enter the market will face higher-average costs of $0D$ associated with their small size $0A$, and thus find it difficult to compete.

Power to pull out • • •

MNEs, like other private sector organizations, seek to maximize profits. They are therefore constantly monitoring the environment to exploit changes in international costs or demand patterns. They thus have no particular loyalty to an area and can pull out, taking with them foreign expenditure (in the case of tour operators) or employment (in the case of manufacturers).

Enclaves and dual development • • •

One possible result of MNE investment is that a development will be exclusively for foreigners and exclude local people. For example, the Coral Resort owned by a Japanese Company on the island of Cebu in the Philippines is guarded by armed security personnel and the beach area is only accessible to Coral Resort guests. Exclusive developments such as these are termed enclaves.

Dual development describes the situation where the economies of developing countries witness the growth of a sophisticated part of the economy often based around MNEs, with high wages, good working conditions, and developed infrastructure. However this may not be well integrated into the rest of the economy so their may exist alongside this sector an impoverished economy which does not benefit from MNE investment.

Resource grabbing • • •

Local resource prices in developing countries (particularly land) are often low in international terms, and developing countries are generally short of capital and foreign exchange. MNEs tend to have ready access to capital and thus are granted planning permission. One result of this is that MNEs may purchase large areas of land relatively cheaply. This resource is then lost to local exploitation which might be appropriate at a future stage of a country's development. At a Japanese golf course development in the Philippines it was calculated that 150 hectares of land were bought for 150 million yen, a fraction of land prices in Japan, and that the development would yield 600 million yen of income by recruiting just 300 members out of an eventual target of 1600 members.

Labour exploitation • • •

One attraction of investment in developing countries for MNEs is that labour legislation, is generally more relaxed and trades unions, less evident or powerful. This means that labour costs can be reduced significantly through low wages, longer working hours, avoidance of sick, pension or holiday pay. Additionally it is generally easier to hire and fire labour as production fluctuates.

Government policy and multinationals

Governments view the activities of MNEs with mixed feelings, on the one hand attempting to encourage them and the increased income, employment and foreign exchange earnings they can bring, but on the other hand conscious of less attractive characteristics.

Government assistance for multinationals

Because of the potential benefits to a host economy, governments often offer incentive packages to MNEs to attract their projects. For example, estimates for Disneyland Paris suggested that the project would create 18 000 jobs in the construction phase and 12 000 jobs in the operating phase as well as earning US $700 million in foreign currency each year. Because of this there was considerable competition between the governments of France, the UK and Spain to provide the most attractive incentive package to attract Disneyland and enable their national economies to benefit from its effects. In the event the French government provided a comprehensive infrastructure package including new roads and rail connections. It assisted Disneyland Paris with land purchase, provided a loan at preferential interest rates and gave planning permission for future linked developments.

Forsyth and Dwyer (2003) examined the benefits and costs of foreign investment in Australian tourism are identified including effects of increased tourist numbers, balance of payments effects, regional socio-economic impacts, technology transfer, changes in industry structure, loss of equity and control, and transfer pricing. They concluded that Australia can maximize the economic gains it achieves from the tourism industry by maintaining a liberal attitude toward foreign investment.

Government resistance to multinationals

Competitive threat • • •

In some cases governments may think that MNE expansion in their country may pose a danger to domestic companies and thus may attempt to limit MNE expansion, as Exhibit 15.3 illustrates.

Power and accountability • • •

Another government concern regarding MNEs is that of their power and accountability. Some MNEs have turnovers that exceed the gross national products (GNPs) of smaller economies, and this can make some governments feel impotent in terms of policy. Similarly, MNEs, through their

---

Exhibit 15.3   Virgin protests

Virgin Atlantic has protested strongly to the competition authorities about BA's Oneworld alliance, despite having its own agreement with Continental Airlines, British Midlands, Malaysian and Ansett. It argues that these mega-alliances are formed to squeeze out smaller independent airlines and will lead to less competition. This view is supported by travel agents Hogg Robinson who note that there is no evidence that the new alliances have brought down prices or raised service standards.

Source: The author (1999).

---

substantial resources, can exert considerable powers lobbying governments to protect and promote their interests. In some cases the nature of a MNE's product or service can be threatening to governments. This is particularly so in media services. News Corporation has worldwide ownership of newspaper titles as well as world satellite television interests. News Corporation is thus able to exert a considerable influence on public opinion.

Transfer pricing and tax losses

Because MNEs conduct business across national frontiers, they can often rearrange their accounts to minimize their tax position. This is known as transfer pricing. Transfer pricing takes advantage of different rates of corporation tax in different countries.

For example, assume there are two countries. Country *A* has business profit tax of 40 per cent and country *B* has a tax of 20 per cent. It will clearly pay an MNE that operates across countries *A* and *B* to ensure that most of its profits are earned in country *B* and thus pay a smaller amount of tax. It does this by adjusting the internal prices of goods traded within the company. For example, if it imports raw materials for its manufacturing plant in country *A* from its plant in country *B*, it can charge itself an artificially high price for these materials. In doing so it will make high profits in country *B* but pay the lower rate of 20 per cent corporation tax on them. The results of this will mean that profits on finished goods sold in country *A* will have been lowered due to the high import charges, thus payments of high corporation tax (40 per cent) in country *A* are minimized. This means that more profits are retained across the MNE's international operations and that country *A* loses tax revenue.

Review of key terms

- Globalization: organization of a firm's production and sales on a worldwide basis.
- MNE: one which has production or service capacity located in more than one country.

- Parent country: base country of MNE.
- Host country: country in which MNE is operating.
- Greenfield development: new investment on a new site.
- National diamond: product or service for which a country has built a world reputation.
- Product life cycle: stages in marketing of product from growth to maturity and decline.
- Tariff barriers: taxes on goods imported into a geographic area (e.g. the EU).
- Code sharing: packaging of interconnecting flights of linked airlines into one flight code.
- Demonstration effect: method by which skills and technology are transferred to a host economy by participation of local labour.
- Enclave: local MNE development which is isolated from the main host economy.
- Resource grabbing: MNE utilizing of host country's resources which prevents later domestic utilization.
- Transfer pricing: adjusting the prices of goods traded internally within MNEs to minimize tax.

Data Questions

Task 15.1   Coca-Cola-nization

The following are some of the factors that the Coca-Cola Company reported in its 2003 annual report that might impact on its operations, earnings, share of sales and volume growth:

- Economic and political conditions, especially in international markets, including civil unrest, product boycotts, governmental changes and restrictions on the ability to transfer capital across borders.
- Unstable economic and political conditions and civil unrest in the Middle East, North Korea or elsewhere, the unstable situation in Iraq, or the continuation or escalation of terrorism.
- Changes in consumer preferences, including changes based on health and nutrition considerations.
- Competitive product and pricing pressures
- Ability to gain or maintain share of sales in the global market as a result of actions by competitors.
- Foreign currency rate fluctuations, interest rate fluctuations and other capital market conditions.
- Adverse weather conditions, which could reduce demand for the company's products.
- The effectiveness of advertising, marketing and promotional programs.
- Fluctuations in the cost and availability of raw materials, the cost of energy, transportation and other necessary services.
- Ability to maintain favourable supplier arrangements and relationships.
- Ability to avoid disruptions in production output caused by events such as natural disasters, power outages, labour strikes, etc.
- Changes in laws and regulations, including changes in accounting standards, taxation requirements.

- Ability to penetrate developing and emerging markets, which also depends on economic and political conditions.
- Ability to acquire or form strategic business alliances with local bottlers.
- The uncertainties of litigation, as well as other risks and unknowns.

Source: Adapted from Coca-Cola Company, 2003 Annual Report.

Recap Questions

1 Describe and analyse the global opportunities and threats to the Coca-Cola Company under as many of the above headings as possible.
2 What are the advantages and disadvantages of Coca-Cola's global operations to:
   (a) Shareholders
   (b) Host countries
   (c) Workers

Task 15.2 Developments in Zanzibar

Zanzibar is an idyllic island off the east coast of Africa. In Nungwi, villagers use rough red planks to make dhow boats and live on a harvest of mangoes, almonds, coconuts, cloves and citrus fruit, and by netting fish from the Indian Ocean. Its future looks set to for radical change with a significant tourism development planned.

The UK-owned East Africa Development Company is coordinating a massive $4 billion investment proposal in northern Zanzibar on the Nungwi peninsula. The East Africa Development Company (EADC) has been granted a 49-year lease renewable for another 49 years for $1 a year to develop the peninsula. As part of the deal, the government has taken a 26 per cent stake in the venture. Forte Meridien, the UK-based hotel group, is one of several UK companies which are partners in the proposals which will become East Africa's biggest holiday resort. The scale of the proposals include a harbour for cruise ships, 14 luxury hotels, holiday villas, three golf courses and a world trade convention centre.

The Nungwi scheme will be one of the world's biggest building projects. The benefits to the multinational companies involved are clear. Zanzibar is a destination with a good year-round climate, land prices are cheap, and so is labour. There is also the prospect of a greenfield site on a large scale. There are also potential benefits to local people in terms of higher-paid jobs and better living conditions if clean water and electricity are introduced. Nungwi village recently suffered an outbreak of cholera when raw sewage contaminated its well.

But Sue Wheat, writing in the *Guardian*, is keen to point out the strong counter-arguments against this development. She notes that although 20 000 people currently live on the site, the plans make no mention of them and suggest that the area is uninhabited. Sue Wheat poses some other key questions raised by the development of the site:

1 Water rationing is currently the norm in this area. How will the development affect water supplies?
2 How will local needs and environment issues be tackled?
3 Where will the 20 000 residents go?
4 Will any jobs created be suitable for the largely fishing and farming communities?

5 Will the resort use local produce and benefit local farmers or will it import foodstuffs to cater for visitor tastes?

Patricia Barnett Director of the pressure group Tourism Concern, is sceptical whether benefits promised to local people will materialize and is campaigning to protect Nungwi.

Source: The author, from press reports (1998, 1999).

Recap Question

Evaluate the costs and benefits of the Nungwi development to:

- The host country.
- The local host community.
- The East Africa Development Company.
- Forte Meridian.

Task 15.3   US Consumers give Adidas, Reebok and Nike, the boot

The 1990s were a period in which Adidas, Reebok and Nike consolidated their positions as global market leaders in sports goods. Demand seemed insatiable and fuelled high prices. Supply was outsourced to take advantage of labour rates in less-developed economies – at one stage Nike was employing Asian workers at around 70 cents a day. The companies were able to exploit this difference in global economic conditions and produce in cheap markets and ship the goods to sell in expensive ones. Profits rose.

But in 1998, the gravy train was derailed and US sports retailers found themselves over-stocked and forced to reduce prices to shift unsold stock. Analysts blame the fact that the brands have become too common along with bad publicity arising from stories of exploitation of workers in poorer countries for the slump in sales. This caused a shareholder panic about the global state of the market. Fears for the survival of trainer footwear caused heavy falls in the shares of sportswear manufacturers and retailers. But in the UK, the markets are holding up. The sports market in footwear is worth £850 million and clothing is worth £1.4 billion with both showing signs of growth. This is reflected in improved share prices. The US overstocking problems have been attributed to the over-optimism of manufacturers who over-supplied the market. The US problems are also seen as a shift in consumer tastes away from big brand sportswear.

This has led Nike to review its advertising campaigns and Reebok to reassess its image. Part of Nike's problem has been global saturation of its brand which is now seen worn by parents and children, rich and poor, and in just about every country in the world. In a change of strategy Nike has cut spending on sponsorship and US advertising. The company aims to makes the Nike brand less obvious, and so relaunch it as an object of desire, rather than the commonplace. Public relation (PR) Director for Reebok, Dave Fogelson said: 'We have cut back on sponsorship of teams because we need a more balanced approach, placing emphasis on outdoor marketing in order to help establish what we represent. We all followed the successful model of the Nike Air Jordans, and in terms of that we created a monster by focusing on the player rather than the shoe. We need to be smarter about marketing our brand.' Adidas has recently acquired the French ski and golf-wear group Salomon in an effort to diversify into the winter sports market.

Source: The author (1999).

Recap Questions

1 What is transfer pricing and how can MNEs benefit from it?
2 What are the other main opportunities available for these trainer footwear companies as MNEs?
3 What are the main threats facing these trainer companies as MNEs?
4 Evaluate the economic benefits and disadvantages faced by governments which host MNE operations.

Multiple choice

1 **Which of these is the least pronounced effect of globalization?**

   (a) Trade in goods and services
   (b) Capital movements
   (c) Movement of people
   (d) The spread of knowledge

2 **Bass plc opens a new Holiday Inn hotel in India. Which of the following will not benefit the host country?**

   (a) The demonstration effect.
   (b) The increased capital expenditure effect.
   (c) The leakage effect.
   (d) The technology transfer effect.

3 **Which of the following is not a possible disadvantage to the host economy of MNEs?**

   (a) Leakages from the economy.
   (b) Threat to local competition.
   (c) Improved know how.
   (d) Enclaves and dual development.

4 **Which of the following statements is false?**

   (a) An enclave may discriminate against local people.
   (b) Transfer pricing may be used by MNEs to avoid taxes.
   (c) MNEs may set up in foreign countries to avoid tariff barriers.
   (d) Multinational investment mean less leakages from the economy than domestic investment.

5 **Which of the following is not an argument against globalization?**

   (a) Workers in developed countries may see their jobs exported.
   (b) A reduction in tariff barriers.
   (c) Loss of sovereignty in economic policy.
   (d) More exposure to economic shocks.

Review questions

1 What MNEs exist in the leisure goods, leisure services and tourism sectors of the economy? What makes these companies MNEs?
2 Why and how are airlines 'going global'?

3 Using a named overseas project of an MNE, evaluate:
   (a) The benefits of the project to the host country.
   (b) The problems of the project to the host country.
   (c) The benefits of the project to the MNE.
4 What is meant by transfer pricing?
5 Why do MNEs invest from and to the UK?

Web sites of interest

Granada Group plc http://www.granada.co.uk
Marriott International http://www.marriott.com
McDonald's Corp. http://www.mcdonalds.com
World Bank http://www1.worldbank.org/economicpolicy/globalization/dollarqa.htm
Nintendo of America Inc. http://www.nintendo.com
Scottish and Newcastle plc http://www.scottish-newcastle.com
Sony Corporation http://www.sony.com
Time Warner Corporation http://www.timewarner.com
Trump Hotels & Casinos Resorts Inc. http://www.trump.com
Wilson Sporting Goods Co. http://www.wilsonsports.com/
Virgin Atlantic http://www.bized.ac.uk/compfact/vaa/index.htm

Part Eight

Environmental Economics

CHAPTER 16

Environmental impacts

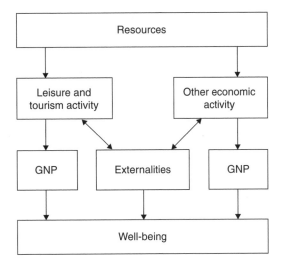

Objectives and learning outcomes

Chapters 12–14 examined the contribution of recreation, leisure and tourism to countries' national economies. Traditionally, economic analysis has measured impacts in terms of readily measurable variables such as employment, balance of payments and gross national product (GNP).

In contrast, the objective of this chapter is to examine the issues raised by environmental economics. Environmental economics involves a wider view of the impact of economic development and growth, taking into account well-being rather than just measuring how much richer people become in monetary terms. Here, issues such as global warming, acid rain and resource depletion have been highlighted as threats to economic growth and even to the future of our species, and critiques and techniques developed by environmental economists can be readily used in the recreation, leisure and tourism sector.

First, questions can be raised about the validity of focusing measures of success solely on the uncritical use of GNP data. Second, environmental accounting techniques seek to include a wide rage of considerations when considering the cost and benefits of particular projects. These include effects on the natural and built environment, as well as raw material and waste product issues. When subjected to environmental scrutiny, the recreation, leisure and tourism sector can display examples of previously unaccounted overall benefits as well as costs. Additionally, as well as being the perpetrator of negative environmental effects, the sector is sometimes the victim of environmental pollution caused elsewhere.

After studying this chapter students will be able to:

- distinguish between growth in GNP and growth in well-being;
- analyse environmental impacts;
- understand environmental externalities,
- distinguish between renewable and non-renewable resources (sources) and analyse the use of such resources;
- understand the significance of waste disposal capacity (sinks) to the economy;
- analyse the effects of the existence of open-access resources on resource use;
- identify the existence of externalities and their contribution to well-being.

Recreation, leisure, tourism and the environment

The environment plays a unique role to much recreation, leisure and tourism for it provides the stage upon which much recreation is enacted. The sector very much depends on the environment for its success. But this provides the dangerous irony for the sector. For the richer the environment, the more recreational activities are drawn to it. The more economic activity, the more the potential negative impacts on the environment and therefore the sector has the potential to destroy the very environment upon which it depends – pristine beaches, coral, attractive countryside, flora and fauna (loss of biodiversity).

Additionally, recreation, leisure and tourism are very dynamic growth sectors in the global economy. By virtue of this they are set to generate more and more environmental impacts as they grow. In particular transport is a key aspect of this sector. The growth in car use and air travel both have potentially serious impacts on the environment in terms of air pollution, casualties, concretization, noise pollution, congestion, global warming, ozone depletion, acid rain and health (see Exhibit 16.1). Another key aspect of the sector is the physical structures and infrastructures that support it and their associated impacts. Add to this the huge amount of waste generated by the sector and the energy consumption of the sector and it is not difficult to see why the sustainability of the sector has become such an important issue. For example, Gielen et al. (2002) have noted that whilst a move towards environmentally benign service industries is widely considered a key strategy for sustainable development the environmental impact of these industries is not negligible. They analyse the environmental impact of Japanese leisure and tourism and their results suggest that leisure and tourism are responsible for 17 per cent of

---

Exhibit 16.1   Intergovernmental Panel on Climate Change (IPCC)

In 1999 the IPCC published a study of the impact of aircraft pollution on the atmosphere and its main findings included:

- Aircraft release more than 600 million tonnes of the world's major greenhouse gas CO_2 into the atmosphere each year.
- Aircraft cause about 3.5 per cent of global warming from all human activities.
- Aircraft greenhouse emissions will continue to rise and could contribute up to 15 per cent of global warming from all human activities within 50 years.
- Nitrogen oxides (NO_2) and water vapour have a more significant effect on the climate when emitted at altitude than at ground level. Hence any strategy to reduce aircraft emissions will need to consider other gases and not just CO_2.
- An increase in supersonic aircraft flying could further damage the ozone layer as aircraft emissions of NO_2 deplete ozone concentrations at high altitudes, where these aircraft would typically fly.
- Aircraft vapour trails or contrails, often visible from the ground, can lead to the formation of cirrus clouds. Both contrails and cirrus clouds warm the Earth's surface magnifying the global warming effect of aviation.

Source: Adapted from www.ipcc.ch/index.htm

the national greenhouse gas emissions, 13 per cent of the national primary energy use and that a considerable part of the national land use is affected by leisure and tourism. They further note that leisure and tourism impact on biodiversity is hard to quantify because of inadequate monitoring systems.

Recreation, leisure and tourism can contribute to environmental impacts at the local or site level and at the global level.

Local environmental impacts

At the local level these can be classified as:

- impacts on natural resources,
- pollution,
- physical impacts.

Impacts on natural resources • • •

Development can put pressure on natural resources particularly in areas where resources are already scarce. In this respect fresh water, is one of the most important natural resources and the recreation and tourism industries have high water usages for golf courses, hotels, swimming pools and personal consumption by tourists. This usage (particularly with its natural industry peaks) has the capacity to create water shortages and waste water disposal problems.

Golf courses require large amounts of water for their every day maintenance and according to Tourism Concern a golf course in a tropical country such as Thailand uses as much water as 60 000 rural villagers. Over extraction of water from wells can cause saline intrusion into groundwater.

Recreational and tourism demands can also put pressure on local resources like energy, food and other raw materials particularly where they are already be in short supply. Over fishing is a possible impact here.

Land resources for recreation and tourism include minerals, fossil fuels, fertile soil, forests, wetland, wildlife and coastal areas. Construction can lead to depletion and deterioration of these resources and loss of scenic landscapes. Many forests have suffered negative impacts of tourism. These include forest fires and clearance for development and tree cutting for fuel. For example, a single trekking tourist in Nepal can use up to 5 kg of wood a day.

Pollution • • •

Recreation and tourism, although often seen as clean in comparison with chemical and smokestack industries, can cause similar pollution as other industries. These effects include:

- air pollutants,
- noise pollution,

- solid waste,
- littering,
- sewage,
- noxious discharges,
- visual pollution.

Recreation and tourism place particular demands on air, road and rail transport. Tourism accounts for more than 60 per cent of air travel and is therefore an important source of air emissions. As incomes increase so long-haul travel becomes more popular. Air pollution from transportation for recreation and tourism has impacts at the local and global level. At the global level carbon dioxide (CO_2) emissions are significant, whilst at the local level pollution around London's Heathrow Airport, for example, often exceeds European Community maximum permitted levels due to a combination of traffic congestion and aircraft movements. This pollution includes carbon monoxide, sulphur dioxide as well as carbon particularates from diesel fuel and can cause asthma and other health problems.

Noise and air pollution also emanates from recreational vehicles such as snowmobiles and jet skis. A survey of snowmobile impacts at Yellowstone National Park, WY, USA found that snowmobile noise could be heard 70 per cent of the time at 11 of 13 sample points.

On average, passengers on cruise ships in the Caribbean each generate 3.5 kg of waste daily which is more than four times the average 0.8 kg generated by the local inhabitants. In mountain areas, trekking tourists generate waste so that the Machu Pichu trail in Peru and Nepal trails have been nicknamed the 'Coca-Cola trail' and 'Toilet paper trail'.

Construction and use of hotels, recreation and other facilities often leads to increased sewage pollution and this has polluted seas and lakes particularly in countries where sewage treatment is undeveloped.

Recreational development can cause severe visual pollution using cheap and standardized buildings which may be totally out of character with local vernacular architecture, or grossly out of proportion or which fail to harmonize with natural features in and around a destination. Cheap land and lack of planning and building regulations can cause a sprawl of tourism and recreation facilities as well as the supporting infrastructure.

Physical impacts • • •

The development and use of recreation and tourism facilities and infrastructure may require blasting, sand and stone mining, concretization and cause erosion, loss of wildlife habitats and loss of natural drainage. Some ecosystems such as alpine regions, rain forests, wetlands, mangroves, coral reefs and sea grass beds are particularly fragile and sensitive to development and change of use. Similarly the development of marinas and beach breakwaters can cause changes in currents and coastlines.

Specific impacts from recreational activities include damage by trampling or mountain bikes on vegetation, the impact of water-based recreation on marine ecosystems such as coral reefs, and animal distress and displacement from safaris.

Global impacts

At the global level environmental impacts of recreation and tourism include:

- loss of biological diversity,
- depletion of the ozone layer,
- climate change.

Loss of biological diversity • • •

Biological diversity means the variety of plant and animal species. Recreation and tourism, can lead to loss of biodiversity where species are hunted, removed or trampled or where the use of natural resources (e.g. vegetation, wildlife, mountain and water) exceed the carrying capacity. Tourists and suppliers may also import species that can disrupt and destroy local ecosystems.

Depletion of the ozone layer • • •

The ozone layer is situated in the upper atmosphere and protects life on earth by absorbing the harmful wavelengths of the sun's ultraviolet (UV) radiation. In particular high exposure to UV radiation can cause skin cancer. The tourism industry seems to contribute to ozone depletion mainly through emissions from jet aircraft with predictions that by 2015 half of the annual destruction of the ozone layer will be caused by air travel.

Climate change • • •

Climate change, or global warming, seems to be worsening because of an increase in the production, and effects of, greenhouse gases in the atmosphere. These greenhouse gasses act as an insulation layer in the atmosphere and trap heat from the sun. CO_2 is one of the most significant greenhouse gases. CO_2 is generated when fossil fuels, such as coal, oil and natural gas are burned (e.g. in industry, electricity generation and automobiles). Additionally since vegetation is an important source of CO_2 absorption the loss of large areas of forest to clearance adds to the accumulation of CO_2.

Recreation and tourism are significant contributors to CO_2 production. It is estimated that recreation and tourism accounts for more than 50 per cent of road traffic and currently air traffic contributes about 2.5 per cent of the total world production of CO_2. However passenger jets are also the fastest growing source of greenhouse gas emissions with the number of international travellers expected to increase from 0.6 million in 1996 to 1.6 billion by 2020.

Economic growth and well-being

Chapter 13 considered the contribution of the leisure and tourism sector to economic growth and development. Economic growth was measured by examining changes in real GNP per capita. Environmental economists point out that such figure may give a misleading impression about improvements in economic well-being for the following reasons:

- The environmental costs of producing goods and services which appear in GNP are not always accounted for. These are called environmental externalities.
- The distribution of the benefits of economic growth is not always even.
- GNP figures may include 'defensive' expenditure. Defensive expenditure is that which would not be otherwise undertaken and is taken to offset environmental externalities.
- The loss of resources to future generations is not accounted for.
- The destruction of the natural environment that can occur from economic development is not given a monetary value.

Exhibit 16.2 demonstrates some of these concepts in relation to the development of an airport.

Exhibit 16.2   Development and well-being

The building and the running of an airport will add to GNP in terms of expenditure on building materials, fixtures and fittings, and access, staffing and consumables. However local residents will suffer from increased noise and atmospheric pollution as well as traffic congestion – none of these costs will appear in GNP data.

Whilst some local residents may benefit in terms of job opportunities, gainers and losers are often different people. The main gainers from the development are the shareholders of the airport company, airlines and tour operators, employees and travellers themselves. Local residents are likely to form only a small fraction of these categories and so the benefits of such growth will be unevenly shared. GNP per capita figures only show average effects of growth.

Because of the extra noise, some residents will buy double glazing, more petrol will be used because of traffic congestion, and roofing contractors will gain more work because of vortex effects of aircraft (the tendency of aircraft engine thrust to cause intense patches of air currents which remove roof tiles). This is defensive expenditure. It is expenditure made to try to combat some of the ill-effects of the development. It does not leave anyone better off than before the development, but it contributes to GNP data, exaggerating the apparent benefits of the development.

Finally the development will involve loss of the natural environment. This represents the loss of an amenity to some people in terms of views or tranquillity or open space, but again this loss fails to register in GNP data.

The discussion in exhibit 16.2 shows the need for caution in equating growth in GNP with growth in well-being. Indeed, some economists have argued that when a wider view of economics growth is taken, the costs may exceed the benefits. Such analysis has caused the questioning of policies which lead to fastest economic growth without regard to the wider consequences and some environmental economists have called for a halt or limit to economic growth.

The New Economics Foundation has produced an Index of Sustainable Economic Welfare (ISEW) as an alternative measure of economic progress to that of GDP. It argues that while in 1997 GDP in the UK was over one and a half times higher than that in 1972, 'during the same period violent crime has quadrupled, the incidence of asthma has tripled, the number of workless households has tripled, car traffic has almost doubled and concentrations of climate changing gases in the atmosphere have grown to perilous levels'.

The ISEW adjusts GDP accounts to take account of a wider understanding of welfare. Its five main adjustments are:

1 Defensive expenditure (spending to offset social environmental costs) are deducted.
2 An allowance is made for long-term environmental damage.
3 Net investment is included.
4 Changes in the distribution of income are valorized to reflect the higher marginal utility derived by extra income earned by poorer people.
5 A value for household labour is included.

Comparisons between changes in GDP and the ISEW over time are striking. Whilst per capita GDP grew at an annual average of 2 per cent between 1950 and 1966 the ISEW only grew by an annual average of 0.6 per cent. But in recent years the indices have actually moved in different directions. Between 1990 and 1996 whilst per capita GDP has risen by an annual average of 1.1 per cent, per capita ISEW has actually fallen by an annual average of 1.3 per cent.

Externalities

The notion of externalities has already been briefly discussed in Chapter 7. Externalities are those costs or benefits arising from production or consumption of goods and services which are not reflected in market prices. Because of this there is little incentive for firms to curb external costs, since they do not have to pay for them. Externalities can be divided into the following categories:

- *Production on production*: This is where one firm's external costs interfere with the operation of another firm, e.g. noise from discos and clubs which creates a noise nuisance to hotel residents.

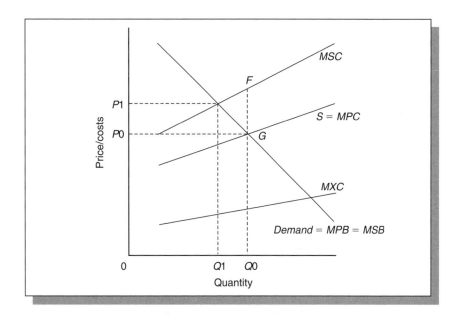

Figure 16.1
External costs, private costs and optimum output. (see text for details)

- *Production on consumption*: This is where industrial externalities affect individuals' consumption of a good or service, e.g. aircraft noise affects people trying to listen to music; increase in crime levels in resorts; visual pollution of hotels, caravans and car parks affects enjoyment of landscape.
- *Consumption on production*: Fox example, this occurs when external costs of consuming a good or service interfere with a firm's production process, e.g. traffic jams caused by a leisure park cause transport delays to local firms.
- *Consumption on consumption*: This is where the external effects of an individual's consumption of a good or service affect the well-being of another consumer, e.g. holiday-makers destroying coral reef, congestion around a football stadium causing inconvenience to other people. Figure 16.1 shows how firms tend to overproduce goods and services which are subject to externalities.

Demand curve D shows the marginal private benefit of consuming the good and, assuming there are no external benefits, it also represents the marginal social benefit. It shows how much consumers are willing to pay for extra units of output. Supply curve S shows the marginal private costs of production, i.e. costs per extra unit of output. Producers will wish to expand their output to $0Q0$ since the price they receive from extra units of production will exceed the costs of extra units of production up to that point. Beyond that point the extra costs of producing each good will exceed the price received for it. Thus $0Q0$ represents the optimal market level of production.

Curve MXC represents marginal external costs, perhaps because of noise or other pollution effects. Adding MXC to MPC generates the marginal social cost curve *MSC*. Notice that now we include external costs, i.e. previously unpriced environmental resources, the level of output $0Q0$ is no longer optimal, since marginal social costs exceed marginal social benefits by the amount *FG*. A reduction in output to $0Q1$ where $MSC = MSB$ would need to take place to provide the optimal social level of production.

The case of sewage discharges into the sea illustrates this point. Whilst there is little marginal private cost to the water companies for pumping sewage into the sea, it represents a loss of well-being to people who want to use the sea. There is a considerable marginal external cost which takes the form of cleaning costs to surf equipment, medical costs to treat infections and loss of earnings caused by sickness. These are readily quantifiable costs to which must be added the general unpleasantness of contact with sewage. Exhibit 16.3 considers some of the externalities posed by tourism development in Greece. It demonstrates the fine balance that has to be achieved in tourism development, with overdevelopment causing degradation of the place itself, which can threaten future demand and prosperity.

Another consequence that may stem from such development is that price inflation and property prices may rise, making it increasingly difficult for those not participating in the development, and thus benefiting from rising wages and profits, to remain in the area. This effect is termed economic displacement and occurs where a traditional and a growing sector of the economy exist side by side. The growing sector may increasingly threaten the traditional sector and participants in the traditional sector may only be able to access limited parts of the growing sector.

It is also possible to identify less obvious, distant, external costs of tourism and leisure developments. For large-scale resort developments, for example, consideration can be given to the sources of raw materials for building and the subsequent effect of quarrying for stone or forest depletion for timber.

Exhibit 16.3   Tourism curse visited on this blessed Aegean isle

The Greek island of Amorgos is rugged, barren and beautiful.

But things are changing fast since locals can now make more money through tourism in 2 months than they could otherwise make in a year.

The tourism boom is taking its environmental toll. There are growing problems with water, sewage and rubbish, although officials are reluctant to acknowledge them.

'If we're careful we'll be all right. Our only real problem is plastic water bottles,' says Mr Vekris, a local mayor. 'You know the quality of our lives has really improved with tourism.'

And indeed it has. It has meant washing machines and colour televisions for local inhabitants, but these are luxuries that will ultimately be at the expense of Amorgos.

Source: Adapted from *The Guardian* (6 September 1999).

Use of resources

Environmental economics distinguishes between two types of resources. Non-renewable resources are those which have a fixed supply. Once they have been used up there will be none left for future generations. Renewable resources are those which are capable of being replenished.

Non-renewable resources

Landscapes, views, open spaces and tranquillity represent non-renewable resources in the leisure and tourism sector. They are used up by general economic development as well as by leisure and tourism development itself. An important consideration concerning the use of non-renewable resources is the rate of depletion and hence the level of resources bequeathed to future generations.

The urgency of this problem can be illustrated as follows: Economic development uses up such resources. It also generates increases in incomes and leisure time and thus the demand for such resources. Thus we have the prospect of dwindling natural resources having to provide for increasing demands and thus degeneration occurring at a quickening pace.

Renewable resources

An important renewable resource for large-scale tourism development in some parts of the world is water. Large-scale development requires considerable resources of fresh water. It is here that the technique of impact assessment is important. Forecasts need to be made of water use against water renewal, although in some circumstances the latter may be supplemented by water diversion schemes. If water is obtained from underground aquifers, these will eventually run dry or be subjected to salt or other pollution if the rate of extraction exceeds the rate of replenishment. This problem is compounded by the free access problem, where it is not in anyone's interests to preserve water if everyone is drawing it from the same source.

Resources such as footpaths, public parks and golf courses also have a renewable resource element to them. If the rate of wear of footpaths for example, exceeds the rate of regeneration of protective vegetation, degradation will occur, as illustrated in Exhibit 16.4 and Plate 16. In this context Havitz and Adkins (2002) discuss the circumstances in which it might be necessary to de-market municipal golf courses where the natural surfaces of the golf course are negatively impacted by overuse.

One of the reasons for such overuse and degradation is that the use of footpaths and public parks is free to the user. In markets where prices prevail, price is an important factor in rationing the demand for scarce resources. Consumers economize on use so as to conserve their limited money income. Where price is zero, there is no incentive to economize. The use of unmetered water illustrates this point. For example, many people leave the tap on when they are cleaning their teeth, using a couple of pints of water where only

Exhibit 16.4 Calls for brake on mountain biking – Nicholas Schoon

The government is pondering whether restrictions on mountain bikes may be necessary because their growing popularity is damaging some of the nation's best scenery.

This week a report to be published by the Council for the Protection of Rural England will highlight mountain biking as one of the ways in which unrestricted countryside leisure and tourism are increasingly harming the environment. The cyclists often use footpaths, although the law says they should be restricted to bridleways and byways. The broad, highgrip tyres they use are stripping out vegetation and leaving deep, muddy furrows.

Walkers and ramblers complain that they are irritated and frightened by mountain bikes that pass them at speed. Some regard the bicycles as an inappropriate, unnatural leisure pursuit in cherished landscapes such as the 11 national parks of England and Wales.

Source: Adapted from *The Independent* (9 May 1994).

Plate 16
Erosion from trampling
and cycling
Source: The author

half a cupful is needed since there is no incentive to economize on use. Figure 16.2 shows the economics behind this. Curve D represents the demand curve for the use of a footpath. As price falls, demand rises. At price $P2$ demand would be $Q2$. If zero price is charged, demand rises to $0Q0$. For some paths this may result in usage which exceeds the limits where the resource can regenerate itself. If $0Q1$ represents the point of use

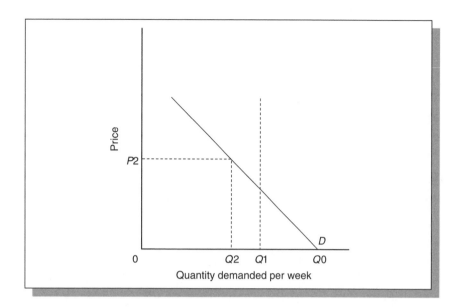

Figure 16.2
Effects of zero price on demand (see text for details)

beyond which regeneration cannot take place, then $Q1Q0$ represents use which causes degeneration of the resource at zero price.

The idea of carrying capacity is related to the regenerative capacity of resources. It has been defined as 'the maximum number of people who can use a site without an unacceptable alteration in the physical environment and without an unacceptable decline in the quality of experience gained by visitors' (Mathieson and Wall, 1982). It should be noted that this definition includes not just the possible degeneration of the physical environment but also the fact that too many visitors may spoil the visitor experience.

The macroeconomy and waste

Figure 16.3 recalls the simple circular flow of income model used earlier to underpin introductory macroeconomic analysis. Factors of production are purchased by firms from households and combined to produce goods and services which are then sold to households. Household expenditure is financed from the income derived from selling factors of production to firms. Additionally there are leakages from the system in the form of taxes, savings and imports, as well as injections into the system of government spending, investment and exports.

However, in its simple form, the model fails to illustrate some key points about the relationship of the economy to the environment. In particular it fails to show the production of waste materials (use of sinks) and the using up of resources (use of sources). In fact the production of waste materials is partially covered by the model and partially not. Exhibit 16.5 illustrates this point.

The article is about Newquay in Cornwall, UK, whose population of 100 000 is swollen by up to a million summer visitors. A key product of the

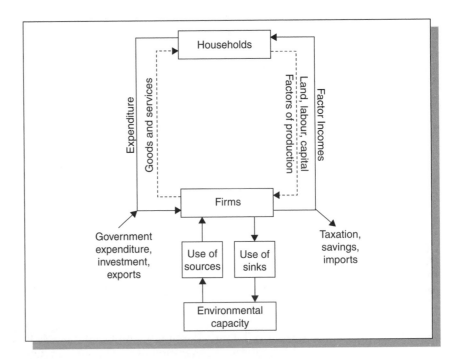

Figure 16.3
The circular flow
of income and
environmental capacity

Exhibit 16.5   Surfing in the sewers

'I've just come back from a surf. The water quality wasn't too bad today because the wind was blowing offshore and the tide was going out. When the wind blows on to the shore and when the tide is high you still get the occasional pad or condom floating by.'

The surfers are far from happy. And it's not hard to see why. A quick walk on to the headland and you notice the air begins to smell rich, sweet and vile. A brown slick drifts out to sea off the point. Tucked away beneath the cliffs is its source – the same old sewage outflow pipe, pumping out output all day long.

Source: Adapted from *The Guardian* (5 August 1994).

---

tourism industry is sewage. This waste is collected and partially treated by South West Water, and this activity is picked up by traditional economics in the simple circular flow diagram as the use of factors of production to perform a service. However the raw sewage that is discharged directly into the sea represents the use of a waste sink and the simple circular flow model does not reflect this.

The circular flow model can show an increase in economic growth caused by tourism – increased expenditure, generating increased incomes which in turn allow increased expenditure – without highlighting a significant threat to such growth in terms of pollution effects. The use of the waste sink is free to South West Water and thus there is little incentive for it to amend its behaviour. There is, although, clearly a limit to the capacity of the sea to assimilate this waste. Where this assimilative capacity is exceeded, degradation of the sea occurs.

Environmental economics seeks to make the link between economic production – in this case tourism – on the one hand, and the production of the ability of the ecosystem to absorb waste on the other. It further seeks to amend economic models to incorporate this relationship so that such economic development can take place without causing feedback which would threaten economic development, or cause an unacceptable level of pollution. Thus Figure 16.3 adds an environmental dimension to the simple circular flow model to highlight that production uses sources and sinks and that the environment has a limited capacity to meet these demands.

Open access and overuse

There is a particular problem posed by open access to resources. It is what Harden (1968) referred to as the tragedy of the commons. The sea is an example of an open-access resource. It does not have a clear owner and therefore it is difficult to exert property rights over it – for example, preventing waste dumping. Because of this there is little incentive to reduce outflows into the sea. The problem becomes more difficult with seas such as the Mediterranean. The Mediterranean coastline is shared by a number of countries. If one country should decide to reduce outflows of sewage into the sea, it will still suffer the ill-effects of the outflows from other countries who might even think that there is now more capacity for their sewage. Exhibit 16.6 goes beneath the sea to record the destruction of an open-access resource. On the same subject Rodgers and Cox (2003) examined the effects of trampling on the survival of Hawaiian corals against different levels of human use. They found that survival dropped from 70 per cent at the low impact site to 55 per cent at the medium impact site. Total loss (0 per cent survival) was reported from the high impact site after only 8 months. High impact was equivalent to less than 200 000 total visitors or 63 people in the water per hour.

The skies are another open-access resource and because of this there is less incentive to reduce pollution for example, by aircraft.

Environmental effects of other sectors on the leisure and tourism sector

The general environmental concerns of global warming, ozone depletion, acid rain and atmospheric pollution each have impacts on the leisure and tourism sector. The early 1990s for example witnessed successive years of poor snow conditions in European ski resorts. Global warming would clearly have an impact on the height of snow cover, thus putting low-level resorts out of business and shortening the length of the ski season. For example, a weather forecasting model at the UK Hadley Centre for Climate Prediction and Research predicts a 3°C increase in UK average temperatures

---

Exhibit 16.6   Reefs under threat

It took thousands of years to create the majestic coral reefs that lie under the earth's oceans. These vast limestone structures have been laid over the centuries by reef-building corals. They are home to a huge diversity of plants and over 200 species of fish.

The Great Barrier Reef, off the coast of Australia extends for some 2000 km and is a magnet for scuba divers. The Belize Barrier Reef stretches for some 250 km off the coast of Belize in central America.

But the reefs are under threat from industry, from agriculture and from tourism. Industrial fishing techniques using dynamite can blow up the fragile polyps that create the reefs. Rain forest clearance smothers the Belize Reef as thickly polluted run-off flows out of the rivers into the oceans.

Meanwhile, the tourism trade is set to kill one of its golden gooses. Whilst some boat operators practise good conservation methods and coach and cajole their clients to respect the coral, the growing size of the tourist tide threatens reef preservation. Boatloads of inexperienced snorkellers and divers regularly inflict unintentional damage, by touching sensitive polyps or smashing coral branches with a kick of a flipper.

But not all the damage is accidental. Some boat operators let their anchors drop on the reefs – the damage is evident by the clouds of debris thrown up. And some tourists seem unable to resist taking home just one small momento ('that won't make any difference'). For those who don't make the dive themselves there are plenty of willing hands – and souvenir shops in reef resorts are often full of rare shells and coral curios.

Source: The author, from press cuttings (January 1995).

---

between 1998 and 2100. This is based on estimated outputs and effects of greenhouse gases. The results are bad news for the Scottish ski industry since more of the precipitation that falls in Scotland will be in the form of rain rather than snow.

Exhibit 16.7 demonstrates alarming possible effects of global warming. CO_2 emissions, the main source of which is fossil-fuel burning, are the main contributor to global warming. Some commentators have predicted an increase in the average surface temperature of the earth of between 2°C and 5°C over the next hundred years if CO_2 emissions double over the same period. However not only are the physics and the chemistry of this calculation fraught with uncertainty, but so are the economics. It is difficult to predict the rate of economic growth and the subsequent demand for fossil-fuel burning for energy provision. Also there is a time lag between the emission of greenhouse gases and the effect on global warming.

Ozone depletion may also affect the leisure and tourism sector. The ozone layer is a layer of gas around the earth which protects it from UV radiation from the sun. Recent thinning of the ozone layer has been attributed to use of CFCs – chlorofluorocarbons – which have been used in the manufacture of spray cans and refrigerators. The main harmful effects of

---

Exhibit 16.7   'Paradise' islands unite against sea-level threat: alarm over global warming – Geoffrey Lean

Fakaofu Atoll, the main island of the watery territory of Tokelau, has just one of the world's 400 million automobiles and it is making a lonely contribution to the island's impending extinction.

Tokelau, a group of islands administered by New Zealand – just $12\,km^2$ of land in more than $250\,000\,km^2$ of Pacific Ocean – is expected, literally, to be wiped off the map by pollution. So are six other scattered strings of atolls, including similar dependencies and independent nations, among them the 1196-island state of the Maldives in the Indian Ocean.

As CO_2 emitted by fuel burned in the world's cars, homes and industries heats up the climate, many scientists believe that the seas will rise and eventually drown such low-lying islands.

Although small may be beautiful, however, it is also vulnerable. These islands' water supplies are usually limited and are increasingly being depleted by the tourism on which at least half their economies depend. Tourism increases pollution – only one-tenth of the sewage produced by the 20 million people who visit the Caribbean each year receives any kind of treatment. Increasingly dirty seas and oil spills imperil economies.

But the greatest threat of all comes from global warming. The highest point on the main island of Kiribas, in the Pacific Ocean, is 2 foot above sea level; and scientists' best estimate is that the seas will rise higher than this over the next century.

Source: Adapted from *The Independent on Sunday* (13 March 1999).

---

ozone depletion are to increase the danger of skin cancer after exposure to the sun. Clearly this may affect the demand for holidays based around sunbathing. Acid rain is the term given to acidic deposits caused mainly by the emission of sulphur dioxide into the atmosphere by industry. Its main effects in the leisure and tourism sector include:

- corrosion of buildings (particularly the stonework found on cathedrals),
- damage to trees (making forest areas less attractive to tourism),
- pollution of rivers and lakes.

The external effects of specific industrial developments can also have an impact on the leisure and tourism sector. Exhibit 16.8 illustrates the effects of the film industry on the tourism sector although it is interesting to note that Maya Bay has now become an tourist attraction because of its starring role in *The Beach*. Additionally, oil spills, like the oil tanker disaster that occurred off the Galapagos Islands (Ecuador) in January 2001, can cause severe short-term damage to tourist attractions. There, a ship loaded with 160 000 gallons of diesel fuel and 80 000 gallons of other petroleum products ran aground spilled nearly all of its load. The tourism potential of the area was seriously affected.

Exhibit 16.8   Lights, camera, destruction

Twentieth-Century Fox, searching for a location to film Alex Garland's best-selling novel, *The Beach*, chose Maya Bay on Phi Phi Ley island, situated off southern Thailand. The film stars Leonardo DiCaprio and Tilda Swington. However, Maya Bay's natural state of scrub bushes did not quite fit the imagination of the producer of the film, Andrew Macdonald. He wanted coconut trees and long clear views over sand and sea and gained permission from the Thai forestry department to give the beach a makeover. The government added its blessing to the project saying that the film would benefit the economy by promoting Thailand.

However, John Vidal reported in *The Observer* that 'More than half of the level section of the beach has now been dug up and the sand dunes broken up. Hundreds of holes have been dug, destroying the roots of plants that hold the dunes together'. The actions of the film unit have attracted the attentions of local environmental groups. They staged a demonstration on the beach wearing DiCaprio masks and protested that the damage caused by digging up plants was damaging the ecosystem and would lead to beach erosion.

Positive environmental effects of leisure and tourism

Although much of the environmental debate focuses on the detrimental effects of economic development, there are also benefits which can be noted. The inflow of foreign tourists to London for example sustains a breadth of theatres that could not be supported by the indigenous population. The existence of tourism in remote rural areas can make the difference between local shops remaining profitable, and therefore open, or not. Similarly the income and interest derived from tourists help to preserve heritage sites, contributing to restoration and upkeep. National parks and forest provide not only facilities for tourism but also preserve habitats for flora and fauna.

Exhibit 16.9 illustrates the potential for tourism to counter global deforestation.

Review of key terms

- Environmental economics: analysis of human well-being as well as the flow of money in the economy.
- Defensive GNP expenditure: expenditure that takes place to defend or protect one party from the external effects of the activities of another (e.g. double glazing as a defence from noise pollution).
- Externalities: those costs or benefits arising from production or consumption of goods and services which are not reflected in market prices.
- ISEW: Index of Sustainable Economic Welfare.

Exhibit 16.9   Deforestation: The tourism alternative

In 1990 about 11 000 km^2 of Amazonian rainforest were cleared and by 1995, that figure had jumped to more than 29 000 km^2. The latter represents an area equivalent to over 6 million football fields. The forest is being subjected to a series of developments which involve its wholesale destruction. These include industrial-scale agriculture schemes, cattle ranching and tropical timber cutting. To support these schemes there have been forest highway projects, energy distribution schemes and resettlement programmes.

The environmental consequences of this destruction are threefold. First, the Amazon rainforest is home to Amerindian settlements. Second, it contains almost 50 per cent of the world's terrestrial species and is a crucial site for maintaining biodiversity. The Amazon rainforest also plays an important role in the global carbon and water cycles. Trees are essential in reducing CO_2 levels in the atmosphere and about one-fifth of the earth's fresh water flows down the river Amazon. Meanwhile, carbon emissions from slash-and-burn clearance programmes add to global warming.

Nigel Sizer, a senior associate with the World Resources Institute and José Goldemberg who has an environment portfolio in the Brazilian government, suggest alternative uses of the forest to prevent its destruction, emphasizing the role leisure and tourism can play: 'Brazil is receiving hundreds of millions of dollars in international assistance administered by the World Bank to reduce deforestation. More careful use of these G-7 funds could go a long way towards combating the crisis ... Investments could be made in alternative development, such as community forestry, non-timber products, education and tourism, instead of subsidizing rainforest destruction'.

Source: The author (1990).

- Non-renewable resources: those which have a fixed supply.
- Renewable resources: those which are capable of being replenished.
- Waste sink: part of the environment where waste products are deposited.
- Assimilative capacity: ability of sink to absorb waste.

Data Questions

Task 16.1   Cashing in on a hole in the sky: David Nicholson-Lord argues that green economics should replace Adam Smith

The adage that every cloud has a silver lining is even truer now that the sun is shining. This month saw the start of an alliance between Boots and the Cancer Research Campaign to promote 'sensible sun behaviour'. The benefits for the Cancer Research Campaign are obvious: extra money for research.

But what's in it for Boots? Here's a clue. There are five 'play safe in the sun' guidelines and at least three involve buying something: sunhats, sunglasses, suncream. Who sells sunglasses? Why, Boots does – in fact it is offering customers discounts if they trade in their old ones. Boots also sells suncream. The lucrative sun-protection market is worth £110 million and Boots has about 47 per cent of it.

The hidden factor in all this is the gap in the ozone layer opening up 20 miles above our heads and letting in carcinogenic radiation. Skin cancer rates in the UK are double those of 20 years ago, and although lazing on foreign beaches is still largely to blame, the ozone factor is catching up fast. In the USA alone, accelerating ozone loss could cause an extra 200 000 skin cancer deaths over the next 50 years. Profit margins on suncreams are about 50 per cent and the market is growing at around 4 per cent a year. Suncreams with a high protection factor make up 70 per cent of it. From a purely business perspective, holes in the ozone layer are exceptionally good news.

There is another, more serious angle to this. When the Treasury does its sums, that portion of the £110 million sun-protection market arising from worries about UV radiation will be added to GNP and will count as economic growth. Thanks to the hole in the ozone layer and the skin cancer epidemic, we will all be that little bit richer. As a way of measuring progress, this is clearly a nonsense, since the quality of our lives will undoubtedly be poorer. Fortunately, some economists are developing a better way of assessing growth.

Later this year the New Economics Foundation, a group of 'green' economists, will produce the UK's first index of sustainable welfare, a form of alternative GNP measuring progress since the fifties, not only in income but in areas such as health, education, diet and environmental quality. These developments signify that the environmental movement is evolving a coherent critique of conventional economic theory which includes a response to the accelerating pace of planetary degradation – global warming in particular. The global free market emerges as one of the villains.

To a generation nourished on the idea that unlimited free trade is a good thing, this may be hard to accept. It rests on the assumptions that, first, cash relationships are invading and destroying areas of community life in which they have no place; and second, far from being a benevolent 'invisible hand' – Adam Smith's phrase – the market is blind to the environmental and social destruction it causes. Hence the global cash economy is a game that only the rich and powerful can win. Which brings us back to Boots and the GNP. In the post-war era, GNP has been transmuted from being a purely statistical tool into a national political goal. Unscrambling it promises to be an exercise both cathartic and revelatory. An index of sustainable economic welfare developed in the USA, for example, shows that while the sum total of economic activity, measuring both 'good' and 'bad' expenditure, has continued to increase, improvements in welfare levelled off in the late sixties and since 1979 have declined. In other words, we have lots more suncream, sunglasses and sunhats – but we can't really enjoy the sunshine any more.

Source: Adapted from *The Independent* (31 May 1993).

Recap Questions

1 'Thanks to the hole in the ozone layer ... we will all be that little bit richer.'
   (a) Explain what is meant by this.
   (b) Explain why 'this is clearly a nonsense'.
2 'The environmental movement is evolving a coherent critique of conventional economic theory.' Explain the meaning of this statement.

3 Explain what economic 'goods' and 'bads' derive from leisure and tourism economic activities.
4 Should green economics replace Adam Smith?
5 Distinguish between GDP and ISEW using this article.

Task 16.2

Table 16.1 illustrates some of the possible economic benefits and costs of recreation, leisure and tourism. Critically review the comprehensiveness of the table, add to it where necessary and use it as a basis to analyse the effects of a leisure or tourism development or provision.

Table 16.1   Leisure and tourism costs and benefits

Benefits	Costs
Satisfaction of wants	Distortion of local prices
Employment	Satisfaction of some wants at the expense of others
Foreign exchange earnings	Imports
Technology transfer	Congestion
Improved health	Aesthetic degradation
Better understanding of things	Pollution
Regeneration in depressed areas	Resource depletion
Engine for economic growth	Erosion
Source of profit	Loss of natural environment
	Loss of local control of resources

Task 16.3   Fasten your seatbelts and prepare for unsustainable take-off

The Heathrow Association for the Control of Aircraft Noise (HACAN) has published data from a number of sources about the effects that airports have on their local environment. These include:

- Sedative use increases by 8 per cent in areas affected by aircraft noise.
- Fourteen per cent more anti-asthma drugs are consumed by people living within 10 km of an airport.
- Transport 2000 calculates that every return air ticket generates an average of four car journeys.
- Dr Meyer Hillman, a transport specialist, has shown that every passenger on a return flight to Florida is responsible for a discharge of 1.8 tonnes of CO_2.
- The Intergovernmental Panel on Climate Change is expected to show that aircraft emissions are responsible for about 10 per cent of the world's CO_2 production.
- Mortality rates are near Los Angeles Airport are 5 per cent higher than in quieter places.
- The reading ability of 12–14-year olds who attend schools under flight paths is reduced by 23 per cent.
- Children exposed to aircraft noise are more likely to develop anxiety disorders.

- Airport expansion means more noise and less countryside.
- CO_2 emissions are forecast to increase by 500 per cent by 2100.
- High-altitude carbon emissions from aircraft are less likely to be reabsorbed by forests or oceans than other emissions, and are therefore more serious threats to the greenhouse effect
- Sulphur dioxide emissions from aircraft on the polar routes contribute to ozone depletion.

Source: HACAN.

Recap Questions

1 What externalities are associated with air travel?
2 Assess the impact of air travel on renewable and non-renewable resources.
3 Are the quiet skies an example of open access overuse?
4 What evidence is there to suggest that the market equilibrium of air traffic exceeds the optimum social equilibrium?
5 How should GDP figures be adjusted to take account of the externalities of air travel?

Multiple choice

1 **Environmental economists would argue that the value of suncream should not appear as part of a country's GNP. The main reason for this is because**

(a) The price of suncream includes sales tax.
(b) Suncream consumption is unevenly distributed throughout the population.
(c) The purchase of suncream represents 'defensive' expenditure.
(d) Suncream is not a necessity.

2 **Which of the following externalities represents the disruption to local traders' profits of an international fixture at a large sports stadium?**

(a) Production on consumption.
(b) Consumption on consumption.
(c) Consumption on production.
(d) All of the above.

3 **Which of the following statements is not true?**

(a) Externalities are those costs arising from production of goods which are not reflected in market prices.
(b) Water is a non-renewable resource.
(c) Non-renewable resources have a fixed supply.
(d) Renewable resources are capable of being replenished.

4 **The use of renewable resources is necessarily unsustainable ...**

(a) In the long-term.
(b) In the short-term.

(c) Where their use is greater than their regenerative capacity.

(d) Where their use is less than their regenerative capacity.

5 Which of the following statements is true?

(a) There are no positive environmental effects of leisure and tourism.

(b) Making resources free will protect them from overuse.

(c) Air travel gives rise to defensive expenditure.

(d) GNP underestimate overall well-being.

Review questions

1 What additions and what subtractions would environmental economists like to see with regard to GNP figures?

2 Distinguish between the four types of externalities.

3 What unpriced externalities arise from the:
   (a) Location of a football stadium?
   (b) Building of the channel tunnel?
   (c) Development of a lakeside campsite?

4 Under what circumstances are renewable resources exhaustible?

5 What environmental problems arise from open-access resources?

Web sites of interest

New Economics Foundation: http://sosig.ac.uk/neweconomics/newecon.html

Tourism Concern: http://www.gn.apc.org/tourismconcern/

Friends of the Earth: www.foe.co.uk

Surfers against Sewage: www.sas.org.uk

United National Environmental Programme – Tourism: http://www.unepie.org/tourism/home.html

British Airways: Environment Report: http://www.british-airways.com/inside/comm/environ/environ.shtml

Learning help in economics and business studies: http://www.bized.ac.uk

CHAPTER 17

Action for
sustainability

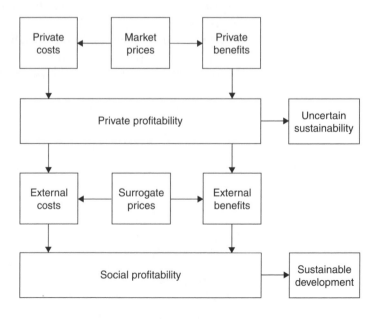

Objectives and learning outcomes

Chapter 16 examined the environmental impacts of the leisure and tourism sector. It considered ways in which the market failed to signal long-term problems of resource depletion, waste production and disposal, and other unpriced externalities. It highlighted the distinction between what was most profitable for firms and what was most profitable for society as a whole. It chronicled a wealth of evidence of undesirable results if the market was left to dictate future developments without any regard for wider environmental considerations.

This chapter examines strategies for utilizing environmental economic analysis to enable development of the leisure and tourism sector to take place with due regard to possible side effects. The aim of such analysis is to prevent the side effects of development causing socially unacceptable damage to the environment or indeed to stifle the very developments themselves. By studying this chapter students will be able to:

- explain the meaning of sustainable development;
- understand the limitations of the price mechanism in allocating resources in respect of environmental considerations;
- utilize different instruments for encouraging sustainability and environmental consideration;
- evaluate a variety of methods to impute value to unpriced externalities;
- understand the range of influences on environmental policy.

Meaning of sustainable development

There is considerable debate about the precise definition of sustainable development. It should also be noted that several levels of sustainability may be considered. At the widest level, sustainability of world economic development embraces those planet-threatening issues of global warming, resource depletion and ozone loss. Sustainability can also be considered at a national economy level, at a local level and at an individual leisure or tourism project level.

Key points in the development of environmental policy include:

- The United Nations Conference on the Human Environment held in Stockholm, 1972. A key outcome here was the creation of the United Nations Environmental Programme (UNEP).
- The 1987 *Brundtland Report* for the World Commission on Environment and Development which defined sustainability as 'development that meets the needs of the present without compromising the ability of future generations to meet their own needs' (World Commission on Environment and Development, 1987: 43). It therefore laid considerable emphasis on what is termed 'intergenerational equity'.

- The 1992 Earth Summit held in Rio, 1992. Here 182 governments agreed to adopt Agenda 21 – a comprehensive action plan for the environment.
- 1995: Agenda 21 guidelines produced for Travel and Tourism Industry by the World Tourism Organisation (WTO), with the World Travel and Tourism Council (WTTC) and the Earth Council (WTO, 1997).
- The Kyoto Conference in 1997. This led to the Kyoto Protocol which set out a 5-year commitment period (2008–12) for signatories to meet emission targets for greenhouse gases (GHGs).
- World Summit on Sustainable Development (WSSD) in Johannesburg, South Africa in 2002. Of relevance to recreation and tourism here was guidance for changing unsustainable patterns of consumption and production; promotion of sustainable tourism development as an issue of protecting and managing the natural resource base for economic and social development; sustainable tourism that contributes to social, economic and infrastructure development and sustainable development in the developing parts of the world.

Common elements in the *Brundtland* approach to sustainable development are first, the rate of use of renewable and non-renewable resources and maintenance of natural capital. Implicit here is that renewable resources should not be used beyond their regenerative capacities. Additionally, where non-renewable resources are used up, future generations should be compensated by the provision of substitute capital in some form so that, at the minimum, a constant stock of capital is maintained across generations. The second key element in the *Brundtland Report* is consideration of the effects of development on local and global waste sinks.

Sustainability has also been defined as growth which is not threatened by feedback, for example, pollution, resource depletion or social unrest. This can be related to tourism destination development. In this case sustainability would be that level of development which did not exceed the carrying capacity of the destination and thus cause serious or irreversible changes to the destination. It is development that can sustain itself in the long run.

It is also possible to consider environmental costs and benefits when considering specific projects. This approach considers the total social and private costs against the total private and social benefits of a project with a view to summarizing its total social value, taking into consideration environmental impacts as well as market profitability. The key principles of sustainability can be summarized as:

- consideration of externalities,
- consideration of depletion of non-renewable resources,
- tailoring of economic activity to the carrying capacity of the environment,
- the precautionary principle,
- the 'polluter pays' principle.

Since the operation of the free market in its present form does not guarantee the inclusion of the above principles in resource allocation, it follows that the implementation of sustainable development will involve modifications of free market activity.

The price mechanism and the environment

The market economy does in fact have an in-built tendency to conserve resources. In the model where competing firms seek to maximize their profits, since profit is defined as total revenue minus total costs, there is a constant pressure to economize minimize costs and hence on resources. Where environmental costs also appear as a firm's costs (e.g. energy use) business objectives and environmental objectives will coincide.

However the current market price of resources is not always an accurate measure of its true cost. This is particularly the case for unpriced open access resources such as the sea. Chapter 16 explored the fact that, whilst the costs of sewage pumping into the sea were minimal for water companies, considerable pollution costs are incurred by other users of the sea. Similarly the loss of landscape and views caused by tourism destination development is not apparent in the profit and loss accounts of the organizations involved. Equally the price mechanism does not give due regard to the future. Overexploitation of non-renewable resources such as coastline, countryside, rivers and mountains may leave future generations materially worse off than the current population. These considerations mean that the market often leads to overproduction and overdevelopment of projects where there are considerable unpriced externalities.

Policy

It is difficult for a country or a sector to introduce effective plans for sustainable development without having a guiding strategy. The following is the UK government strategy for sustainable development (www.sustainable-development.gov.uk/uk_strategy).

'Our strategy for sustainable development has four main aims. These are:

- social progress which recognizes the needs of everyone;
- effective protection of the environment;
- prudent use of natural resources;
- maintenance of high and stable levels of economic growth and employment.

For the UK, priorities for the future are:

- more investment in people and equipment for a competitive economy;
- reducing the level of social exclusion;
- promoting a transport system which provides choice, and also minimizes environmental harm and reduces congestion;
- improving the larger towns and cities to make them better places to live and work;

- directing development and promoting agricultural practices to protect and enhance the countryside and wildlife;
- improving energy efficiency and tackling waste;
- working with others to achieve sustainable development internationally.

Government policy will take account of 10 guiding principles:

- putting people at the centre;
- taking a long-term perspective;
- taking account of costs and benefits;
- creating an open and supportive economic system;
- combating poverty and social exclusion;
- respecting environmental limits;
- the precautionary principle;
- using scientific knowledge;
- transparency, information, participation and access to justice;
- making the polluter pay'.

What is noticeable about this strategy is that as well as environmental sustainability it places emphasis on economic sustainability (i.e. it seeks a balance between the environment and economic growth) as well as equality and social exclusion.

It should be noted that intergovernmental organizations such as UNEP also publish principles for sustainable tourism (www.uneptie.org/pc/tourism/policy/principles.htm).

Approaches to sustainability

There are a variety of different approaches to encourage sustainability. These are identified in Table 17.1 under the three categories of regulation, market approaches and soft tools.

These approaches function at different operational levels. Regulation generally functions at the national and international level. The next level is the market level. Here it is possible to use taxes and subsidies to influence the demand and supply of goods and services towards improved environmental ends. Soft tools such as eco-labelling may also be used to influence consumption at the consumer level.

Table 17.1 Approaches to environmental control and improvement

Regulations	Market approaches	Soft tools
Planning	Ownership	Tourism eco-labelling
Environmental impact assessment	Taxes, subsidies and grants	Certification/award schemes
	Tradable rights and permits	Guidelines, treaties and agreements
Laws and regulation	Deposit–refund schemes	Citizenship, education and advertising
Special status designation	Product and service charges	

Regulation

Direct regulation methods, sometimes known as command and control (CAC), involve the government setting environmental standards. These might take the form of water quality standards or planning regulations.

Planning permission • • •

This is a type of preventative control and by and large these are more effective. Planning permission is a preventive control seeking to stop developments that do not meet planning guidelines. Planning guidelines are devised to ensure that developments consider wider environmental issues and impacts. Enforcement is relatively straightforward since building may not commence without the necessary permission.

Environmental impact assessment • • •

Projects over a certain size are often required to undertake an Environmental impact assessment. This generally takes the form of a cost–benefit analysis that it includes the wider costs and benefits to society in addition to those accruing privately to firms and individuals. For a project or development to be socially acceptable the sum of the benefits to society (including external and private benefits) must exceed the sum of the cost to society (including external and private costs). This may be written as:

$$\Sigma B > \Sigma C$$

where Σ means 'the sum of', B is to the benefits to society and C, the costs to society.

A problem arises from using this equation in its raw form. When we measure costs and benefits, some happen immediately, and some happen at some future date. People would prefer to have money today than in the future. This is because £100 today is worth more than a promise of £100 in 10 years since it can earn interest in the intervening period. Therefore, future values must be adjusted to give present values. This is known as discounting and the rate used to discount is generally related to the long-term interest rate. The formula for finding a present value is:

$$\frac{B_t}{(1+r)_t}$$

where B_t is the benefit in year t and r is the discount rate.

Thus incorporating discounting techniques to the formula for social acceptability for projects gives:

$$\frac{B_t}{(1+r)_t} > \frac{C_t}{(1+r)_t}$$

where C_t is the benefit in year t.

There is considerable debate amongst environmental economists about the use of discount rates since, if environmental damage resulting from a project results in the distant future, then its effects are minimized in cost–benefit analysis by discounting. It is felt by some that this attributes too little significance to, for example, the potential damage caused by storing nuclear waste.

These types of control are sometimes criticized for their bureaucratic nature and the extra costs that are generated.

Retrospective controls and laws • • •

Retrospective controls include the setting of environmental control targets, after the externality-producing project has been commissioned. These include limits to aircraft and other noise, and water quality levels. Litter laws and penalties also fall under this category. Critics argue that such control methods themselves use considerable resources in monitoring and policing the limits and that non-compliance rates can be high. Figure 17.1 in the next section compares their effectiveness with green taxes.

Special designation • • •

Some sites have been granted special status designation as a way of promoting conservation and controlling development. These designations have varying degrees of statutory backing. For example, in the UK there are designated Sites of Special Scientific Interest (SSSIs) and Areas of Outstanding Natural Beauty (AONBs). SSSIs are sites which are considered to be of special interest because of flora, fauna, geological or physiographical features. AONBs are designated by the Countryside Commission to conserve areas of natural beauty.

The IUCN (the World Conservation Union) has also identified categories of protected areas, with a view to international collaboration and standardization for conservation. The categories include:

* Strict nature reserve/wilderness area (protected area managed mainly for science or wilderness protection.
* National park: protected area mainly managed for ecosystem protection and recreation.
* Natural monument: protected area managed mainly for conservation of specific natural features.
* Habitat/species management area: protected area managed mainly for conservation through management intervention.
* Protected landscape/seascape: protected area managed mainly for landscape/seascape conservation and recreation.
* Managed resource protected area: protected area managed mainly for the sustainable use of natural ecosystems.

Market approaches

Market approaches focus on manipulation of prices rather than use of regulations as a method of achieving environmental goals. The key to economic approaches is the adjustment of market prices in an attempt to reflect more fully the environmental costs and benefits of activities. The aim is to make producers and consumers adapt their behaviour in the light of these adjusted prices. In this way, pursuit of self-interest can bring environmental improvements. Approaches under this category include:

- ownership;
- taxes, subsidies and grants;
- tradable rights and permits;
- deposit-refund schemes;
- product and service charges.

Ownership • • •

Since free-access resources are often overused (e.g. the sea as a waste sink), privatization of such resources is sometimes advocated. For example, ownership of a lake is an incentive to enforce property rights. In such a case the use of the resources (e.g. for sewage disposal) would have to be bought and thus a price would be charged for a hitherto free service. The price would fluctuate, like all market prices, to reflect the demand and supply of the service.

Tenancy also gives a less strong incentive for environmental care than ownership. In New Zealand this has been addressed by offering concessions to operate in some National Parks and some conservation areas on a tradable basis. This means that if concessionaires move on they may sell their permit. This gives a strong incentive to tenants to invest in environmental improvements that can be recouped in an improved selling price of a concession.

Some argue there may be little incentive for an organization in the private sector to consider cost–benefit analysis when appraising a project. It will, instead, attempt to satisfy its shareholders by seeking to maximize profits. Public ownership is thus advocated to improve environmental performance. In principle a public sector organization has an incentive to consider social costs and benefits, since external costs will fall upon the electorate. The actual way in which public sector organizations approach externalities will depend upon the demands of the government. Voluntary sector organizations may have aims and objectives which encompass consideration of the full social costs and benefits. Exhibit 17.1, describing National Trust conservation work, illustrates this.

Taxes, subsidies and grants • • •

Typical of economic approaches are taxes which can be used to raise prices to discourage consumption of goods and services with harmful environmental impacts, and subsidies which can be used to reduce prices and

---

Exhibit 17.1 Issues

As a major conservation charity, the Trust does its utmost to practise what it preaches: it therefore aims to minimize adverse effects of its activities on the environment. Surveys of sewage and farm-waste discharges were largely completed in 1993, and innovative ways of treating waste and of minimizing it in the first place are being brought in.

The Trust also committed itself to reducing its energy consumption and to producing full environmental impact assessments for all proposals exploiting renewable energy.

Source: The National Trust; *The Year in Brief 1993–4.*

---

encourage consumption of goods and services with beneficial environmental impacts. Taxation is also a way of promoting the polluter pays principle (PPP) adopted by the Organization for Economic Co-operation and Development (OECD) in 1972. In this case producers of goods and services who cause environmental impacts are required to pay taxes which are sufficient to cover the costs of ameliorating environmental impacts.

Curtis (2002) investigated carbon dioxide (CO_2) emissions per tourist bed which he found to average 748.8 kg CO_2 per year in the Cairns region of Queensland, Australia. He notes that moderate emissions reductions can be made by way of increased energy efficiency but that excess emissions by luxury hotels/resorts need further action. An investment in carbon sinks is recommended (i.e. in forests or other means of CO_2 absorption), or alternately a carbon tax amounting to \$5.23 per bed per year, or based on emissions, \$15.38 per tonne of CO_2 per year.

Transport is a key issue here. The importance of transport to countryside tourism and recreation is emphasized by the Council for National Parks (1997: 14–15), which found that 'of the 76 million visits made annually to UK National Parks 91 per cent are made by car'. Because the environmental effects and impacts of air and car travel are considerable, there are repeated calls for taxation to make transport prices more fully reflect environmental costs. In particular there is pressure to increase taxes on car and air travel. Friends of the Earth (UK) also have a campaign directed at air travel. Called The Right Price for Air Travel it is pressing for air ticket prices to reflect the true environmental costs of flying. It notes that currently plane tickets and kerosene are free of value added tax (VAT). In addition there are no excise duties on kerosene nor any environmental taxes on air travel. However against this it is noted that air travel is responsible for significant noise pollution and nitrogen oxide emissions. It is forecast that half of the annual destruction of the ozone layer will be caused by air traffic in 2015 (De Clerck and Klingers, 1997: 4–5).

Control of emissions and production of waste may also be achieved using taxation. For example, taxes on non-returnable beverage containers (e.g. Finland) can encourage the use of returnable containers and therefore reduce the amount of containers left as litter. The Landfill Tax (UK, 1996)

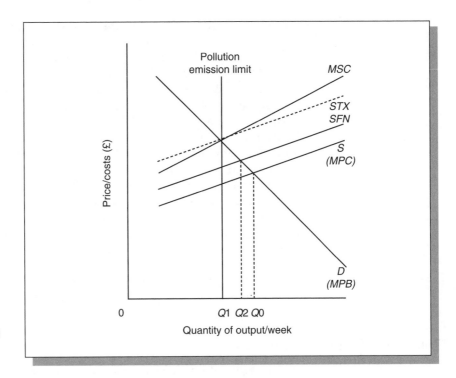

Figure 17.1
Comparison of taxation and direct environmental control (see text for details)

aims to encourage waste producers to produce less waste, recover more value from waste and to seek more environmentally friendly methods of waste disposal.

Figure 17.1 compares the operation of an environmental tax with a direct environmental control. D represents the demand curve and marginal private benefit for a product. S represents the supply curve and marginal private costs (MPCs) of production. Profit-maximizing firms will continue to produce where the price paid for extra sales (indicated by the demand curve) is greater than the extra costs of production (MPC). They will thus produce a level of output of $0Q0$.

However, in this example, production causes pollution, and external costs. Adding these to MPC generates the marginal social cost (MSC) curve. The socially optimum level of output is now found at $0Q1$ since production should be increased at all points where marginal private benefit (MPB; indicated by how much consumers are willing to pay for extra units of the good) exceeds marginal social cost.

The imposition of a pollution tax is designed to make the firm internalize the previously external costs of pollution and integrate environmental considerations. A pollution tax which raised the S or MPC curve to STX would cause the firm's private profit-maximizing level of output to coincide with the social profit-maximizing level of output at $0Q1$. A similar result could be achieved by imposing a pollution emission limit at $0Q1$. A system of fines would be needed to enforce such pollution limits. The system of monitoring of standards and imposition of fines is not totally effective, though. If, considering the likelihood and level of fine, the firm's MPC

were only increased to *SFN*, then the firm would produce a level of output of 0*Q2* – thus the system of direct control would be less effective than the system of taxation. It would also incur administrative costs.

One of the economic justifications for taxes on alcohol is to reduce consumption and thus minimize externalities in use (being drunk and disorderly). It is interesting to speculate whether scenes such as those described in Exhibit 17.2 are less common in countries such as Norway and Sweden where there are much higher alcohol taxes than in the UK.

In reality, although administrative costs are lower than for direct controls, there are several problems in setting an environmental tax. These include imputing monetary value to pollution costs, long-term pollution costs and the relating of pollution levels to output levels. A further criticism of environmental taxes and environmental charging is their regressive nature, in that their effects will hit the poor proportionately more than the rich. In theory this problem might be addressed by compensating the poor by income tax adjustments.

Subsidies (e.g. to public transport) are often used to encourage the supply of goods and services which have positive environmental impacts.

Tradable rights and permits ● ● ●

Tradable rights and permits are often associated with quotas that are set by governments for pollution levels. Tradability means that the overall quota

---

Exhibit 17.2   Emergency: Britons having fun – Sandra Barwick

It was New Year's Eve, but the mood was not exactly festive in the accident and emergency department of St Thomas' Hospital. 'We do not normally have vomit bowls laid out at reception', sighed the assistant director, Susan White, 'but those are what we are going to need'. The first casualty arrived, at 11.25, prone on his trolley, visible only in patches: large hairy legs, a pair of immobile trainers, some vomit-speckled hair. 'He's had a combination of beer, champagne and something else', said the ambulanceman, deadpan. 'We think he's Spanish'. A faint cry of 'Waaaa-aaaa' came from the trolley as it was wheeled away.

At midnight, the chimes of Big Ben came over the television. In they came, one after the other, bound to their trolleys. Almost all were men in their late teens or early 20s, in dirty jeans over which they had vomited. Outside the minor surgeries department a line of men sat or lay: punchmarks embedded on their cheeks, bottled broken on their heads, noses broken, lips cut. One had been bitten, one had had a cigarette stubbed out on his eye.

'Happy New Year', the ambulanceman said with ironic detachment to their prone charges.

Source: Adapted from *The Independent* (2 January 1993).

can be achieved flexibly with companies buying and selling quotas to each other. Permits are issued allowing a given level of pollution. For example, the total number of noise units for aircraft could be stipulated for a particular airport. These permits are then tradable. Supporters of this system stress its flexibility. Some aircraft operators can reduce noise pollution more cheaply than others. They can do so and sell permits to those who find it expensive to reduce noise pollution. Thus the total amount of pollution is limited, but how it is achieved is likely to involve flexibility and lowest costs.

The Waitomo glow worms cave (Plimmer, 1994: 2–3) demonstrates the use of permits applied to environmental impacts. CO_2 emissions from visitor numbers were threatening the glow worms. A permit was introduced which did not stipulate visitor numbers but rather fixed a maximum quota for CO_2 levels. This left the way of achieving environmental improvement flexible, so that revenues could be protected by appropriate visitor management.

Since global warming and the limitation of carbon emissions were key aspects of the Kyoto agreement, carbon trading has become more closely studied. This can involve not just firms (such as airlines) trading carbon emission quotas amongst themselves but could involve trading emission rights against the carbon sink functions of forests. The sink function of forests comes from their ability to absorb carbon from the atmosphere and Thoroe (2003) argues the need for a more intensive inclusion of forest sinks in the international regulations, as well as the assignment of responsibility for the conservation of sinks.

Deposit-refund schemes • • •

These schemes provide incentives for recycling. It is possible to introduce such schemes at a local outlet to encourage the return of cans and bottles and reduce littering at a site, but because visitors often bring in products bought from elsewhere, initiatives on a national scale are likely to be more successful. For example, in Austria a refundable deposit scheme is used to encourage recycling of beverage containers. Exhibit 17.3 illustrates a system that operates in Manitoba, Canada.

Product and service charges • • •

Charges for car parking can be used to encourage a switch towards the use of public transport. Additionally, road pricing for motorway use exists in some EU countries (e.g. France and Spain), but not in others (e.g. UK and Germany). London now operates a Congestion Charging scheme where motorists are charged £5 to enter the central zone. This has reduced traffic flows by approximately 25 per cent.

Soft tools

Soft tools represent another set of instruments to promote sustainability. They are voluntary by nature and attempt to change behaviour sometimes

---

Exhibit 17.3   Deposit refund schemes in Manitoba, Canada

Manitoba currently operates several systems to redeem some of the 470 million beverage containers sold annually in the province:

1 A system of deposits on domestic beer and refillable soft drink bottles encourages recovery of up to 98 per cent of beer bottles but only 50 per cent of beer cans. Deposit containers are redeemed at point of sale.
2 A recycling program to collect and recycle non-deposit alcohol beverage containers on a fee-for-service basis. The current payout rate is 5 cents per pound for glass (a 750 ml bottle is approximately 1 pound).

Container returns as per cent of sales in Manitoba

	1988
Beer bottles	98
Beer cans	48
Aluminium cans	24
Plastic bottles	4
Liquor containers	0

Source: Manitoba Environment http://www.gov.mb.ca/conservation/env-issues.html

---

by improved information, sometimes by advice, sometimes by persuasion and sometimes by forming specific networks. They include the following:

- tourism eco-labelling;
- certification/award schemes;
- guidelines, treaties and agreements;
- citizenship, education and advertising.

Tourism eco-labelling • • •

The focus of this approach to sustainability is the consumer in the marketplace. Leisure and tourism consumers themselves have power to change the environmental effects of goods and services by purchasing those which are environmentally friendly. The idea here is to supply consumers with additional environmental information to enable then to make a more informed choice in the purchase of goods and services. Just as foods are labelled to indicate their contents, an eco-label provides information concerning key environmental data related to a good or service supplied. The rationale behind eco-labelling is first to give consumers additional environmental information upon which to base their comparison of goods and services before purchase. Second, an eco-label can stimulate producers to achieve environmental improvements in the products in order to gain competitive advantage. The complex nature of tourism services makes eco-labelling in this area difficult, but a number of examples exist such as the Green Globe scheme.

Certification/award schemes • • •

Certification schemes exist in order to authenticate and give credibility to environmental claims made by organizations and to provide marks that can be recognized by consumers and producers. The Blue Flag scheme for beaches is a good example here and Buckley (2002) discusses the other examples of effective eco-label schemes such as Green Globe 21 and the National Eco-tourism Accreditation Programme for Australia. Award schemes are often used as ways of rewarding and publicizing good practice. The Tourism for Tomorrow (UK) is an annual award given for contribution to sustainable tourism.

Guidelines, treaties and agreements • • •

A variety of organizations produce guidelines and codes of conduct for good environmental practice in countryside areas. For example, the World Conservation Union (IUCN, 1995) has published a guide for conservation planning in countryside areas. These are a series of guidance notes supported by illustrative case studies. Similarly the Federation of Nature and National Parks of Europe (FNNPE, 1993) produced a report *Loving Them to Death* which includes guidelines for managers for developing sustainable tourism in protected areas, along with case studies and recommendations to governments.

Citizenship, education and advertising • • •

The focus of this approach to sustainability is on the individual acting in the role of consumer, or worker or opinion former. In order for consumers to fulfil their full power in purchasing 'green' goods and services do this they first need raised consciousness about the environmental effects of their purchases. Here improved environmental education is an important method so that citizens are more aware of the environmental effects of actions and consequently act to change their own actions and influence others to do the same. Examples include building environmental education into the curriculum, specialist university courses, information and interpretation for visitors to tourism sites, the role of interest groups in raising consciousness and advertising campaigns to change behaviour. Plate 17 illustrates a campaign in Bondi Beach, New South Wales, Australia to discourage the dropping of litter on the beach.

Pricing the environment

In the realm of purely private costs and benefits it is relatively straightforward for firms to determine a profit-maximizing level of output. The costs

Plate 17
Don't be a tosser
Source: The author

of inputs are readily available and selling prices can be gauged from scanning the competition, from historical data and, ultimately, are determined in the market. There are thus some firm figures which inform production levels.

However, when we move into the arena of external costs and benefits we encounter the problem of missing markets and thus find pricing difficult. We can easily calculate the costs of aircraft use in terms of fuel, staffing and depreciation, but how do we measure the cost of aircraft noise? We clearly need to address this problem if we are to attempt to modify economic behaviour. For without some indication of the costs of environmental impacts it is impossible to set effective levels of taxation or decide upon other interventions in a rational way. Several methods have been developed by environmental economists to impute value for unpriced goods or services and these are now explained.

Willingness to pay method

Here survey techniques are used to find households' willingness to pay (WTP) for the preservation of an environmental asset – for example, a piece of woodland threatened by a road development. The survey can include people who are currently visiting the asset and those who do not visit it but care about it. The total valuation of the asset can then be found by multiplying the average WTP by the number of people who enjoy the asset. The main difficulty of using the WTP method is whether respondents reply to the hypothetical WTP question in the same way as they would if faced with actual payment.

Hedonic pricing method

Hedonic pricing values environmental resources by considering their effect on the prices of goods or services that have readily observable market prices. House prices are a convenient yardstick for this exercise. House prices are affected by a number of factors – condition, number of rooms, central heating, garden size and nearness to transport and shops. They are also affected by environmental factors, for example, prices will be depressed by the presence of aircraft noise and increased by the presence of a park.

Hedonic pricing method (HPM) involves the collection of data recording price, and the presence or absence of all the salient determinants of price. Once a price can be established to reflect the non-environmental factors (number of rooms, etc.) then the effects of the environmental factor under analysis (e.g. aircraft noise) can be attributed to variations in the price of houses with otherwise similar characteristics. An imputed cost can then be attributed for aircraft noise nuisance. Difficulties involved with HPM mainly centre around the large number of differences that occur between houses, and the changes in other factors such as interest rates during data collection.

IeGoffe (2000) used the hedonic price method to assign monetary values to some of the external effects of agricultural and silvicultural activities in France. The renting price of rural self-catering cottages, or gîtes was examined and it was found that intensive livestock farming caused the renting-price of gîtes to decrease, whereas permanent grassland had the opposite effect.

Travel cost method

The assumption behind this method of environmental asset valuation is that there is a relationship between the travel costs that a visitor has incurred to visit a tourism or recreational site and their valuation of that site. The attraction of this method is that travel costs for visitors by car are readily measurable as they consist mainly of petrol costs. A survey records the distance visitors travelled to the site, and technical details about their car. From this, travel costs are calculated. This is then compared to the number of visits the individual makes per year to the site.

Figure 17.2 illustrates a typical scatter diagram which might result from plotting travel costs against number of visits, after adjusting for other factors such as income differences. A typically shaped demand curve $D0$ relates the price of visiting the site (measured by travel costs) to the demand (the number of visits per year). A total value of the site for recreational use can be obtained from this information.

There are however problems which arise in using travel cost method (TCM). First travelling involves use of time which represents an additional cost for many people. Second, some people may arrive on bicycle or on foot and thus register no travel cost, even though their actual valuation of the site may be positive. Third, people may combine visiting the site with other activities on the same journey and it is difficult to unscramble the contribution of travel costs to each.

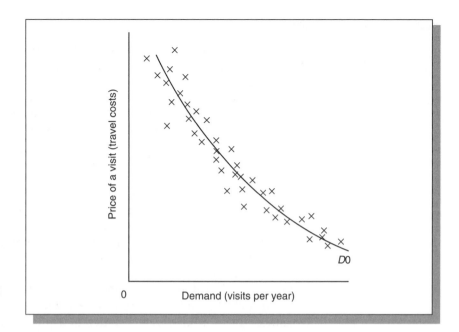

Figure 17.2
Use of TCM to construct a demand curve for a tourism/recreational site

Dose–response method

This valuation method depends upon the availability of data linking the effects of pollution to a response in, for example, human health or crop production. The effects of sewage pollution in the sea could be measured in terms of medical resources needed to remedy pollution-induced sickness, and loss of earnings.

Replacement cost technique

This might offer a way of measuring some of the environmental effects of acid rain. For example, the cost of restoration of buildings damaged by such pollution could be measured and thus the cost of acid-rain pollution measured.

Mitigation behaviour method

Some pollution effects result in households undertaking defensive expenditure which can be measured in the market. The existence of aircraft noise pollution, for example, may lead households to fit double glazing to mitigate its effects. This defensive expenditure can be summed to find costs incurred from the pollution.

Exhibit 17.4 provides estimates of the economic environmental costs of climate change, local noise and local air quality (LAQ) of UK passenger air traffic and the study was commissioned by government in order to inform its environmental management policy for air travel.

Exhibit 17.4   Aviation and the environment: using economic instruments

1 The 'cost of carbon'

This represents the cost to society resulting from climate change effects caused by releasing carbon into the atmosphere as CO_2. The cost of global environmental damage caused by climate change is estimated and then related to the amount of carbon released as CO_2, giving a damage cost per tonne of carbon.

It was concluded that 'a value of approximately £70/tC (2000 prices, with equity weighting) seems like a defensible illustrative value for carbon emissions in 2000. This figure should then be raised by £1/tC in real terms for each subsequent year'.

The £70 per tonne of carbon value takes no account of uncertainties including the probability of:

- the so-called 'climate catastrophe' (e.g. melting of the West Antarctic ice sheet, Gulf Stream suppression, etc.);
- the 'socially contingent impacts' of climate change (e.g. famine, mass migration, etc.);
- the costs of impacts post 2100.

The estimated CO_2 emissions from UK passenger flights are:
2003: 8.2 millions of tonnes.
2003: 19.0 millions of tonnes.

2 Total climate change costs

As well as CO_2 effects, air travel also causes climate change due to the emissions of other gases and vapour trails. The total of these are called radiative effects. Taking all radiative effects into account the estimated total climate change costs of UK passenger flights are:
2000: £1.4 billion.
2003: £4.8 billion.

3 Noise costs

Based on the hedonic studies, monetary values for the effect of aircraft noise at Heathrow Airport ranged between 36 and 40 pence per passenger. The total cost of noise impacts for all airports has been estimated at around £25 million for 2000.

4 Local Air Quality

The study by CE Delft in 2002 on the *External Costs of Aviation* estimates that the external LAQ costs of aviation vary between €1–2 per passenger (equivalent to £119–236 million for all UK passengers).

Adapted from http://www.hm-treasury.gov.uk/media//8E752/Aviation_
Environment.pdf

Exhibit 17.5   BA and the environment

BA is committed to improving its environmental performance, and reducing the adverse impacts of its activities on the global and local environment. The two key issues identified for the airline industry are:

- The local environmental impact of aircraft noise and emissions around airports.
- The global climate change effect of CO_2 and other aircraft emissions.

For noise management we support the International Civil Aviation Organization (ICAO) recommended Balanced Approach. The four key elements of this are:

- reductions at source – quieter aircraft;
- land-use planning;
- operational procedures;
- operational restrictions.

A similar balanced approach – using a combination of instruments – can also be taken to managing Local Air Quality. We support the use of accurate modelling to assess air quality impact and to understand the contribution of aircraft relative to other sources.

Climate change is a major concern for us. The climate change impact of aviation arises from:

- CO_2 from aircraft burning fossil fuels.
- Other effects in the upper atmosphere, linked to emissions of nitrogen dioxide, particles and water vapour.

The combined effect – the 'radiative forcing' generated by aviation – is estimated to account for about 3.5 per cent of the total warming generated by human activity.

We believe that the best long-term mechanism for ensuring aviation takes account of its CO_2 emissions is through international emissions trading. We work within both ICAO and IATA to promote this.

We are committed to taking voluntary action to improve fuel efficiency and reduce global warming emissions.

In addition to all of these activities we have a corporate priority to improve waste management. We seek to improve the efficiency of use of all the resources we deploy and manage our waste and effluent responsibly and effectively.

Source: Adapted from www.britishairways.com/travel/crenvhome/public/en_gb

Firms' environmental policies

Increasingly, individual firms are appointing environmental managers, compiling environmental policies and conducting environmental audits and action plans. There are several motives for this. First, anticipation of government controls may save money in the long run or even preclude their need. Second environmental action leads to savings on input costs. Finally an improved market image may result. Leadership in this area has come from the WTTC, the WTO both of which have published guidelines. Organizations such as British Airways (BA) produce a regular environmental report setting and monitoring targets for:

- noise,
- emissions,
- waste,
- congestion,
- tourism and conservation.

And a statement of BA's environmental policy is illustrated in Exhibit 17.5.

Review of key terms

- Sustainable development: development which can endure over the long run.
- Intergenerational equity: ensuring future generations do not inherit less capital than the current one.
- Natural capital: raw materials and the natural environment.
- Regenerative capacity: limit to harvesting of renewable resource whilst maintaining stock level.
- Social cost–benefit analysis: comparison of full social costs and benefits of a project.
- Discounting: adjusting future monetary values to present monetary values.
- Willingness to pay method: discovery of what people would be prepared to pay for a currently unpriced resource.
- Hedonic pricing method: imputing a price for an environmental externality by determining its effect on other prices.
- Travel cost method: imputing the value of a site by measuring the cost of travel to it.
- Dose–response method: measuring effects of pollution in monetary terms.
- Replacement cost technique: measuring costs of pollution by calculating restoration costs.
- Mitigation behaviour method: measuring costs of pollution by counting defensive expenditure.
- Command and control: direct regulations (e.g. water quality regulations).
- Market-based incentives: adjusting prices to reflect external costs.
- Polluter pays principle: polluter pays the full cost of pollution effects.

Data Questions

Task 17.1 Tourism: a taxing business

The following extracts reveal different attitudes to taxes on tourism.

Tourism taxation

Taxes on the tourism industry can stifle growth if they are not equitable and applied after careful consultation between fiscal authorities and the tourism sector, according to a report, Tourism Taxation, prepared by the WTO. Graham Wason from management consultants Deloitte Touch who prepared the report says 'Governments have realized that taxing tourism is an easy way to gain extra revenue without upsetting their own voters and the industry is very concerned about the upward trend'. He identified 40 different types of taxes levied on the tourism industry throughout the world and noted that tax rates were increasing. 'It is not realistic to say we do not want to be taxed. If we did not pay taxes there would be no money for improving airports or roads or to invest in necessary social services, but it is important that tourism is not unfairly taxed'.

The report notes that charges for entry and exit visas are among the worst taxes on tourism with some countries such as the Marshall Islands charging $20 to enter the country and another $20 to leave. Consultant Oliver Bennet suggests, 'It is much better to encourage people to come into the country and then to tax them on consumption while they are there'. Other problems noted are when governments change taxes without giving tour operators sufficient time to incorporate the changes into their pricing structures. Euro MP Petrus Cornelissen urged the EU to give tourism priority treatment because of its ability to create new jobs. He particularly criticized plans to scrap duty-free shopping in 1999 which threatened the jobs of 100 000 people employed directly or indirectly in the sector. He said, 'Taxfree shops are not just a bonus for travellers, they are a major source of revenue for the airport authorities, enabling airport fees to be kept at lower levels'.

Source: WTO Press Release.

Taxing the Seychelles

The government of the Seychelles has imposed a $100 environmental tax on tourists payable on arrival at the airport. The tax is being imposed in order to limit visitor numbers and provide funds for environmental projects. In 1998 about 130 000 tourists a year visited the island and the government wants to encourage an upper limit of 180 000 so as not to overcrowd the beaches. The tax is also part of a strategy to maintain the upmarket image for the island. Keith Betton of the Association of British Travel Agents thinks that the tax is a bad idea. 'The bottom end of the market is very price sensitive. This could send people to other holiday destinations like Mauritius'.

Source: The Guardian.

Enough is enough

More than 75 groups in 23 countries are protesting today (6 November 1998) as part of Friends of the Earth Europe's Right Price for Air Travel campaign. They are calling on governments and the European Union to introduce a kerosene tax for all flights within the EU as well as emissions-related charges and stricter noise and emissions around airports. Air travel is the fastest-growing source of greenhouse gas emissions. It is responsible for about 7 per cent of global warming, including 3 per cent of global CO_2 emissions.

Yet a 50-year-old international agreement means airlines pay no duty on the fuel they use, whereas motorists and long-distance coach operators have to pay over 40 pence per litre. Even train companies pay 3 pence per litre for their diesel. Roger Higman, Friends of the Earth's senior transport campaigner, said: 'Flying is the most polluting form of transport there is. Yet airlines pay no duty on the fuel they use and therefore have little incentive to conserve fuel or control their emissions. The tax exemption gives airlines an unfair advantage over other forms of transport, encouraging people to travel in the least environmentally friendly way. The Chancellor ... must back European moves to end this loophole by taxing airlines for the fuel they use'.

Source: Friends of the Earth Press Release (6 November 1998).

Different accounts of aircraft pollution

- *Pat Malone*
  Aircraft emissions are not covered by international agreements seeking to limit emissions of greenhouse gases (GHGs). At the Kyoto environmental summit last year they were specifically exempted because negotiators could not agree on how to pin responsibility on individual nations.
  Aircraft burn 3 per cent of all fossil fuels used on earth, and their turbines produce between 1.5 billion and 2.2 billion tonnes of CO_2 every year.
  Passenger jets may be responsible for as much as 10 per cent of all GHG emissions – according to some estimates – with their pollution being injected directly into the upper atmosphere as a kind of 'intravenous fix' for global warming.

  Source: *The Observer* (8 November 1998).

- *Pierre Jeanniot, Director-General, International Air Transport Association*
  Allow me to correct some of Pat Malone's assertions on air pollution (News, 8 November): 'Aircraft produce between 1.5 and 2.2 billion tonnes of CO_2 every year'. The true figure is closer to 0.5 billion tonnes, that is, 2.5 per cent of the world total from the burning of fossil fuels.
  'Passenger jets may be responsible for as much as 10 per cent of all GHG emissions.' CO_2 emissions from air traffic contribute about 1.5 per cent of man-made annual input to global warming. Cumulative emissions of exhaust gases from air traffic are thought to be around 3 per cent.

  Source: Letter to *the Observer* (22 November 1998).

Recap Questions

1 What kinds of taxes are imposed on tourism?
2 Explain the relationship between demerit goods, merit goods, public goods, taxation and tourism.
3 Why is elasticity of demand an important consideration in setting tax levels?
4 Evaluate the case for scrapping duty free tax concessions.
5 What are the arguments for and against taxation of aviation fuel?
6 What factors should determine the amount of tax imposed on aviation fuel.
7 In what ways could taxes on tourism be used to maximize employment and minimize environmental damage?
8 Compare taxation with other instruments for achieving environmental improvements in the leisure and tourism sector.
9 Why is it important to accurately assess the environmental impacts of air travel? Why do disagreements such as those noted above make life difficult for economists?

Task 17.2   Environment: under deafening skies

Residents of the tiny village of Longford barely flinch any more. Living within a few hundred yards of one of Heathrow's two runways, they have become accustomed to the deafening roar of transatlantic jumbos as they heave themselves into the skies. Lunchtime conversation under umbrellas outside the White Horse stops involuntarily every few minutes to allow the ear-splitting din to die down. The plane passes, chatter resumes ... for a moment. 'You get used to it', the locals shrug philosophically.

Many work or have worked at the airport. They have learned to rely for their sanity on the hours of relative peace when Heathrow switches its operations to the south runway. Until then, those at home tend to spend most of the time locked behind double glazing. It might seem bad now, but with a dramatic increase in the number of passengers forecast by the aviation industry and consequent expansion plans, environmentalists are fearful of what lies ahead. At Heathrow, already the world's busiest international airport, work is nearing completion on a fifth terminal (T5) which will double the airport's annual capacity to nearly 80 million passengers. Clusters of opposition groups have mushroomed around the country's main airports to fight the expansion plans. The argument they have to counter is the creation of much-needed jobs and the economic shot-in-the-arm which the aviation industry claims they would bring. Rita Pearce, who has lived in Longford for 23 years and worked for Pan-American at Heathrow for 16, now believes enough is enough.

The pollution has already taken its toll on her family's health, she says – she has had pleurisy 5 times in 2 years and her two daughters have developed asthma – and she believes increased air traffic and the introduction of night flights from October will make life there unbearable. 'It is going to be absolute hell', she said. If planning permission for the fifth terminal is granted, in addition to the main terminal building with up to three satellites, there are plans for three giant car parks, with access provided by a new spur road from the M25 spanning the Colne Valley Park, described by Friends of the Earth as a unique river valley in the capital, important for wildlife and recreation. The plans also assume the M25 will be widened to 14 lanes in the Staines area to the south-west. The sewage works, meanwhile, occupying the site of T5 has been shifted on to green belt land to the north-west of the airport. Families in the area do not believe reassurances that T5 will not require a third runway. A report has suggested that BA had drawn up plans for a new Heathrow runway to the south of the existing two.

Source: Adapted from *The Guardian* (23 July 1993) (1995, 2004).

Recap Questions

1 Draw up a list of private and social costs and benefits of the development of T5.
2 In what ways could you attempt to measure the monetary value of the costs and benefits?
3 Under what economic circumstances should the T5 development go ahead?
4 Under what circumstances should a third runway be opened?

Task 17.3   Show them the way to go Dome

January 1999's *Transport Retort* (the magazine of Transport 2000) reported on transport plans for the expected 70 000 daily visitors to the Millennium Dome in Greenwich, London. These include a tube link, satellite park-and-ride schemes, and car access only for orange badge holders. The government has promised a car-free event.

However, it is estimated that 25 per cent of visitors will make part of their journey by car or taxi. This means about one and a half million car journeys assuming two people to a car. Greenwich already suffers from poor air quality – during 1997, ozone, nitrogen dioxide and particulates* were higher than international health guidelines on at least 20 days – and the Dome will make things worse. This is especially serious for the 20 per cent of children who have asthma and the 10 per cent of adults who are unable to work because of a long-term respiratory illness. Public opinion has forced a reduction in inner-city park-and-ride schemes because they increase local congestion and pollution and arguably contribute to car dependency. However, a 1000-car site is still planned at Woolwich just across the river. In addition, traffic is likely to increase because of the new Sainsbury's (1400-car park) and the Millennium Eco-village (paradoxically including a 1423-car park).

Greenwich council admit that many people may try to leave their cars just outside the mile-and-a-half parking exclusion zone. In the mid-1990s, various organizations devised methodologies for measuring some of the external effects of road transport in the UK. The figures for air and noise pollution were approximately £20 000 million and £3000 million, respectively, congestion costs about £19 000 million and the cost of death and injuries about £3000 million depending on the valuation put on a life. *Transport Retort* in July 1998 listed other impacts of road transport including:

- Stress for travellers and residents.
- Loss of green space for roads and parking.
- Worsening health for increasingly car-dependent people (sedentary lifestyles in place of walking and cycling).
- Loss of independent mobility for children, senior citizens and non-car owners because of deteriorating public transport.

Other external costs include the cost of providing street lighting and the associated light pollution, long-term damage to buildings through vibration, and the deaths each year of about 1 million domestic and wild animals.

Sources: Compiled by Nigel North from:
Transport Retort (January 1999) 'Dome Alone';
Transport Retort (July 1998) diagram 'quantified health effects of traffic are only the tip of the iceberg'.
Blue Print 5, 'The True Costs of Road Transport' Maddison, Pearce et al. (1996) Earthscan.
Royal Commission Report (1995) *Transport and the Environment*, Oxford University Press.
How Vehicle Pollution Affects Our Health (1994) Ashden Trust.

Recap Questions

1 What are externalities? List the external costs of road transport mentioned in the article.
2 In the estimates of external costs, each of the 3600 lives lost annually is valued at about £700 000. Some international studies argue that this figure should be closer to £2 million. With this new figure calculate the total measured external costs of road transport for the UK.
3 The special taxation (petrol duty and vehicle excise duty) paid by motorists is estimated at £26 000 million for 1998–9. Comment on the argument that motorists pay too much tax.

---

*Particulates are tiny pieces of solid or liquid matter that are small enough to go through natural body filters and penetrate the lungs. They are emitted by exhausts because of incomplete combustion of fuel. Some of the chemicals are carcinogenic (cause cancer).

4 The article lists some impacts which are not measured. Suggest ways to attempt to measure those external effects.
5 What practical policies would you suggest to persuade visitors to the Dome to leave their cars at home?

Multiple choice

1 **The setting of air noise limits around airports is an example of:**

(i) An attempt to control external costs.
(ii) A command and control method of environmental damage control.
(iii) Privatization of a free access resource.
(iv) A perfect market.

Which of the above is true?

(a) All of the above.
(b) (i) only.
(c) (i) and (ii) only.
(d) (ii) and (iii) only.

2 **Measurement of the social costs of sewerage dumping at sea, by counting the costs to surfers of sewerage related illness, uses which of the following methods?**

(a) Hedonic pricing method.
(b) Dose–response method.
(c) Willingness to pay method.
(d) Polluter pays principle.

3 **Which of the following is true of 'intergenerational equity'?**

(a) It was the main policy outcome of the Kyoto conference.
(b) It means not causing resource impoverishment for the future.
(c) It means trying to reduce extremes of poverty.
(d) It involves equating marginal private and marginal social costs.

4 **Which of the following is not true?**

(a) Greenhouse gases are a main cause of global warming.
(b) Ozone depletion causes an increase in penetration of UV rays.
(c) CO_2 is a key greenhouse gas.
(d) CO_2 is a key cause of ozone depletion.

5 **Which of the following is not a principle of sustainable development?**

(a) The endogenous growth principle.
(b) Tailoring of economic activity to the carrying capacity of the environment.
(c) The precautionary principle.
(d) The 'polluter pays' principle.

Review questions

1 List the various stakeholders that would wish to influence a named leisure or tourism development and identify their viewpoints.
2 Explain the various ways in which the cost of aircraft noise could be imputed.
3 What is the approximate present value of £100 due in a year's time, if the discount rate is 10 per cent?
4 What are the essential elements of sustainable development?
5 What are the five key stages in social cost–benefit analysis?

Web sites of interest

BA Environmental Report: http://www.british-airways.com/inside/Comm/environ/environ.shtml
WTTC: www.wttc.org/
Green Globe: a worldwide environmental management and awareness programme for the travel and tourism industry http://www. greenglobe.org/
Tourism Concern: http://www.tourismconcern.org.uk
Friends of the Earth: www.foe.co.uk
Surfers against sewage: www.sas.org.uk
UNEP – tourism: http://www.unepie.org/tourism/home.htm

CHAPTER 18

Critique, alternative perspectives and change

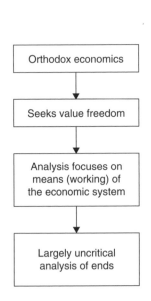

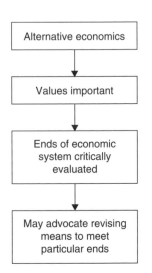

Objectives and learning outcomes

The point of departure for this chapter is Richard Lipsey's (1973) once ubiquitous economics textbook that went under the title *Positive Economics*. This text represents the influential core of orthodox economics. It is likely that this, or similar economic texts were the undergraduate bibles of those representatives of the International Monetary Fund (IMF) who travel the world lecturing the poorest countries on the importance of a balanced State budget, the merits of privatization and tight monetary control.

The problem with this text was that it sold its approach – *positive economics* – as the only meaningful approach to economics. It elevated this approach to an orthodoxy that was eloquently critiqued by Omerod (1994) in *The Death of Economics*. In doing so it reduced economics to a set of theories laden with restrictive assumptions. The theory of perfect competition is a good example. The theories had to simplify because the actual real world of economics is too complex and messy to model otherwise. So the theories were constructed with many limiting assumptions that allowed them to function with mathematical precision. But of course the more assumptions that preceded theory building, the less useful the theories became in explaining or predicting real world behaviour. At the same time *Positive Economics* promoted the free market as a natural and irrefutable entity. It elevated it to the status of say gravity. That is something that was natural and that humans were subservient to. The counterpart to this was that it also demoted human agency to a walk on part on the stage of free-market economics. Humans were assigned the role of *homo economicus* that is to say they made rational economic decisions based around maximizing their satisfaction from a limited income. Firms were assigned the role of profit maximizers and the world was therefore assigned a set of economic rules by which to develop itself.

The world which *Positive Economics* so confidently pitched itself against was the world of normative thought. Positive economics dealt with facts. Disputes over facts could be resolved by resort to evidence or logic. In contrast, normative thought was based on opinion or values or aspirations. Since, the argument went that there was no way of resolving a dispute over opinion, normative thought should be banished from economics which could make its case more securely based on facts. A positive approach put economics on the same kind of secure foundations as physics, chemistry and biology.

So *Positive Economics* explained why there were differences in wages, the benefits of Free Trade, how markets acting freely would deliver economic and allocative efficiency and how consumers maximized their satisfaction. In other words individual markets, national economies and indeed the global trading economy could all theoretically work like a well-oiled machine. Indeed this approach to economics seems to devote its entire effort to understanding the means by which the economy works rather than putting the ends of economic endeavour up for scrutiny.

To quote Omerod (1994: 3):

'The world economy is in crisis … [and] the orthodoxy of economics, trapped in an idealized, mechanistic view of the world, is powerless to assist.'

The purpose of this chapter is to question the way orthodox or conventional economics takes the lead in explaining how things work according to what appear to be natural or neutral principles. This chapter invites a critical look at the economic aspects of the world of recreation, leisure and tourism as it has developed and asks normative questions. Has this world developed in a way that is good? Are there better ways of constructing this world and how could we go about achieving this?

By studying this chapter students will be able to:

- understand the limitations of conventional economics;
- understand the Marxian critique of capitalism;
- critically evaluate the economic state of recreation, leisure and tourism;
- articulate desirable economic ends;
- explain alternative approaches to reaching desired economic ends.

Marx versus orthodox economics

Joan Robinson (1942) in her *Essay on Marxian Economics* wrote of the fundamental differences between Marxian and traditional orthodox economists. She notes first, that 'orthodox economists accept the capitalist system as part of the eternal order of nature while Marx regards it as a passing phase in the transition from the feudal economy of the past to the socialist economy of the future'. Second, she notes that orthodox economists assume that all of the members of economic society share a common interest while 'Marx conceives of economic life in terms of a conflict of interest between owners of property [the bourgeoisie] who do no work and workers [the proletariat] who own no property. Robinson is thereby adverting to the fact that orthodox economists take the market or capitalist economic system for granted and work within it to explain its mechanisms. They take it as a given. Marx on the other hand holds the whole system up for inspection and examines its consequences paying particular attention to the conflict of class interests and the possibility of another system – that of socialism.

Marx's *Manifesto of the Communist Party* represents a powerful critique of capitalist economics and Exhibit 18.1 reproduces some key extracts from it.

Exhibit 18.1   Karl Marx and Frederick Engels: Manifesto of the Communist Party 1848 (extracts)

The history of all hitherto existing society is the history of class struggles...

The modern bourgeois society that has sprouted from the ruins of feudal society has not done away with class antagonisms. It has but established new classes, new conditions of oppression, new forms of struggle in place of the old ones.

Our epoch, the epoch of the bourgeoisie, possesses, however, this distinct feature: it has simplified class antagonisms. Society as a whole is more and more splitting up into two great hostile camps, into two great classes directly facing each other – bourgeoisie and proletariat...

Each step in the development of the bourgeoisie was accompanied by a corresponding political advance in that class.... The bourgeoisie has at last, since the establishment of Modern Industry and of the world market, conquered for itself, in the modern representative state, exclusive political sway. The executive of the modern state is but a committee for managing the common affairs of the whole bourgeoisie.

The bourgeoisie ... has resolved personal worth into exchange value, and in place of the numberless indefeasible chartered freedoms, has set up that single, unconscionable freedom – Free Trade. In one word, for exploitation, veiled by religious and political illusions, it has substituted naked, shameless, direct, brutal exploitation. The bourgeoisie has stripped of its halo every occupation hitherto honoured and looked up to with reverent awe. It has converted the physician, the lawyer, the priest, the poet, the man of science, into its paid wage labourers. The bourgeoisie has torn away from the family its sentimental veil, and has reduced the family relation into a mere money relation.

The bourgeoisie cannot exist without constantly revolutionizing the instruments of production, and thereby the relations of production, and with them the whole relations of society.... The need of a constantly expanding market for its products chases the bourgeoisie over the entire surface of the globe. It must nestle everywhere, settle everywhere, establish connections everywhere...

All old-established national industries have been destroyed or are daily being destroyed. They are dislodged by new industries, whose introduction becomes a life and death question for all civilized nations, by industries that no longer work up indigenous raw material, but raw material drawn from the remotest zones; industries whose products are consumed, not only at home, but in every quarter of the globe. In place of the old wants, satisfied by the production of the country, we find new wants, requiring for their satisfaction the products of distant lands and climes. In place of the old local and national seclusion and self-sufficiency, we have intercourse in every direction, universal inter-dependence of nations...

The bourgeoisie, by the rapid improvement of all instruments of production, by the immensely facilitated means of communication, draws all, even the most barbarian, nations into civilization. The cheap prices of commodities are the heavy artillery with which it forces the barbarians' intensely obstinate hatred of foreigners to capitulate. It compels all nations, on pain of extinction, to adopt the bourgeois mode of production; it compels them to introduce what it calls civilization into their midst, i.e., to become bourgeois themselves. In one word, it creates a world after its own image.

The bourgeoisie has subjected the country to the rule of the towns. It has created enormous cities, has greatly increased the urban population as compared with the rural, and has thus rescued a considerable part of the population from the idiocy of rural life. Just as it has made the country dependent on the towns, so it has made barbarian and semi-barbarian countries dependent on the civilized ones, nations of peasants on nations of bourgeois, the East on the West.

The bourgeoisie ... has agglomerated population, centralized the means of production, and has concentrated property in a few hands. The necessary consequence of this was political centralization. Independent, or but loosely connected provinces, with separate interests, laws, governments, and systems of taxation, became lumped together into one nation, with one government, one code of laws, one national class interest, one frontier, and one customs tariff...

In proportion as the bourgeoisie, i.e. capital, is developed, in the same proportion is the proletariat, the modern working class, developed – a class of labourers, who live only so long as they find work, and who find work only so long as their labour increases capital. These labourers, who must sell themselves piecemeal, are a commodity, like every other article of commerce, and are consequently exposed to all the vicissitudes of competition, to all the fluctuations of the market.

Owing to the extensive use of machinery, and to the division of labour, the work of the proletarians has lost all individual character, and, consequently, all charm for the workman. He becomes an appendage of the machine, and it is only the most simple, most monotonous, and most easily acquired knack, that is required of him. Hence, the cost of production of a workman is restricted, almost entirely, to the means of subsistence that he requires for maintenance, and for the propagation of his race. But the price of a commodity, and therefore also of labour, is equal to its cost of production. In proportion, therefore, as the repulsiveness of the work increases, the wage decreases. What is more, in proportion as the use of machinery and division of labour increases, in the same proportion the burden of toil also increases, whether by prolongation of the working hours, by the increase of the work exacted in a given time, or by increased speed of machinery, etc.

Modern Industry has converted the little workshop of the patriarchal master into the great factory of the industrial capitalist. Masses of labourers, crowded into the factory, are organized like soldiers. As privates of the industrial army, they are placed under the command of a perfect hierarchy of officers and sergeants. Not only are they slaves of the bourgeois class, and of the bourgeois state; they are daily and hourly enslaved by the machine, by the overlooker, and, above all, in the individual bourgeois manufacturer himself. The more openly this despotism proclaims gain to be its end and aim, the more petty, the more hateful and the more embittering it is...

The proletariat goes through various stages of development. With its birth begins its struggle with the bourgeoisie. At first, the contest is carried on by individual labourers, then by the work of people of a factory, then by the operative of one trade, in one locality, against the individual bourgeois who directly exploits them. They direct their attacks not against the bourgeois condition of production, but against the instruments of production themselves; they destroy imported wares that compete with their labour, they smash to pieces machinery, they set factories ablaze, they seek to restore by force the vanished status of the workman of the Middle Ages.

At this stage, the labourers still form an incoherent mass scattered over the whole country, and broken up by their mutual competition.... But with the development of industry, the proletariat not only increases in number; it becomes concentrated in greater masses, its strength grows, and it feels that strength more. The various interests and conditions of life within the ranks of the proletariat are more and more equalized, in proportion as machinery obliterates all distinctions of labour, and nearly everywhere reduces wages to the same low-level. The growing competition among the bourgeois, and the resulting commercial crises, make the wages of the workers ever more fluctuating. The increasing improvement of machinery, ever more rapidly developing, makes their livelihood more and more precarious; the collisions between individual workmen and individual bourgeois take more and more the character of collisions between two classes. Thereupon, the workers begin to form combinations (Trade Unions) against the bourgeois; they club together in order to keep up the rate of wages; they found permanent associations in order to make provision beforehand for these occasional revolts. Here and there, the contest breaks out into riots.

Now and then the workers are victorious, but only for a time. The real fruit of their battles lie not in the immediate result, but in the ever-expanding union of the workers. This union is helped on by the improved means of communication that are created by Modern Industry, and that place the workers of different localities in contact with one another. It was just this contact that was needed to centralize the numerous local struggles, all of the same character, into one national struggle between classes. But every class struggle is a political struggle...

Finally, in times when the class struggle nears the decisive hour, the progress of dissolution going on within the ruling class, in fact within the whole range of old society, assumes such a violent, glaring character, that a small section of the ruling class cuts itself adrift, and joins the revolutionary class, the class that holds the future in its hands...

Of all the classes that stand face to face with the bourgeoisie today, the proletariat alone is a genuinely revolutionary class. The other classes decay and finally disappear in the face of Modern Industry; the proletariat is its special and essential product...

In the condition of the proletariat, those of old society at large are already virtually swamped. The proletarian is without property; his relation to his wife and children has no longer anything in common with the bourgeois family relations; modern industry labour, modern subjection to capital, the same in England as in France, in America as in Germany, has stripped him of every trace of national character. Law, morality, religion, are to him so many bourgeois prejudices, behind which lurk in ambush just as many bourgeois interests...

All previous historical movements were movements of minorities, or in the interest of minorities. The proletarian movement is the self-conscious, independent movement of the immense majority, in the interest of the immense majority. The proletariat, the lowest stratum of our present society, cannot stir, cannot raise itself up, without the whole superincumbent strata of official society being sprung into the air.... The modern labourer ... instead of rising with the process of industry, sinks deeper and deeper below the conditions of existence of his own class. He becomes a pauper, and pauperism develops more rapidly than population and wealth. And here it becomes evident that the bourgeoisie is unfit any longer to be the ruling class in society, and to impose its conditions of existence upon society as an overriding law.... Society can no longer live under this bourgeoisie, in other words, its existence is no longer compatible with society.

The essential conditions for the existence and for the sway of the bourgeois class is the formation and augmentation of capital; the condition for capital is wage labour. Wage labour rests exclusively on competition between the labourers. The advance of industry, whose involuntary promoter is the bourgeoisie, replaces the isolation of the labourers, due to competition, by the revolutionary combination, due to association. The development of Modern Industry, therefore, cuts from under its feet the very foundation on which the bourgeoisie produces and appropriates products. What the bourgeoisie therefore produces, above all, are its own grave-diggers. Its fall and the victory of the proletariat are equally inevitable.

Marx develops a number of key ideas which include:

- history can be seen as a series of class struggles;
- the basic conflict between the bourgeoisie and the proletariat;
- the representation of bourgeois interests by government;
- the deterioration of the conditions of the proletariat;
- the globalization of capitalism;
- the constant change of capitalism;
- the commercial crises of capitalism;
- the inevitable victory of the proletariat over the bourgeoisie.

So what is the relevance of Marx to the economic provision of recreation, leisure and tourism? Perhaps we should start with its problems. Although communism represented an important force in the 20th century, by the 21st century it is largely on the wane. Some interesting exceptions remain.

China in name is still communist but hardly in action, Cuba is both in name and action and Nepal is subject to regular attack from Marxist revolutionary groups. But in general there appears to be no threat of imminent revolution. Indeed in many parts of the world worker power (particularly as measured by Trade Union membership) is in decline. Capitalism has its recurrent minor crises but government economic intervention has been successful in preventing prolonged or profound crises. The conditions of workers have generally improved by most measures – more holidays, better conditions, and better pay so that they are able to become part of consumer society.

But Marxian analysis still offers some important insights. First, it encourages a deep inspection of the whole project of capitalism rather than blind acceptance of it. It reminds us that the prevailing economic system is not a natural or given phenomenon and critique encourages us to ask whether the system is providing the kind of economic ends that we desire. Second, it encourages us to ask whose interests are being served by capitalism. Third, it encourages us to ask whose interests are served by governments. Fourth, whilst it is clear that the absolute poverty of the proletariat has declined, the relative gap between owners of capital and workers seems to be widening. Perhaps more significantly there seems to be an underclass of those who are unable to access the mainstream economic system and thus we can witness the extraordinary contrasts of poverty and plenty a few blocks away in major cities of the world. Fifth, we may see the globalization of capitalism as replacing other competing value systems in societies throughout the world through its overwhelming power. But perhaps most significantly whilst national class antagonisms seem to have subsided, internationally the gap between rich and poor is extreme. Indeed it appears that in many parts of the world the conditions of the poor remain stubbornly wretched (Plate 18).

Plate 18
Delivering coal by handcart, China
Source: The author

Critical evaluation of the economic state of recreation, leisure and tourism, and desirable economic ends

So, as we embark upon the 21st century we may remark upon how wrong Marx was in his analysis of capitalism. Revolutions seem to be taking the world population not into communism but out of it. Capitalism is as brash, dynamic and delivering goods and services by the bucket load. In terms of leisure and tourism those on average incomes in the North America, the European Union and Australasia have access to a dazzling array of recreation, leisure and tourism opportunities in the form of gyms, satellite television, sports, recreational activities, and domestic and foreign holidays. Moreover there has, in general, been a release from the harsh conditions of work described by Marx. Fewer people work in factories or endure hard physical work. In short we've never had it so good.

Economic development in some parts of the world based on tourism means that generations of workers have been able to completely miss out the squalid conditions associated with the Industrial Revolution of the UK for example, and achieve economic growth using the relatively clean industry of tourism.

Karl Marx famously said that religion was the opium of the masses. By this he meant that strong religious beliefs meant that people were not alive to their plight in the world. Religion provided both a discipline encouraging unquestioning respect for authority and a kind of a drug providing meaning and the promise of a good after-life in return for a well-spent life on earth and good deeds. It could be said that in the present age leisure is the opium of the people. It provides a feel good factor and a diversion from more profound politico-economic issue.

It therefore seems appropriate to end this book with a wake up call concerning the less desirable ends that are delivered as part and parcel of our economic prosperity based upon free market economics. This will take the form of a number of questions and issues for consideration.

1 Travel has given us the opportunity to move freely around the globe, dropping in and out of distant lands and cultures. This raises two questions:
  – Are we happy with the intense poverty that we have to step around in many parts of the world? The World Bank estimated that in 1999 1.2 billion people worldwide had consumption levels below $1 a day – 23 per cent of the population of the developing world – and 2.8 billion lived on less than $2 a day. Table 18.1 shows examples of world poverty wherein Ethiopia and Uganda 82 per cent of the population are living on less than $1 a day. This notion of poverty, disease and starvation in a world of unparalleled affluence is surely the most profound disgrace to the modern world. Table 18.2 shows the distribution of world gross domestic product (GDP) amongst the world population. Note the paradox in distribution between India which has 21 per cent of the world population but only 5 per cent of world GDP and the USA which has 5 per cent of the world population but 21 per cent of world GDP.

Table 18.1 World poverty

Year of survey	Country	Percentage of population below $1 a day	Percentage of population below $2 a day
2000	Bangladesh	36	83
2000	Ethiopia	82	98
1994	India	35	80
1996	Nepal	38	83
1996	Uganda	82	96
1998	Vietnam	18	63

Source: Adapted from IMF, www.worldbank.org/data

Table 18.2 Distribution of world output (2002)

Area/example	Percentage of world GDP	Percentage of world population
Advanced economies	55.7	15.4
e.g. United States	*21.1*	*4.7*
Developing economies	38.1	78.1
e.g. India	*4.8*	*20.8*
Countries in transition	6.3	6.4
e.g. Russia	*2.7*	*2.3*

Source: Adapted from IMF, World Economic Outlook 2003.
www.imf.org/external/pubs/ft/weo/2003

- Is it just that many people are excluded and denied access to developed countries in search of better conditions?
2 But even limited travel in our own countries also raises questions about poverty:
   - Why is there such a big gap between rich and poor?
   - Why does the economy generate squalor and affluence within close proximity?
   - Why do those who work hardest often get the lowest wages?
3 Factory life and harsh working conditions are disappearing from the developed world. However, the production of many leisure goods – computers, CD players, sports shoes, equipment and clothing – often takes place in factories and sweatshops in less developed countries with poor wages and tough working conditions. Exhibit 18.2 reports on conditions in a garment factory in Honduras. Cruise ships provide an

---

Exhibit 18.2 Industrial Embroidery, Choloma, Honduras

This is a small factory with approximately 370 workers, where silk screening and embroidery work is done for many labels including Nike, Old Navy/Gap, Tommy, Polo Jeans, Hanes, Osh Kosh, and other brands.

The factory operates 24 hours a day, seven days a week. The night shift in the silk screening department runs from 6:00 p.m. to 6:00 a.m., four nights a week. During the shift the workers get just one 30-minute break at 1:00 a.m. The workers describe conditions as very tense, with constant pressure from management to reach production goals. 'The factory demands a lot – too much' the workers say.

Temperatures in the silk screening department can reach 94 to over 100 degrees. The workers explain, 'we sweat like we're under the sun'. The factory is very labour intensive with little mechanization. Four workers manage each 'octopus', a silk screening machine, which has 12–14 arms, each arm applies different colours to the garment to make up the image and lettering. The shirts are mounted on a wooden ironing board.

The 'octopus' can silk screen one shirt each minute, meaning the labour cost involved in silk screening each shirt is less than seven cents. The workers are on their feet all night, constantly walking in a circle as they attend the machine. From the machine the shirts go through a dryer. This is why the factory is so hot even at night.

The workers describe facing constant relentless pressure to work faster to meet their production goals. Speaking during working hours is prohibited. Bathroom visits are monitored. One woman said that 'the supervisors are constantly watching you and if you take more than two minutes they scold you'.

The workers say they are completely exhausted when they leave at the end of the shift. The basic wage at the factory is 576.10 lempiras a week, or $33.15. But by racing to meet their high production goals, and putting in 10–21.5 hours of overtime each week, the fastest workers can earn from $50.37 to $75.12 a week, which would be between 93 cents and $1.15 an hour.

Source: Adapted from The National Labour Committee report on factory conditions describes conditions in the Inhdelua Free Trade Zone in Honduras.

---

alarming example of the very good life on the upper decks and the very bad life below decks:

– Are we happy that others work long hours with low pay and in bad working conditions to provide us with cheap goods?

4 Economic growth brings higher wages and material prosperity. But are we happy with the balance between economic growth and environmental damage including:

– global warming;
– atmospheric pollution;

 – traffic congestion;
 – noise pollution;
 – the concretization of the natural environment.
5 As economic growth increases crime seems to grow too. The fear and effects of crime can be profound:
 – Have we properly understood the relationship between crime and the economy?
6 The government collects taxes and spends them on our behalf:
 – Are we happy with the amount of taxes raised?
 – Are we happy with the way in which our money is spent on for example, education, health, defence, leisure, etc.?
7 Although we seem to grow richer each year it is not clear that we grow happier:
 – Are we satisfied with our work/life balance?
 – Do we work too many hours?
 – Has consumerism meant the loss of our spiritual dimension?
8 When we examine the profiles of Chief Executive Officers and board members of major companies including those in leisure and tourism we find a strong imbalance:
 – Can we defend the disproportionate representation of white males in positions of economic power?
9 Are we happy to allow child prostitution and sex tourism?
10 A richer society does not appear to be a healthier one:
 – Are we happy to encourage cigarette smoking to cause terrifying death by lung cancer?
 – Why is obesity such a problem in wealthy societies? (See Exhibit 18.3.)
11 Why are we still plagued by war and terrorism – are there any economic reasons for this?
12 It appears that in a free market we all have access to recreation, leisure and tourism:
 – Why do some groups seem to suffer from social exclusion from these and other areas of life?

Of course, you may well have different answers to these questions – or even want to pose a different set of questions but the point about this discussion is that it raises issues that do not often surface through a study of positive economics and encourages thought about the desirable ends of economic activity.

Practical approaches

This section examines some practical approaches to some of the issues outlined in the previous sector. In fact in some cases the issues have been covered in previous chapters. For example, the issues surrounding environmental economics have been discussed in Chapters 16 and 17. Similarly policies to discourage demerit goods (cigarettes) and encourage merit goods (fitness) were tackled in Chapter 7. Work/leisure issues were covered in Chapter 4.

Exhibit 18.3   Report: Broadcasting Bad Health: Why Food Marketing Needs to be Controlled

- The Food Commission published a report *Broadcasting Bad Health: Why Food Marketing Needs to be Controlled* in 2003. It claimed that companies including KFC, Burger King, McDonald's, Nestlé, Coca-Cola, Pepsi and Mars were using free toys, cartoon characters and gimmicky packaging to push 'high-calorie, low-nutrition food' on youngsters.
- It further noted that for every $1 spent globally by the World Health Organization (WHO) on preventing obesity, high blood pressure and other diseases caused by fatty western diets, the global food industry spent $500 promoting them.
- The report said food advertising accounted for about 50 per cent of all advertising in children's programmes and of that amount, around 75 per cent was for fast or convenience food.
- Co-author of the report, Kath Dalmeny, said, 'Junk foods and sugary drinks are supported by enormous advertising budgets that dwarf any attempt to educate children about healthy diets'.
- WHO has identified as 'probable' or 'convincing' the link between obesity, heart disease and certain types of cancers with the consumption of fatty foods and heavily sweetened drinks. It also pointed to a rising tide of diet related diseases in developing countries such as India and China.

Source: The author, from press cuttings.

Trade Unions

Trade Unions can act as powerful groups to protect the interest of workers. It may be argued that the growth of Trade Unions had an important effect in raising the living standards and working conditions of the proletariat so that the kind of revolutionary class conflict predicted by Marx failed to occur.

Exhibit 18.4 illustrates the aims and activities of the GMB – Britain's general union which has a lot of members in the leisure industries. It also shows their campaign to ensure equal pay for women.

Pressure groups

There are a number of pressure groups that exist to achieve particular aims in leisure, recreation and tourism and engage in broader campaigns which have relevance to these subjects.

Exhibit 18.4   The GMB Union

The Food and Leisure Section of the GMB is composed of members working in:

- Food and drink manufactures.
- Hotel and catering.
- Tourism and leisure.
- Food and drink retail.
- Food and drink distribution.
- Sports.

The section has been developed to meet and overcome problems being encountered now in these industries. Problems that will be those of British industry in general in years to come:

- Development of European Works Councils.
- Continuous changes in ownership due to takeovers and mergers.
- Large transnationals who do not identify with a region, or the UK.
- Part time workers.
- Greater employment of women.
- Temporary/seasonal work.
- Work Life balance.
- Partnership.

Major Employers with GMB members include:

- Forte.
- Bass.
- ASDA.
- Bourne Leisure.
- Butlins.

- Haven.
- RoadChef.
- Jarvis.
- Whitbread.

Make Equal Pay a Reality

GMB has been at the forefront of the fight for equality within Trade Unions, at the workplace and within society for many years. Women make up nearly 40 per cent of their members. One of their campaigns is called 'Make Equal Pay a Reality'.

There is a gender pay gap of 19 per cent between women and men full time workers. Much of the difference in pay can be accounted for by employer infringement of equal pay legislation, albeit, in many cases, unintentional. Whether unintentional or not, this breach of legislation cannot be allowed to continue. It can be resolved by equal pay reviews. However, despite requests, many organizations are not voluntarily carrying out equal pay reviews. The GMB is now lobbying the government to end this situation and to make pay reviews compulsory.

Source: GMB web site www.gmb.org.uk

Tourism Concern • • •

The mission of Tourism Concern is to effect change in the tourism industry by campaigning for fair and ethically traded tourism. It does this through a number of activities:

- *Tourism for communities*: Tourism Concern has been working since 1989 to raise awareness of the negative impacts of tourism, economic, cultural, environment and social. A major part of their work is advocacy. 'Communities often find they have tourism imposed on them by governments and foreign developers and tourism businesses; that there is little linkage between tourism especially at a mass scale – and local industry, such as agriculture; that land and natural resources are frequently co-opted, often illegally; and that their cultural traditions are appropriated and commercialized'(www.tourismconcern.org.uk).
- *The tourism industry*: Tourism Concern seeks to work with the tourism industry trying to convince those who run and manage holidays that tourism can support local people, cultures, environment and economies, while still be exciting and enjoyable.
- *Campaigning*: Tourism Concern has been campaigning on human rights and tourism for several years. Campaigns include the displacement of the Maasai from their homes in East Africa and 'Trekking wrongs: porters' rights' which highlights the terrible conditions porters who accompany trekkers endure in mountain environments.
- *Fair Trade in tourism*: This involves Tourism Concern working with the travel industry to make things fairer for people living in destinations and showing individual holiday-makers how they can play their part.
- *Community tourism*: Here Tourism Concern has worked closely with people from over 40 countries to create their own locally run tours or lodgings.

Greenpeace • • •

Greenpeace is a non-profit organization, with a presence in 40 countries across Europe, the Americas, Asia and the Pacific. It does not accept donations from governments or corporations but relies on contributions from individual supporters and foundation grants. It does this to maintain its independence.

Greenpeace focuses on worldwide threats to biodiversity and the environment and its main campaigns seek to:

- Stop climate change.
- Protect ancient forests.
- Save the oceans.
- Stop whaling.
- Say no to genetic engineering.
- Stop the nuclear threat.

- Eliminate toxic chemicals.
- Encourage sustainable trade.

Oxfam • • •

One of the main aims of this charity and pressure group is the relief of poverty. To do achieve this, it offers direct help to those in poverty, lobbies governments for change and organizes campaigns:

- It seeks to help people organize so that they might gain better access to the opportunities they need to improve their livelihoods and govern their own lives. It also works with people affected by humanitarian disasters, with preventive measures, preparedness, as well as emergency relief.
- It conducts high-level research and lobbying aiming to change international policies and practices in ways which would ensure that poor people have the rights, opportunities and resources they need to improve and control their lives.
- It instigates popular campaigning, alliance building and media work designed to raise awareness among the public of the real solutions to global poverty, to enable and motivate people to play an active part in the movement for change, and to foster a sense of global citizenship.

An example of its campaigning is the NikeWatch Campaign:

> Ever wondered, as you slipped on your sneakers or pulled on a pair of jogging shorts, what life might be like for the person who made them? Nike promotes sport and healthy living, but the lives of workers who make Nike's shoes and clothes in Asia and Latin America are anything but healthy. They live in severe poverty and suffer stress and exhaustion from overwork. Oxfam Community Aid Abroad is part of an international campaign to persuade Nike and other transnational corporations to respect workers' basic rights (www.caa.org.au/campaigns/nike/).

On the other hand Cukier (2002) conducted research that challenged the negative image of tourism employment that he argues has largely been derived from a developed country context and has not been based on empirical research within the tourism sector. His research is based on interviews conducted with 240 tourism workers in the coastal resort villages of Sanur and Kuta in Bali, Indonesia. The study examined the appropriateness of existing conceptions of tourism employment and determined empirically the degree to which these conceptions are appropriate to developing countries. He concluded that tourism employment is a generally positive phenomenon from the perspective of tourism employees. Tourism employment is accorded a relatively high status, provides many opportunities for women and migrant workers, and is generally well remunerated, especially when compared to traditional employment options.

New Economics Foundation

New Economic Foundation (NEF) is an independent think and do tank located in London which exists to 'inspire and demonstrate real economic well-being'. It aims to improve quality of life by promoting innovative solutions that challenge mainstream thinking on economic, environment and social issues. Economic, social and environmental justice are central to its philosophy and it aims to put people and the planet first. NEF seeks to combine rigorous analysis and policy debate with practical solutions on the ground, often run and designed with the help of local people. The main ways in which NEF works are through:

- practical local projects and tools for change;
- in-depth research;
- campaigning;
- policy discussion;
- raising awareness through the media and publications;
- incubation of new organizations and campaigns that can create long-term change in society.

Radical approaches to regeneration ● ● ●

NEF has developed a number of programmes and tools which seek to build regeneration of poor communities from the grassroots level. Specifically the tools seek to mobilize a community's resources, engage the community in the process of regeneration, and inspire the community to take action. The key tools are:

- *BizFizz*: a one-stop shop led by an enterprise coach that fosters business development by mobilizing all the local networks and resources a community possesses.
- *Plugging the leaks*: a tool, based around a one-day workshop, which leads the community through a process of understanding how their local economy works and facilitates ideas for improving it.
- *Local Alchemy*: a process of community-led economic analysis, visioning and planning which leads to a strategy for long-term economic renewal.
- *LM3*: a measuring tool that enables anyone to assess how a particular business or initiative impacts the local economy, and how to improve that impact.

Radical economic research and reconfiguration ● ● ●

In the area of alternative economic research NEF produces *The Real World Economic Outlook* (Pettifor, 2003). This publication examines the global economy from a radical perspective: that of economic and environmental justice. This is in contrast to the IMF publication the *World Economic Outlook* which offers an orthodox analysis of the world economy.

The 2003 report investigates the situation of those impoverished and harmed by financial globalization and it pinpoints globalization's true legacy: debt and deflation. Globalization is analysed not as a spontaneous event of economic and technological development, but as a deliberate strategy to place finance at the centre of local, national and global communities. The authors argue that globalization has proved disastrous not only for the environment and for billions of people in poor countries, but increasingly for economies in the west. They show that one of the major outcomes of globalization – falling prices for labour, goods and services – will make it more difficult for individuals, households, governments and corporations to repay the debts acquired through financial liberalization. It argues that ordinary people have been lured into a trap of debt and deflation without due consideration for the consequences. Additionally the report demonstrates how a globalized, finance-centred economy has led to a dramatic increase in inequality, both within and between countries.

Free trade/fair trade

Chapter 14 discussed the theoretical arguments for free trade and the General Agreement on Trade in Services (GATS) agreement. However, as well as bringing lower consumer prices, more choice and greater economic efficiency, free trade also has key drawbacks. In particular, there appears to be an imbalance of power and trading terms between rich and poor countries. Exhibit 18.5 offers a critique from Tourism Concern of aspects of GATS.

It is because of concerns of Free Trade on the interests of poorer countries that the Fair Trade lobby has arisen.

The key principles of Fair Trade (Fair Trade Federation, 2003) include:

- *Creating opportunities for economically-disadvantaged producers*: At the heart of Fair Trade is the aim of poverty alleviation and sustainable development. It lays a particular emphasis on creating opportunities for workers and suppliers who have been economically-disadvantaged or marginalized by the conventional trading system.
- *Gender equity*: Another key principle is to ensure that women's work is properly valued and rewarded. The aim of Free Trade is to ensure that women are always paid for their contribution to the production process and are empowered in their organizations.
- *Transparency and accountability*: Fair Trade advocates transparent management and commercial relations so that trading partners and customers are fully aware of the way in which the business works.
- *Capacity building*: Fair Trade aims to develop producer independence and growth in similar organizations. This can be achieved by assistance in developing management skills, improved access to markets and financial and technical expertise.
- *Payment of a fair price*: This is at the heart of Fair Trade. A fair price is one that has been agreed through dialogue and participation and is set in the regional or local context. It should cover production costs but

Exhibit 18.5   The downside of GATS

There is evidence that GATS may promote the interests of companies over people and the environment. GATS and the corporate globalization it promotes, does not necessarily support sustainable development. Many countries have made commitments to liberalize tourism under GATS, but few are able to retain powers to restrict developments that threaten eco-systems and local communities.

There are various obligations under the GATS. One called 'most favoured nation' means that companies can always set up tourism busi-nesses in countries signed up to GATS. Another obligation – termed 'national treatment' – means that foreign businesses must be treated in the same way as domestic businesses.

Consequently, host governments, cannot compel tourism transnation-als to employ local labour or use local materials and products instead of importing them. This prevents destinations from optimizing local eco-nomic benefits. Nor will governments be able to implement special measures to secure a competitive base for domestic businesses against foreign investment.

On paper the purpose of these commitments is to ensure a transparent and anti discriminatory 'level playing field'. They should also help com-panies benefit from liberalized trade in other countries. Having such 'recip-rocal rights' is particularly important for Southern countries wanting to gain market access in Northern countries. However, in a very unequal world, this may benefit some rather than all.

GATS could definitely pose problems for destinations with a large pro-portion of small or underdeveloped businesses, with a lot of informal sec-tor tourism businesses, or with poor technological and capital resources. If countries also have weak, political and democratic governance which prevents poor communities from gaining access to national and inter-national markets, the implications for ordinary people involved in tourism are also negative.

Far from reducing poverty, liberalization under GATS has meant Southern countries are bracing themselves for an onslaught of foreign investment in the form of takeovers and acquisitions within their newly budding tourism industries. Northern countries are, however, not recipro-cating equally by opening up their markets to the service exports of Southern countries. This is particularly the case in relation to labour under the mode of 'supply of natural persons'. Barriers to a two-way flow of labour include restrictive immigration rules in developed nations. Other barriers include licensing, technical standards setting and grant subsidies for the domestic sectors in tourism for Southern countries.

GATS entails no specific obligation on companies to trade in host coun-tries according to internationally agreed conventions on environmental sustainability and human rights, including labour rights. Consequently governments could face real difficulties in trying to limit negative environ-mental, social and cultural impacts in their country. These include trying to restrict the mushrooming of foreign-owned developments including all-inclusive hotels, which are often highly controversial amongst local people because they contribute so little to the local economy. Governments also face difficulties in making the employment of local workers or the use of local products and materials a condition of foreign investment. It could also render a government powerless to stop tourism development on indigenous land and sacred sites, in response to community protests. If host governments attempted to control foreign investment in any way, once they had committed to GATS they could be legally challenged by investing companies under the dispute settlement procedure within the World Trade Organization.

Source: Fair Trade in Tourism, the bulletin of Tourism Concern's Fair Trade in Tourism Network, Issue 3 (Winter 2001/Spring 2002).

additionally enable production that is socially just and environmentally sound. It includes the principle of equal pay for equal work by women and men and prompt payment by trading partners.

- *Working conditions*: Fair Trade entails ensuring a safe and healthy working environment. Where children are part of the labour force the principles of the UN Convention on the Rights of the Child are adhered to.
- *Environmental sustainability*: Fair Trade encourages producers to engage in production practices that manage and use local resources sustainably.

Pro-poor tourism

Ashley et al. (2000) note that

In the tourism sector, national governments and donors have generally aimed to promote private sector investment, macro-economic growth and foreign exchange earnings, without specifically taking the needs and opportunities of the poor into account in tourism development.

They make the additional point that

Donor-supported tourism master plans focus on creating infrastructure, stimulating private investment and attracting international tourists. Investors are often international companies and local élites, whose profits are generally repatriated abroad or to metropolitan centres. Links with the local economy are often weak, with the possible exception of employment.

This view is supported by various case studies including that of Mvula (2001) who reports on the impacts of wildlife tourism to South Luangwa National Park, Zambia on the rural local communities that reside there. She assesses local people's attitude towards tourism in the area and solicits their views on how the benefits to the community could be increased. Her findings show that the community want more involvement with tourism and tourists. She indicates, however, that the benefits of tourism currently reach few local people and that in some instances inequality and discrimination are evident in the employment practice of the local tourism industry. Mvula points to community tourism based on cultural heritage as a potential way of maximizing the benefits of tourism to communities, while minimizing the impacts.

These observations have given rise to the concept of pro-poor tourism (PPT). PPT is tourism that results in increased net benefits for poor people. PPT is not a specific product or niche sector but rather it is an approach to developing and managing tourism and its aim is to enhance the linkages between tourism businesses and poor people. In this way tourism's contribution to poverty reduction can be increased and poor people can be empowered to participate more effectively in the development and provision of tourism products. There are a variety of links with different types of 'the poor' that need to be considered. These include staff, neighbouring communities, land-holders, producers of food, fuel and other suppliers, operators of micro tourism businesses, craft-makers, other users of tourism infrastructure (roads) and resources (water), etc. PPT strategies are various and can range from increasing local employment to building mechanisms for consultation. The critical success factor in PPT is not the type of company or the type of tourism, but that an increase in the net benefits that go to poor people can be demonstrated. By net benefits is meant the surplus of gains over the costs of tourism to the target 'poor' population.

The SNV-Nepal project is a good example of PPT in action and provides a good example of the import substitution process – whereby the goods and services required by the tourism industry are encouraged to be produced and supplied locally rather than from Kathmandu. In this project the Dutch Development Agency SNV, works through its District Partners Programme (DPP) with district and village development committees, non-government organizations (NGOs) and the private sector to 'benefit women and disadvantaged groups at village level' in the remote Humla district of north-west Nepal.

The focus of the project is at the local level – on specific enterprises and communities along a trekking trail. The emphasis of the PPT strategy is on local mobilization through the development of community-based organizations and business planning and training designed to enable the poor to develop micro-enterprises and to take up employment opportunities. The outcomes of the project include:

- the development of micro-enterprise plans, of which 32 have been approved;
- plans to develop hot springs and village tours;

- plans for a multiple use Visitors Centre to provide a focal point for the local provision of tourism services such as portering, mules, horses, etc. and produce, such as vegetables, to trekking agents and tourists;
- construction of toilets along the trekking trail;
- a US $2 per tourist trail maintenance tax;
- an understanding of the challenges of breaking into the existing well-established and connected tourism elite.

Endnote: markets, ethics and power

It should be clear that the study of economics does not include any real analysis of power or ethics in society. The study of positive economics implies a quite passive analysis of how the economy works. Power is seen as something neutral and a study of positive economics only describes power in economics in terms of what causes market changes. So where does power lie in the economic world? Clearly it lies mainly with those who have highest incomes, accumulated capital and healthy profit. For it is this spending power which dictates the answers to those questions posed at the beginning of this book:

- What to produce?
- How to produce it?
- Where to produce it?
- Who is it produced for?

It is therefore equally clear that those with low incomes and no accumulated capital have very little influence in determining how these basic economic questions will be answered.

At the same time it can be seen that economics does not necessarily deliver solutions that are ethically sound. Ethics is concerned with our values – and our distinctions between good and bad. What this chapter has attempted to show is that the ends that result from economic activity (i.e. the outcomes of the playing out of economic forces) may not be the ones that we would choose from an ethical perspective. For when we examine the outcomes of:

- What has been produced?
- How it has been produced?
- Where it has been produced?
- Who has benefited from production? …

… we may well feel that from an ethical point of view these outcomes are not always appropriate.

And so it seems appropriate to end this book on a power/political note. On the one hand we may not mind about the outcomes of economic activity and just accept them as inevitable. Or we might agree that economic outcomes are the best that we can have. But if we have a vision of alternative, of better ends of economic activity, then we must intervene to initiate change. And we can do that at many levels:

- We all have some power at the individual level and here we may change our own consumption patterns. We can effectively withhold our money votes from economic outputs we disapprove of and vote for those we favour.
- At the individual level we can also make our ethical views known by letterwriting to newspapers, to politicians. We can influence our friends by discussion and argument.
- We can also lever up our individual power by grouping with other people. This can mean contributing to or joining a pressure group that campaigns on an issue we support. Or it may mean supporting or joining a broader political party. But at the very least it must mean exercising our right to vote where we have one.

Review of key terms

- Positive economics: deals with facts.
- Normative economics: includes values and opinions.
- Marxian analysis: conflict of interest between owners of property [the bourgeoisie] who do no work and workers [the proletariat] who own no property.
- *The Real World Economic Outlook's* critique: globalization brings problems of debt and deflation.
- Ricardo: expounded theory of the benefits of Free Trade.
- Fair Trade: payment of a fair price for traded goods and services.
- PPT: tourism that results in increased net benefits for poor people.

Data Questions

Task 18.1   The German Ideology

The ideas of the *ruling class* are in every epoch *the ruling ideas*, i.e. the class which is the *ruling material force* of society, is at the same time its *ruling intellectual force*. The class which has the means of material production at its disposal has control at the same time over the means of material production, so that thereby, generally speaking, the ideas of those who lack the means of material production are subject to it.

Source: From Marx and Engels *The German Ideology*.

Recap Questions

1 What is meant by the terms in italics?
2 What did Marx and Engels mean by this statement?
3 To what extent is this statement true today?

Task 18.2   Social exclusion in countryside leisure in the United Kingdom

This project was commissioned by the Countryside Recreation Network (CRN) to develop its understanding of issues of social exclusion and inclusion in countryside recreation…

A review of the literature reveals a range of definitions of social exclusion. The consensus amongst definitions is that social exclusion always involves a set of processes, that through particular institutional arrangement, one social group does to another. Exclusion is often associated with poverty, unemployment, isolation, discrimination and vulnerability. Some authors and institutions prefer to use the term social inclusion. They are exploring the same phenomenon, but feel that inclusiveness is a more positive concept.

Studies identify four groups whose participation rates in countryside recreation are low: young people, low-income groups, ethnic minorities and disabled people. However, one should not assume that all members of such groups are excluded.

Welfarist social policy argues that the state should endeavour to correct perceived 'inequalities' in recreation participation. Merit good arguments suggest that the state ought to provide leisure because everyone benefits from it (other merit goods include the police and basic education). More recently, ideas of citizenship have underpinned attempts to create more inclusive leisure policy. In these, the state limits its role in leisure provision/management and the citizenry shares the responsibility for its own leisure.

In relation to countryside recreation, there is evidence of major variations in participation between different groups. Age, health and disability, socio-economic group and ethnicity all influence participation in countryside recreation. There is compelling evidence of low participation rates amongst ethnic minorities, poorer socio-economic groups and an inference that disabled and ethnic minorities may feel stigmatized in their use of the countryside.

Source: *The Role of the Countryside in Addressing Social Exclusion.*
A Report for the Countryside Recreation Network, by Bill Slee and Derren Jones of Aberdeen University and Nigel Curry, Countryside and Community Research Unit.

Recap Questions

1 What is social exclusion?
2 How would orthodox economists explain the provision of recreation provision?
3 Is social exclusion a useful term in orthodox economics?
4 Which groups tend to suffer from social exclusion?
5 Is social exclusion an important issue?
6 In what ways might social exclusion be tackled?

Task 18.3   Ethical tourism

We need more than just rules for ethical tourism. Rules are often ignored or flouted according to expediency. They do not necessarily result in improved outcomes. Therefore this article is concerned with two main themes. First it is about ethical tourism action. The term action is deliberately used to locate the discussion in contrast to the discourse that is mainly about reflection.

The reflective discourse around ethical tourism has attracted criticism as 'promise without practice'. Indeed it was well over a decade ago when Krippendorf cautioned that:

> ...the 'thinkers' who sit in their studies are political lightweights. Their recommendations will remain politically anaemic theories as long as there is no pressure on the politicians from the general public – both tourists and their hosts... What we need then are rebellious tourists and rebellious locals. (1987: 107)

The second theme of the article is education and students. What is sought is not necessarily rebellious students but students who act in the tourism world – whether as tourists, or tourism professionals or political activists – with a strong and developed sense of critical knowing. This is a knowing not just of the narrow professional competence that may be characterized as vocationalism but which extends to an ethical competence. Action thus informed is designed to promote change for the promotion of a better tourism society and world.

Source: Tribe, J (2002) Education for responsible tourism action, *Journal of Sustainable Tourism*, **10** (4), 309–324.

Recap Questions

1 What is ethical tourism and what might be its typical features?
2 How might ethical tourism differ from current tourism products?
3 Why is there a difference between ethical tourism and actual tourism?
4 To what extent does the study of economics help us to understand ethical tourism?
5 In what ways can we promote ethical tourism?

Multiple choice

1 **Which of the following is a criticism of Paul Omerod of orthodox economics?**

   (a) It is trapped in an idealized, mechanistic view of the world.
   (b) It explains differences in wages.
   (c) It explains the benefits of Free Trade.
   (d) It deals in values.

2 **Which of the following is not part of Marxian analysis?**

   (a) History can be seen as a series of class struggles.
   (b) There is basic conflict between the bourgeoisie and the proletariat.
   (c) The victory of the proletariat over the bourgeoisie is inevitable.
   (d) International trade brings gains to all its participants.

3 **Which of these is not a feature of the GATS agreement on Free Trade?**

   (a) Signatories if the agreement are free to impose import duties.
   (b) Foreign owned companies must have free access to domestic markets.

(c) Concessions granted to any one country must also be made available to all other signatories of the Agreement.

(d) Foreign investors must be treated on an equal basis with domestic investors.

4 **Which of the following is not a feature of Fair Trade?**

(a) Gender equity.
(b) Payment of a fair price.
(c) A safe and healthy working environment.
(d) Guaranteed quality of goods traded.

5 **In a free market economy what is produced is determined by:**

(a) Ethical considerations.
(b) Fairness.
(c) Purchasing power.
(d) Human needs.

Review questions

1 What is orthodox economics?
2 How does the economics of the New Economics Foundation differ from that of orthodox economics?
3 What are the key points in Marx's analysis of capitalism?
4 Why did Marx's prediction of a proletariat revolution not materialize?
5 How does Fair Trade differ from Free Trade – what are its advantages and disadvantages?
6 How could consumers and producers ensure that their tourism is pro-poor?
7 What are your personal points of satisfaction and dissatisfaction with the recreation, leisure and tourism opportunities offered by the market economy?

Web sites of interest

www.greenpeace.org
www.propoortourism.org.uk
www.tourismconcern.org.uk
www.oxfam.org.uk
www.fairtradefederation.com
www.neweconomics.org/

References and further reading

Aguiló, E., Alegre, J. and Sard, M. (2003). Examining the market structure of the German and UK tour operating industries through an analysis of package holiday prices. *Tourism Economics*, **9** (3), 255–78.

Aksu, A. and Tarcan, E. (2002). The Internet and five-star hotels: a case study from the Antalya region in Turkey. *International Journal of Contemporary Hospitality Management*, **14** (2), 94–7.

Archer, B. (1996). Economic impact analysis. *Annals of Tourism Research*, **23** (3), 704–7.

Archer, B. and Fletcher, J. (1996). The economic impact of tourism in the Seychelles. *Annals of Tourism Research*, **23** (1), 32–47.

Archer, B. H. (1982). The value of multipliers and their policy implications. *Tourism Management*, December, 236–41.

Archer, B. H. (1984). Economic impact: misleading multipliers. *Annals of Tourism Research*, **11**, 517–18.

Archer, B. H. (1995). Importance of tourism for the economy of Bermuda. *Annals of Tourism Research*, **22**, 918–30.

Archer, B. H. and Owen, C. A. (1971). Toward a tourist regional multiplier. *Regional Studies*, **5** (4), 289–94.

Ashley, C. (2000). *The Impacts of Tourism on Rural Livelihoods: Experience in Namibia*. ODI Working Paper No. 128.

Ashley, C. and Roe, D. (1998). *Enhancing Community Involvement in Wildlife Tourism: Issues and Challenge*. Wildlife and Development Series No. 11. London, IIED.

Ashley, C., Boyd, C. and Goodwin, H. (2000). Pro-poor tourism: putting poverty at the heart of the tourism agenda. *Natural Resource Perspectives*. London, ODI.

Ashworth, G. A. and Voogd, H. (1990). *Selling the City*. Chichester, Wiley.

Ashworth, G. J. and Dietvorst, A. G. J. (eds) (1995). *Tourism and Spatial Transformations: Implications for Policy and Planning*. Wallingford, CAB International.

Balaguer, J. and Cantavella-Jordá, M. (2002). Tourism as a long-run economic growth factor: the Spanish case. *Applied Economics*, 2002 **34** (7), 877–84.

Barke, M., Towner, J. and Newton, M. (eds) (1995). *Tourism in Spain*. Wallingford, CAB.

Begg, D., Fischer, S. and Dornbusch, R. (2002). *Economics*, 7th edn. Europe, McGraw-Hill Education.

Bergstrom, J. A., Cordell, H. A., Ashley, G. A. and Watson, A. A. (1990). Economic impacts of recreational spending on rural areas: a case study. *Economic Development Quarterly*, **4** (1), 29–39.

Blazević, B. and Jelusić, A. (2002). Croatian balance of payment and tourism. *Tourism and Hospitality Management*, **8** (1/2), 127–42.

Bouchet, P. (2002). A new consumer trend amongst the elderly: high-end tourism, *Loisir et Societe*, **25** (2), 377–96.

Bourdieu, P. (1984). *Distinction: A Social Critique of the Judgement of Taste*. London, Routledge and Kegan Paul.

Boviard, A., Tricker, M. and Stoakes, R. (1984). *Recreation Management and Pricing*. London, Gower.

Bramham, P., Henry, I., Mommaas, H. and Van der Poel, H. (eds) (1993). *Leisure Policies in Europe*. Wallingford, CAB International.

Braun, B. and Soskin, M. (1999). Theme park competitive strategies. *Annals of Tourism Research*, **26** (2), 438–42.

Briguglio, L., Archer, B., Jafari, J. and Wall, G. (eds) (1996). *Sustainable Tourism in Islands and Small States: Issues and Policies*. London, Pinter.

Briguglio, L., Butler, R., Harrison, D. and Filho, W. (eds) (1996). *Sustainable Tourism in Islands and Small States: Case Studies*. London, Pinter.

Brooker, M. (2002). How to raise finance for the small hotel enterprise – a way forward. *Hospitality Review*, **4** (1), 13–20.

Brown, F. (1998). *Tourism: Blight or Blessing?* Oxford, Butterworth-Heinemann.

Bryman, A. (1995). *Disney and His Worlds*. London, Routledge.

Buckley, R. (2002). Tourism ecolabels. *Annals of Tourism Research*, **29** (1), 183–208.

Buhalis, D. (2003). *eTourism: Information Technology for Strategic Tourism Management*. Harlow, UK, Prentice-Hall.

Bull, A. (1995). *The Economics of Travel and Tourism*. Harlow, Longman.

Burns, P. (1998). From Communist to common-weal: reflections on tourism training in Romania. *Tourism Recreation Research*, **23** (2), 45–52.

Burns, P. and Holden, A. (1995). *Tourism: A New Perspective*. Hemel Hempstead, Prentice-Hall.

Butler, R., Hall, R. and Jenkins, M. (eds) (1998). *Tourism and Recreation in Rural Areas*. Chichester, Wiley.

Canina, L. (2001). Acquisitions in the lodging industry: good news for buyers and sellers. *Cornell Hotel and Restaurant Administration Quarterly*, **42** (6), 47–54.

Canina, L., Walsh, K. and Enz, C. (2003). The effects of gasoline-price changes on room demand: a study of branded hotels from 1988 through 2000. *Cornell Hotel and Restaurant Administration Quarterly*, **44** (4), 29–37.

Carney, D. (ed.) (1998). *Sustainable Rural Livelihoods: What Contribution Can We Make?* London, DFID.

Cater, E. and Lowman, G. (1994). *Ecotourism: A Sustainable Option*. Chichetser, Wiley.

Coalter, F. (1998). Leisure studies, leisure policy and social citizenship: the failure of welfare or the limits of welfare? *Leisure Studies*, **17** (1), 21–36.

Coccossis, H. and Nijkamp, P. (eds) (1995). *Sustainable Tourism Development*. London, Ashgate.

Commonwealth of Australia (2003). *Tourism White Paper*. Canberra, Department of Communications.

Conlin, M. and Baum, T. (eds) (1995). *Island Tourism: Management Principle Sand Practice*. London, Wiley.

Cooke, A. (1994). *Economics of Leisure and Sport*. London, ITBP.

Cooke, A. (1994). *The Economics of Leisure and Sport*. London, International Thomson Business Press.

Cooper, C. and Wanhill, S. (eds) (1997). *Tourism Development: Environmental and Community Issues*. Chichester, Wiley.

Croall, J. (1995). *Preserve or Destroy? Tourism and the Environment*. London, Caloust Gulbenkian Foundation.

Cukier, J. (2002). Tourism employment issues in developing countries: examples from Indonesia. In *Tourism and Development: Concepts and Issues* (R. Sharpley and D. Telfer, eds). Clevedon, UK, Channel View Publications.

Cullen, P. (1997). *Economics for Hospitality Management*. London, ITBP.

Curtis, I. (2002). Environmentally sustainable tourism: a case for carbon trading at Northern Queensland hotels and resorts. *Australian Journal of Environmental Management*, **9** (1), 27–36.

Cushman, G., Veal, A. A. and Zuzanek, J. (eds) (1996). *World Leisure Participation: Free Time in the Global Village*. Wallingford, CAB International.

Dardis, R., Soberon-Ferrere, H. and Patro, D. (1994). Analysis of leisure expenditures in the United States. *Journal of Leisure Research*, **25** (4), 309–21.

Davidson, R. (1994). *Business Travel*. Harlow, Longman.

Davidson, R. (1998). *Tourism in Europe*, 2nd edn. Harlow, Longman.

Davidson, R. and Maitland, R. (1997). *Tourism Destinations*. London, Hodder and Stoughton.

Dawson, S., Blahna, D. and Keith, J. (1993). Expected and actual regional economic impacts of Great Basin National Park. *Journal of Park and Recreation Administration*, **11** (1), 45–57.

De Clerk, P. and Klingers, J. (1998). The right price for air travel? *Tourism in Focus*, 25.

Deegan, J. and Dineen, D. A. (1997). *Tourism Policy and Performance: The Irish Experience*. London, ITBP.

Deloitte and Touche, IIED and ODI (1999). *Sustainable Tourism and Poverty Elimination Study*. A report to DFID, UK.

Department of the Environment (1990). *Tourism and the Inner City*. London, DOE.

Diamantis, D. and Fayed, H. (2002). The general agreement on trade in services (GATS) and its impact on tourism. *Travel and Tourism Analyst*, **3**, 87–99.

Dickinson, B. and Vladimir, A. (1996). *Selling the Sea: Inside Look at the Cruise Industry*. Chichester, Wiley.

Doganis, R. (1991). *Flying Off Course: The Economics of International Airlines*. London, Routledge.

Doganis, R. (1992). *The Airport Business*. London, Routledge.

Dumazedier, J. (1967). *Toward a Society of Leisure*. London, Macmillan.

Dwyer, L., Forsyth, P. and Prasada, R. (2002). Destination price competitiveness: exchange rate changes versus domestic inflation. *Journal of Travel Research*, **40** (3), 328–36.

Eadington, W. R. and Redman, M. (1991). Economics and tourism. *Annals of Tourism Research*, **18**, 41–56.

Eaton, B. (1996). *European Leisure Business: Strategies for the Future*. Cambridge, Elm.

Eckard, E. (2001). The origin of the reserve clause: owner collusion versus 'public interest'. *Journal of Sports Economics*, **2** (2),113–30.

Edgecombe, S. (2003). Leisure provision as a public good and the need for another bottom line. *Australian Parks and Leisure*, **6** (1), 22–3.

Elliot, J. (1997). *Tourism: Politics and Public Sector Management*. London, Routledge.

English, Donald, B.K. and Bergstrom John, C. (1994). The conceptual links between recreation site development and regional economic impacts. *Journal of Regional Science*, **34** (4), 599–611.

Fair Trade Federation (2003). *Report on Fair Trade Trends in US, Canada and the Pacific Rim*. Washington, Fair Trade Federation.

Fayed, H. and Westlake, J. (2002). Globalization of air transport: the challenges of the GATS. *Tourism Economics*, **8** (4), 431–55.

Fleming, W. R. and Toepper, L. (1990). Economic impact studies: relating the positive and negative impacts to tourism development. *Journal of Travel Research*, Summer, 35–42.

Fletcher, J. E. (1989). Input–output analysis and tourism impact studies. *Annals of Tourism Research*, **16**, 514–29.

FNNPE (The Federation of Nature and National Parks of Europe) (1993). *Loving Them to Death?* Grafenau, Germany, FNNPE.

Forsyth, P. and Dwyer, L. (2003). Foreign investment in Australian tourism: a framework for analysis. *Journal of Tourism Studies*, **14** (1), 67–77.

France, L. (ed.) (1997). *Earthscan Reader in Sustainable Tourism*. London, Earthscan.

Frechtling, D. (2001). *Forecasting Tourism Demand*. Oxford, Butterworth-Heinemann.

Fredman, P. and Heberlein, T. (2003). Changes in skiing and snowmobiling in Swedish mountains. *Annals of Tourism Research*, **30** (2), 485–8.

Friedman, T. (1999). *The Lexus and the Olive Tree*. New York, Anchor Books/ Doubleday.

Gee, C. Y. (ed.) (1997). *International Tourism: A Global Perspective*. Madrid, World Tourism Organisation.

Gee, C. Y., Makens, J. C. and Choy, D. J. L. (1997). *The Travel Industry*. New York, Van Nostrand Reinhold.

Gielen, D., Kurihara, R. and Moriguchi, Y. (2002). The environmental impacts of Japanese tourism and leisure. *Journal of Environmental Assessment Policy and Management*, **4** (4), 397–424.

Glyptis, S. (ed.) (1993). *Leisure and the Environment: Essays in Honour of Professor J. A. Patmore*. London, Belhaven Press.

Go, F. M. and Pine, R. (1995). *Globalization Strategy in the Hotel Industry*. London, Routledge.

Goffe le, P. (2000). Hedonic pricing of agriculture and forestry externalities, *Environmental and Resource Economics*, **15** (4), 397–401.

Goodwin, H. J., Kent, I., Parker, K. and Walpole, M. (1997). *Tourism, Conservation and Sustainable Development*. Final report to the Department for International Development.

Grant, B. (2002). Over 65 and ready to play. *Australian Leisure Management*, **35**, 36–8.

Gratton, C. and Kokolakakis, T. (2003). A bright future. *Leisure Management*, September, 38–40.

Gratton, C. and Taylor, P. (2000). *Economics of Sport and Recreation*. London, E and FN Spon.

Hall, C. M. (1994). *Tourism and Politics: Policy, Power and Place*. Chichester, Wiley.

Hall, C. M. (1997). *Tourism in the Pacific Rim: Development Impacts and Markets*, 2nd edn. Harlow, Longman.

Hall, C. M. and Jenkins, J. M. (1995). *Tourism and Public Policy*. London, ITBP.

Hall, C. M. and Lew, A. (eds) (1998). *Sustainable Tourism: A Geographical Perspective*. London, Addison Wesley.

Hall, C. M. and Page, S. J. (1996). *Tourism in the Pacific: Issues and Cases*. London, ITBP.

Hall, M. (ed.) (1998). *Sustainable Tourism: A Geographical Perspective*. Harlow, Longman.

Hamzaee, R. and Vasigh, B. (1997). An applied model of airline revenue management. *Journal of Travel Research*, **35** (4), 64–8.

Hanlon, P. (1996). *Global Airlines: Competition in a Transnational Industry*. Oxford, Butterworth-Heinemann.

Hardin, G. (1968). The tragedy of the commons. *Science*, **162**, 1243.

Harris, R. and Leiper, N. (eds) (1995). *Sustainable Tourism: An Australian Perspective*. Oxford, Butterworth-Heinemann.

Harris, R., Heath, N., Toepper, L. and Williams, P. (1998). *Sustainable Tourism: A Global Perspective*. Oxford, Butterworth-Heinemann.

Harrison, D. (ed.) (1992). *Tourism and the Less Developed Countries*. Chichester, Wiley.

Harrison, L. C. and Husbands, W. (eds) (1996). *Practising Responsible Tourism*. Chichester, Wiley.

Havitz, M. and Adkins, K. (2002). Demarketing leisure services: the case of municipal golf courses. *Journal of Park and Recreation Administration*, **20** (2), 90–110.

Haywood, L. and Butcher T. (1994). *Community Leisure and Recreation: Theory and Practice*. London, Focal Press.

Holloway, C. J. (1998). *The Business of Tourism*. Harlow, Longman.

Hyland, A., Puli, V., Cummings, M. and Sciandra, R. (2003). New York's smoke-free regulations: effects on employment and sales in the hospitality industry. *Cornell Hotel and Restaurant Administration Quarterly*, **44** (3), 9–16.

Indra, D. (2001). The effect of the events of September 11, 2001 on world tourism, *Turizmus Bulletin*, **5** (4), 47–50.

Inkpen, G. (1998). *Information Technology for Travel and Tourism*, 2nd edn. Harlow, Longman.

Inskeep, E. (1997). *Tourism Planning*. New York, Van Nostrand Reinhold.

Ioannides, D. and Debbage, K. G. (eds) (1998). *The Economic Geography of the Tourist Industry: A Supply-Side Analysis*. London, Routledge.

IUCN (The World Conservation Union) (1995). *Best Practice for Conservation and Planning in Rural Areas*. Gland, Switzerland, IUCN.

Jamieson, W. (2001). *Promotion of Investment in Tourism Infrastructure*. New York, UN ESCAP.

Jensen, T. (1998). Income and price inelasticities by nationality for tourists in Denmark. *Tourism Economics*, **4** (2).

Johnson, J. (2003). Grey power: the future is now. *Parks and Recreation Canada*, **60** (5), 26–7.

Johnson, P. and Thomas, B. (eds) (1992). *Perspectives on Tourism Policy*. London, Mansell.

Johnson, P. and Thomas, B. (eds) (1992). *Choice and Demand in Tourism*. London, Mansell.

Johnson, R. L. and Moore, E. (1993). Tourism impact estimation. *Annals of Tourism Research*, **20**, 279–88.

Jones, P. and Pizam, A. (eds) (1993). *The International Hospitality Industry: Organisational and Operational Issues*. Harlow, Longman.

Knowles, T. (1996). *Corporate Strategy for Hospitality*. Harlow, Longman.

Knowles, T. and Egan, D. (2000). Recession and its implications for the international hotel industry. *Travel and Tourism Analyst*, **6**, 59–76.

Koch, E., with de Beer, G. and Elliffe, S. (1998). SDIs, tourism-led growth and the empowerment of local communities in South Africa. *Development Southern Africa* Special Issue, **15** (5), Summer 1998.

Kotas, R., Teare, R., Logie, J., Jayawardena, C. and Bowen, J. (eds) (1996). *The International Hospitality Business*. London, Cassell.

Kottke, M. (1988). Estimating economic impacts of tourism. *Annals of Tourism Research*, **15**, 122–33.

Krippendorf, J. (1987). *The Holiday Makers*. Oxford, Butterworth-Heinemann.

Lawson, F. (1998). *Tourism and Recreation Development*. London, Focal Press.

Lea, J. (1998). *Tourism and Development in the Third World*. London, Routledge.

Leiper, N. (1999). A conceptual analysis of tourism-supported employment which reduces the incidence of exaggerated, misleading statistics about jobs. *Tourism Management*, **20** (5), 605–13.

Linder, S. (1970). *The Harried Leisure Class*. New York, Columbia University Press.

Lipsey, R. (1973). *An Introduction to Positive Economics*. London, Weidenfeld and Nicolson.

Lockhart, D. G. and Drakakis-Smith, D. (eds) (1996). *Island Tourism: Trends and Prospects*. London, Pinter.

Lundberg, D., Stavenga, M. and Krishnamoorthy, M. (1995). *Tourism Economics*. Chichester, Wiley.

Mathieson, A. and Wall, G. (1992). *Tourism: Economic, Physical and Social Impacts*. Harlow, Longman.

McCormack, F. (1994). *Water Based Recreation: Managing Water Resources for Leisure*. Cambridge, Elm.

McNeill, L. (1997). *Travel in the Digital Age*. Chichester, Bowerdean Publishing.

Medlik, S. (1994). *The Business of Hotels*. Oxford, Butterworth-Heinemann.

Middleton, V. T. C., with Hawkins, R. (1998). *Sustainable Tourism: A Marketing Perspective*. Oxford, Butterworth-Heinemann.

Milne, S. S. (1987). Differential multipliers. *Annals of Tourism Research*, **14**, 499–515.

Mowforth, M. and Munt, I. (1998). *Tourism and Sustainability: New Tourism in the Third World*. London, Routledge.

Mules, T. (2001). Globalization and the economic impacts of tourism. In *Tourism in the Twenty-first Century: Reflections on Experience* (B. Faulkner, G. Moscardo and E. Laws, eds). London, Continuum.

Mvula, C. (2001). Fair trade in tourism to protected areas – a micro case study of wildlife tourism to South Luangwa National Park, Zambia. *International Journal of Tourism Research*, **3** (5), 393–405.

National Park Service (1990). *Economic Impacts of Protecting rivers, Trails, and Greenway Corridors – A Resource Book*. California, US Department of the Interior National Park Service.

Newman, T., Curtis, K. and Stephens, J. (2003). Do community-based arts projects result in social gains? A review of the literature. *Community Development Journal*, **38** (4), 310–22.

O'Hagan, J. and Jennings, M. (2003). Public broadcasting in Europe: rationale, licence fee and other issues. *Journal of Cultural Economics*, **27** (1), 31–56.

Omerod, P. (1994). *The Death of Economics*. London, Faber and Faber.

Oppermann, M. (ed.) (1997). *Pacific Rim Tourism*. Wallingford, CAB International.

Oppermann, M. and Chon, K.-S. (1997). *Tourism in Developing Countries*. London, ITBP.

Page, S. (1994). *Transport for Tourism*. London, ITBP.

Page, S. A. and Getz, D. (eds) (1997). *The Business of Rural Tourism: International Perspectives*. London, ITBP.

Pattullo, P. (1996). *Last Resorts: The Cost of Tourism in the Caribbean*. London, Cassell.

Peacock, M. (1995). *Information Technology in the Hospitality Industry*. London, Cassell.

Pettifor, A. (2003). *Real World Economic Outlook*. Hamphire, UK, Palgrave Macmillan.

Pitegoff, B. and Smith, G. (2003). Measuring the return on investment of destination welcome centres: the case of Florida. *Tourism Economics*, **9** (3), 307–23.

Plimmer, N. (1994). Everyone benefits? The case of New Zealand. *Environment and Development Report*, London, WTTC.

Poon, A. (1993). *Tourism, Technology and Competitive Strategies*. Wallingford, CAB.

Porter, M. (1980). *Competitive Strategy: Techniques for Analysing Industries and Competitors*. New York, Free Press.

Porter, M. (1990). *The Competitive Advantage of Nations*. Basingstoke, Macmillan.

Price, M. F. (ed.) (1996). *People and Tourism in Fragile Environments*. London, Wiley.

PricewaterhouseCoopers (2002). Analysis of UK hotel employment trends and hotel sector performance. *Hospitality Directions – Europe Edition*, **6**, 8–12.

PricewaterhouseCoopers (2003). UK hotel sector must wait until 2004 for a strong rebound. *Hospitality Directions – Europe Edition*, **8**, 21–7.

Priestley, G. K., Edwards, J. A. and Coccossis, H. (eds) (1996). *Sustainable Tourism? European Experiences*. Wallingford, CAB International.

Putnam, R. (2000). *Bowling Alone: The Collapse and Revival of American Community*. New York, Simon and Schuster.

Ravenscroft, N. (1992). *Recreation Planning and Development*. Basingstoke, Macmillan.

Riley, M., Ladkin, A. and Szivas, E. (2002). *Tourism Employment: Analysis and Planning*. Clevedon, UK, Channel View Publications.

Ritzer, G. (1993). *The McDonaldization of Society*. Thousand Oaks: CA Pine Forge Press.

Robertson, R. (1992). *Globalization: Social Theory and Global Culture*. London, Sage.

Robinson, J. (1942). *An Essay on Marxian Economics*. Basingstoke, MacMillan and Co.

Robinson, L. and Taylor, P. (2003). The performance of local authority sports halls and swimming pools in England. *Managing Leisure*, **8** (1), 1–16.

Rodgers, K. and Cox, E. (2003). The effects of trampling on Hawaiian corals along a gradient of human use. *Biological Conservation*, **112** (3), 383–9.

Russell, B. (1994) (original 1932). *In Praise of Idleness and Other Essays*. London, Routledge.

Ryan, C. (2003). *Recreational Tourism: Demand and Impacts*. Clevedon, UK, Channel View Publications.

Sable, K. and Kling, R. (2001). The double public good: a conceptual framework for 'shared experience' values associated with heritage conservation. *Journal of Cultural Economics*, **25** (2), 77–89.

Salma, U. (2002). Indirect economic contribution of tourism to Australia. *Bureau of Tourism Research Tourism Research Report*, **4** (2).

Schor, J. (1992). *The Overworked American: The Unexpected Decline of Leisure*. New York, Basic Books.

Shackley, M. (1996). *Wildlife Tourism*. London, ITBP.

Shah, K. (2000). *Tourism, the Poor and Other Stakeholders: Asian Experience*. ODI Fair-Trade in Tourism Paper. London, ODI.

Sharpley, R. (2003). *Tourism and Leisure in the Countryside*. Cambridge, Elm Publications.

Shaw, G. and Williams, A. (eds) (1997). *The Rise and Fall of British Coastal Resorts; Cultural and Economic Perspectives*. London, Pinter.

Sheldon, P. J. (1997). *Tourism Information Technology*. Wallingford, CAB International.

Sheldon, Pauline J. (1990). A review of tourism expenditure research. In *Progress in Tourism, Recreation and Hospitality Management* (C. P. Cooper, ed.). London, Belhaven Press.

Shone, A. (1998). *The Business of Conferences in the Hospitality and Leisure Industries.* Oxford, Butterworth-Heinemann.

Sinclair, M. T. and Stabler, M. J. (eds) (1991). *The Tourism Industry: An International Analysis.* Wallingford, CAB International.

Sinclair, M. T. and Stabler, M. J. (1997). *The Economics of Tourism.* London, Routledge.

Smeral, E. (2003). A structural view of tourism growth. *Tourism Economics*, **9** (1), 77–93.

Smith, M. K. (2003). *Issues in Cultural Tourism Studies.* London, Routledge.

Song HaiYan, Romilly, P. and Liu XiaMing (2000). An empirical study of outbound tourism demand in the UK. *Applied Economics*, **32** (5), 611–24.

Spotts, D. M. and Mahoney, E. (1991). Segmenting visitors to a destination region based on the volume of their expenditures. *Journal of Travel Research*, Spring, 24–31.

Stabler, M. J. (ed.) (1997). *Tourism and Sustainability: Principles to Practice.* Wallingford, CAB International.

Sugiyarto, G., Blake, A. and Sinclair, M. T. (2003). Tourism and globalization: economic impact in Indonesia. *Annals of Tourism Research*, **30** (3), 683–701.

Swarbrooke, J. and Horner, S. (1998). *Consumer Behaviour in Tourism: An International Perspective.* Oxford, Butterworth-Heinemann.

Szymanski, S. (2000). Hearts, minds and the restrictive practices court practice. In *Football in the Digital Age: Whose Game is it Anyway?* (S. Hamil, J. Michie, C. Oughton and S. Warby, eds), pp. 191–204. Edinburgh, Mainstream Publishing Co (Edinburgh) Ltd.

Tate, P. (2002). The impact of 9/11: Caribbean, London and NYC case studies. *Travel and Tourism Analyst*, **5**, 1.1–1.25.

Taylor, D., Fletcher, R. and Clabaugh, T. (1993). A comparison of characteristics, regional expenditures, and economic impact of visitors to historical sites with other recreational visitors. *Journal of Travel Research*, **32** (1), 30–5.

Taylor, F. (1993). *To Hell with Paradise, A History of the Jamaican Tourism Industry.* University of Pittsburgh Press.

Teare, R. and Olsen, M. (eds) (1992). *International Hospitality Management: Corporate Strategy in Practice.* London, Longman.

Teare, R., Canziani, B. F. and Brown, G. (eds) (1997). *Global Directions: New Strategies for Hospitality and Tourism.* London, Cassell.

Theobald, W. (ed.) (1998). *Global Tourism: The Next Decade*, 2nd edn. Oxford, Butterworth-Heinemann.

Thomas, B. and Townsend, A. (2001). New trends in the growth of tourism employment in the UK in the 1990s. *Tourism Economics*, **7** (3), 295–310.

Thomas, R. (ed.) (1996). *The Hospitality Industry, Tourism and Europe.* London, Cassell.

Thoroe, C. (2003). Sink effects of forestry inadequately rewarded? *Forst und Holz*, **58** (3), 55–8.

Torkildsen, G. (1992). *Leisure and Recreation Management.* London, Spon.

Tourism Forecasting Council (1998). A major new investment tool. *Forecast – Tourism Forecasting Council*, **4** (2), 28–31.

Tribe, J. (1997). *Corporate Strategy for Tourism.* London, ITBP.

Veal, A. (2002). *Leisure and Tourism Policy and Planning.* Wallingford, UK, CABI Publishing.

Veblen, T. (1967). *The Theory of the Leisure Class.* New York, Viking Press.

Waddoups, C. (2001). Unionism and poverty-level wages in the service sector: the case of Nevada's hotel-casino industry. *Applied Economics Letters*, **8** (3), 163–7.

Wagner, J. E. (1997). Estimating the economic impacts of tourism. *Annals of Tourism Research*, **24** (3), 592–608.

Wahab, S. and Pigram, J. J. (eds) (1997). *Tourism, Development and Growth: The Challenge of Sustainability.* London, Routledge.

Weaver, D. (1998). *Ecotourism in the Less Developed World.* CAB International.

Wells, A. T. (1993). *Air Transportation.* London, ITBP.

West, G. and Gamage, A. (2001). Macro effects of tourism in Victoria, Australia: a nonlinear input–output approach. *Journal of Travel Research*, **40** (1),101–9.

Wheatcroft, S. (1994). *Aviation and Tourism Policies: Balancing the Benefits.* London, ITBP.

Williams, A. M. and Shaw, G. (eds) (1991). *Tourism and Economic Development: Western European Experiences.* Chichester, Wiley.

Williamson, P. and Hirsch, P. (1996). Tourism development and social differentiation in Koh Samui. In *Uneven development in Thailand* (M. Parnwell, ed.), pp. 186–203. Aldershot, UK, Avebury.

Witt, S. F. and Witt, C. A. (1992). *Modelling and Forecasting Demand in Tourism.* London, Academic Press.

World Commission on Environment and Development (1987). *Our Common Future.* Oxford, OUP.

WTO (1991). *Tourism to the Year 2000: Qualitative Aspects Affecting Global Growth.* Madrid, World Tourism Organisation.

WTO (1993). *Investments and Financing in the Tourism Industry.* Madrid, World Tourism Organisation.

WTO (1994). *GATS Implications for Tourism.* Madrid, World Tourism Organisation.

WTO (1996). *Tourism and Environmental Protection.* Madrid, World Tourism Organisation.

WTO (1996). *Tourism and New Information Technologies.* Madrid, World Tourism Organisation.

WTO (1997). *Agenda 21 for the Travel and Tourism Industry.* Madrid, World Tourism Organisation.

WTO (1997). *Asia Tourism – Towards New Horizons.* Madrid, World Tourism Organisation.

WTO (1997). *Compendium of Tourism Statistics.* Madrid, World Tourism Organisation.

WTO (1997). *Multilateral and Bilateral Sources of Financing for Tourism Development.* Madrid, World Tourism Organisation.

WTO (1997). *Senior Tourism.* Madrid, World Tourism Organisation.

WTO (1997). *Yearbook of Tourism Statistics.* Madrid, World Tourism Organisation.

Yale, P. (1995). *The Business of Tour Operations.* Harlow, Longman.

Yeoman, I. and Ingold, A. (eds) (1997). *Yield Management: Strategies for the Service Industries.* London, Cassell.

Zhou, D. Yanagida, J. F. Chakravorty, U. and Leung, P. (1997). Estimating economic impacts from tourism. *Annals of Tourism Research*, **24** (1), 76–89.

Index